Offenders' Memories of
Violent Crimes

Wiley Series in

The Psychology of Crime, Policing and Law

Series Editors

Graham Davies and Ray Bull

University of Leicester, UK

The Wiley Series in the Psychology of Crime, Policing and Law publishes concise and integrative reviews on important emerging areas of contemporary research. The purpose of the series is not merely to present research findings in a clear and readable form, but also to bring out their implications for both practice and policy. In this way, it is hoped that the series will not only be useful to psychologists but also to all those concerned with crime detection and prevention, policing, and the judicial process.

For other titles in this series please see www.wiley.com/go/pcpl

Offenders' Memories of Violent Crimes

Edited by

Sven Å. Christianson

Stockholm University and Sundsvall Forensic Psychiatric Hospital, Sweden

John Wiley & Sons, Ltd

Copyright © 2007   John Wiley & Sons Ltd, The Atrium, Southern Gate, Chichester,
West Sussex PO19 8SQ, England

Telephone   (+44) 1243 779777

Email (for orders and customer service enquiries): cs-books@wiley.co.uk
Visit our Home Page on www.wiley.com

Other Wiley Editorial Offices

John Wiley & Sons Inc., 111 River Street, Hoboken, NJ 07030, USA

Jossey-Bass, 989 Market Street, San Francisco, CA 94103-1741, USA

Wiley-VCH Verlag GmbH, Boschstr. 12, D-69469 Weinheim, Germany

John Wiley & Sons Australia Ltd, 42 McDougall Street, Milton, Queensland 4064, Australia

John Wiley & Sons (Asia) Pte Ltd, 2 Clementi Loop #02-01, Jin Xing Distripark, Singapore
129809

John Wiley & Sons Canada Ltd, 22 Worcester Road, Etobicoke, Ontario, Canada M9W 1L1

Wiley also publishes its books in a variety of electronic formats. Some content that appears
in print may not be available in electronic books.

Anniversary Logo Design: Richard J. Pacifico

Library of Congress Cataloging in Publication Data

Offenders' memories of violent crimes / edited by Sven Å. Christianson.
    p.   cm.
    Includes bibliographical references and index.
    ISBN-13: 978-0-470-01507-0 (cloth : alk. paper)
    ISBN-10: 0-470-01507-1 (cloth : alk. paper)
    ISBN-13: 978-0-470-01508-7 (pbk. : alk. paper)
    ISBN-10: 0-470-01508-X (pbk. : alk. paper)
    1. Forensic psychology.   2. Violent offenders.   3. Amnesia.   4. Criminal
    investigation—Psychological aspects.   5. Criminal psychology.   6. Forensic psychology.
    I. Christianson, Sven-Åke.
    RA1148.O33 2007
    364.3—dc22   2006023994

British Library Cataloguing in Publication Data

A catalogue record for this book is available from the British Library

ISBN-13 978-0-470-01507-0 (hbk)   978-0-470-01508-7 (pbk)

Typeset in 10/12pt Century Schoolbook by Integra Software Services Pvt. Ltd,
Pondicherry, India
Printed and bound in Great Britain by TJ International Ltd, Padstow, Cornwall
This book is printed on acid-free paper responsibly manufactured from sustainable forestry
in which at least two trees are planted for each one used for paper production.

Contents

About the Editor

Sven Å. Christianson is a Professor of Psychology, Ph.D., Chartered Psychologist, and chief of the Research Unit for Forensic Psychology, at the Department of Psychology, Stockholm University, Sweden. He is also an Adjunct Professor at Sundsvall Forensic Psychiatric Hospital, Sweden. Dr Christianson has authored or co-authored over one hundred papers published in peer reviewed psychological and medical journals and anthologies, and has written or edited several books regarding crime, trauma, and memory, for example *Handbook of Emotion and Memory* (1992), *Traumatic Memories* (1994), *Crime and Memory* (1996), *Advanced Interrogation and Interviewing Technique* (1998) and *Police Psychology* (2004). The objective of his current research programme is to gain an understanding of the relationship between emotion and memory, with a research focus on victims', bystander witnesses' and offenders' memories of violent and sexual crimes. Dr Christianson has been a consultant in numerous murder, rape and child sexual abuse cases, and he is a sought after speaker and psychological expert witness.

List of Contributors

Sven Å. Christianson, Department of Psychology, Stockholm University, SE-106 91 Stockholm and Sundsvall Forensic Psychiatric Hospital, Box 880, SE-851 24 Sundsvall, Sweden

Maaike J. Cima, Department of Medical and Clinical Psychology, Maastricht University, P.O. Box 616, 6200 MD Maastricht, The Netherlands

Barry S. Cooper, Forensic Psychiatric Hospital, Forensic Psychiatric Services Commission, 70 Colony Farms Road, Port Coquitlam, B.C., V3C 5X9, Canada

Naomi Doucette, University of New Brunswick - Saint John, Department of Psychology, Box 5050, Saint John, N.B., E2L 4L5, CANADA

Ceri Evans, Canterbury Regional Forensic Service, Hillmorton Hospital, Private Bag 4733, Lincoln Road, Christchurch, New Zealand

Ronald P. Fisher, Department of Psychology, Florida International University, 3000 N.E. 151st Street, Academic One, Room 324, North Miami, FL 33181, U.S.A.

Ingrid Freij, Department of Psychology, Stockholm University, SE-106 91 Stockholm, Sweden

Pär Anders Granhag, Department of Psychology, Göteborg University, PO Box 500, SE-405 30 Göteborg, Sweden

Gisli H. Gudjonsson, Department of Psychology, Institute of Psychiatry, De Crespigny Park, Denmark Hill, London SE5 8AF, UK

Hugues Herve', Forensic Psychiatric Hospital, 70 Colony Farm Rd., Port Coquitlam, B.C., V3C 5X9, Canada

Carole Hill, University of Aberdeen, School of Psychology, William Guild Building, Old Aberdeen, AB24 2UB, UK

Ulf Holmberg, Department of Behavioural Sciences, Kristianstad University, SE-291 88 Kristianstad, Sweden

Marko Jelicic, Department of Experimental Psychology, Maastricht University, P.O. Box 616, 6200 MD Maastricht, The Netherlands

Elke Kalbe, Max-Planck-Institute for neurological Research, Gleueler Str. 50, D-50931 Köln, Germany

Hans J. Markowitsch, Physiological Psychology, University of Bielefeld, P.O.B. 10 01 31, D-33501 Bielefeld, Germany

Amina Memon, University of Aberdeen, School of Psychology, William Guild Building, Old Aberdeen, AB24 2UB, UK

Harald L.G.J. Merckelbach, Department of Experimental Psychology, Maastricht University, P.O. Box 616, 6200 MD Maastricht, The Netherlands

Gillian Mezey, St George's University of London, Division of Mental Health, Jenner Wing, Cranmer Terrace, Tooting, London SW17 ORE, UK

Kim van Oorsouw, Department of Experimental Psychology, Maastricht University, P.O. Box 616, 6200 MD Maastricht, The Netherlands

Tom Pakkanen, Department of Psychology, Åbo Akademi University, FIN-20500 Åbo, Finland

Valerie Perez, Valerie Perez, 15290 SW 104th Street, Building 4, Number 12, Miami, FL 33196. U.S.A.

Stephen Porter, Dalhousie University, Department of Psychology, Halifax, Nova Scotia, B3K 4J1, CANADA

Pekka Santtila, Department of Psychology, Åbo Akademi University, FIN-20500 Åbo, Finland

Eva von Vogelsang, Swedish National Criminal Police Analysis Section, Investigative Analysis & Offender Profiling Unit, P.O Box 12256, SE-102 26 Stockholm, Sweden

Aldert Vrij, Department of Psychology, University of Portsmouth, King Henry Building, King Henry 1 Street, Portsmouth, PO1 2DY, UK

David B. Wexler, College of Law, University of Arizona, Tucson Arizona 85721, USA

Michael Woodworth, Ph.D., University of British Columbia - Okanangan, Department of Psychology, Irving K. Barber School of Arts and Sciences, 3333 University Way, Kelowna, B.C. V1V 1V7, Canada

John C. Yuille, Department of Psychology, University of British Columbia, 2136 West Mall, Vancouver, B.C. V6T 1Z4, Canada

Series Preface

The Wiley Series on the Psychology of Crime, Policing and the Law publishes integrative reviews of important emerging areas of contemporary research. The purpose of the series is not merely to present research findings in a clear and readable form, but also to bring out their implications for both practice and policy. In this way, it is hoped that the series will not only be useful to psychologists, but also to all those concerned with crime detection and prevention, policing and the judicial process.

The current volume has a focus on offenders' memories of violent crimes. This is a relatively new and challenging topic not only for psychologists but also for investigators and the courts. For a considerable number of years some people seem to have accepted the notion that victims in certain types of cases (e.g., violent rapes) may have difficulty in providing a comprehensive account of what took place, so can the same notion be applied to offenders?

In the opening chapter the editor (and co-authors) sets the scene for the remaining 14 chapters and asks whether empirical and theoretical foundations are actually available for the notion of offenders being unable to remember their crime. A following chapter then presents an innovative approach that emphasises the roles of emotions and individual differences. The major results from a very substantial, recent study of violent crime perpetrators are then reviewed, with the instrumentality of violence emerging as an important factor.

Young offenders commit violent crimes. Analyses of the accounts provided years later by such perpetrators noted that many of them had intrusive memories of their crimes, some of them appeared to have amnesia (at least partial) for the events, but few seemed to have full amnesia (i.e. could remember nothing). Of course, when appearing to have difficulty remembering their violent crimes, offenders may be trying to deceive. A chapter in this volume quite rightly addresses this crucial issue.

After this, the volume considers the possibility of whether in the near future brain imaging techniques could be used in violent crime investigations (e.g. of suspects) and the extent to which there might be a neural basis for criminal behaviour.

The role of malingering (e.g. feigning amnesia for a crime) is then extensively considered. In one chapter this is interestingly set within a particular murder case, and in another chapter a broader overview is presented, which notes that simulating amnesia seems to be quite a popular strategy for trying to minimise responsibility for a violent crime and that severe emotional arousal on the part of the offender and/or the taking of drugs/alcohol should not too readily be accepted as evidence for amnesia. A further chapter has a focus on how to assess the authenticity of crime-related amnesia.

How best to interview offenders is a crucial question regarding their (apparent) recall of violent crimes and one third of this volume's chapters are devoted to this issue. While the general public in most countries in the world could be under the impression that their police officers receive appropriate training in how to interview suspects, such training is relatively rare. One chapter overviews the extensive training now available to police officers in the UK and the contrasting approach that has historically been taken in the USA. Another chapter examines research on the relationship between interviewing and confessions, noting that some suspects' vulnerabilities may result in false confessions. A further chapter focuses on how best to interview co-operative suspects.

Since some people claim to have no memory of the violent crime they are being accused of having committed, interviewing to detect deception is a topic of high relevance to this volume. A comprehensive overview of this topic is therefore presented. Also of importance is the under-researched notion that aspects of the crime (e.g. the behaviour of the offender at that time) could act as a guide concerning how to interview the alleged offender (i.e. the suspect).

This volume concludes with a thought-provoking chapter that suggests that interviewing alleged violent crime offenders in a humanitarian way could be more effective than doing so in a coercive way. While such an idea could make sense from a psychological point of view, investigators (e.g. police officers), lawyers, politicians, and the general public may find it initially hard to grasp why this should be. This book will succeed in its aim when such readers come to realise the complexities of the topic of gathering offenders' memories of violent crimes.

RAY BULL
University of Leicester

Preface

Although research on offenders' memories has been relatively sparse, especially compared to research on victims' and witnesses' memories, it hardly constitutes a new theme in psychological research. Experimental and clinical studies have been conducted on this issue for almost 100 years, yet work on offenders' memories has never been compiled into a comprehensive volume. In recent years, researchers and practitioners have shown increasing interest in offenders and in the way offenders remember and tell about their crimes. The present volume is the first of its sort; its aim is to provide an up-to-date account of the current state of knowledge in the area of offenders' memories. It goes without saying that forensic psychology is a rapidly growing field, and the present book should prove to be a timely and valuable source for the increasing number of psychologists and other practitioners who have professional interests and responsibilities relating to crime, criminals, the police and the legal system.

The book presents a mixture of literature reviews, recently published or unpublished findings and theory on such topics as memorial patterns in perpetrators, instrumental and reactive offenders, traumatized offenders, crime-related amnesia, crime-related brain activation, detecting lies and deceit, confabulation and false confessions, expert witnesses' and lay people's opinions, and interviewing techniques. The present volume also discusses methodological difficulties and ethical dilemmas associated with different paradigms and procedures currently used to study offenders' remembering of and narratives on violent crimes. Furthermore, the book presents broader theoretical perspectives to guide future research on offenders' memories and testimonies.

The book is divided into three sections. The first section includes chapters that focus on theoretical aspects of offenders' memories. Some of the specific questions discussed include the following: What is the nature of eyewitness memory in offenders? Have offenders' memories special characteristics that differ from those of victims and bystander witnesses? What factors can explain different memorial patterns in perpetrators' memories for violence? Are acts of instrumental violence remembered differently than acts of reactive violence? Do offenders with heightened levels of antisocial psychopathology remember differently than other offenders do?

The second section is concerned with aspects of assessment and evaluation, and explores offenders' memories, with particular emphasis on crime-related amnesia. Specific questions to be discussed are: How can we explain memory loss for criminal offences? What methods can be used to evaluate the authenticity of crime-related amnesia? What factors play the most crucial role in malingered amnesia? Is there a neural basis for criminal or antisocial behaviour and will different amnesia conditions show different brain activation patterns when studied using functional imaging techniques? How do intoxication, personal characteristics, expectations or lowered levels of intelligence affect offenders' memory? What are the beliefs among lay people and mental health professionals regarding offenders' memories and crime-related amnesia?

The final section contains chapters on interviewing issues. Among the specific questions discussed are: What factors can enhance the possibilities for suspects to provide useful investigative information? What interviewing techniques are effective in terms of accurately identifying suspects as truthful or untruthful? How can the interviewer recognize confabulation and false confessions in suspects? Can crime-scene features be used to predict interrogation behaviour among homicide offenders? What is the impact of offenders' well-being on their remembering of and narration on violent offences?

In taking on this book project, I attempted to bring together as strong a team of international researchers as possible, whose research covers a broad spectrum of topics concerning offenders' memories and narration. Fortunately enough, almost everyone I approached chose to participate, and all contributors have shown the greatest co-operativeness imaginable. The study of offenders' memory of violent and sexual crimes is an interdisciplinary undertaking of interest to clinical and experimental psychologists, psychiatrists, psychotherapists, social workers, judges, lawyers as well as police forces, penal institutions, probation services and other agencies that deal with offenders. In the process of editing this comprehensive volume, I have learned a great deal. I have also become convinced that the content of this book will further the knowledge and understanding of criminal behaviour of both students and professionals working in the areas of clinical psychology, forensic psychology and law enforcement.

I wish to express my gratitude to the contributors for finding time in their busy schedules, for their responsiveness to suggestions and for their willingness to add to the quality of this book. Many thanks to Karen Williams for her help in correspondence and editing. I am grateful to John Wiley & Sons for taking on this particular book project, and I would like to thank Matthew Duncan, Ruth Graham, Gillian Leslie, Carole Millett, Claire Ruston, and associates for their assistance in getting the book to press so quickly and efficiently. Finally, I am particularly grateful to Lina Leander for her love and support while this project was underway.

Sven Å. Christianson

Part 1

Theoretical Aspects of Offenders' Memories

CHAPTER 1

Searching for Offenders' Memories of Violent Crimes

Sven Å. Christianson, Ingrid Freij and Eva Von Vogelsang

Some 15 years ago, Professor John Yuille notified the first author about a book entitled *The Violent Years of Maggie MacDonald* (Gould & MacDonald, 1987). In the mid-sixties, Margaret MacDonald, a 33-year-old citizen of Toronto, stabbed her abusive common-law husband to death. Margaret claimed to be amnesic for the crime. She claimed to have no memory whatsoever of the act of killing, but remembered events immediately before and after the killing (Gould & MacDonald, 1987; Porter, Birt, Yuille & Herve, 2001). The case attracted enormous media attention, and it was revealed that Margaret had been abandoned and abused as a child, experienced life as a sex-slave, prostitute, alcoholic and drug addict, and had been exposed to violence throughout her life. Due to her history of longstanding abuse, Margaret herself and the women's movement in Canada regarded her as a victim rather than a perpetrator. Eventually, she was acquitted of murder and received a probation sentence. Less than a year later, she killed her second husband and was sentenced to life imprisonment.

Offenders' Memories of Violent Crimes. Edited by Sven Å. Christianson.
© 2007 John Wiley & Sons, Ltd.

Among laypeople, a large majority believe that it is perfectly possible for an offender to develop complete amnesia for a crime and that, in certain types of homicide, dissociative amnesia is a highly plausible scenario. Mental health professionals who appear as expert witnesses in such cases often assume that this type of memory loss is the joint effect of strong emotions and excessive drug or alcohol use. The question is whether there is an empirical and theoretical foundation for such assumptions. The outcome of Maggie's case reveals the importance of, and need for, a more thorough understanding of offenders' memories and shows that a naive understanding of violent behaviour and the effects of crime-related trauma on memory may result in immense personal, social and financial costs to society. The more we learn about the individuals who commit violent crimes, the better society can investigate such crimes and assess the likelihood that a violent criminal will re-offend.

The case of Margaret MacDonald taps into many of the theoretical and applied issues covered in the present volume, such as understanding the relationship between emotion/trauma and memory, post-traumatic stress disorder, crime-related amnesia, offender characteristics, forensic interviewing, detection of deception, development of criminal behaviour, recidivism and treatment prognosis. In this introductory chapter, we will discuss some of these issues and, at the same time, outline the content of the other chapters in this volume.

EFFECTS OF EMOTION AND TRAUMA ON MEMORY

Understanding the effects of trauma on memory is crucial if we are to evaluate offenders' accounts of violent events. During the past decades, an interest in understanding the relationship between emotion and memory has gradually increased among researchers and practitioners in diverse disciplines such as the cognitive, neurological, clinical and forensic sciences. For both theoretical and applied reasons, the need for scientific research on this issue has been particularly evident in forensic psychology. Numerous studies have been conducted on arousal and memory, emotional stress and memory, eyewitness memory, and trauma and amnesia (see Christianson, 1992a, b; Reisberg & Heuer, 2004, for reviews). These studies have shown that there is no single effect of trauma on memory, but instead a variety of patterns, where memories for details vary in both amount and accuracy. As pointed out in the comprehensive model presented by Hervé, Cooper and Yuille in this volume (Chapter 2), there are a variety of predisposing, precipitating and perpetuating biopsychosocial factors that interact to guide an offender's memory.

The vast majority of existing research on memory and emotion concerns non-violent settings, and with respect to violent settings, the research in forensic psychology has focused on bystander witnesses and victims of crime. Only a few studies have focused on offenders' memories, and the topics of trauma and offenders' memories have most often been studied separately. Moreover, although it is not unusual for offenders to develop post-traumatic stress disorder (PTSD) symptoms in response to their own crimes (Pollock, 1999, see also Evans & Mezey Chapter 4, this volume), the trauma literature and international conferences on psycho-traumatology seldom include research on trauma and PTSD in offenders. This limited body of research on trauma and memory in offenders is partly due to the interests of researchers and partly to practical obstacles. First and foremost, clinicians and other practitioners in the field of psychological trauma are focused on victims of accidents, catastrophes and crime. Our understanding – based on discussions with professionals engaged in clinical practice and research regarding, for example, rape victims, battered women, children who witnessed domestic violence or been beaten or subjected to sustained sexual abuse – is that professionals' empathy with the victims more or less excludes any mental involvement in the offenders' reactions and possible trauma development. That is, as a scientist, you either have the victim or the perpetrator perspective, and because trauma is inherently associated with victims, few scholars with an interest in psychological trauma end up studying perpetrators. Thus, among the several rationales for writing this book is the need for a compiled source of knowledge regarding the effects of emotion and trauma on offenders' memory of violent crimes.

It is also important to acknowledge some of the methodological and experiential differences associated with studying the relationship between memory and emotion in offenders as opposed to victims and bystander witnesses. As pointed out by Porter, Woodworth and Doucette in this volume (Chapter 5), there are several practical, methodological and ethical obstacles to conducting research on offenders. These obstacles concern collecting any in-person data from incarcerated offenders or problems associated with offenders as a vulnerable population, problems in advertising the study or encouraging participation in the absence of monetary gain, potential self-selection bias, the need for minimising the presence of security staff during the research interview (to maintain anonymity/confidentiality), and ensuring the safety of interviewers. The problem of credibility is always present in forensic settings, but it is reasonable to assume that guilty suspects and perpetrators may choose to withhold or distort information about their experiences to a higher degree than do victims and witnesses, even in a confidential research interview.

EMOTIONS IN REACTIVE AND INSTRUMENTAL OFFENDERS

It is important to understand how emotional reactions in response to crime can vary among victims, bystander witnesses and offenders. While victims and bystander witnesses almost exclusively experience negative emotions in response to violent crimes, perpetrators' experiences may vary from trauma to extreme pleasure between and during crimes. Some offenders experience extremely negative emotions during and after criminal acts, and this is especially significant among offenders who have committed *reactive* violent crimes as opposed to *instrumental* violent crimes (Dodge, 1991; Pollock, 1999). In reactive homicide, the violence leading to the death of another person can be construed as some sort of impulsive response. The attack is spontaneous, immediate and emotion driven. Victim provocation is evident, but there is no apparent external goal other than to harm the victim following a provocation/conflict (e.g., rage and despair associated with crimes of passion). A purely reactive homicide is an immediate, rapid and powerful affective response (e.g., manslaughter). However, in some cases, the crime may contain some degree of planning. For example, the offender may leave the scene to get a weapon and return for revenge, but without a 'cooling off' period between provocation and attack. Victims are typically a spouse or someone well known to the offender. The offender experiences a high level of angry arousal at the time of the violent event. The fact that reactive homicide tends to evoke extremely negative feelings in perpetrators is illustrated by statistics showing that 58% of them develop PTSD symptoms in response to their own crimes (Pollock, 1999). Of course, it can not be ruled out that at least some of these perpetrators fake PTSD symptoms (e.g., Rosen & Phillips, 2004). Nevertheless, PTSD symptoms can be found among offenders and are an under-researched theme.

In instrumental homicide, the violence leading to death is planned and proactive. A homicide is purely instrumental when the murder is clearly goal directed (e.g., a means to fulfil sexual or material needs or to experience a thrill), with no evidence of an immediate emotional or situational provocation, and when the victim is of little personal significance to the offender (e.g., robberies, rape or sexual homicide). Self-reported lack of arousal and anger during the offence are common in this group of offenders. Thirty-four per cent of instrumental homicide offenders developed PTSD symptoms subsequent to their crime, which is fewer compared to reactive homicide offenders (Pollock, 1999), but still a significant number. However, many instrumental offenders may also experience neutral or even positive emotions before, during and after the crime, and some phases of the crime may also be associated with negative emotions, while other phases are associated with positive emotions. For example, a rape may originally have been a planned event (i.e., an instrumental crime). However, during its execution, an unexpected complication (e.g., victim resistance) may have created a reactive situation such that the rapist became so aggravated by the victim's response and his own inability to dominate and control the victim that he felt compelled to kill the victim. Thus, some components of a crime event may be instrumental and others reactive (cf., instrumental–reactive violence), and this may result in differential memory for different parts of an event. The analysis of a memory (e.g., its level of detail, affect, etc.), accordingly, must be coordinated with the instrumental/reactive aspect of each part of the event. Evidently, the instrumental–reactive dichotomy is not always easy to make (see for critical review, Bushman & Anderson, 2001), but we do believe that it helps with conceptualising links between types of violence and their psychological consequences.

SEARCHING FOR OFFENDERS' MEMORIES ALONG PATHS TO VIOLENT CRIME

In order to extend our distinction between instrumental and reactive violence, we may break down the commission of violence into even smaller parts. Violence is a process of discrete, sequential and recognizable behaviours, a process that can be envisioned as a path leading from the initial grievance to the ultimate violence (Calhoun & Weston, 2003). According to Calhoun and Weston, individuals of violent intent 'move from developing the idea for committing violence through various individual steps leading to the violent act' (p. 57). These actions are only noticeable if we knew where to look and what to look for. In their model, the authors discuss a method of assessing threat, as threat is frequently part of an escalating spiral leading to violence. Seeing the requisite behaviours in their entirety and in sequence further enhances the threat manager's ability to identify potential problems, assess the actual degree of risk, and decide on the best strategy for managing that risk. A number of telltale signs in each step may help an investigator to identify possible actions. We use Calhoun and Weston's model of the path to intended violence to understand and analyse steps of discrete, sequential and recognisable *homicide* actions, which should be possible for the offender to recall. Assessing homicide offenders' memories of these steps provides insight into their motives and intents.[1] The first step, *Grievance*, which always must exist, concerns, for example, feelings of anger, frustration, jealousy, revenge, sense of loss, injustice or sense of mission, or any other reason for being aggravated or wronged in some way. The next step, *Ideation*, is about deciding to use, consciously selecting, and accepting the use of violence to correct the wrong or to fulfil sexual fantasies or material needs or to experience a thrill. As examples of signals of violence, some offenders discuss their fantasies, needs or thoughts with others, some identify with other assailants, and some fixate on violence in general or specific acts of violence and regard violence as the only alternative to solving their problem. The third step includes *Research and Planning*. That is, once an individual decides on violence, he or she must do some planning regarding the best way to execute the assault (where to find the target, type of weapon, etc.). As discussed by Calhoun and Weston, research and planning may be extensive and elaborate, but not every case involves extensive planning or research, which was obvious in John Hinckley's attempt to assassinate President Ronald Reagan: Hinckley's decision was made the very same morning, when he learned from the *Washington Post* that Reagan was scheduled to make a luncheon speech at the Washington Hilton, which was not far from his hotel. Typical signs of research/planning are information gathering, target research (daily activities of the target), suspicious inquires (e.g., among the target's relatives or fellow workers) and target surveillance.

After the completion of research and planning, the offender moves on to the fourth step, the stage of *Preparations*. Preparations are activities (e.g., practising firing a gun) that can be disguised, carried out in secret, but that are most often noticeable and often involves interaction with others. Common preparation activities are assembling equipment, acquiring a weapon, arranging for transportation, choosing clothing (costume), etc. Because the offender knows that the path to violence has an end point, he or she can prepare for achieving that end (e.g., planning for suicide, leaving written messages to various family members, or making out a last will and testament).

---

[1] The steps described in this chapter are a mixture of descriptions from Calhoun and Weston (2003) and our own elaborations made to suit the actions of homicide offenders.

In the fifth step, *Breach*, the offender must position him/herself in proximity to the target. Getting close can be as simple as strolling the streets at night as potential victims are heading back home from an evening downtown, or driving an unregistered, illegal taxi or delivering newspapers early in the morning. Getting close to a victim is both noticeable and potentially preventable, and it requires considerable effort by the offender to avoid detection. The sixth and final step of the Calhoun and Weston model is the *Attack*. Taking this step requires considerable commitment and nerve. As discussed by Calhoun and Weston, a number of intended assassins did not become actual assassins because the assassination simply proved to be too difficult. In interviews with several rape and homicide offenders, the first author has learned that the attack itself often deviates from what was planned or is aborted due to the behaviour of the victim or surrounding circumstances.

As pointed out by Calhoun and Weston (2003), 'Since the process resembles a path, the perpetrator can move in either direction along it, reaching one level and then moving forward or retreating to a previous level. Time means nothing along the path. Traversing it can take months, even years, or it can be covered in hours, even minutes' (p. 58). While the description above concerns instrumental violence, the model may also be applicable to reactive violence.[2] However, in reactive violence, the two steps of 'research/planning' and 'preparation' are not involved, that is, the offender moves directly from 'ideation' to 'action', and for reactive homicide offenders, it is often but a small step from idea to action.

In addition to the translation of Calhoun and Weston's six steps above, the present authors suggest that homicide offenders may also proceed into two additional steps or recallable actions, such as actions upon the victim's body post-mortem and disposal of the body. We call step seven *Realisation*. After the attack, and when the perpetrator has incapacitated or killed his/her victim, thereby gaining control, he/she can, if desired, act out his/her fantasies. These may be sexual and/or violent in nature, and for some perpetrators they can be likened to a constant companion along the path leading to the violent act. In the perpetrator's mind, thoughts surrounding the violent act are refined to the point of perfection. If the location and situation allow (i.e., no witnesses present), the perpetrator can act out

---

[2] The corresponding term for reactive violence in Calhoun and Weston's (2003) model is 'impromptu violence', which is defined as a spontaneous, unplanned usually emotional, violent outburst spawned by the circumstances of the moment.

his/her fantasies through sexual acts, insertion of objects into bodily orifices or by mutilating or damaging the victim's body.

Post-crime Behaviour is our term for the eighth and final step. The perpetrator's behaviour following the crime is commonly aimed at avoiding discovery. For example, the dead body may be moved, the crime scene cleaned and the weapon and other technical evidence removed from the scene or destroyed. It happens that the crime scene and the body are arranged so as to mislead (so-called 'staging') and make the crime appear to be something else, e.g., an accident. Manipulation and moving of the body may also be part of the perpetrator's fantasy. Perhaps he/she wishes the discovery of the body to be shocking. This can be achieved by, e.g., placing the naked body in a public place and in an obscene posture, with legs spread open.

Just as analyses of the perpetrator's behaviour in the first six steps can help us identify the motives and driving forces underlying the crime, post-crime behaviour and strategies can provide information on the perpetrator and his/her possible personality disorders and mental capacity. For example, efficient and rational post-crime behaviour may indicate that the perpetrator's mental capacity is sound.

As previously mentioned, the model is also applicable to perpetrators who have committed reactive acts of violence, thus perpetrators for whom the step between thought and action is probably short. These steps may even converge into the same sequence. Certain steps in the process may not occur, and this also applies to our proposed step seven, *Realisation*. Step eight, *Post-crime Behaviour*, is probably found to varying extents in reactive perpetrators as well. Active post-crime behaviour is rational behaviour, which would seem to require some degree of presence of mind on the part of the perpetrator. In cases where the perpetrator of a reactive crime claims memory loss, the prerequisites for recovering memory for step eight would seem to be better than those for recovering memory for the previous, often more impulsive and emotional steps.

In searching for offenders' memories, it is important to focus not only on the content, but also, as pointed out by Evans and Mezey in this volume (Chapter 4), to look at the different forms of memories of violent crime (e.g., amnesia versus intrusive memories), the different aspects of the violent event at different times of recall, and memories at different phases of the crime (e.g., the type of cognitive processing preceding, during and after the assault). The path of violence presented above may be useful in analysing and assessing offenders' memories of violent crime in more detail. For example, a homicide offender who claims amnesia for his/her crime should be asked about each step along the path to the homicidal violence. We consider that it is highly unlikely for an offender to be genuinely amnesic for all steps in the path to the intended or reactive violence (see also Chapter 7 by Merckelbach & Christianson, this volume).

THE REACTIVE VERSUS INSTRUMENTAL DICHOTOMY: THEORETICAL AND PRACTICAL ASPECTS

Although a distinction between reactive and instrumental homicide may oversimplify a highly complex behaviour with multiple motivations and manifestations (Bushman & Anderson, 2001), this distinction is relevant for several theoretical and practical reasons. First, it is often possible to classify with some degree of accuracy whether homicidal behaviour is predominantly reactive or instrumental. Second, by using the reactive versus instrumental dichotomy, various psychological characteristics of offenders can be predicted, such as types of emotions in different types of violence, patterns of memory responses, crime motivation, focus of attention and personality disorder. Third, knowledge about an offender obtained by studying crime scene characteristics and types of crime will generate the foundation for interrogation strategies. That is, the systematic analysis of offenders' memories of impulsive (reactive) or planned (instrumental) crimes might help criminal investigators in selecting strategies for interviewing perpetrators who either confess, deny having committed the crime or claim memory loss.

Regarding offender characteristics, Woodworth and Porter (2002) found that 27% of their sample of 125 Canadian offenders could be classified as psychopaths. Over 90% of the psychopaths were instrumental offenders. Because psychopaths would be expected to exhibit a general lack of affective interference and absence of empathy and remorse, and because of the pre-homicide fantasies often found among psychopaths, negative emotional reactions are less likely to occur in this group of offenders. Naturally, antisocial and psychopathic offenders may appear among those who commit violence that is classified as instrumental. (See also van Oorsouw & Cima, Chapter 8, this volume, regarding personality characteristics of individuals claiming amnesia for their crimes.)

The reactive and instrumental types of violence may also be associated differently with the emotional experiences of guilt and shame, as discussed by Santtila and Pakkanen in this volume (Chapter 13). Because the victim is often important in reactive offences, guilt is a likely emotion, which motivates reparative action including confessing. Among instrumental offenders, the victims themselves are not important, but are used in order to satisfy offenders' needs and, consequently, feelings of guilt are less likely. According to Santtila and Pakkanen, the instrumental offender is more likely to feel shame, which has the effect of decreasing the motivation for revealing what has happened and confessing to the crime.

The dichotomy between reactive and instrumental violence may also provide hints about the offender's focus of attention during the crime, that is, whether it is internal (directed towards one's own emotions) or external (directed towards event-related details) at the time of the crime. Cooper and Yuille (Chapter 3; but see also Hervé, Cooper & Yuille, Chapter 2, both in this volume) argue that the affect associated with reactive violence is likely to result from internal (e.g., subjective) resources, because the motivation for reactive violence is, by definition, internal (e.g., rage, anger). In instrumental violence, on the other hand, the focus of attention is often directed to external (e.g., event-related) sources, partly due to external motivation of instrumental violence (e.g., financial or a special type of victim). Consequently, if the offender has focused on the source of affect during a reactive act of violence (e.g., an internal source such as rage), he/she would likely have relatively poorer memory for the details of the event as opposed to an instrumental offender, who would more likely focus on the event itself.

Because there is a high degree of premeditation and preparation in instrumental homicides, one may expect that such offences would be easier for the offender to remember. In cases of sexual murder – especially in offenders who plan to commit subsequent homicides – the victim's actions and reactions and sexual components, etc, are often compared to a script fantasy that foregoes the murder. Premeditated fantasies and the act of murder are replayed over and over in the offender's mind, and the more the offender goes over the event in his/her mind (i.e., elaborative rehearsal; Craik & Lockhart, 1972), the more firmly the event will be stored. However, in reporting about their offences, instrumental offenders, and especially psychopaths, are more likely than other offenders to 're-frame' the level of instrumentality involved (i.e., exaggerate the reactivity). In comparing official reports and offenders' self-reported descriptions, Porter and Woodworth (2006) found that psychopaths were more likely to commit instrumental (premeditated, goal-driven) homicides. Interestingly, the instrumentality difference disappeared when offenders' narratives were examined, such that psychopaths exaggerated the reactivity of their violence, by minimising the degree of planning/premeditation and exaggerating the victim's role in, as well as the spontaneity of the offence (see also Porter, Woodworth & Doucette, Chapter 5, this volume).

Furthermore, instrumental offenders are expected to experience a more optimal level of intra-crime arousal, which facilitates remembering the offence. On the other hand, a state of extreme arousal (anger and rage) among reactive offenders may result in dissociative amnesia for their criminal behaviour. Whereas genuine dissociative memory reactions (amnesia) are unlikely to occur in instrumental offenders, several authors have argued that dissociative amnesia is typical of crimes that are unplanned, involve a significant other and are committed in a state of strong agitation (e.g., Kopelman, 1995; Loewenstein, 1991). Thus, dissociative amnesia would typically occur in the context of, what has been termed here and elsewhere, 'reactive homicide' (Pollock, 1999; see above). The underlying idea is that extreme levels of arousal during the crime may hamper memory at a later point in time. Thus, a failure in retrieval processes would underlie dissociative amnesia: the offender, who eventually has come to his/her senses, finds it impossible to access memories stored during a moment of turbulence. A term often used in the Anglo-Saxon literature to describe amnesia as a consequence of strong emotions (e.g., rage) is 'red-out'. In the words of Swihart, Yuille and Porter (1999): 'Apparently, an individual can get so angry with his/her intimate partner that s/he can severely beat or kill that partner and then not remember doing so: that is, they can experience a red-out resulting in circumscribed amnesia' (p. 200). Merckelbach and Christianson (Chapter 7, this volume) discuss other more recent theoretical assumptions that apply to dissociative amnesia in offenders and the way in which extreme emotions/traumatic memories affect memory encoding.

CLAIMS OF CRIME-RELATED AMNESIA

Although there are cases in which emotional events, especially highly arousing and traumatic ones, are poorly retained–for example, victims of rape, torture, sexual abuse and war, who have experienced extreme states of negative emotions possibly in combination with brain damage, may show a temporary inability to remember a traumatic event – these cases are rare (e.g., Christianson & Engelberg, 1999; Christianson & Nilsson, 1989; McNally, 2005; Terr, 1990; van der Kolk & Fisler, 1995). Findings from both real-life studies and experimental studies on non-criminal witnesses suggest that certain characteristics of negative emotional events are perceived and retained in an automatic fashion. In particular, experimental research reveals that there is a superior advantage for the detection and recognition of stimuli indicative of threatening situations (Christianson, 1997). A study by Christianson,

Loftus, Hoffman and Loftus (1991) showed that the level of memory performance for subjects presented with emotional stimuli (involving, e.g., blood) at very short exposure durations (180 ms) was almost identical to that found for subjects presented with the same emotional stimuli at longer exposure durations. Another finding is that the level of recognition is higher for unpleasant stimuli (pictures of victims of crime, traffic accidents, war, malady, famine) as compared to neutral scenes (people in everyday situations) and positive stimuli (e.g., sexual pictures of nudes in very sensual summer scenes) (Christianson & Fällman, 1990). Neuropsychological studies suggest that individuals are able to process fear-related visual stimuli in the absence of attention because emotional stimuli activate the amygdala, even when individuals are unaware that the information has been presented (e.g., Vuilleumier, Armony, Clarke, et al., 2002).

Some research also suggests that we are predisposed to retain certain characteristics of emotional information that had a survival value in earlier stages of evolution. In line with Öhman (1979, 1991), we argue that when people are exposed to a stressful event, critical stimulus features, such as bloodstains, may be extracted and evaluated as emotionally significant and thus activate an orienting response. Due to attention-demanding stimulus characteristics and personal involvement, controlled conceptual resources are subsequently allocated for further analysis of the stimulus. In short, critical details will be extracted by pre-attentive mechanisms and controlled processes will subsequently be allocated to the emotionally relevant information. This mode of processing would hypothetically promote memory for central detail information, but impair memory for peripheral details that are irrelevant and/or spatially peripheral to the emotion-eliciting event. In support of this assumption, there is the main finding, from both laboratory studies and studies of real-life events, that emotions improve memory for central details, or the gist of an event, but at the same time undermine memory for peripheral aspects of the event (see Christianson, 1992; Reisberg & Heuer, 2004, for reviews).

In most laboratory studies on witnesses of violent content, emotion has generally been evoked by some salient visual stimulus (e.g., facial injuries, the sight of a slashed throat, a child's bleeding eyeball or wounded legs). It may be, then, that these 'attention magnets' (Reisberg & Heuer, 2004) and not the emotional arousal have been the cause of the observed narrowing of memory. In examining memory for thematically-induced arousal in either laboratory events or in naturally-occurring emotional memories, results indicate that emotionality improves memory for all aspects of these events, with no memory narrowing (Laney, Campbell, Heuer & Reisberg, 2004; Laney,

Heuer & Reisberg, 2003). Although caution is appropriate when applying laboratory results to real-life events in general and to offenders in particular, there are indications of selective focusing in real-life situations, especially in extreme cases of negative emotional impact, for example shooting situations (Karlsson & Christianson, 2003; 2006), rape cases (Christianson & Nilsson, 1989), and in cases of repeated child sexual abuse (Christianson & Lindholm, 1998; Terr, 1990). Some recent experimental research offers further support for the idea that extremely affective details may temporarily interfere with subsequent information, a phenomenon termed emotional blindness or attentional rubbernecking (Most, Chun, Widders & Zald, in press). Obviously, such anterograde effects only occur to the effect that individuals find the material genuinely emotional. Considering instrumental offenders as discussed above, one would expect that their external focus along with their more optimal level of arousal would promote memory for certain critical details of the crime event.

In comparison with victims of violent crime or bystander witnesses, it is much more common that suspects or perpetrators of violent crimes display difficulties in remembering emotion-laden events (Christianson & Merckelbach, 2004; Schacter, 1986; Taylor & Kopelman, 1984). In fact, claims of amnesia are often made in the context of murder or manslaughter cases (25–40% of those who are found guilty of homicide claim to be amnesic or to have a complete memory loss, Schacter, 1986; Taylor & Kopelman, 1984). There are, however, other crime categories in which claims of amnesia do occur, for example in cases of sexual crime (Bourget & Bradford, 1995), domestic violence (Swihart, Yuille & Porter, 1999) and fraud (Kopelman, Green, Guinan, Lewis & Stanhope, 1994; see Christianson & Merckelbach, 2004 for a review), and the large majority of these claims are circumscribed to the crime itself (Bradford & Smith, 1979).

As discussed by Jelicic and Merckelbach in this volume (Chapter 9), there are different ways to explain memory loss for criminal offences. A common explanation is that crimes committed in a state of altered consciousness, such as in extreme rage, anger or psychosis, are stored in an exceptional context (Porter, Birt, Yuille & Hervé, 2001). Later, when the offender has returned to a more calm or normal state, retrieval of crime-related memories will be obscured due to the discrepancy between the internal state at encoding and that at retrieval and be largely inaccessible (cf., so-called red-outs and dissociative amnesia as discussed earlier). Crime-related amnesia may also be related to problems at encoding and storage due to intoxication, head injuries and brain diseases (cf., organic amnesia). For example, a large proportion of violent offenders are intoxicated owing to alcohol and/or drug use, which undermines the ability to encode and consolidate detailed information in memory. Brain dysfunction due to organic causes is discussed at further length in the chapter by Markowitsch and Kalbe in this volume (Chapter 6), but see also the case reports presented by Merckelbach and Christianson (Chapter 7). Still another explanation pertains to failures in meta-memory, i.e., some offenders may truly believe they are amnesic while in fact they are not (see Chapter 8 by van Oorsouw & Cima, this volume, for a thorough discussion, but see also below).

An alternative explanation, which is in contrast to the previous explanations for memory loss in offenders, is that offenders are deliberately simulating their memory problems. That is, amnesia may be used as a calculated defence strategy, partly to avoid or reduce responsibility and punishment (obstruct police investigation), but also to avoid emotional memories of the crime. These strategies prevent the offender from working through the factors underlying his/her homicidal behaviour. Such memory avoidance behaviour might have a far-reaching impact on recidivism, which is illustrated by the following case. A young man (AD) left his hometown by car, and after several hours of driving, he stopped to call his parents-in-law to tell them that something terrible had happened at their daughter's home and that they must go there. The parents soon found their daughter stabbed to death in her apartment. During the police investigation, AD claimed to have no memory of what had happened to his fiancé. He could not provide any details, he could not deny or confess to the crime. He served a sentence of eight years in prison and claimed to be amnesic throughout that period. After being released, he soon moved in with a woman, who was found shortly thereafter strangled to death in his apartment. As in the first murder, AD claimed to be amnesic. In the second investigation, however, an interrogator who used an empathetic style (characterised by cooperation, an obliging manner, a positive attitude, helpfulness and personal interest in his case) interviewed him. Owing to this positive contact, AD revealed that he had remembered both acts of killing from the beginning. As to his motive for simulating amnesia, he said that even a murderer should not be treated as he had been during the police investigations in the first murder. This case not only pinpoints the risk of recidivism, but also stresses the importance of interviewing suspects in such a way that does not provide motivation for denial or amnesia in suspects (see chapters by Hill & Memon, Chapter 10, and Holmberg, Christianson & Wexler, Chapter 15, this volume).

The case of AD as well as the case of Margaret McDonald, presented at the very beginning of this chapter, suggests that claims of crime-related amnesia represent a risk factor. Indeed, in their large-scale study involving 308 forensic patients in high security settings, Cima, Nijman, Merckelbach, Kremer and Hollnack (2004) found that such claims were especially prominent among recidivists. This outcome also suggests that claims of crime-related amnesia are related to a criminal career (prior convictions). In the Cima et al. (2004) study, the most pronounced difference between offenders claiming amnesia and the controls was that the former were older and had more prior convictions (i.e., experience). Also, as argued by Van Oorsouw and Cima in this volume, it may well be that offenders who were familiar with the penal system have had more opportunities to experience the advantages of claiming (partial) amnesia for their crime. Along the same lines, Santtila and Pakkanen (Chapter 13, this volume) discuss whether criminal background, in terms of convictions and previous prison experience, and age of the suspects are relevant factors in understanding the effects of confessing or denying. For example, 'those with previous convictions may be more likely to be aware of their legal rights and through their familiarity with the interrogative situation more likely to be able to cope with the associated social pressures (Gudjonsson, 2003)' and to understand when it is more advantageous to confess or to resist confessing. In this volume, Gudjonsson provides a thorough discussion of confessions and false confessions (Chapter 11).

HOW MOTIVATED ARE OFFENDERS TO FORGET?

In order to assess the motivation among offenders to forget their crimes or simulate amnesia, we asked the offenders themselves about the occurrence of amnesia and their evaluation of other homicide offenders (Christianson, Holmberg, Bylin & Engelberg (2006)). A total of 182 convicted homicide and sexual offenders serving their sentences in Swedish prisons were contacted by post and ask to complete a questionnaire. The questionnaires were distributed to all inmates by the Swedish Prison and Probation Administration. More than 50% were willing to participate ($n = 83$). More specifically, half of the homicide offenders and half of the sexual offenders, with ages ranging from 20–63 years and with sentences ranging from 1.3 years to life imprisonment, volunteered to provide information. The questionnaire consisted of items about offenders' experiences of Swedish police interviews, about their attitudes towards allegations of these serious crimes (see Holmberg & Christianson,

2002), but also about memory and amnesia.[3] One item in the questionnaire asked about their estimation of how often offenders generally deliberately feign loss of memory for the crime in order to avoid conviction. Only 2% of the homicide offenders thought that perpetrators of this type of crime never feign memory loss to some degree.

Another question asked was whether they had ever felt that they truly wanted to forget the crime event. Fifty-three per cent of the homicide offenders and 35 % of the sexual offenders answered positively to this item. These results suggest that homicide offenders are highly motivated to forget their offences. Overall, the results showed higher proportions of homicide offenders who claimed to be amnesic or to have a vague memory for the crime as compared to sexual offenders. This difference between homicide and sexual offenders is probably related to the fact that sexual offences are planned (instrumental), and that instrumental offences are less frequently associated with amnesia than are reactive offences (see below). To the specific question of whether they had experienced a complete or partial loss of memory for the crime event, 58 % of homicide and 45 % of sexual offenders claimed that they had. A subsequent question pertained to the vividness of their memory for the crime event. Among the homicide offenders, only 23 % claimed to have a very vague memory for the crime event. Keeping in mind that 58 % claimed to have a complete or partial amnesia for their crime at some point, and that only 23 % had a vague memory at the time of the interview, one must assume that 35 % (58 − 23) have had some sort of memory recovery.

CLAIMS OF AMNESIA AMONG INSTRUMENTAL AND REACTIVE HOMICIDE OFFENDERS

In analysing offenders' memories of violent crimes, the distinction between instrumental and reactive violence permits exploring several important issues: For example, which type of offender is more likely to commit an act of reactive violence as opposed to instrumental violence? Does the quality and veracity of memories differ between

---

[3] To increase confidentiality and inmates' trust in participating in the study, and to avoid censorship from the correctional staff, the pre-stamped envelopes were pre-addressed to a public authority (Stockholm University). The Swedish Law on treatment of offenders in prison (§25, The Swedish Law, SFS 1974: 203) states that letters from inmates to public authorities should be forwarded without any censorship, accordingly the offenders were expected to be truthful in their anonymous answers to the questions.

acts of instrumental violence and reactive violence? Which type of violence is more likely to lead to genuine amnesia? Some answers to these questions are offered in an ongoing study, in which rates of amnesia are being assessed among instrumental versus reactive homicide offenders (Christianson & von Vogelsang, 2006). Christianson and von Vogelsang collected data from 146 homicide cases. Of these, 89 were coded as primarily reactive and 57 as primarily instrumental. Rage and relational themes were the two most common crime motives among reactive offenders, whereas sexual and thrill themes were the most common motives among instrumental offenders. Ninety per cent of the reactive offenders reported negative emotions at the time of the crime and 75 % reported such emotions for the period after the crime. In the instrumental group, 55 % experienced negative emotional arousal during and 42 % after the crime. This pattern is in line with previous research (e.g., Pollock, 1999) revealing that 58 % of those who had committed reactive homicide showed PTSD symptoms compared to 36 % among the instrumental murderers.

In comparing offenders' memory before, during and after the crime, Christianson and von Vogelsang (2006) found that it was more common to have complete memory loss for what happened during the crime than for information immediately before and after the crime. This pattern was evident for both groups, but was most pronounced in the reactive group. Note that this pattern is opposite to what is normally found when studying memory for emotional events (Christianson, 1992). That is, subjects typically remember the emotion-inducing event quite well, but show impaired memory for information preceding and/or succeeding the highly arousing event (Most et al., in press).

Forty-seven per cent of the reactive offenders and 28 % of the instrumental offenders claimed amnesia for the offence in the beginning of the police interviews. Twenty-three per cent (20 offenders) of the reactive offenders and 14 % (8 offenders) of the instrumental offenders consistently claimed to be amnesic for the act of killing throughout the investigation. Averaged across the two groups, this percentage is 19 %, which is quite similar to percentages reported in other studies on amnesia for homicide (e.g., Cima, Nijman, Merckelbach, Kremer & Hollnack, 2004; Pyzsora, Barker & Kopelman, 2003; Taylor & Kopelman, 1984).

The question arises of whether these percentages associated with the instrumental and reactive offenders reflect true proportions of genuine amnesia for homicidal violence. There are several methods that can be used to evaluate the authenticity of crime-related amnesia. Jelicic and Merckelbach (Chapter 9, this volume) review four strategies that have been proposed in the literature: (a) using certain characteristics of the amnesia and/or the defendant (i.e., symptoms of extreme specificity) as clues to distinguish true from feigned amnesia; (b) using standard malinger questionnaires or tests that, by means of self-report scales, assess clinically atypical or bizarre symptoms and preferences; (c) assessing the defendant's knowledge of the crime and the crime scene by means of symptom validity tests; and (d) using physical lie detection techniques such as the Guilty Knowledge Test/Relevant-Irrelevant Test, and Control Question Test. Strategies for detecting deception either by analysing what people say, observing nonverbal behaviour or measuring physiological responses are discussed at further length by Vrij and Granhag (Chapter 12, this volume)

In assessing the authenticity of the crime-related amnesia claimed by 19% of subjects in the Christianson and von Vogelsang (2006) study, symptoms of extreme specificity that are often associated with malingering were scrutinised. Drawing on a review by Porter and Yuille (1995), some clues will be listed. First, many amnesic offenders say that they recall events immediately preceding and following the crime, with a circumscribed memory loss for the act of killing itself. This typical pattern of remembering and forgetting was also claimed by Margaret MacDonald, whose case was described in the very beginning of this chapter. This pattern is quite unusual in clinical cases of both organic and dissociative amnesia, where more blurred demarcations between remembering and forgetting are found. Second, Schacter (1986) argued that false claims of amnesia are characterised by a sudden onset and low ratings on feeling-of-knowing judgements. If, for example, a murder suspect is asked about the possibility of recurrence of memories after being provided with cues, recognition alternatives, more time to think about the event, additional interrogations, a visit to the crime scene, etc., the malingerer is usually dogmatically negative. On a related note, malingerers typically report that they are not helped by an interviewing method known as the Cognitive Interview (Fisher & Geiselman, 1992; see also Chapter 14, this volume). This method incorporates: (a) reinstatement of both environmental and personal context; (b) reporting everything regardless of its perceived importance; (c) recounting the line of events in different temporal orders (forward or backward), and (d) reporting events from a variety of perspectives. Although the cognitive interview may not break a suspect who intentionally wishes to withhold information, one should expect him/her to retrieve more information as a result of these well-established memory-enhancing techniques. Malingerers usually say that they do not profit from these techniques.

Third, Porter and Yuille (1995) pointed out that malingerers are also more likely to relate symptoms of extreme specificity (e.g., 'I cannot recall anything from noon until midnight') and to recount symptoms of extreme severity.

Fourthly, suspects often blame their amnesia on intoxication. Yet, as pointed out by Parwatikar, Holcomb and Menninger (1985), amnesia for crime is unlikely to be purely dependent on an intoxicated state. In their study on drivers arrested during large traffic-control actions by the Dutch police, van Oorsouw, Merckelbach, Ravelli, Nijman and Mekking-Pompen (2004) found that claims of alcohol amnesia (blackout) were predominantly made by those involved in an accident. More specifically, 85% of the drivers who claimed amnesia were involved in a serious motor vehicle accident, whereas 35% of those not claiming amnesia were involved in such an accident. Interestingly, during the time of the arrest, blood-alcohol concentrations (BACs) in those who claimed amnesia were not higher than BACs of arrested drivers who did not claim amnesia. This illustrates that the combination of amnesia and intoxication claims may serve face-saving purposes (see also Kalant, 1996). A more thorough discussion of the relation between alcohol and substance abuse and crime memories/claims of crime-related amnesia (cf., blackouts) is provided by van Oorsouw and Cima in Chapter 8 of this volume.

In evaluating the 19% of subjects who claimed amnesia in the Christianson and von Vogelsang (2006) study, certain characteristics were found to be common in this group. To begin with, 46% of the offenders were dogmatic about their amnesia (e.g., 'It doesn't matter if you ask me 5, 10 or even more times, I will never remember anything about what happened that evening'). A second feature was that 79% claimed to have total memory loss, for example, 'My memory is like a black hole, everything is gone'. In clinical cases of both organic and dissociative amnesia, patients have islands of memories or fragments from the amnesic part of the event rather than a total memory loss. Further, claims of sharp limits for the beginning and end of the amnesia were quite common among (e.g., 'from the moment I stepped out of the restaurant door, until I sat in the police car, everything is lost'). Fifty-four per cent described this type of circumscribed amnesia, which is an atypical pattern in clinical settings. Other symptoms of extreme specificity in the homicide offenders who consistently claimed to be amnesic for the act of killing were that memory loss varied between interviews (50%), that critical information was lost during interviews (38%) or that there was no recovery whatsoever. References to intoxication were also quite common. However, a closer look at the total sample revealed that 67% were intoxicated by alcohol during the crime (88% of the reactive offenders and

39% of the instrumental offenders), but only 19% of them claimed amnesia.

In the Christianson and von Vogelsang (2006) sample, almost all homicide offenders who consistently claimed to be amnesic for the act of killing showed three or more symptoms of extreme specificity. Given these characteristics, one may assume that forensic experts are well advised to consider the possibility of malingering in claimants of amnesia. There are, of course, several possible explanations for why offenders try to feign amnesia, as discussed elsewhere in this volume. Remaining silent is a more elegant way of evading answering cross-examination questions. It may also be an excuse used to avoid painful discussions about crime details with social workers or therapists. Among reactive offenders, it may be a strategy for psychological survival – a way to handle both the past, which has led to the act of crime, and the immediate present, being a murderer. But it may also be a strategy used among instrumental offenders (especially sexual murderers) to protect 'precious' memories. Doubt should arise specifically in cases when suspects with a diagnosis of psychopathy claim amnesia. Psychopaths do not experience the extreme negative emotions that may undermine encoding of information, but could instead experience very pleasant emotions during the crime. Psychopaths also have a tendency towards pathological lying and malingering (Porter & Yuille, 1995). In keeping with this, Cima et al. (2003) found, in their sample of psychiatric prison inmates, that those who claimed amnesia displayed more antisocial characteristics, but also scored higher on an instrument that taps into malingering tendencies.

Furthermore, psychiatric experts often have a pathology bias, and amnesia may elicit a cascade of psychiatric experts' willingness to explain the offender's deviant behaviour, for example, 'Well, he shows no regret, but on the other hand, he is amnesic'. Alternatively, amnesia may be used as an explanation when practitioners fail to obtain a statement (narrative) from a suspect/client. Perhaps, we are nursing a myth when we believe that people can be amnesic for such a unique, emotional, often once-in-a-lifetime event as murder. Of course, offenders can forget about certain details of the event, but the question is whether an offender can be amnesic with respect to the complete act of killing. Recent findings suggest that this is very unlikely.

On the other hand, some features may indicate that a claim of crime-related amnesia is bona fide. First, in some cases amnesic offenders may give themselves up or, at least, make no effort to avoid capture (Gudjonsson, Kopelman & MacKeith, 1999; Kopelman, 1987; Taylor &

Kopelman, 1984; see also case NN in Chapter 7, this volume). Second, there is a consistency in how they describe their amnesia, and many of their descriptions *do* in fact resemble those given by other people with psychological forms of amnesia – the memories being locked away in the back of the mind and difficult to retrieve, and sometimes there being islands or fragments of preserved memory within the amnesic gap, rather as in the amnesia that follows head injury. Third, it should be noted that victims of offences, such as rape victims, sometimes describe very similar amnesic gaps (Mechanic, Resick & Griffin, 1998), and eyewitnesses often make errors in recall; in neither case are their motives impugned. Fourth, alcoholic blackouts are very common in heavy drinkers, and many offenders have a long alcohol history, including previous blackouts, and very high BACs at the time of their alleged offence. Finally, it should be noted that amnesia on its own does not have any bearing upon criminal responsibility or accountability in most countries. The only exceptions are the very rare instances in which automatism is an issue, in which amnesia is a necessary but not sufficient condition for raising an automatism defence. In practice, amnesia can be damaging to mounting a defence, and can hinder a defendant's instructions to his/her lawyers.

For the expert witness, it may be difficult to differentiate between dissociative, organic or feigned amnesia. This has to do with the fact that simulators can give a compelling imitation of someone with a dissociative or organic amnesia. It is only with the help of structured interviews focusing on certain memory characteristics and tests (see Jelicic & Merckelbach, Chapter 9, this volume) that an expert will be able to identify simulators. Ultimately, it is a matter for the jury to decide whether they believe a defendant's account, including any claim of amnesia. The expert is there only to advise triers of fact on the circumstances in which amnesia may or may not arise, and the decision in any particular case is a matter for the jury. The question is how well informed appointed expert witnesses and judges are about the characteristics of genuine versus feigned amnesia, and what their beliefs are about the plausibility of developing complete amnesia for a crime.

EXPERTS' BELIEFS ABOUT CRIME-RELATED AMNESIA

Among laypeople, it seems that a large majority believe that it is perfectly possible for an offender to develop complete amnesia for his/her crime. This was evident in a study by Merckelbach, Cima and

Nijman (2002). The authors administered a vignette to 54 laypersons, in which a homicide and the aftermath were described. In
the vignette, a court-appointed mental health professional concluded
that the crime-related amnesia was a result of 'alcohol and drug use
in combination with strong emotions'. The laypersons were asked
whether they thought this was a plausible scenario in this type of
crime. Eighty-two per cent indicated that they thought it was. Seventy-
six per cent also felt that the court was very wise to appoint a forensic
expert. When asked about the origins of the amnesia, 70% believed
that alcohol and emotions were responsible.

The issue of whether or not offender-claimed crime-related amnesia
might be genuine may have little or no effect on ordinary people's daily
lives, nor on other people close to them. There are instances, however,
in which these perceptions have the potential to seriously influence
and even harm the life of others, i.e. when laypeople in their professional roles as judges, lawyers, prosecutors or police officers let false
knowledge guide their decision-making process. One way for professionals working within the field of criminal justice to overcome this
lack of knowledge is to consult an expert witness. Professionals should
rely on expert witnesses to overcome their own lack of technical knowledge, and these expert witnesses should in turn base their opinions
on what the psychological literature says about dissociative amnesia,
simulated amnesia and organic amnesia. One would expect judges,
prosecutors and other trained professionals to possess a greater knowledge of witness statement constituents, based on their education and
experience, than do laypeople not working in the field of criminal
justice, but also greater than laypeople in the field, such as politically
appointed jurors.

In a study by Christianson and Freij (2006), 245 judges, 128 police
officers and 214 jurors were asked to rate the degree to which they
considered certain factors to be plausible causes of genuine amnesia
in an offender. The authors' hypothesis was that the two professional
groups would show lower ratings than would the group of laypeople,
i.e. they would agree to a lesser extent that a certain factor might
cause amnesia. The authors did find statistically significant between-
group differences in the ratings, but post-hoc tests revealed no clear
direction of these differences (see Table 1.1).

Christianson and Freij (2006) conducted another study with a more
experimental design to explore whether professionals working in criminal justice share the belief that an offender can develop complete
amnesia for his/her crime. The authors had two main objectives: first
to further investigate possible between-group differences and, second,
to examine whether case-specific information affected group beliefs.

Table 1.1 Professionals' and laypersons' beliefs about plausible factors causing genuine amnesia for the crime event in an offender[1]

Variable	Judges ($n = 245$)	Jurors ($n = 214$)	Police Officers ($n = 128$)
Physical injuries	4.89	4.83	4.59
Extreme emotions of fear/terror[2]	4.35	4.96	4.41
Extreme emotions of anger/rage[2]	3.70	4.26	3.68
Very short crime course of event[2]	3.14	3.45	2.76
Unplanned/unforeseen crime course of event[2]	3.18	3.51	2.95
Sleep ambulism[3]	4.00	3.51	3.64
Repression because of guilt and anxiety[2]	4.24	4.64	4.28
Effects of alcohol[2]	5.05	4.95	4.36
Effects of narcotics[2]	5.12	5.42	4.66
Prolonged drug abuse[2]	5.00	5.41	4.62
Influences from others[3]	3.99	4.18	3.74
Mental disease[3]	5.41	5.36	5.05
Mental disabilities[2]	4.33	4.92	4.23

[1] Answers were given on a Likert scale from 1 = Not at all, to 7 = Very much. Numbers here are mean values.
[2] Significant between-group differences, $p < .01$.
[3] Significant between-group differences, $p < .05$.

A vignette was constructed describing a homicide case in which an offender, after a night out visiting a restaurant, stabbed another person to death. The offender claimed amnesia for the homicide. The offender and the victim in this case were involved romantically and shared a history of violence and assault. Two case-specific conditions were manipulated: the gender of the offender and the perceived cause of memory loss (alcohol intoxication or extreme emotional stress). Thus, the vignette had four possible conditions. The vignette was randomly administered to 336 judges and 118 police officers and prosecutors. They were asked to carefully read the vignette and to answer two questions concerning whether or not the claimed amnesia could be considered genuine (yes/no) and to what degree they believed alcohol (in one condition) and extreme emotion (in one condition) to be a plausible cause of genuine amnesia. Over all conditions, the majority of judges (64%) and half of police officers/prosecutors indicated that the claimed amnesia could be considered genuine. This between-group difference was statistically significant. When examining the specific conditions separately, similar trends were discovered. The strongest significant difference was found in the male offender/extreme emotion condition, where 70% of judges but only 37% of police officers/prosecutors believed the claimed amnesia to be genuine. Regarding the ratings of the degree to which alcohol or extreme emotions could be plausible causes of the claimed amnesia, no statistically significant difference was found between the two groups over the four conditions. However, trends similar to those described above emerged showing that the judges were more likely to favour the presented factor as a possible cause of amnesia. This trend was strongest in the male offender/alcohol condition. The authors also administered the vignette to 77 mental health professionals and 103 students. A majority (69% and 83%, respectively) of both groups also indicated that the claimed amnesia could be genuine, with similar trends over all four conditions. Both groups rated the plausibility of a genuine amnesia higher than did the professional groups.

MEMORY-UNDERMINING EFFECTS OF SIMULATED AMNESIA

Are perpetrators who claim amnesia liars? Instead of giving a direct answer, let us consider the complexity of remembering and sharing homicide offences. As discussed by van Oorsouw and Cima in this volume (Chapter 8), feigning amnesia not only obstructs legal and therapeutic processes but might also undermine memory for the crime. In a simulation study by Christianson and Bylin (1999), subjects were presented with a case vignette of a murder and were instructed to identify themselves with the offender. Next, one group of subjects was told to play the role of an amnesic offender during a task that consisted of a series of questions about the case. The control group was encouraged to perform as well as they could on this task. After a week, subjects returned to the lab and, again, answered questions about the case. This time, all subjects were instructed to perform as well as they could. During the first session, subjects who played an amnesic role gave fewer correct answers than did control subjects, which is not remarkable. It only shows that the 'amnesic' subjects took their role seriously. However, at the one-week follow-up test, ex-simulators were still performing under the level of control subjects. Along with the results of similar studies (van Oorsouw & Merckelbach, 2004), these results show that simulating amnesia has memory-undermining effects.

There are several explanations for why simulated amnesia may sometimes develop into real memory problems. One emphasises lack of rehearsal of crime details. People generally have a tendency to remove stressful thoughts, feelings and memories from their conscious awareness. Not only victims and bystanders but also perpetrators display an aversion to remembering traumatic events. Cognitive aversion is not static, however, but is dependent on the amount of psychological stress that is experienced. Thus, a major obstacle to recalling events of an unpleasant or traumatic nature is that intentional retrieval of such personal memories seems to be related to processes strategically aimed at inhibiting the reactivation of associated emotion (Philippot, Schaefer & Herbette, 2003). The finding is consistent with the notion of mood maintenance as well as the phenomenon of overgeneral memories (Williams et al., 2000). By remaining at a general or abstract level of information, individuals attempt to avoid the reactivation of acute and painful emotions felt in specific experiences of personal or forensic relevance. The perpetrator may have an even stronger motivation to engage in cognitive avoidance. It is common among reactive homicide offenders, as well as among victims of repeated sexual and physical abuse, to develop strategies to avoid thinking about the event. Many homicide offenders do not have a background of sharing personal negative experiences and have developed, from an early age, avoidance skills that involve distortion, displacement and stop-thinking activity. Over time, strategies of this kind, which underlie active avoidance, may cause links and associations to specific event details to become less robust (e.g., Wegner, Quillian & Houston, 1996). This circumstance, in turn, will limit access to detailed information.

Another possibility is that simulators think of a new version that better fits their wish to be less responsible for the crime. This type of processing would imply that perpetrators who feign amnesia confuse their own version with the original event and subsequently have difficulties understanding how their own memory has changed. This might result in source monitoring errors (Johnson, Hashtroudi & Lindsay, 1991). Still another explanation is that expectancies are the driving force behind the memory-undermining effect of simulating amnesia. People who initially played the role of an amnesic person may have a strong expectation that they will perform poorly on subsequent memory tasks. This, in turn, may give rise to a 'self-fulfilling prophecy' when the person is given such a memory task. This phenomenon is also known from studies on placebo effects. Subjects who receive a placebo in combination with the story that it is a memory-undermining substance later perform less well on memory tasks than do control subjects (Kvavilashvili & Ellis, 1999; see also van Oorsouw and Cima, Chapter 8, this volume).

The general tendency towards avoiding reactivation of unpleasant memories and emotions or a confused version of the original event may, nonetheless, be overcome with the application of the memory-enhancing principles of the Cognitive Interview (CI) when assisting a person's information retrieval. As discussed by Fisher and Perez in this volume (Chapter 14), care is taken to allow sufficient time for an individual to recall all unique characteristics of a particular event before trying to retrieve details that are not immediately accessible. In applying the principles of the CI, plenty of time is allowed to recreate the circumstances surrounding an event, including time to recreate the emotional feelings associated with the event. As the interviewee is allowed to take the time he/she feels is necessary, the information is retrieved successively at a pace that is tolerable to the individual being assisted (see interviewing techniques discussed in Chapters 10, 11, and 15 in this volume). Further, nonverbal information pertaining to body movements and sensory perception (sights, colours, sounds, olfactory and gustatory details) may not only take time to access in memory in their own right but may be particularly imbued with salient emotions. Thus, reactivation of such details may be especially strenuous and painful. Many clinicians, therefore, let the person talk about his/her experience in the third person, that is, as if the event had happened to someone else and as if he/she had merely been an observer. This procedure does not always yield a detailed description but it is a suitable first attempt at recall, for example, when working with victims of rape or sexual abuse, for whom shock, shame and violated integrity bar any sharing of the most intimate details of their traumata.

BEING A RECIPIENT OF MEMORIES OF VIOLENT CRIME

In order for an offender to be willing to confront and tell about his/her crime, thus confronting his/her own feelings and the victim's reactions, there is a need for a recipient of potentially traumatising memories, someone who is skilled in listening to and prepared to receive reports of gruesome, shocking experiences from other people. Details of murder are not easy to listen to and many listeners disclose, either verbally or non-verbally, that they feel very uneasy when listening to details of violence. Besides confrontations with death exposure, many professionals receive potentially traumatising information merely by interviewing crime victims and suspects. A number of studies have shown that exposure to gruesome events and human suffering on a daily basis creates stress in professionals (Anderson, Litzenberger & Plecas, 2002; Brysiewicz, 2002). Iliffe (2000) conducted structured interviews with 18 counsellors about their experiences of working with perpetrators and survivors of domestic violence. The counsellors revealed experiences of horror when hearing women narrate about severe abuse. General feelings of heaviness, churning stomach and nausea, as well as feeling shaken were responses that the counsellors perceived when women narrated about violent events. The responses the counsellors experienced sometimes generated a need to distance themselves somewhat from what they heard, and when they became too distanced from their client's narration, they saw the negative impact of their avoidance. Croft (1995) argues that some police officers may feel reluctant to use the technique of re-establishing the context of the crime event, a technique emphasised in the cognitive interview (Fisher & Geiselman, 1992). Mentally reconstructing the event in a victim's or an offender's mind may be seen by the police officer as promoting unbearable feelings in re-experiencing the crime event. Such emotive considerations may be put forward to justify a police officer's reluctance to confront details of crime.

In a study on police officers' attitudes towards interviewing crime victims and suspects, Holmberg, Christianson and Karlsson (2006) found that police officers perceived themselves as having a calm attitude and allowing time for comments in interviewing both crime victims and suspects. But results also showed a higher degree of stress-related symptoms from interviewing *suspects* as compared with victims. Holmberg et al. also found that the vast majority of the investigative officers conducted only one or two interviews with crime victims and that almost half conducted only one or two interviews with suspects. These findings suggest that police officers may be unaware of the mechanisms and prerequisites related to traumatised victims and suspects, or that they may consider they have no need for further information than what has been revealed through one or two interviews. An alternative assumption might be that some police officers are inclined to avoid closer contact with suffering or despicable people in order to avoid secondary or vicarious traumatisation (see, e.g., Croft, 1995; Figley, 1995; Pearlman & MacIan, 1993). Karlsson and Christianson (2003) found that many Swedish police officers considered themselves as inadequately prepared and trained for stress-evoking events such as investigating brutal murders, especially when children are involved. Furthermore, research on psychotherapists (Pearlman & MacIan, 1993; Pearlman & Saakvitne, 1995) indicates that frequent work with rape victims and sexually and physically abused children was associated with intrusive thoughts and avoidance, but also that coping ability was of great importance, such that absence of protecting factors increased the risk of vicarious traumatisation. We can probably expect the same effects on forensic psychiatry staff for example, who must assess and treat individuals who have perpetrated serious violent or sexual crimes. A psychologist once told the first author about how upset she was the first time she was to meet with a 'murderer' (for a therapy session). We can assume that her client, the murderer, perceived her discomfort and consequently behaved in an agitated manner, which in turn confirmed the psychologist's bias that the murderer was a strange and, in the psychologist's eyes, threatening person (the man had stabbed his partner to death during a violent fight but was not otherwise considered a violent person). Perhaps police officers, as well as mental health personal working with convicted violent offenders, are not fully aware of their own affective responses to repetitive contacts with offenders of violent crimes. They may develop a distancing perspective as a defence against the negative aspects of the crime that they have to investigate. This may result in various consequences for the investigative duty, such as avoiding different crime-relevant details, terminating the interview too quickly or providing poor documentation from the interview. As discussed above, perhaps mental health practitioners too are inclined to accept amnesia in a homicide offender due to the grisly details of the murder.

Perhaps protecting factors play a part in that police officers often seek a confession, which, from their perspective, is an ideal starting point for a perpetrator to tell his story about the crime. However, many offenders and especially those who have committed reactive violence are not focused on the crime, but more on their own reactions and want to understand how it all could have happened. One would assume that better preparation among health personal and police officers might promote a different attitude towards multiple and in-depth interviews with offenders of violent and gruesome crimes. In Chapter 10 of this volume, Hill and Memon discuss training for investigators and present guidelines on investigative interviewing as a tool to determine how and why a crime occurred, and who committed the crime (see also Holmberg, Christianson & Wexler, Chapter 15, this volume).

SUMMARY

In searching for offenders' memories, we need to understand the basic principles of the relationship between emotion and memory. We also need to know that emotions may vary both within and between offenders (e.g., from extreme pleasure to trauma), and that these emotions are closely related to the motivation for committing the crime (e.g., reactive versus instrumental). Violent crime suspects may deny crime or claim crime-related amnesia as a strategy to evade responsibility and to avoid psychological stress related both to the past and to the immediate present, for example, being a murder suspect. In analysing offenders' memories of homicidal violence, our data indicate that offenders have a strong motivation for feigning amnesia and that their claimed amnesia most often has symptoms of extreme specificity, indicating malingering. It should be noted that malingering per se may have memory-undermining effects. Among professionals working in criminal justice as well as mental health professionals, a majority believe that it is perfectly possible for an offender to develop complete amnesia for homicide, and that the memory loss may be an effect of strong emotions or excessive drug or alcohol use. In this chapter, we have presented arguments for why this approach is dubious and suggested that laypeople as well as professional groups, including judges and psychologists/psychiatrists, often do not possess relevant knowledge about offenders' paths to reactive or intended violence or about crime-related amnesia. A critical aspect in searching offenders' memories is the context in which an offender has to remember and tell about the crime. We argue that it is of immediate importance that the interviewer not only be skilful in investigative interviewing but also well prepared to receive reports of gruesome details and aware of his/her own affective and protective responses.

REFERENCES

Anderson, G.S., Litzenberger, R. & Plecas, D. (2002) Physical evidence of police officer stress. *Policing: An International Journal of Police Strategies & Management*, **25**(2), 399–420.

Bourget, D. & Bradford, J.M.W. (1995) Sex offenders who claim amnesia for their alleged offense. *Bulletin of the American Academy of Psychiatry and Law*, **23**, 299–307.

Bradford, J.W. & Smith, S.M. (1979) Amnesia and homicide: The Padola case and a study of thirty cases. *Bulletin of the American Academy of Psychiatry and Law*, **7**, 219–231.

Brysiewicz, P. (2002) Violent death and the South African Emergency nurse. *International Journal of Nursing Studies*, **39**, 253–8.

Bushman, B.J. & Anderson, C.A. (2001) Is it time to pull the plug on the hostile versus instrumental aggression dichotomy? *Psychological Review*, **108**, 273–9.

Calhoun, F.S. & Weston, S.W. (2003) *Contemporary threat management: A practical guide for identifying, assessing and managing individuals of violent intent*. San Diego: Specialized Training Services.

Cima, M., Merckelbach, H., Hollnack, S. & Knauer, E. (2003). Characteristics of psychiatric prison inmates who claim amnesia. *Personality and Individual Differences*, **35**, 373–80.

Cima, M., Nijman, H., Merckelbach, H., Kremer, K. & Hollnack, S. (2004) Claims of crime-related amnesia in forensic patients. *International Journal of Law and Psychiatry*, **27**, 215–21.

Christianson, S.Å. (1992a) Emotional stress and eyewitness memory: A critical review. *Psychological Bulletin*, **112**, 284–309.

Christianson, S.Å. (Ed.) (1992b) *Handbook of Emotion and Memory: Research and Theory*. Hillsdale, N.J.: Erlbaum Associates Publishers.

Christianson, S.Å. (1997) On emotional stress and memory: We need to recognize threatening situations and we need to 'forget' unpleasant experiences. In David G. Payne and Frederick G. Conrad (Eds), *Intersections in basic and applied memory research*. (pp. 133–156). Hillsdale, N.J.: Erlbaum Associates Publishers.

Christianson, S.Å. & Bylin, S. (1999) Does simulating amnesia mediate genuine forgetting for a crime event? *Applied Cognitive Psychology*, **13**, 495–511.

Christianson, S.Å. & Engelberg, E. (1999) Memory for emotional events. In T. Dalgleish & M. Power (Eds), *The handbook of cognition and emotion* (pp. 211–28). Chichester: John Wiley & Sons, Ltd.

Christianson, S.Å. & Fällman, L. (1990) The role of age on reactivity and memory for emotional pictures. *Scandinavian Journal of Psychology*, **31**, 291–301.

Christianson, S.Å. & Freij, I. (2006) *Experts' beliefs about crime-related amnesia*. Manuscript in preparation.

Christianson, S.Å., Holmberg, U., Bylin, S. & Engelberg, E. (2006) *Homicide and sexual offenders' motivation to forget their crimes*. Manuscript in preparation.

Christianson, S.Å. & Lindholm, T. (1998) On the fate of traumatic memories in childhood and adulthood. *Development and Psychopathology*, **10**, 761–80.

Christianson, S.Å., Loftus, E.F., Hoffman, H. & Loftus, G.R. (1991) Eye fixations and memory for emotional events. *Journal of Experimental Psychology: Learning, Memory, and Cognition*, **17**, 693–701.

Christianson, S.Å. & Merckelbach, H. (2004) Crime-related amnesia as a form of deception. In P.A. Granhag & L.A. Strömwall (Eds). *The detection of deception in forensic contexts* (pp. 195–225). Cambridge: Cambridge University Press.

Christianson, S.Å. & Nilsson, L.-G. (1989) Hysterical amnesia: A case of aversively motivated isolation of memory. In T. Archer & L.-G. Nilsson (Eds), *Aversion, avoidance, and anxiety: Perspectives on aversively motivated behavior*. (pp. 289–310). Hillsdale, NJ: Lawrence Erlbaum Associates.

Christianson, S.Å. & von Vogelsang, E. (2006) *Reactive and instrumental homicide offenders who claim amnesia for their crime*. Unpublished manuscript.

Craik, F.I.M. & Lockhart, R.S. (1972) Levels of processing: A framework for memory research. *Journal of Verbal Learning and Verbal Behavior*, **11**, 671–84.

Croft, S. (1995) Helping victims to remember. *Police*, November, 13–14.

Dodge, K.A. (1991). The structure and function of reactive and proactive aggression. In D.J. Pepler & K.H. Rubin (Eds). *The development and treatment of childhood aggression*, (pp. 224–253). Hillsdale, NJ: Erlbaum.

Figley, C.R. (Ed.) (1995) *Compassion fatigue: Coping with secondary traumatic stress disorder in those who treat the traumatized.* New York: Brunner/Mazel, Inc.

Fisher, R.P. & Geiselman, R.E. (1992) *Memory-enhancing techniques for investigative interviewing. The cognitive interview.* Springfield, Illinois: Charles C. Thomas Publisher.

Gould, A. & MacDonald, M. (1987) *The violent years of Maggie MacDonald.* Scarborough, Ontario: Prentice-Hall, Canada.

Gudjonsson, G.H. (2003) *The Psychology of Interrogations and Confessions: A Handbook.* Chichester: John Wiley & Sons, Ltd.

Gudjonsson, G.H., Kopelman, M.D. & MacKeith, J.A.C. (1999). Unreliable admissions to homicide: A case of misdiagnosis of amnesia and misuse of abreaction technique. *British Journal of Psychiatry,* **174**, 455–9.

Holmberg, U, & Christianson, S.Å. (2002) Murderers' and sexual offenders' experience of police interviews and their inclination to admit or deny crimes. *Behavioral Sciences and the Law,* **20**, 31–45.

Holmberg, U., Christianson, S.Å. & Karlsson, I. (2006) *Stressful event exposure as related to police officers' attitudes towards interviewing victims and suspects.* Manuscript submitted for publication.

Iliffe, G. (2000) Exploring the counselor's experiences of working with perpetrators and survivors of domestic violence. *Journal of Interpersonal Violence,* **15**(4), 393–413.

Johnson, M.K., Hashtroudi, S. & Lindsay, D.S. (1991) Source monitoring. *Psychological Bulletin,* **14**, 3–28.

Kalant, H. (1996) Intoxicated automatism: Legal concept vs. scientific evidence. *Contemporary Drug Problems,* **23**, 631–48.

Karlsson, I. & Christianson, S.Å. (2003). The phenomenology of traumatic experiences in police work. *Policing: An International Journal of Police Strategies & Management,* **3**, 419–38.

Karlsson, I. & Christianson, S.Å. (2006). Police officers involved in a manhunt of a mass murder: Memories and psychological responses. *Policing: An International Journal of Police Strategies & Management,* **29**, 524–40.

Kopelman, M.D. (1987) Crime and amnesia: a review. *Behavioural Sciences and the Law,* **5**, 323–42.

Kopelman, M.D. (1995) The assessment of psychogenic amnesia. In A.D Baddeley, B.A. Wilson & F.N. Watts (Eds). *Handbook of Memory Disorders* (pp. 427–448). New York: John Wiley & Sons, Inc.

Kopelman, M.D., Green, R.E.A., Guinan, E.M., Lewis, P.D.R. & Stanhope, N. (1994) The case of the amnesic intelligence officer. *Psychological Medicine,* **24**, 1037–45.

Kvavilashvili, L. & Ellis, J.A. (1999) The effects of positive and negative placebos on human memory performance. *Memory,* **7**, 421–37.

Laney, C., Campbell, H.V., Heuer, F. & Reisberg, D. (2004) Memory for thematically arousing events. *Memory & Cognition,* **32**, 1149–59.

Laney, C., Heuer, F. & Reisberg, D. (2003) Thematically-induced arousal in naturally-occuring emotional memories. *Applied Cognitive Psychology,* **17**, 995–1004.

Loewenstein, R.J. (1991) Psychogenic amnesia and psychogenic fugue: A comprehensive review. *American Psychiatric Press Review of Psychiatry,* **10**, 189–222.

McNally, R.J. (2005) Debunking myths about trauma and memory. *Canadian Journal of Psychiatry,* **50**, 817–22.

Mechanic, M.B., Resick, P.A. & Griffin, M.G. (1998) A comparison of normal forgetting, psychopathology, and information-processing models of reported amnesia for recent sexual trauma. *Journal of Consulting and Clinical Psychology*, **66**, 948–57.

Merckelbach, H., Cima, M. & Nijman, H. (2002) Daders met geheugenverlies [Offenders with memory loss]. In P.J. van Koppen, D.J. Hessing, H. Merckelbach & H. Crombag (Eds). *Het Recht van Binnen: Psychologie van het Recht.* (pp. 667–85). Deventer: Kluwer.

Most, S.B., Chun, M.M., Widders, D.M. & Zald, D.H. (in press). Attentional rubbernecking: Cognitive control and personality in emotion-induced blindness. *Psychonomic Bulletin & Review*.

Öhman, A. (1979) The orienting response, attention, and learning: An information processing perspective. In H.D. Kimmel, E.H. van Olst & J.F. Orlebeke (Eds), *The orienting reflex in humans* (pp. 443–72). Hillsdale, NJ: Lawrence Erlbaum Associates.

Öhman, A. (1991) Orienting and attention: Preferred preattentive processing of potentially phobic stimuli. In B.A. Campell, R. Richardson, & H. Hayne (Eds), *Attention and information processing in infants and adults: Perspectives from human and animal research*, (pp. 263–95). Hillsdale, NJ: Lawrence Erlbaum Associates.

Parwatikar, S.D., Holcomb, W.R. & Menninger, K.A. (1985) The detection of malingered amnesia in accused murderers. *Bulletin of the American Academy of Psychiatry and Law*, **13**, 97–103.

Pearlman, L.A. & MacIan, P.S. (1993) Vicarious traumatization among trauma therapists: Empirical findings on self-care. *Traumatic Stress Points: News for the International Society for Traumatic Stress Studies*, **7**(3), 5.

Pearlman, L.A. & Saakvitne, K.W. (1995) Treating therapists with vicarious traumatizations and secondary traumatic stress disorders. In Figley, C.R. (Ed.), *Compassion fatigue; Coping with secondary traumatic stress disorders in those who treat the traumatized* (pp. 150–177). New York, NY: Brunner/Mazel, Inc.

Philippot, P., Schaefer, A. & Herbette, G. (2003) Consequences of specific processing of emotional information: Impact of general versus specific autobiographical memory priming on emotion elicitation. *Emotion.* **3**, 270–83.

Pollock, Ph.H. (1999). When the killer suffers: Post-traumatic stress reactions following homicide. *Legal and Criminological Psychology*, **4**, 185–202.

Porter, S., Birt, A.R., Yuille, J.C. & Hervé, H.F. (2001) Memory for murder: A psychological perspective on dissociative amnesia in legal contexts. *International Journal of Law and Psychiatry*, **24**, 23–42.

Porter, S. & Woodworth, M. (2006) Patterns of violent behaviour in the criminal psychopath. In C. Patrick (Ed.), *Handbook of psychopathy* (pp. 481–94). New York, NY: The Guilford Press.

Porter, S. & Yuille, J.C. (1995) Credibility assessment of criminal suspects through statement analysis. *Psychology, Crime, and Law*, **1**, 319–31.

Pyszora, N.M., Barker, A.F. & Kopelman, M.D. (2003) Amnesia for criminal offences: A study of life sentence prisoners. *Journal of Forensic Psychiatry & Psychology*, **14**, 475–90.

Reisberg, D. & Heuer, F. (2004) Memory for emotional events. In D. Reisberg, & P. Hertel (Eds), *Memory and emotion. Series in affective science*, (pp. 3–41). Oxford: Oxford University Press.

Rosen, G.M. & Phillips, W.R. (2004) A cautionary lesson from simulated patients. *Journal of the American Academy of Psychiatry and the Law*, **32**, 132–3.

Schacter, D.L. (1986) Amnesia and crime: How much do we really know? *American Psychologist*, **41**, 286–95.

Swihart, G., Yuille, J. & Porter, S. (1999). The role of state-dependent memory in red-outs. *International Journal of Law and Psychiatry*, **22**, 199–212.

Taylor, P.J. & Kopelman, M.D. (1984). Amnesia for criminal offences. *Psychological Medicine*, **14**, 581–8.

Terr, L. (1990). *Unchained memories: True stories of traumatic memories, lost and found.* New York: Basic Books.

Van der Kolk, B.A. & Fisler, R. (1995) Dissociation and the fragmentary nature of traumatic memories; Review and experimental confirmation. *Journal of Traumatic Stress*, **8**, 505–25.

Van Oorsouw, K. & Merckelbach, H. (2004) Feigning amnesia undermines memory for a mock crime. *Applied Cognitive Psychology*, **18**, 505–18.

Van Oorsouw, K., Merckelbach, H., Ravelli, D., Nijman, H. & Mekking-Pompen, I. (2004) Alcohol black out for criminally relevant behavior. *Journal of the American Academy of Psychiatry and the Law*, **32**, 364–70.

Vuilleumier, P., Armony, J.L., Clarke, K., Husain, M., Driver, J. & Dolan, R.J. (2002) Neural response to emotional faces with and without awareness: Event-related fMRI in a parietal patient with visual extinction and spatial neglect *Neuropsychologia*, **40**, 2156–66.

Wegner, D.M., Quillian, F. & Houston, C.E. (1996) Memories out of order: Thought suppression and the disturbance of sequence memory. *Journal of Personality and Social Psychology*, **71**, 680–91.

Williams, J.M.G., Teasdale, J.D., Segal, Z.V. & Soulsby, J. (2000) Mindfulness-based cognitive therapy reduces overgeneral autobiographical memory in formerly depressed patients. *Journal of Abnormal Psychology*, **109**, 150–5.

Woodworth, M. & Porter, S. (2002). In cold blood: Characteristics of criminal homicides as a function of psychopathy. *Journal of Abnormal Psychology*, **111**, 436–45.

CHAPTER 2

Memory Formation in Offenders: Perspectives from a Biopsychosocial Model of Eyewitness Memory

Hugues Hervé, Barry S. Cooper and John C. Yuille

INTRODUCTION

In spite of more than 100 years of eyewitness research, no comprehensive theory exists to explain either the between-subject memory variability found in eyewitnesses' accounts of criminal events or the within-subject mechanisms that lead to changes in eyewitnesses' accounts over time. In this chapter, we present a biopsychosocial model of eyewitness memory adapted for the offender context.[1] As scientist-practitioners, our goal was to develop an empirically anchored theory that can both explain research findings and

---

[1] The model presented was developed to address memory formation with special attention to eyewitness memory and, therefore, is greater in its scope than presented here.

Offenders' Memories of Violent Crimes. Edited by Sven Å. Christianson.

guide clinical practice. As such, our model reflects the current state of knowledge in the areas of affect, memory, trauma and crime, and emphasises both individual differences and group similarities. As practitioners, our interest was to make sense of the observed memory variability in the real world, not in unravelling the specific neuropsychophysiological mechanisms underlying this variability.[2] In other words, we took a top-down, rather than a bottom-up, approach that emphasised external validity. As theorists, we wanted to account for the variability in offenders' accounts of their crimes and, therefore, propose a comprehensive theory.

The proposed model is unique in two ways. Firstly, while we support the prevailing view that eyewitnesses' memories are strongly influenced by their emotional reactions, we argue that these emotional reactions are more complex and variable from one individual to another than previously proposed. Secondly, being well aware that emotional reactions, as well as memory formations, do not occur in a vacuum, we propose that there are a variety of predisposing, precipitating and perpetuating biopsychosocial factors that interact to guide an eyewitnesses' memory and provide a framework for their integration. After reviewing the eyewitness memory literature in terms of research approaches, identified memory patterns and prevailing theories, we introduce our view of emotional processing and delineate its implications for eyewitness memory formation. We then present our biopsychosocial model of eyewitness memory and its implications for research and practice.[3]

EYEWITNESS LITERATURE

Research Approaches

Eyewitness memory is the first hand account of a crime by a witness (perpetrator, victim or bystander). Eyewitness memory is one of the largest areas of study in forensic psychology, with most investigations being analogue in nature. Unfortunately, this over-reliance on laboratory research has limited the growth of the field.[4] For

---

[2] Viewing these mechanisms as important, however, we hope others will explore them further.

[3] For brevity, topics adequately reviewed elsewhere were summarised, with references provided. We acknowledge that a more thorough review of the literature would help clarify certain aspects of our model but our goal was simply to introduce our model. We plan to publish a book that more extensively explains our model and its implications.

[4] The lack of statistical techniques that can capture the complexity of memory processes, while accounting for individual differences, is another limiting factor.

ethical reasons, such research precludes the examination of how actual violence/trauma – naturalistic situations denoted by significant stress/arousal – impacts memory; instead the focus is on the effects of low-intensity stress upon memory within sterile environments, resulting in findings of questionable generalisability (Tulving & Madigan, 1970). Indeed, although examining memory for such events is important, archival and field studies consistently reveal that memory for witnessed events is more varied, as seen in case law and clinical anecdotes, than suggested by laboratory research (Cutshall & Yuille, 1989; Kuehn, 1974; Tollestrup, Turtle & Yuille, 1994; Yuille & Cutshall, 1986); the former reveal memory patterns that the latter simply cannot yield (Yuille & Daylen, 1998), greater memory heterogeneity between eyewitnesses who view the same event (Cooper, Kennedy, Hervé & Yuille, 2002), and that memory is sensitive to a variety of post-encoding distortions (van der Kolk, McFarlane & Weisaeth, 1996). Rather than acknowledging these facts, some laboratory researchers have focused on criticising naturalistic research on methodological grounds, arguing for internal over external validity.[5] This focus on internal validity has obvious theoretical implications: The results of an experiment that can control all extraneous effects – effects that typify real-life experiences – can more readily be explained by unidimensional models. Archival research and field studies, however, draw out the need for a multidimensional theoretical formulation.

Identified Memory Patterns

Given the contrasting findings between analogue, archival and field studies, it is only through their combination that the full range of eyewitness memory patterns emerges (Tulving, 1991). With this in mind, eyewitness research has revealed 10 memory patterns (Yuille & Daylen, 1998): normal forgetting, active forgetting, dissociative amnesia, state dependent memory, red out, remarkable memory, script memory, dissociative memory with either an external or internal focus, and created memory (Table 2.1).[6] These patterns represent the end product of a mixture of processes (e.g., time-based forgetting, memory avoidance, affect-moderated encoding/retrieval, dissociation, etc.) that delineate memory quantity (i.e., amount of event-related

---

[5] For example, a reviewer once commented: 'In the process of bringing the investigation to a real-life scenario, the researcher has lost the essence of the weapon focus effect' (anonymous reviewer, 2000).

[6] Yuille and Daylen's (1998) categories were supplemented to reflect subsequent research.

Table 2.1   Identified memory patterns displayed by eyewitnesses

Normal Forgettting	Occurs for events of non-significance (i.e., routine/benign). Memory initially relatively good in terms of quantity and quality but benign nature causes superficial encoding prone to time-based forgetting and distortions. One of three patterns inducible in analogue research; may apply to some aspects of arousing events (e.g., peripheral details).
Active Forgetting	Occurs for events of significance. Memory initially good in terms of quantity and quality but, due to conscious avoidance of the memory and its triggers, loss of memory quantity (part/whole) occurs over time. Avoidance can lead to paradoxical effect: memory enhancement.
Dissociative Amnesia	Occurs for events of extreme significance (trauma) with loss of memory quantity (part/whole) developing during or following event; rule out organic causes. Poorly understood but not believed to reflect state-dependent effects and/or active forgetting, although latter may be a contributing factor.
State Dependent Memory	Occurs for events of significance and non-significance. Robust empirical support for latter: memory quantity reflects similarity between encoding and retrieval context (environment and internal state), with loss of detail reflecting extent of discrepancy. With regards to latter, memory thought to be dependent on similarity in affective state between encoding and retrieval.
Red Out	Occurs for events of significance; evidence limited to offenders. Results when affect is substantially altered (typically by rage), causing altered state of consciousness resulting in amnesia for violent act, with acts preceding/following being recalled. May reflect special case of dissociative amnesia but likely an extreme form of state-dependent memory.
Remarkable Memory	Occurs for events of significance (positive or negative) with memory (part/whole) generally being detailed, accurate, and retained over long intervals.
Script Memory	Occurs for repeated events of non-significance (e.g., day-to-day activities) or significance to which individual has habituated (e.g., repeated unchanging victimisation/offending). Memory reflects blending of episodes into one generalised memory ('script') that is retained over time.
Dissociative Memory	Occurs for events of significance leading to dissociative symptoms during or following event, with memory reflecting dissociative experience:
	External Focus: If the dissociative experience results in 'out of body experience,' event is perceived from an external perspective, resulting in memory of unique

	quality characterised by observer perspective (e.g., looking in from detached, alternative viewpoint) as opposed to typical field perspective (i.e., through one's own eyes). Validity established but veracity of observer memories is unknown.
	Internal Focus: If the dissociative experience results in partial/total loss of contact with reality, memory is significantly limited. If partial, focus will be on internal state, with memory evidencing little quantity but subjective qualities (i.e., event-specific affective/mental state; e.g., fear, mental confusion). If total, focus reflects dissociation into fantasy life, resulting in detailed but event-unrelated memory, with event-incongruent subjective qualities.
Created Memory	False/illusory memory of event of non-significance or significance developed via suggestion or (theoretically) active fantasy life (fantasy becomes reality). Inducible in analogue research; field examples largely induced via suggestive/coercive therapeutic/investigative practices; also self-induced.

Labels meant to highlight dominant processes leading to pattern.

details; e.g., full recollection to amnesia) and quality (i.e., type [e.g., central vs peripheral], nature [e.g., field vs observer perspective] and accuracy [e.g., distorted to created details]).[7] The first five deal with different patterns of memory loss, while remarkable and script memories reflect the long-term retention of memories. Dissociative memories reflect event-related processes affecting memory quantity and quality, and created memories are a product of suggestion, not of events, and therefore reflect quality. These categories are not mutually exclusive. For example, a perpetrator may show remarkable memory for the central details of a robbery but normal forgetting for its peripheral aspects. While the former might remain largely unaltered, the latter, given the reconstructive nature of memory, will fluctuate from one retelling to another (Erdelyi & Kleinbard, 1978), resulting in about 60% of the total details remaining equivalent over time (Conway, 1997).[8] In addition, this list is not meant to be exhaustive but, rather, to represent the memory patterns stemming from known cognitive/affective processes. Clearly, other patterns could

---

[7] As our intention was to explain eyewitness memory formation, accuracy refers solely to how well one's memory reflects the witnessed event, not to the instrumental distortion of memory.

[8] An assumption of our model is that memory is not reproductive but reconstructive in nature (Schacter, 1996).

be added by considering additional influences (e.g., substance abuse leading to alcohol-induced blackout; Goodwin, 1995). Such moderating and mediating influences are, therefore, woven into the present theory.

Prevailing Theories

A fundamental assumption in the eyewitness literature is that memory is highly sensitive to emotion-mediated distortions (Christianson, 1992), with most investigators adopting a unidimensional view of emotion reflecting either valence (positive/negative) *or* arousal (high/low; Revelle & Loftus, 1990). However, emotional processing is much more complex: it includes both physiological (i.e., arousal) and cognitive responses (Mandler, 1984), the latter – when thinking in dimensional terms – reflecting both valence and arousal (Russell, 1989). Furthermore, scant attention has been given to the effects of physiological arousal on memory, independent of cognitive processes.[9] This is remarkable given that trauma/crime create, by definition, strong arousal reactions (van der Kolk et al., 1996) and investigators generally interpret their findings in light of theories that propose memory is mediated by arousal (Christianson, 1992).

According to the Yerkes–Dodson 'law' (Yerkes & Dodson, 1908), the relationship between arousal and performance is curvilinear. Under this view, increases in arousal initially facilitate memory until it reaches an optimal level, at which point further increases in arousal have negative effects. Christianson (1992) points to numerous findings that suggest, as far as the central details of emotional events are concerned, high arousal can benefit all stages of memory, suggesting that the Yerkes–Dodson law has limited application for explaining eyewitness memory results. Accordingly, Christianson and others turned to Easterbrook's (1959) cue-utilisation hypothesis, which proposes that arousal reduces attentional mechanisms (i.e., restricts the range of cues attended to), that is, one's ability to engage in parallel processing (Easterbrook, 1959). Initially, this restriction benefits performance by allocating all available resources to the task at hand so that central (relevant) information is attended to at the detriment of peripheral (irrelevant) information, as seen in numerous analogue studies. Theoretically, as stress mounts to real-world levels,

---

[9] Laboratory studies have thus far largely focused on the cognitive representation of arousal.

the reduction in cue utilisation eventually includes central information, thereby increasingly limiting encoding, doing so in a manner suggested by the Yerkes–Dodson law. As such, we do not discount this process and, instead, view it as occurring in parallel with the cue-utilisation effect, as supported by contemporary views of basic memory consolidation (Humphreys & Revelle, 1984; Walker, 1958). At low levels of arousal, information transfer (IT) between short-term memory (STM) and long-term memory (LTM) is relatively poor, thereby hindering LTM formation. At moderate levels of arousal, IT improves, resulting in a larger amount of information being transferred from STM to LTM. With further increases in arousal, a larger amount of event-related information is sampled and placed within limited STM resources. At a certain point, STM becomes overloaded, as IT cannot keep up, resulting in certain memories never being transferred to LTM. Presumably, within the IT stream, central information – being more affectively loaded (see below) – is given priority over peripheral information.

While we endorse the view that high arousal influences parallel processing and memory transfer, we believe this disruption to be more complex as it leads to a variety of memory consequences. The inability of these theories to explain this variability, as well as post-encoding distortions, highlights the need for a more ecologically valid theoretical approach. Towards this aim, van der Kolk and colleagues (1996), based on their research on trauma victims, suggested extreme arousal in a personally threatening scenario causes a dissociation of the emotional/sensory aspects of memory from the narrative aspects. They do not propose that emotional stress affects the allocation of attentional resources, as proposed by Easterbrook (1959), but that it simply breaks the links between various cognitive processes, leaving each, however, intact in memory. Unfortunately, this theory has yet to be validated and is proving difficult to investigate. Furthermore, although we agree that some eyewitnesses may have access to a variety of memories (sensory to narrative), we question the premise that attentional and memory processes would fail to produce an encoding bias (e.g., narrative over sensory or vice versa).

EMOTIONAL PROCESSING

Most theorists agree that emotional experiences reflect two correlated, yet independent mechanisms: A biological system mediating arousal responses to emotional events and a cognitive system that evaluates the significance of emotional events, each communicating with the other (Mandler, 1984). Within this framework, arousal refers to physiological activity produced by the autonomic nervous system (ANS), thereby setting the quantitative aspects of experienced emotions. ANS arousal (ANSA) also serves to prepare the organism for action, while concurrently signalling the mental system to remain alert and attentive – both of which are likely to impact memory. As ANSA is non-specific (i.e., does not produce a specific emotional response; Schachter, 1971), the cognitive system must perform a meaning analysis of the event in question to determine its emotional connotation (Mandler, 1984). Mediated by the central nervous system, it ascribes the particular quality of the emotion (e.g., pleasant vs unpleasant), which in turn serves to either decrease or increase ANSA (Mandler, 1984). Although these interpretative cognitions may be engendered by arousal, they are primarily defined by the general situation and current cognitive state of the organism, which themselves affect memory. Thus, it is the joint product of these systems that construct emotions as we know them: 'Arousal provides the intensity of the emotional state, and cognition provides its quality' (p. 119; Mandler, 1984). Since affect moderates memory formation, eyewitness memory research must consider each system and how they may differ across individuals and situations.

Individual Differences: Arousal Sensitivity and Affective Focus

Advancements in the study of affect (Blascovich, 1990, 1992; Mandler, 1984) suggest one's arousal sensitivity (i.e., biological sensitivity to ANSA) is a major factor mediating affective responses to events and, as such, memory for such events. Differing across individuals, it is viewed as a normally distributed dimension, with hypersensitives (low arousal threshold) and hyposensitives (high arousal threshold) defining the end points of the continuum (Blascovich, 1992; Figure 2.1). Since the labelling of environmentally elicited affect requires the perception of the ensuing ANSA, arousal sensitivity sets the threshold at which point an event becomes emotionally relevant (i.e., as it reaches/surpasses optimal levels). Table 2.2 provides a selective portrayal of how arousal affects hypersensitives and hyposensitives. As can be seen, the same situation can lead to a higher level of perceived arousal in hypersensitives than in hyposensitives.

Blascovich (1990, 1992) further postulated that arousal sensitivity delineates which aspect of the emotional response is paid most attention, doing so indirectly via its effect on cognitive development.

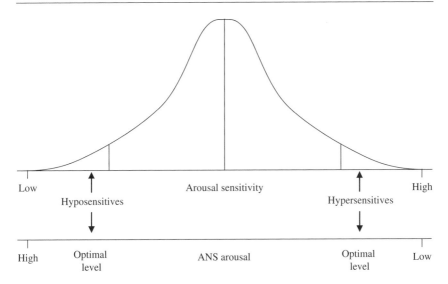

Figure 2.1 Theoretical distribution of ANS arousal sensitivity and consequent optimal arousal levels

Being sensitive to physiological changes, hypersensitives have learned to attend to internal (somesthetic) over external (environmental) cues when labelling their affect, while hyposensitives, being relatively indifferent to physiological changes, have learned to rely on external rather than internal cues. In line with this theory, Feldman (1995) found people to be either arousal-focused (i.e., an affective response strongly based on one's reaction to an emotional event) or pleasure-focused (i.e., an affective response strongly based on the interpretation of the emotional event) when evaluating their emotional reactions, as well as emotional events in general. Consequently, one would expect hypersensitives to have more physiologically based (emotional-sensory) memories and hyposensitives to have more cognitively based (autobiographical/narrative) memories for emotional events. Indeed, it is not uncommon to see eyewitnesses with a clear narrative-like memory without any accompanying affect or emotional memories without a clear narrative (van der Kolk & Fisler, 1995).

Given that this multidimensional emotional response and the manner in which it varies from one eyewitness to the next permeate all levels of our model, we now turn our attention to their influences on memory formation, following which our model and its implications for research and practice are presented.

Table 2.2 Hypothetical arousal perception and arousal-mediated effects on attention, memory, and suggestibility based on trait arousal sensitivity and intensity of event-related arousal

Event-related Arousal Effects	Hypersensitive	Hyposensitive
Extremely low		
Perceived arousal	Very low/Uncomfortable	Extremely low/Intolerable
Attentional bias	External>Internal	External<<<Internal
External[1]	Central>Peripheral	Peripheral
Internal[2]	Cognitive>Sensory	Cognitive<<<Sensory
Memory distortions	RM/AF>NF/SM>DM(EF)/SDM (NF/SM)[4]	DM(IF)/SDM>RM/AF (NF/SM)[4]
Suggestibility[3]	Mild/Internal	Extreme/External
Very low		
Perceived arousal	Low/Comfortable	Extremely low/Distressing
Attentional bias	External=Internal	External<<Internal
External[1]	Central=Peripheral	Central<<Peripheral
Internal[2]	Cognitive=Sensory	Cognitive<<Sensory
Memory distortions	NF/SM	RM/AF/DM(IF)/SDM (NF/SM)[4]
Suggestibility[3]	None[5]	Moderate/External
Low		
Perceived arousal	Medium/Optimal	Very low/Uncomfortable
Attentional bias	External≤Internal	External<Internal
External[1]	Central≤Peripheral	Central<Peripheral
Internal[2]	Cognitive<Sensory	Cognitive<Sensory
Memory distortions	RM/NF/SM	RM/AF>NF/SM>DM(IF)/SDM (NF/SM)[4]
Suggestibility[3]	Mild/External	Mild/External
Medium		
Arousal perception	High/Uncomfortable	Low/Comfortable
Attentional bias	External<Internal	External=Internal
External[1]	Central<Peripheral	Central=Peripheral
Internal[2]	Cognitive<<Sensory	Cognitive=Sensory
Memory distortions	RM/AF>NF/SM>DM(IF)/SDM (NF/SM)[4]	NF/SM
Suggestibility[3]	Moderate/External	None[5]
High		
Perceived arousal	Very High/Traumatic	Medium/Optimal
Attentional bias	External<<Internal	External≥Internal
External[1]	Central<<Peripheral	Central≥Peripheral
Internal[2]	Cognitive<<<Sensory	Cognitive>Sensory
Memory distortions	RM/AF/DM(IF)/SDM(RO) (NF/SM)[4]	RM/NF/SM
Suggestibility[3]	High/External	Mild/Internal

Very high		
Perceived arousal	Extremely high/Unbearable	High/Uncomfortable
Attentional bias	External<<<Internal	External>Internal
External[1]	Peripheral	Central>Peripheral
Internal[2]	Cognitive<<<Sensory	Cognitive>>Sensory
Memory distortions	DM(IF)/SDM(RO)> RM/AF(NF/SM)[4]	RM/AF>NF/SM> DM(EF)/SDM (NF/SM)[4]
Suggestibility[3]	Extreme/External	Moderate/Internal
Extremely high		
Perceived arousal	Extremely high/Debilitating	Very high to Extremely high/Traumatic to debilitating
Attentional bias	Internal	External≫Internal to internal
External[1]	N/A	Central>>Peripheral to central
Internal[2]	Sensory	Cognitive>>>Sensory to sensory
Memory distortions	DA	DM(EF)/SDM(RO)≥ RM/AF (NF/SM)[4]to DA
Suggestibility[3]	Extreme/External	High to extreme/Internal to External

NF = Normal Forgetting; AF = Active Forgetting; DA = Dissociative Amnesia; RM = Remarkable Memory; SDM = State-Dependent Memory; RO = Red Out; SM = Script Memory; DM = Dissociative Memory; [1] = Central and peripheral information objectively defined; [2] = Cognitive and sensory information of environmentally elicited affective response; [3] = Refers to both susceptibility level and type, the latter stemming from attentional bias (Created Memory not specified as reflects post encoding psychosocial factors); [4] = Occurs only if individual, due to personal history, habituated to event; [5] = While increasingly likely over time, suggestibility not provided as reflects state more than trait effects.

EMOTIONAL PROCESSING AND EYEWITNESS MEMORY FORMATION

Arousal Sensitivity

Physiologically, emotions reflect ANS reactions that lead to an orientation response characterised by a narrowing of attention onto the central aspects of the scene at the exclusion of peripheral details. This reaction intensifies as arousal rises, with memory distortions occurring at disturbing (traumatic) levels. Not everyone, however, experiences arousal in the same manner, with hypersensitives and hyposensitives being, respectively, susceptible and resistant to its effects. Being biologically pre-defined, early socialisation will, within limits, fine-tune one's trait arousal sensitivity (trait sensitivity), which will then remain relatively resistant to long-term changes. However, there are a host of variables that can affect it at the state level (e.g., pre-trauma affect, threat level; see later), thereby functionally rendering individuals relatively hypersensitive or hyposensitive within a specific event (state sensitivity). Regarding memory, arousal sensitivity will dictate the point during arousal augmentation when one will experience the affect as traumatic and, consequently, display arousal-mediated attentional distortions, with more prototypical individuals showing greater effects. Given that hypersensitives are likely to interpret arousing events as traumatic at lower levels of arousal than hyposensitives, the former should display memory distortions earlier in the arousal stream and across a wider range of arousal levels than the latter (Table 2.2).

Cognitive System

Psychologically, emotions reflect cognitive interpretations. Throughout development, individuals learn to emotionally differentiate objects, situations and people (Mandler, 1984). New emotional events are then interpreted in light of both their current characteristics and one's emotional learning history. Clearly, interpretive sophistication will depend on one's cognitive capacities and, as such, neurocognitive functioning is thought to exert the most influence on this system. Given the developmental nature of this system, arousal sensitivity, temperament/personality, acculturation and certain more transient factors are also quite influential (see later). Together, these factors produce idiosyncratic cognitive filters through which events are interpreted, which should be evident in eyewitnesses' accounts. For example, while the statement of an intellectually limited offender should be relatively short, concrete and possibly echoing interpretative confusion (e.g., failure to fully understand the gravity of the situation, misinterpretation of social cues, etc.), that of an intellectually intact offender should evidence more complex and abstract language, more detail and relatively little interpretive confusion. Psychological profiles of interviewees could therefore help clarify their idiosyncratic responses.

The Interplay of Arousal Sensitivity and the Cognitive Interpretative System

A central aspect of emotional responses is that each component – ANSA and cognition – feeds back into the other, the end product having further memory effects. Arousal sensitivity, being innate to the organism, shapes the development of the cognitive system. Throughout development, hypersensitives and hyposensitives, respectively, avoid and seek out, arousing experiences (Ellis, 1987). As a result, arousal sensitivity sets the parameters of one's emotional learning environments, information used to make sense of future emotional events. While hypersensitives will label events based on how they affect them emotionally, that is, along an arousal dimension (positive events as unexciting and negative events as arousing), hyposensitives will label events based on event-specific features, that is, along a valence continuum (low arousing as bad and high arousing as good) – labels that should be reflected in eyewitnesses' statements. For example, a hyposensitive (psychopathic) sex offender, when asked to describe how he felt when he raped for the first time replied:[10] 'Pumped up, a real high. Yeah, I know it was wrong, but thinking about it still gives me a buzz'. When asked about the death of his mother after a long illness, his most salient comment was: 'The funeral was a real drag. I went to sleep'. Further examination clearly indicated this man evaluated events and experiences solely in terms of their ability to arouse or stimulate him. Indeed, he stated, 'If something gives me a rush, gets the adrenaline flowing, that's good. If it doesn't, that's bad. End of story' (personal communication, Hare, 1997).

By influencing the type of emotional information deemed subjectively relevant (central), arousal sensitivity also indirectly delineates what will be encoded into memory. On the one hand, hypersensitives have a very alert physiological system that, once engaged, sends a strong signal that is quickly experienced as disturbing. As a result, they – throughout development – have become especially attuned to, and focused upon, their internal states, all the while avoiding arousal-eliciting sources (Figure 2.2). Attention paid to the scene will be aimed at decreasing the intensity of the situation by, for example, locating an escape route (peripheral information). In other words, as arousal rises, they increasingly focus on peripheral information at the detriment of central information (Table 2.2; Figure 2.3). This reaction is akin to a phobic individual who, although peripherally aware of the phobic stimuli, continuously searches for a way to escape the situation (Thorpe & Salkovskis, 1998). On the other hand, hyposensitives have a relatively numb physiological system that not only takes greater stimulation to engage but, once engaged, sends a relatively weak signal that takes time to be experienced as disturbing. Being intrinsically under-stimulated, they have become especially attuned to, and focused upon, external stimulation, with sensory-emotive functioning being of secondary importance (Figure 2.2). Seeing no need to shy away from arousal-eliciting events, they use this (central) information to

---

[10] Psychopathy, throughout this chapter, refers to the concept defined by the Hare Psychopathy Checklist-Revised (Hare, 2003).

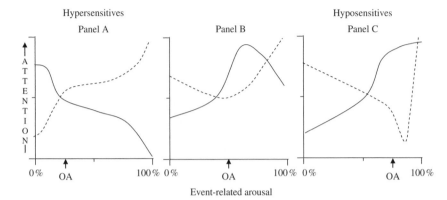

Figure 2.2 Theorised orintation response (external vs internal attentional focus) based on event-related arousal and arousal sensitivity (OA = optimal arousal)

────── Central information (i.e., objectively defined)
─ ─ ─ ─ Peripheral information (i.e., objectively defined)

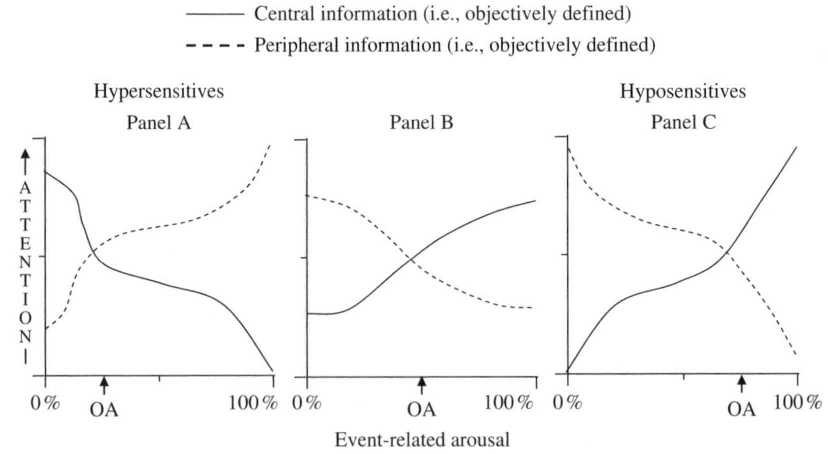

Figure 2.3 Theorised external orientation response (central vs peripheral attentional focus) based on event-related arousal and arousal sensitivity (OA = optimal arousal)

make sense of their affective experiences, with their internal states and benign (peripheral) aspects of the event receiving little attention – an effect that becomes increasingly pronounced as arousal increases (Table 2.2; Figure 2.3). This reaction is akin to that of experienced law enforcement personnel who, although vaguely aware of their internal state and of surrounding activities during an armed standoff, focus their attention on the situation at hand. Any awareness of their own sensations and surroundings is likely to be of short duration and of secondary importance and, therefore, less likely to be encoded. Consequently, hyposensitives should generally make better eyewitnesses than hypersensitives (i.e., encode more central than peripheral information). For example, a psychopathic offender, when asked about his memory for perpetrated acts of violence reported: 'I remember everything I do and do everything I want'. Certain situations (e.g., imminent threat of death), however, will, by definition, trigger potent ANS reactions that will surpass even the hyposensitive's tolerance to arousal and, therefore, deserve attention (if only briefly; see Mandler, 1984). In essence, while peripheral to the investigative process, the sensory experience takes on a subjectively central role, suggesting that extremely arousing events will engender encoding of one's sensory experience, the extent of which reflecting one's arousal sensitivity (Figure 2.4).

Given the dynamic nature of events and emotions, interpretive cognitions are continuously being updated, with each update dampening or stimulating the arousal component of the affective response, which in turn influences attention and IT from STM to LTM.[11]

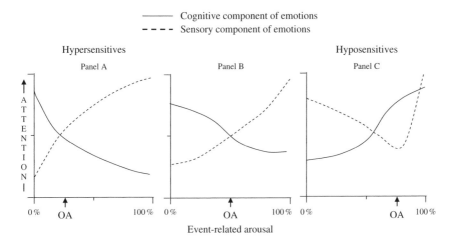

Figure 2.4 Theorised internal orientation response (cognitive vs sensory attentional focus) based on event-related arousal and arousal sensitivity (OA = optimal arousal)

---

[11] Under relaxed situation, the reverse pattern should be observed, a la Yerkes–Dodson.

Within arousing/criminal events, stimulating effects will quickly be interpreted by hypersensitives as significant, thereby leading them to further focus upon their internal (sensory) state and, to a lesser extent, subjectively relevant peripheral information. In addition, their already taxed STM resources will quickly become overloaded, thereby precluding LTM consolidation to benefit from efficient IT, especially for central information. The same situation, however, will take longer to be interpreted as significant by hypersensitives (if at all). When perceived as significant, it will cause them to increasingly focus upon central information and, to a lesser extent, their internal (cognitive) state at the detriment of peripheral information, with STM becoming increasingly taxed but not necessarily overloaded, thereby allowing LTM consolidation to benefit from IT efficiency. Conversely, dampening effects, reducing the stress on STM resources (especially for hypersensitives) and, therefore, allowing efficient IT to LTM, should result in hypersensitives encoding, in addition to their subjective experience, a wider range of peripheral information and possibly some subjectively relevant central information, and in hyposensitives encoding, in addition to central information, an increasing amount of subjectively relevant peripheral information, with their internal state becoming increasingly of secondary importance. That emotions are dynamic in nature highlights the fact that dampening and stimulating effects will have specific memory impacts depending when in the arousal sequence they become engaged, which explains why eyewitnesses may display a variety of memory patterns to the same event.

Finally, arousal sensitivity and mental ability will delineate one's predominant type of feedback during stressful/criminal events. In general, hypersensitives, who shy away from stimulation, and individuals of limited intellect, who are less able to make sense of their surroundings, are prone to catastrophise their experience and, therefore, engage ANS stimulation, while hyposensitives, who fear-not stimulation, and the intellectually intact, who can use their intellect to their advantage, may rationalise their situation, resulting in ANS dampening.

A BIOPSYCHOSOCIAL MODEL OF EYEWITNESS MEMORY

Overall, it appears that the quality and quantity of crime-related memories depends on the interaction between characteristics of the witness and event (Yuille & Daylen, 1998), a notion that permeates our theoretical approach. A central assumption of our model is that one's emotional response during a stressful/criminal event will delineate both the quality and quantity of the ensuing memory. We stress the fact that emotional reactions are multidimensional in nature, reflecting both physiological and psychological processes that differ across individuals. Believing that emotional reactions, as well as memory formation, do not occur in a vacuum, we postulate that eyewitness memory variability stems from specific and interacting predisposing, precipitating and perpetuating biopsychosocial factors (i.e., factors that bias witnesses to respond to an event in a particular manner, affect witnesses during the event, and influence memory retention and reconstruction, respectively).[12] These factors generally exert their effect on memory indirectly by affecting primarily one's arousal sensitivity and/or secondarily one's interpretive system. Although receiving some empirical attention, these factors have yet to be incorporated into a comprehensive theory and, therefore, we propose a framework for their integration (see Figure 2.5).

Predisposing Factors

Predisposing factors are either innate traits or experiences that occur prior to the event in question and, as such, serve to delineate the typical response that someone will have to a stressful event. In other words, they serve to set the parameters of memory formation for the to-be-remembered event. This knowledge can then be used to predict the range in quantity and quality of memory that an eyewitness should display.

Biological variables

As highlighted previously, arousal sensitivity delineates the emotional impact of criminal events. This trait differs across individuals, from hypersensitives to hyposensitives, and development, with sensitivity theoretically increasing with age (Zuckerman, 1979). While males generally score lower on measures of arousal sensitivity and higher on measures of sensation seeking than females (Keogh, 2004; Zuckerman, 1979), it remains unknown whether these differences are innate and/or the result of early socialisation, and it may be the case that they, in part, reflect differences in the expression (rather than experience) of arousal sensitivity. Accordingly, investigators are urged to evaluate sensitivity on a case-by-case basis rather than by making group-based generalisations. Indeed, while primarily biologically predefined, there

---

[12] We distinguish between biological, psychological, and social factors as we view each of these realms as having important influences on memory in their own right.

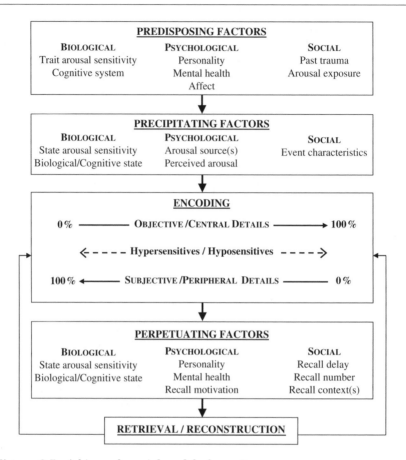

Figure 2.5 A biopsychosocial model of eyewitness memory

are a host of variables that may affect sensitivity development, as well as one's state sensitivity (see below). Irrespective if trait or state, hypersensitives will fall prey to arousal-mediated memory distortions earlier and over a wider range of arousal levels as compared to hyposensitives (see Figure 2.1).

Neurocognitive functioning is another innate trait with important implications for memory formation as it effects all stages of memory, namely: attention and working memory for delineating encoding quantity; spatial and language functioning for encoding quality; and memory functioning and processing speed storage, and executive and language abilities for the quantity and quality of retrieval, respectively. In light of feedback mechanisms, neurocognitive abilities also influence the quantity and type of information sampled from the environment.

Furthermore, the commission of crime, engendering ANS stimulation may disrupt mental processing, especially in the cognitively impaired. Considering an individual's neurocognitive strengths and weaknesses, which change throughout development and evidences minor gender differences at certain developmental stages, is therefore crucial to the understanding of his/her memory capabilities. This is especially significant in the offender context in which both innate (e.g., FAE) and acquired (traumatic brain injury; chronic substance abuse) neuropsychological impairments are found in disproportionate amounts, with acquired brain injuries – especially that affecting frontal lobe functioning (e.g., frontal lobe syndrome) – potentially leading to permanent changes in one's arousal sensitivity (i.e., from hyper to hypo or vice versa; e.g., Damasio, 1994). Of note, such brain damage should be accompanied with relatively abrupt changes in behaviour and memory characteristics (e.g., a previously instrumentally violent offender with good memory for his/her acts, becoming predominantly reactive in his/her violence and evidencing significant affect-mediated memory distortions).

Psychological variables

Arousal sensitivity has also been linked to personality, with introverts and borderlines being hypersensitives, and extroverts, sensation seekers and psychopaths being hyposensitives (Ellis, 1987; Eysenck, 1967; Zuckerman, 1979), suggesting that different personality types may succumb to arousal-mediated distortions at different points in the arousal stream. For example, the psychopath, who is theoretically the most arousal hyposensitive of all individuals (Blackburn, 1979; Hare, 1965), is likely to feel little traumatic arousal, at times even experiencing what others consider traumatic as pleasurable, and, therefore, will be relatively immune to arousal-mediated distortions (Christianson et al., 1996). By adding unique cognitive filters, personality also influences how events will be interpreted (Blair et al., 1995), with interpretations becoming increasingly idiosyncratic as personality becomes disordered in nature. Given that personality disordered individuals are prone to succumb to cognitive distortions in times of stress – such as engendered by crime – their eyewitness accounts should evidence personality specific distortions. For example, the narcissistic offender, believing in his/her invincibility, may recall an offence as much less threatening than a catastrophising borderline offender. Unfortunately, little is known regarding the role of personality on memory for crime (although see Oorsouw & Cima, Chapter 8, this volume).

Psychiatric status, with its links to arousal sensitivity and effects on cognition, is another important predisposing variable to consider. Some Axis I disorders may serve to delineate the intensity and quality of emotional responses, a point with memory implications. For example, individuals prone to anxiety are likely to be more sensitive to arousal fluctuations than individuals with no such history, thereby rendering them hypersensitive in stressful/criminal events irrespective of their trait sensitivity. Such disorders are also likely to have a significant impact on event-related interpretations. For example, a schizophrenic offender, given his/her fantasy world, is likely to have a more idiosyncratic – but not necessarily invalid – interpretation than would a non-schizophrenic. Like personality, little is known regarding the influence of Axis I disorders on eyewitness memory.

Finally, one's pre-crime affective state (be it chronic or acute in nature) will help define, in part, how arousing an event may be. As this factor has received no empirical attention, we speculate that, in regards to offenders, if one's pre-crime state coincides with the affect engendered by the commission of the offence, such as seen in acts of instrumental violence – as they serve to satisfy pre-defined goals – then their should be relatively little added ANSA and, therefore, minimal memory distortions. However, should the nature of the offence significantly alter one's affective state and do so in a negative manner, as seen in reactive types of offences, then significant ANSA should be experienced, resulting in memory distortions. By creating a uniquely intense affective experience, this latter process may be one pathway leading to state-dependent memories, as well as to the 'red out' phenomenon (Swihart, Yuille, & Porter, 1999). As this particular pathway is relatively independent of one's arousal sensitivity, hyposensitives should be as susceptible to this process as hypersensitives.

Social variables

Although one's trait sensitivity, being based in biology, is more resistant to change than one's cognitive system, both are nevertheless affected by past experiences (Mandler, 1984), thereby delineating one's state sensitivity to an interpretation of current events. While cultural and gender socialisation are likely to significantly influence the manner in which events are interpreted and, therefore, encoded, little is known regarding the influence of these factors on eyewitness memory.

Nevertheless, research suggests that one's personal history will affect one's future reactions. Highly arousing and unpleasant experiences will sensitise people so that future traumatic events are physiologically and/or cognitively experienced as more disturbing than would have normally been the case (e.g., Porter, 1996; Terr, 1991; van der Kolk et al., 1996), thereby functionally rendering individuals hypersensitives, irrespective of their trait sensitivity. This view is consistent with the diagnostic formation of PTSD, a defining feature of which is hyperarousal/hypervigilance (American Psychiatric Association [APA], 1994). In contrast, high-intensity experiences that desensitise people to future arousing events render individuals hyposensitive, irrespective of their trait sensitivity. As such, desensitisation may explain the formation of script memories, as subsequent related events will be interpreted as more benign than would otherwise have been the case and, therefore, not require event-specific encoding. For example, while the novice offender might experience both fear and excitement during his/her first break and enter – resulting in an affectively loaded memory that deserves detailed encoding – the repeat offender, interpreting his/her action as a routine event – not unlike going to work – experiences little affect, thereby creating no need for detailed encoding; instead, the event will be integrated into his/her script for how his/her break and enters typically unfold. Given that initial events are more 'remarkable' than subsequent ones, one's script should be more heavily influenced by initial than subsequent events, especially with increases in delay between encoding and recall (i.e., more recent events may be initially intact but quickly evidence normal forgetting). This effect may occur even for repeated traumas but only if the individual experiences the new trauma as relatively benign (i.e., has become desensitised). It is important to highlight that script memories are not mutually exclusive from other ones and, consequently, investigators should be open to the possibility that scripts include various types, quantities and qualities of memories. For example, habituation may result in a false sense of safety that, when challenged (i.e., script violations; e.g., the unexpected arrival of the homeowners during a routine break and enter), leads to high arousal, resulting in the violation being ascribed emotional significance and, therefore, encoded. That is, departures will be encoded not as benign but as remarkable.

Precipitating Factors

Precipitating factors are specific to the circumstances of the event and, based on the parameters set by predisposing factors, further fine-tune memory formation (Figure 2.5).

Table 2.3 Hypothetical ANSA intensity changes across offence stages for eyewitnesses based on arousal sensitivity

	Hypersensitive			Hyposensitive		
	Offender	Victim	Witness	Offender	Victim	Witness
Pre-offence	High	Low	Low	Low	Low	Low
Offence	Very high	Extremely high	High	Medium	High	Medium
Post-offence	High	Very high	Medium	Low	Medium	Low

Biological variables

Engaging in criminal conduct results in ANS stimulation that, moderated by one's arousal sensitivity and cognitive capacities, affects both attention and memory. Hyper- and hyposensitive individuals not only experience arousal differently but, in light of affective feedback, also experience different arousal changes as the situation unfolds (excitatory vs inhibitory effects), suggesting that investigators consider the dynamic nature of offences, and the resulting changes in affective states, when taking eyewitnesses' accounts (see Table 2.3). Of special importance, are significant and unexpected changes (be it real or perceived) as such changes are likely to be potent ANSA moderators – especially for hypersensitives, with changes reducing threat perception decreasing ANSA and those increasing threat perception increasing ANSA.

As arousal reaches traumatic levels, it can have a debilitating memory impact by fully allocating attention either internally (for the hypersensitive; Table 2.2) or externally (for the hyposensitive; Table 2.2), both processes serving to dampen ANSA. That is, ANSA that surpasses an individual's traumatic threshold is likely to cause a dissociation (Spiegel & Cardeña, 1991) between the processing of internal and external cues, leaving only one source of information available for encoding. Obviously, each response would result in different memory consequences (Table 2.2). While the hypersensitive, focused inward, is likely to turn to his/her fantasy life and, therefore, experience a sense of derealisation (a feature of PTSD; APA, 1994), the hyposensitive, completely focused outward, is likely to take an observer perspective (Cooper, Cuttler, Dell & Yuille, [in press)] and, therefore, experience depersonalisation (another feature of PTSD; APA, 1994). Obviously, in terms of investigative value, the former process, leading to a dissociative memory with internal focus, is devastating and the latter, while engendering minor qualitative distortions, results in memories of investigative value (disociative memory with external focus). As noted previously, 'traumatic and unbearable' levels of arousal are likely to force all individuals internally (Table 2.2), with hypersensitives being prone to dissociate into fantasy and hyposensitives to focus exclusively upon their subjective experience, the only psychological responses left to reduce ANSA to manageable levels.

ANS stimulation also influences behaviour (e.g., fight vs flight) and, therefore, memory for the act (e.g., escape vs confrontation) in a manner consistent with one's arousal sensitivity. Hypersensitive offenders will want to get things over quickly, with unexpected/delaying events causing spikes in ANS reactions. They are likely to be highly focused on their internal states, especially when complications occurs, at which point escape will be of paramount importance. Hyposensitives, however, feel less rushed and less disturbed by complications, which they are likely to tune-out until unavoidable, at which point confrontation will be the likely course of action. The end result is that hypersensitives' memories will be characterised by more peripheral than central information, with hyposensitives showing the opposite pattern (Table 2.2).

Any factor that affects these biological responses should be considered when interviewing offenders about their crimes. One such factor is substance use, with depressants reducing ANS reactions and stimulants increasing them. Of course, substance use also affects one's cognitive capacities, with depressants slowing processing speed, stimulants increasing processing speed, and psychogenics adding unique cognitive filters. Additionally, they may result in state-dependent memories or block encoding altogether (e.g., alcohol-induced blackouts).

Psychological variables

While arousal sensitivity will delineate the type of trauma-related information allocated attention (i.e., internal vs external), it is the affective load attached to an event that will predominantly dictate how well and for how long a memory will be recalled (Table 2.2). Indeed, there exists good evidence that emotional events are better recalled than non-emotional events (Christianson, 1989, 1992; Thompson, Morton & Fraser, 1997). However, there also exists evidence that highly emotional events can result in significant memory loss (Yuille & Daylen, 1998). While the topic of much debate, this paradoxical effect is explainable when viewing emotional processing as multidimensional (Figure 2.6). The cognitive component of emotions, injecting personal significance to events, increases the saliency of memory traces by adding the number of cues available for memory reconstruction,

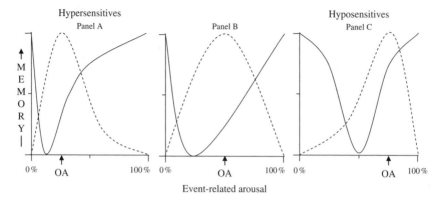

——— Quality (i.e., cognitive component of emotions infusing memory with subjective significance)

– – – – Quantity (i.e., physiological/arousal component of emotions impacting STM/IT/LTM)

Figure 2.6 The theorised relationship between memory (quality and quantity) and emotions based on a multidimensional model of emotions (cognitive and physiological components), event-related arousal, and arousal sensitivity (OA = optimal arousal)

that is, details indirectly related to the event.[13] This process is moderated by one's psychosocial history, including past experiences, personality, psychiatric status and crime-related motivation, which serves to add idiosyncratic interpretive filters. The physiological component of emotions also adds informative value to memories but, given the Yerkes–Dodson principle, only to a certain point. That is, it can increase the size of the memory trace by accelerating IT from STM to LTM, resulting in a greater number of cues available during memory reconstruction, that is, details directly related to the event. However, as arousal intensifies, limited STM resources become increasingly taxed, resulting in an increasing number of details not being transmitted to LTM. Therefore, objectively significant events that are subjectively interpreted as relatively benign (i.e., low-to-moderate intensity; e.g., benign, opportunistic crimes; day-to-to day criminal activities), although initially remembered quite well, will be subjected to normal forgetting (Table 2.2). Conversely, events interpreted as significant but non-traumatic (i.e., moderate-to-high intensity; e.g., obsessively planned crimes; unique/novel criminal activities) will be remembered quite well and for long periods of time, thereby

---

[13] Interestingly, this may explain the creation of remarkable memories at low arousal levels (Table 2.2).

leading to remarkable memories (Table 2.2). However, as interpretations become traumatic in nature, memory distortions (quantity and quality) will be increasingly evident (Table 2.2), with debilitating levels leading to dissociative amnesia – presumably by overwhelming memory consolidation altogether. As with other factors, this process is moderated by one's arousal sensitivity, with hypersensitives ascribing greater affective significance to arousing events than hyposensitives (Table 2.2).

Cuing an ANS response, criminal events also result in an orientation response that guides attention towards the source of the arousal (Burke, Heuer & Reisberg, 1992). Evidence indicates different memory effects occur depending on whether or not the arousal-source is part of the to-be-remembered event (Christianson, 1992). With respect to eyewitness memory, the source of the arousal is, in part, external; that is, caused by the crime being committed. Of course, offences may involve various arousal sources (e.g., victim, accomplice, factors that increase risk of apprehension), the attentional importance of which reflects one's meaning analysis and, therefore, being subjectively defined. If the sources are ascribed similar importance, then the resulting memory is likely to reflect their combination, thereby affecting quality. However, when one source is deemed more important than the others then it will receive encoding priority, thereby affecting quantity.

Event-unrelated arousal may also surface as a result of previous experiences (e.g., in the form of flashbacks). For example, the current crime may cue memories of past crimes (i.e., state-dependent memories), resulting in two arousal sources competing for limited attention. Memory distortions (e.g., combination of past and current events) can occur if the event-unrelated arousal dominates the processing stream (Christianson, 1992). In essence, they would form a type of script memory but one that is associated with a much greater affective load, and therefore containing more details, than habituation-initiated scripts, a difference that can be used to differentiate them during investigative efforts. If the combined affective load is uniquely experienced, then another form of state-dependent memory may emerge, with both emotional states needing to be present for retrieval to be successful. However, if the remembered event takes a significantly dominant role in the processing stream, then it may lead to total amnesia for the event proper, leaving the offender only able to report about peripheral information (e.g., events that preceded/followed the actual offence), as seen in the 'red out' phenomenon (Swihart et al., 1999).

The arousal source may also reflect motivational factors that initiated the crime. For example, a reactive murder committed in a fit of jealousy is likely to involve two arousal sources: The murderous act and the jealous feelings motivating that act. Following Christianson's (1992) logic, event-unrelated arousal may take a dominant role for the murderer, resulting in an internal focus (e.g., feeling of betrayal/anger) and, therefore, memory deficits regarding the homicidal act. This process may provide another pathway to the 'red out' phenomenon. In such cases, the rage state, a defining feature of red outs, likely won over event-related information in the competition for attention. Thus, offenders who engage in reactive, emotionally driven crime/violence, where the motivation is internal and intense, should have relatively impaired memories of their crimes (Cooper & Yuille, Chapter 3 this volume). Ego-dystonic instrumental offences (e.g., being forced to rob to pay a debt; Hervé, Petitclerc & Hare, 1999), including multiple arousal sources, as well as potent ANSA, should also result in memory distortions. In contrast, offenders who engage in ego-syntonic instrumental offences (including violence), where the goal is more cognitively than emotionally driven, as well as external in nature, should have better memories for their crimes (Cooper & Yuille, Chapter 3 this volume).

Social variables

The encoding context, helping to define the subjective meaning of events, has its own effect on memory by delineating the intensity and quality of affective responses and, therefore, the affective load attached to memory. For example, Tollestrup et al. (1994) have shown that many fraud victims exhibit normal forgetting. As this victim is unaware that a crime has been committed until some time has elapsed, the event will initially be interpreted (encoded) as benign and, therefore, quickly forgotten (Yuille & Daylen, 1998). Similarly, certain types of events are likely to be interpreted as more significant than others and, therefore, to result in remarkable memories (e.g., one's first offence). Of note, if the event in question has never before been experienced, then, by definition, it will result in a unique emotional reaction, suggesting another pathway to state-dependent memories or, in its extreme, to the 'red out' phenomenon.

Another contextual variable is the feeling of personal safety during the event. For example, victims and injured victims report less crime-related information than witnesses and non-injured victims, respectively (e.g., Christianson & Hubinette, 1993; Kuehn, 1974). Clearly, highly arousing events where there is obvious danger evoke deeper and more personal sensations/cognitions, and therefore memory distortions, than those that, although highly arousing, do not suggest imminent danger. In terms of offenders, immediate and negative personal consequences should therefore have serious effects on memory formation. For example, being arrested in the commission of the act (imminent loss of personal freedom) is likely to result in greater ANS arousal than being arrested during the course of the investigations, the former resulting in greater memory distortions (especially for the latter part of the act) than the latter. It should be noted, however, that the perception of danger is likely to be affected by other variables as well, such as arousal sensitivity, past sensitising and desensitising experiences and personality (e.g., by creating a sense of vulnerability or invincibility), suggesting that personal safety is, in part, subjectively defined. As noted previously, while culture and gender socialisation are likely to affect how events are interpreted (including threat perception), as well as one's event-specific behavioural reactions, these factors have yet to receive focused research attention.

Perpetuating Factors

Precipitating factors, which include many of the variables listed above, follow the to-be-remembered event and act to either increase or decrease the quantity and quality of memory. As memory is reconstructive in nature, it is susceptible to distortions each time it is retrieved, with initial accounts reflecting encoding-based distortions and, to a lesser extent, retrieval biases. As each retelling results in re-encoding (Figure 2.5), subsequent recollections are prone to increasingly evidence distortions reflecting the additive process of retrieval biases (Figure 2.5), especially for subjectively peripheral information. Unfortunately, such distortions may become memory reality (i.e., historical vs narrative truth; Hyman & Loftus, 1998; Nash, 1994), thereby permanently contaminating memory. Accordingly, the earlier one can get an account of the event under investigation the closer it will resemble historical truth, especially when dealing with a hypersensitive offender.

Biological variables

Arousal sensitivity is a significant perpetuating factor in light of its impact on memory decay (see above), recall motivation, and memory reconstruction. As hyper- and hyposensitives differ in their desire to broach (rehearse) arousing topics, the former will likely intrinsically avoid arousing memories, while the latter will savour them, thereby weakening and strengthening memory trace (quantity), respectively. In addition, when recall occurs, the attentional biases noted above will presumably influence the reconstructive process of memory, with hypersensitives focusing on internal/peripheral information and hyposensitives on external/central information. If recall engenders ANSA, the attentional bias will be even more pronounced. Consequently, over-repeated recalls, peripheral and central information becomes differentially resistant to the effects of decay.

As noted previously, neurocognitive functioning affects all stages of memory. At retrieval, the impact of deficits is likely to become increasingly pronounced over time and retellings, again highlighting the urgency in seeking eyewitnesses' accounts. In the intellectually impaired, event-related distortions should be relatively more pronounced for abstract/subjective details (e.g., assumptions or interpretations, such as intentions, motivations, and social dynamics) than concrete/objective details (e.g., facts such as who did what).

Psychological variables

Psychological variables exert their impact on when, why, and how recall occurs. For example, decay for high-intensity events, such as violence, will be affected by rehearsal (to self or others). If the violence was reactive or otherwise ego-dystonic in nature, the individual is unlikely to be intrinsically motivated to broach the topic, especially details of a shameful nature, thus weakening memory trace over time. If, however, the motivation was instrumental and/or ego-syntonic, the individual may relish the experience, thereby strengthening memory trace. Personality and psychiatric status will also affect recall motivation, as well as sensitivity to external recall incentives, post-event coping strategies, response style, and the cognitive filters through which memory is reconstructed (e.g., Christianson et al., 1996; Cooper, 2005; Porter, Birt, & Yuille, 2000) – all of which influence memory reconstruction, with distortions augmenting over-repeated recalls.

Affect at recall, which may partly be delineated by one's pre-recall affective state (as discussed in the predisposing section), is also important as it can cue memory, as seen in mood-dependent research. However, emotional reactions at the time of recall may also bias memory retrieval and, consequently, distort memory reconstruction, presumably more so for hyper- than hyposensitives. Investigators should therefore aim to induce as little of an emotional reaction at recall as possible.[14] Of note, despite their often dramatic presentation, psychopaths and other hyposensitives are not likely to be overtaken by affect during interviews and, thus, will not be subject to such effects.

---

[14] Confrontational interviewing techniques are therefore counter-indicated when seeking eyewitness accounts.

Given the evidence that the commission of ego-dystonic offences can lead to post-traumatic stress responses in offenders (Pollock, 1999), and such responses effect memory processes (Cooper, 2005), enquiring about such responses and their precipitants (e.g., dissociation) is crucial. On the one hand, individuals may attempt to actively avoid thinking of the event proper (a symptom of PTSD) by consciously avoiding peripheral cues of moderate affective intensity that could lead to recall of central, traumatising memories. If successful, this coping strategy could result in fewer memory triggers for the 'feared' event being available for reconstruction over time and, therefore, to active forgetting, with subjectively central information decaying faster than peripheral information. On the other hand, a PTSD response may lead to intrusive thoughts and/or flashbacks about the event that results in ANSA of an intensity and quality similar to that experienced during the event (APA, 1994).[15] In hypersensitives, such added arousal may be overwhelming, thereby engendering active forgetting or, in its extreme, post-event dissociative amnesia. Unlike encoding-based amnesic processes that result in the complete lack of encoding of event-related information, retrieval-based amnesic patterns would reflect the cognitive dissociation of the memory's sensory narrative connections leaving both, however, intact in storage (van der Kolk et al., 1996). Presumably, the information loss resulting from the latter reaction might be retrievable following, for example, successful and carefully conducted treatment. In the hyposensitive, however, the intrusion-related arousal might never become unbearable. As such, every recollection is accompanied with a manageable level of arousal that serves to enhance memory (quantity), thereby suggesting another pathway to remarkable memories. However, given the unique cognitive filters ascribed by such factors as personality, some distortion (quality) is unavoidable over time since traumatised individuals, needing to make sense of their experience, must reconstruct their memories as they see fit until they can safely integrate them within their world view.

Indeed, the manner by which individuals cope with their experiences can have significant effects on memory. For example, substance abuse, a common phenomenon in the offender context, may serve to blunt one's affective response to event-related memories, facilitate memory avoidance or add unique filters through which events are recalled, with the first two weakening the memory trace and the last distorting its quality.

---

[15] Theoretically, memory intrusiveness could reflect either sensory or narrative information (van der Kolk et al., 1996), with hypersensitives being more susceptive to the former and hyposensitives to the latter.

Social factors

While culture and gender socialisation are likely to delineate, for example, the type of information one is willing to share, response to authority figures, response style and one's reaction to particular recall contexts (e.g., investigative vs therapeutic), little is known about these moderating factors. The recall context, however, will impact what type of information is sought and, thus, what is recalled. For example, investigative interviews, in which the aim is to elicit an account of a crime, are focused solely on event-related information, while therapeutic encounters, in which the motivation is successful treatment, are equally focused on event and sensory related information, if not more so on the latter. Unfortunately, these contexts solidify different types of memories, leaving other memories vulnerable to the effects of decay and/or suggestibility. In addition, recall motivations, which can vary from ego-syntonic to ego-dystonic and from truthful to deceitful, are likely to be accompanied with their own emotional and cognitive reactions, which can serve to further contaminate memory.

The manner in which memories are elicited is also critical. For example, the negative impact of leading questions is well established (Bruck, Ceci & Hembrooke, 1998). In addition to jeopardising criminal investigations, leading interviews facilitate memory distortions. Several investigators have been able to implant (false) emotional memories (Loftus & Pickrell, 1995), highlighting the malleability of memory, particularly in suggestible individuals. For example, research indicates that introverted individuals with a dissociative disposition who are interviewed by extroverted interviewers that utilise suggestive/leading questions are most likely to fall prey to the 'creation' of memories (Porter, Yuille, & Lehman, 1999). Biased interviewing techniques are especially likely to negatively impact the quantity and quality of accounts provided by neurocognitively impaired individuals, not because they are necessarily more suggestible but because of the functional consequences of their impairments (e.g., poor language comprehension leading to misunderstandings; tendency to mask deficit – not ask for clarification) and of biased interviewing approaches (e.g., induces ANSA that disrupts already taxed cognitive functioning and increases the likelihood of affect-mediated memory distortions). Given the positive effects of cued recall on memory (Fisher & Geiselman, 1992), the use of this strategy is, however, likely to facilitate memory reconstruction, especially in the neurocognitively impaired, but only if unbiased interviewing techniques are adopted (e.g., leading questions are avoided; cued recall is used once an uninterrupted free narrative is provided; Fisher, 1995; Yuille, Marxsen & Cooper, 1999).

Time-based forgetting suggests a positive correlation between retrieval delay and suggestibility. The type of information an individual will be suggestible to will likely depend on his/her arousal sensitivity. Recall that dissociative experiences disrupt the encoding of central information in hypersensitives and of sensory/peripheral information in hyposensitives. Accordingly, while the hypersensitive, given his/her access to sensory/peripheral information, will be suggestible to central information (Table 2.2), the hyposensitive, given his/her relatively intact memory for central information, is more likely to be suggestible to sensory/peripheral information (Table 2.2). Arousal sensitivity would further dictate that hypersensitives become suggestible at lower and across a wider range of arousal levels than hyposensitives (i.e., have a larger suggestibility window; Table 2.2).

While hypersensitives are less likely than hyposensitives to be intrinsically motivated to recall their crimes, offenders are nevertheless routinely required to provide accounts of their offences throughout their involvement with the criminal justice system. A unique feature of this context is that inaccuracies in central information can often be corrected in light of collateral information. Consequently, if elicited in an unbiased manner, offenders' memories for their crimes should evidence a relative resistance to decay, with the hypersensitive's account becoming increasingly less detailed (i.e., loss of peripheral information but retention of the gist of the offence and context-pertinent details [e.g., risk-related]) and that of the hyposensitive's evidencing good retention of central information but variable retention of peripheral details (i.e., peripheral details will reflect personality based response style [e.g., theatrical] and context-induced motivations [e.g., positive impression management]). More generally, however, externally motivated recall with a potential for negative outcome (e.g., police interrogations leading to loss of personal freedom; therapeutic inducement of memory that person is not ready to cope with) will engender significant ANSA, doing so more intensely for hyper- than hyposensitives, resulting in pronounced retrieval-based attentional biases.

Of course, offenders may also consciously distort their version of events in their attempts to escape justice and/or protect accomplices, a factor mediated by personality (O'Connell, 1960; Parwatikar, Holcomb, & Menninger, 1985; Porter, Birt, Yuille & Hervé, 2001). Unfortunately, such distortions, given the reconstructive nature of memory, may become memory reality and, therefore, reduce the accuracy of both central and peripheral information. Just as active forgetting can lead to memory decay, active confabulation can lead to memory strengthening.

IMPLICATIONS FOR RESEARCH AND PRACTICE

In relation to methodological issues, the proposed model suggests the involvement of different mechanisms within analogue and field studies. On the one hand, laboratory experiments, which induce low-to-moderate levels of arousal, may not engender any affect-related memory impairments. Studies that require recall of emotional scenes will engage a cognitively initiated emotional reaction of little-to-no ANS value and, therefore, observed-memory effect will generally reflect interpretative differences – especially in hyposensitives (e.g., Christianson et al., 1996), suggesting such studies are most useful in unravelling the variables that influence interpretations (e.g., learning history, mental ability, affective focus, personality, psychiatric status). Studies that employ mock witness scenarios that oblige participants to experience rather than interpret an event, should, however, induce some ANSA (albeit of a moderate intensity at best) and, therefore, ANSA-mediated memory effects (e.g., orientation response). In this case, arousal sensitivity will have an impact, albeit a limited one, with hypersensitives being more likely than hyposensitives to display emotion-mediated memory distortions. However, these distortions will reflect different aspects of the arousal continuum than predicted in naturalistic settings (low/moderate vs intense/traumatic), which – according to the Yerkes–Dodson law – should result in a reversal in attentional foci. That is, as arousal decreases, hypersensitives should become increasingly focused on central/external events and hyposensitives on peripheral/internal ones (Table 2.2). While typical analogue paradigms have demonstrated the former, the latter will require new methodologies to be investigated (e.g., creating an eyewitness paradigm within a sensory deprivation environment).

On the other hand, field and archival studies deal with intense, personally relevant situations that result in emotional reactions that include *both* potent ANS reactions and considerable cognitive processing that significantly affects memory. Since the effects investigated in field and archival research reflect the combination of a greater number of factors (predisposing, precipitating, and perpetuating biopsychosocial influences) than that investigated in the laboratory, each of which potentially varies from one witness to the next, naturalistic studies should result in more heterogeneous memory outcomes than laboratory studies. That is, one should expect a great deal of consistency both within and between laboratory studies and a great deal of variability both within and between field studies, which appears to be the case. Accordingly, while the generalisability of analogue research is inherently limited, the external validity of such research can be increased by forcing participants to experience rather than evaluate to-be-remembered events, using complex paradigms in which the influence of many factors are concurrently evaluated, and developing individualised ANSA-inducing stimuli (i.e., of personal relevance), the latter of which being effectively used in the study of memory for phobic objects (Radomsky & Rachman, 2004).

The proposed theory suggests that the assessment of eyewitness memory requires more than an examination of the amount and accuracy of information provided. As developed throughout this chapter, there are a host of variables that influence the quantity and quality of memory. Inherent in our theory is the view that emotional reactions are both dynamic and subjective in nature and, as such, so is memory. Thus, any understanding of affect-mediated responses has to be considered from the vantage point of the witness. The implications are two fold. First, central and peripheral information will be subjectively defined, only periodically in a manner analogous to the investigator. Second, memory patterns should be expected to change over time. Indeed, a witness with an initial remarkable memory may later develop dissociative amnesia for the same event. Obviously, certain changes in memory patterns should be viewed more cautiously than others. For example, the truthfulness of an offender who states that he/she has developed a remarkable memory although having previously reported that he/she dissociated into event-unrelated fantasy at the time of the offence should be questioned.

Whether in research or practice, we strongly recommend investigative interviews to focus upon, not only on the memory in question, but on the following variables: the individual's arousal sensitivity, neurocognitive strengths and weaknesses, personality, psychiatric history (including past traumas), and dissociative disposition; if the individual was under the influence of drugs/alcohol at the time of the event and, if so, the type and quantity; the level of arousal and type of affect (positive to traumatic) experienced during the event and whether or not this changed as the event unfolded; if the individual dissociated at the time of the event or experienced any other psychiatric symptoms (e.g., panic attack); if there was a time in which the individual was unable to recall all or part of the event; if the individual has/had PTSD in relation to the event; if the individual made efforts to avoid thinking about the event and/or used other coping strategies (e.g., substance abuse); the number of previous recalls (to self and others); the individual's affective state at recall (s); and the recall context(s). Each of these factors will impact eyewitness memory and influence the eyewitness' recall capacity.

In terms of credibility assessment, the pattern of memory that a witness reports should be predictable based on the proposed model (Table 2.2), with the range of memory patterns anticipated being predicted by predisposing factors, the evidenced pattern(s) making sense in light of precipitating factors, and deviations being explained by perpetuating factors (Figure 2.5). Otherwise, the credibility of the witness' account should be questioned. In other words, while a border-line claiming poor memory for a reactive act of violence is explainable, a psychopath claiming poor memory for a highly rewarding instrumental crime should raise concern.

CONCLUSION

The present chapter outlined a 'working' biopsychosocial model of eyewitness memory adapted for the offender context. Unlike previous theories, this model assumes that emotional reactions are not uni-dimensional and static but multidimensional and dynamic, reflecting both physiological and cognitive processes. It is proposed that eyewitness memory variability results from individual differences in both of these emotional processes, differences moderated/mediated by a variety of interacting predisposing, precipitating and perpetuating biopsychosocial factors. Various memory predictions were put forward, predictions that attempted to explain the memory variability across and within witnesses in field/archival research, as well as the mechanisms leading to different findings between analogue and naturalistic research.[16] Obviously, much more research is needed in this area and, consequently, this model and its predictions remain speculative. This is, in part, why this model is referred to as a 'working' model. We not only expect but invite our peers to comment and criticise this theory, either in part or in whole, as our primary goal was to generate discussion regarding how to integrate various research findings, findings that have typically been heatedly debated.

AUTHOR NOTE

The views expressed are those of the authors, and do not necessarily reflect the position of the Forensic Psychiatric Services Commission.

---

[16] These were not meant to be exhaustive but, instead, to exemplify the manner in which the model should be applied.

Preparation for this article was supported, in part, by doctoral fellowships to the first and second authors and an operating grant to the third author from the Social Sciences and Humanities Research Council of Canada (SSHRC). The authors are grateful to Kristin Kendrick, Dorothee Griesel and Caroline Greaves for their helpful comments on earlier drafts of this chapter, as well as Dr Sven Christianson and anonymous reviewers for their constructive feedback. Separate parts of this paper were presented at the Canadian Psychological Association's 2002 Annual Convention, the Society for Applied Research on Memory and Cognition's 2003 Conference, and the Society for the Scientific Study of Psychopathy 2005 Conference.

Please address all correspondence concerning this manuscript to: Hugues Hervé, Ph.D., Forensic Psychiatric Hospital, 70 Colony Farm Road, Port Coquitlam, British Columbia, V3C 5X9; telephone (604) 524–7950; fax (604) 660–1206; or email: hherve@forensic.bc.ca.

REFERENCES

American Psychiatric Association (1994) *Diagnostic and statistical manual of mental disorders*, (Rev. 4th ed.), Washington, DC: Author.

Blair, R.J.R., Sellars, C., Strickland, I., Clark, F., Williams, A.O., Smith, M., et al. (1995) Emotion attributions in the psychopath. *Personality and Individual Differences*, **19**, 431–7.

Blackburn, R. (1979) Cortical and autonomic arousal in primary and secondary psychopaths. *Psychophysiology*, **16**, 143–50.

Blascovich, J. (1990) Individual differences in physiological arousal and perceptions of arousal: Missing links between Jamesian notions of arousal-based behaviours. *Personality and Social Psychology Bulletin*, **16**, 665–75.

Blascovich, J. (1992) A biopsychosocial approach to arousal regulation. *Journal of Social and Clinical Psychology*, **11**, 213–37.

Bruck, M., Ceci, S.J. & Hembrooke, H. (1998) Reliability and credibility of young children's reports: From research to policy and practice. *American Psychologist*, **53**, 136–51.

Burke, A., Heuer, F. & Reisberg, D. (1992) Remembering emotional events. *Memory and Cognition*, **20**, 277–90.

Christianson, S.Å. (1989) Flashbulb memories: Special, but not so special. *Memory and Cognition*, **17**, 435–43.

Christianson, S.Å. (1992) Emotional stress and eyewitness memory: A critical review. *Psychological Bulletin*, **112**, 284–309.

Christianson, S.Å., Forth, A.E., Hare, R.D., Strachan, C., Lidberg, L. & Lars-Hakan, T. (1996). Remembering details of emotional events: A comparison between psychopathic and nonpsychopathic offenders. *Personality and Individual Differences*, **20**, 437–43.

Christianson, S.Å. & Hubinette, B. (1993) Hands up! A study of witness' emotional reactions and memories with bank robberies. *Applied Cognitive Psychology*, **7**, 365–79.

Conway, M.A. (1997) Introduction: What are memories? In M.A. Conway (Ed.), *Recovered memories and false memories*, (pp. 1–22). Oxford: Oxford University Press.

Cooper, B.S. (2005) *Memory for mayhem*. Unpublished Doctoral dissertation. University of British Columbia, Vancouver, British Columbia, Canada.

Cooper, B.S., Cuttler, C., Dell, P. & Yuille, J.C. (in press). Dissociation and amnesia: A study in male offenders. *International Journal of Forensic Psychology*.

Cooper, B.S., Kennedy, M.A., Hervé, H.F. & Yuille, J.C. (2002) Weapon focus in sexual assault memories of prostitutes. *International Journal of Law and Psychiatry*, **25**, 181–91.

Cutshall, J.L. & Yuille, J.C. (1989) Field studies of eyewitness memory of actual crimes. In D.C. Raskin (Ed.), *Psychological methods in criminal investigation and evidence* (pp. 97–124). New York: Springer.

Damasio, A.R. (1994) *Descartes' error: emotion, reason, and the human brain*, New York, NY: Grosset/Putnam.

Easterbrook, J.A. (1959) The effect of emotion on cue utilization and the organization of behavior. *Psychological Review*, **66**, 183–201.

Ellis, L. (1987) Relationship of criminality and psychopathy with eight other apparent behavioral manifestations of sub-optimal arousal. *Personality and Individual Differences*, **8**, 905–25.

Erdelyi, M.H. & Kleinbard, J. (1978) Has Ebbinghaus decayed with time? The growth of recall (hypernesia) over days. *Journal of Experimental Psychology: Human Learning and Memory*, **4**, 275–89.

Eysenck, M.W. (1967) *The biological basis of personality*. Springfield, IL: Thomas.

Feldman, L.A. (1995) Valence focus and arousal focus: Individual differences in the structure of affective experience. *Journal of Personality and Social Psychology*, **69**, 150–66.

Fisher, R.P. (1995) Interviewing victims and witnesses of crime. *Psychology, Public Policy, and the Law*, **1**, 732–64.

Fisher, R.P. & Geiselman, R.E. (1992) *Memory-enhancing techniques for investigative interviewing: The cognitive interview*. Springfield, Illinois: Charles C. Thomas.

Goodwin, D.W. (1995) Alcohol amnesia. *Addiction*, **90**, 315–17.

Hare, R.D. (1965) Psychopathy, fear arousal and anticipated pain. *Psychological Reports*, **16**, 499–502.

Hare, R.D. (2003) *Manual for the Hare psychopathy checklist-revised* (2nd ed.). Toronto, ON: Multi-Health Systems.

Hervé, H., Petitclerc, A.M. & Hare, R.D. (1999, May) *Violence-related motivations in psychopathic and nonpsychopathic offenders: Egosyntonic versus egodystonic motivations*. Poster presented at the 60th Annual Convention of the Canadian Psychological Association. Halifax, Nova Scotia.

Humphreys, M.S. & Revelle, W. (1984) Personality, motivation, and performance: A theory of the relationship between individual differences and information processing. *Psychological Review*, **91**, 53–184.

Hyman, Jr. I.E. & Loftus, E.F. (1998) Errors in autobiographical memory. *Clinical Psychology Review*, **18**, 933–47.

Keogh, E. (2004) Investigating invariance in the factorial structure of the anxiety sensitivity index across adult men and women. *Journal of Personality Assessment*, **83**, 153–60.

Kuehn, L.L. (1974) Looking down a gun barrel: Person perception and violent crime. *Perceptual and Motor Skills*, **39**, 1159–64.

Loftus, E.F. & Pickrell, J.E. (1995) The formation of false memories. *Psychiatric Annals*, **25**, 720–5.

Mandler, G. (1984) *Mind and body*. New York, NY: Norton.

Nash, M.R. (1994) Memory distortion and sexual trauma: The problem of false negatives and false positives. *The International Journal of Clinical and Experimental Hypnosis*, **XLII**, 346–62.

O'Connell, B.A. (1960) Amnesia and homicide: A study of 50 murderers. *British Journal of Delinquency*, **10**, 262–76.

Parwatikar, S.D., Holcomb, W.R. & Menninger, K.A. (1985) The detection of malingered amnesia in accused murderers. *Bulletin of the American Academy of Psychiatry and Law*, **13**, 97–103.

Pollock, P.H. (1999) When the killer suffers: Post-traumatic stress reactions following homicide. *Legal and Criminological Psychology*, **4**, 185–202.

Porter, S. (1996) Without conscience or without active conscious? The etiology of psychopathy revisited. *Aggression and Violent Behavior*, **1**, 179–89.

Porter, S., Birt, A.R. & Yuille, J.C. (2000) Negotiating false memories: Influence of interviewer and rememberer characteristics on memory distortion. *Psychological Science*, **11**, 507–10.

Porter, S., Birt, A.R., Yuille, J.C. & Hervé, H.F. (2001) Memory for murder: A psychological perspective on dissociative amnesia in legal contexts. *International Journal of Law and Psychiatry*, **24**, 23–42.

Porter, S., Yuille, J.C. & Lehman, D.L. (1999) The nature of real, implanted, and fabricated memories for emotional childhood events: Implications for the recovered memory debate. *Law and Human Behavior*, **23**, 517–37.

Radomsky, A.S. & Rachman, S. (2004) The importance of importance in OCD memory research. *Journal of Behavioral Therapy and Experimental Psychiatry*, **35**, 137–51.

Revelle, W. & Loftus, D.A. (1990) Individual differences and arousal: Implications for the study of mood and memory. *Cognition and Emotion*, **4**, 209–37.

Russell, J.A. (1989) Measures of emotion. In R. Plutchik & H. Kellerman (Eds), *Emotion: Theory, research, and experience*, **4**. (pp. 83–111). Toronto, Ontario: Academic Press.

Schachter, S. (1971) *Emotion, obesity, and crime*. New York, NY: Academic Press.

Schacter, D.L. (1996) *Searching for memory*. New York: Basic Books.

Spiegel, D. & Cardeña, E. (1991) Disintegrated experience: The dissociative disorders revisited. *Journal of Abnormal Psychology*, **100**, 366–78.

Swihart, G., Yuille, J.C. & Porter, S. (1999) The role of state dependent memory in 'red outs.' *International Journal of Law and Psychiatry*, **125**, 199–212.

Terr, L.C. (1991) Childhood traumas: An outline and overview. *American Journal of Psychiatry*, **148**, 10–20.

Thompson, J., Morton, J. & Fraser, L. (1997). Memories for the marchioness. *Memory*, **5**, 615–38.

Thorpe, S.J. & Salkovskis, P.M. (1998) Selective attention to real phobic and safety stimuli. *Behavioral Research and Therapy*, **36**, 471–81.

Tollestrup, P.A., Turtle, J.W. & Yuille, J.C. (1994) Actual victims and witnesses to robbery and fraud: An archival analysis. In D. Ross, D. Read & S. Ceci (Eds), *Adult eyewitness testimony: Current trends and developments*, (pp. 144–62). New York: Press syndicate of the University of Cambridge.

Tulving, E. (1991) Memory research is not a zero-sum game. *American Psychologist*, **46**, 41–2.

Tulving, E. & Madigan, S.A. (1970) Memory and verbal learning. *Annual Review of Psychology*, **21**, 437–84.

Van der Kolk, B.A. & Fisler, R. (1995) Dissociation and the fragmentary nature of traumatic memories: Overview and exploratory study. *Journal of Traumatic Stress*, **8**, 505–25.

Van der Kolk, B.A., McFarlane, A.C. & Weisaeth, L. (1996) *Traumatic stress: The effects of overwhelming experience on mind, body, and society.* New York: The Guilford Press.

Walker, E.L. (1958) Action decrement and its' relation to learning. *The Psychological Review*, **65**, 129–42.

Yerkes, R.M. & Dodson, J.D. (1908) The relation of strength of stimulus to rapidity of habit-information. *Journal of Comparative Neurological Psychology*, **18**, 459–82.

Yuille, J.C. & Cutshall, J.L. (1986) A case study of eyewitness memory of a crime. *Journal of Applied Psychology*, **71**, 291–301.

Yuille, J.C. & Daylen, J. (1998) The impact of traumatic events on eyewitness memory. In C. Thompson, D. Herman, D. Read, D. Bruce, D. Payne & M. Toglia (Eds), *Eyewitness memory: Theoretical and applied perspectives*, (pp. 155–78). Mahwah, New Jersey: Lawrence Erlbaum Associates.

Yuille, J.C., Marxsen, D. & Cooper, B.S. (1999) Training investigative interviewers: Adherence to the spirit, as well as to the letter. *International Journal of Law and Psychiatry*, **22**, 323–36.

Zuckerman, M. (1979) *Sensation seeking: Beyond the optimal level of arousal.* Chichester: John Wiley & Sons, Ltd.

CHAPTER 3

An Investigation of Violent Offenders' Memories for Instrumental and Reactive Violence

BARRY S. COOPER AND JOHN C. YUILLE

This chapter provides an overview of part of a recently completed study of eyewitness memory in a sample of violent crime perpetrators (Cooper, 2005). Founded in a biopsychosocial theory of eyewitness memory (Hervé, Cooper & Yuille, Chapter 2, this volume), a number of variables empirically and theoretically associated with eyewitness recall were examined. In the following sections, the relevant background literature to this study is reviewed. First, the importance and uniqueness of investigating offenders' eyewitness memories for violence is reviewed. Second, an overview of different types of violence is presented including their relevance to recall. Third, the relevant literature on offenders' memories of violence is discussed. Finally, the method, results and discussion are presented.

As discussed by Christianson (Chapter 1, this volume), the investigation of offenders' memories for their violent crimes is of central

Offenders' Memories of Violent Crimes.   Edited by Sven Å. Christianson.
© 2007 John Wiley & Sons, Ltd.

importance to the criminal justice system. For example, the police need to know what types of narrative accounts to expect when interviewing suspects in order to examine credibility; the triers of fact benefit from similar knowledge with respect to defendants of crime. Similarly, institutional psychologists require knowledge concerning the variables associated with offenders' memories in the context of examining their accounts of their crimes (e.g., concerning risk assessments for the National Parole Board). Despite such centrality, little research has focused on offenders' memories for their crimes, that is, their eyewitness accounts of their own criminal actions. In part, this lack of research formed the impetus for the present study.

Most research on memory for violent crime has concerned the examination of accounts of victims and witnesses. Such research is clearly important and has been applied to many facets of the criminal justice system. However, there are certain issues of investigation permitted by the offender context that cannot be examined in the typical witness and victim context. For example, victims and witnesses are often negatively affected by their criminal experiences. They may perceive the events as stressful and/or traumatic both at the time of their experiences and in the aftermath (Cooper, Kennedy & Yuille, 2004; Darves-Bornoz, 1997; Mechanic, Resick & Griffin, 1998). No research indicates victims or witnesses view criminal victimisation as emotionally positive. Thus, in the victim/witness context, only negative affect can be examined in relation to eyewitness memory. In contrast, clinical-forensic experience and anecdotal evidence suggests offenders may experience a number of different emotions during the commission of violence. These emotions range from extreme pleasure (e.g., excitement, happiness; Hare, 1993; Porter & Woodworth, 2002) to extreme displeasure (e.g., rage, fear; Dutton, 1995; Swihart, Yuille & Porter, 1999). Furthermore, research indicates some offenders develop post traumatic stress disorder (PTSD) in relation to their own violent actions (Pollock, 1999; Spitzer et al., 2001). Accordingly, by studying offenders' memories for their crimes, the full range of affective responses (from pleasure to trauma) can be assessed and the effects of these responses on memory can be examined. The literature suggests an offender's memory for a perpetrated violent event depends on the type of violence employed and the type of affect associated with such violence. These issues are expanded on below.

TYPES OF VIOLENCE

In terms of violence, the instrumental-reactive distinction has received the most empirical attention in the aggression literature (e.g., Chase,

O'Leary & Heyman, 2001; Cornell et al., 1996; Hervé, Petticlerc & Hare, 1999). Although the exact terminology of this dichotomy is found under a variety of categorisations (e.g., reactive–proactive; Hubbard, Dodge, Cillessen, Coie & Schwartz, 2001; Poulin & Boivin, 2000; hostile–instrumental, impulsive–premeditated, hot blooded–cold blooded; Bushman & Anderson, 2001; impulsive–instrumental; Tweed & Dutton, 1998; expressive–instrumental; Salfati, 2000), the underlying meaning is essentially the same. On the one hand, instrumental, or proactive, violence requires forethought and is essentially a means to an end (Woodworth & Porter, 2002). For example, instrumental violence could be employed for an individual to acquire money, goods, and/or sexual gratification. On the other hand, reactive, or hostile, violence requires provocation (be it real or perceived) and typically occurs in the context of negative emotional arousal (Berkowitz, 1983, 1990; Cornell et al., 1996; Dutton, 1995). Although the instrumental–reactive dichotomy is not without criticism due to its overly broad division of a complex behaviour (i.e., violence/aggression; e.g., Bushman & Anderson, 2001; Woodword & Porter, 2002), the division has shown utility in the sexual violence, general violence (Brown & Forth, 1997; Serin, 1991), and domestic violence literatures (e.g., Chase et al., 2001; Tweed & Dutton, 1998).

MEMORY FOR INSTRUMENTAL AND REACTIVE VIOLENCE

The reactive–instrumental division is theoretically associated with differential eyewitness recall (Hervé et al., 2002, 2003; Chapter 2 this volume). For example, Porter et al. (2001) and Swihart et al. (1999) suggest instrumental violence should lead to high-quality recall, as instrumentally motivated offenders are likely to fantasise about the violence prior to engaging in it. Using a more multidimensional view, Hervé et al. (under review; Chapter 2 this volume) suggest memory for perpetrated violence is dependent on the type of violence used and the affect associated with the violence. For example, Hervé et al. propose that, because the motivation for reactive violence is, by definition, internal (e.g., rage, anger) as opposed to the external motivation of instrumental violence (e.g., financial), the affect associated with reactive violence is likely to result from internal (e.g., subjective) as opposed to external (e.g., event-related) sources. Accordingly, if an individual were focused on the source of affect during a reactive act of violence (e.g., an internal source such as rage), the individual would likely have relatively poorer memory for the details of the event. That is, poorer memory in comparison to if the event was instrumental in nature and the source of affect was associated with the event itself. In the latter case, one would expect high quality recall, particularly if the event was instrumentally egosyntonic and the perpetrator was hyposensitive to arousal.

In spite of its theoretical association with memory, little research has directly examined the memory consequences of committing such divergent types of violence (see Chapter 1 Christianson et al.; Chapter 13 Santtila & Pakkanen, both this volume). There is some research, however, suggesting reactive acts of violence are associated with reports of amnesia. For example, Taylor and Kopelman (1984) found the non-instrumental motivation of homicides to be a factor related to claims of amnesia in a sample of homicide offenders. Other research suggests negative valence (e.g., rage, jealousy) during the commission of violence is detrimentally associated with recall (Hopwood & Snell, 1933; O'Connell, 1960). Indeed, some researchers have suggested that it is possible for a perpetrator to become so enraged that a different state of consciousness is attained and, consequently, the perpetrator acts in a rigid, derealised manner and is later amnesic for the violent act itself. Such memory loss has been referred to as a 'red out' (Swihart et al., 1999).

In support of the red out phenomenon, researchers have delineated strong negative emotions (e.g., rage) as contributory to amnesia, an effect that occurs irrespective of intoxication (Guttmacher, 1960; O'Connell, 1960; Parwatikar, Holcomb & Menninger, 1985). Indeed, there are many instances of domestic violence where offenders claimed amnesia for battering incidents in the absence of alcohol ingestion (Dutton, 1995). Although many of these cases could be construed as malingering, there are cases in which the offender admitted responsibility and provided a detailed memory for certain reprehensible acts (e.g., necrophilia) but claimed amnesia for less shocking, but nevertheless, criminal actions (e.g., multiple stabbings; see Porter et al., 2001). Although theoretically appealing and supported by anecdotal evidence, no published research has directly examined the red out phenomena. Red outs were not empirically examined in the present research. However, as each participant was asked to provide multiple memories of perpetrated violence, it was anticipated that anecdotal support for the red out phenomenon would be found.

Considering the research and theoretical speculations reviewed above, the relationship between the type of violence employed (e.g., reactive vs instrumental) was investigated in the present research in terms of both affect and memory. That is, a sample of violent offenders was asked to recall memories of perpetrated acts of both instrumental and reactive acts of violence. The present study was the first within-subject examination of such issues. Based on the research and theory reviewed above, it was hypothesised that instrumental acts of violence would be recalled better than reactive acts of violence. It was anticipated that the effect would be mediated by valence.

In order to examine issues related to dissociative amnesia for violence, the participants were also asked to recall a time in which they committed an act of violence and, at the time of data collection, had little or no memory for the act of violence.

METHOD

Participants

As part of a larger study (Cooper, 2005), 150 male incarcerated violent offenders were interviewed at either Mountain Institution (58%) or Kent Institution (42%). Both institutions are federal penitentiaries situated around the Fraser Valley in British Columbia, Canada. In Canada, all offenders serving time for at least two years are incarcerated in federal penitentiaries governed by the Correctional Service of Canada (CSC). Mountain Institution is a medium-security protective custody institution housing over 500 federal offenders. Kent institution is a maximum-security institution containing approximately 300 offenders who are separated into five distinct populations. Prior to data collection, ethical clearance for the present research was obtained from the University of British Columbia and the CSC. Descriptions of the study were posted throughout the institutions. Word of mouth was also an avenue used to elicit participation. To be eligible for participation, participants must have had at least one conviction for a violent or a sexual offence. They were also required to read and comprehend English. Interested participants contacted the psychology department at their respective institutions via a written request to schedule an interview session. As well, some participants approached the researchers in person to schedule an interview session. Participants received a $10 honorarium for their participation. The interviews took place in either a private office in the psychology department or in a private office in the participants' living units. On average, each interview took approximately 5 hours to complete (including the completion of the questionnaires). Some of the interviews took considerably longer than 5 hours (e.g., 12 hours) and were completed in a span of two days. Breaks in the interviews were frequently taken due to institutional requirements (e.g., meals, count and lockdowns).

The participants mean age was 34.93 ($SD = 10.58$; range: 19–77). Sixty-five per cent were Caucasian, 17% were Aboriginal and approximately 18% reported a mixture of ethnic backgrounds. The participants reported an average of 11.25 years of education ($SD = 2.13$; range: 4.5–18) and indicated being incarcerated for a mean of 6.23 ($SD = 5.88$; range: .08–27) years for their index (i.e., most recent) offences.

Materials

Assessment of arousal and valence

The Affect Grid (Russell, 1980; Russell, Weiss & Mendelsohn, 1989) is a two-dimensional measure of arousal and valence. It is a single-item scale that assesses the dimensions of arousal–sleepiness (i.e., arousal) and pleasure–displeasure (i.e., valence). The scale can be used as a measure of arousal and valence to assess a number of possible criterion variables (e.g., current mood), depending on the objectives of the study in question (Russell et al., 1989). That is, the Affect Grid has general instructions that can be adapted to the goals/needs of specific studies. For the purposes of the present chapter, participants were asked to rate their emotional state during the main part of each event with the Affect Grid. They were asked to place a single mark on the grid during each administration. Both the valence and arousal scores range from 1 to 9. Higher scores reflect higher levels of positive valence and arousal, respectively. Across four studies, Russell et al. (1989) demonstrated the Affect Grid to have sound interrater reliability, split-half reliability, and both convergent (with other measures of arousal and pleasure) and discriminant (between the dimensions of arousal and pleasure) validity.

Assessment of memory characteristics

The Memory Characteristics Questionnaire (MCQ; Johnson, Foley, Suengas & Raye, 1988) is a 39-item self-report questionnaire that assesses the phenomenological qualities of memory (e.g., vividness, detail, coherence, etc.) for an event (for review, see Johnson, 1988). Research shows the MCQ can differentiate between true and false memories of word lists (e.g., Mather, Henkel & Johnson, 1997), videotaped events (Henkel, Franklin & Johnson, 2000), and childhood experiences (Johnson et al., 1988). Participants responded to each MCQ question on a 7-point Likert scale (e.g., 1 = a vague memory for an event; 7 = a clear distinct memory for an event) regarding each provided memory. Participants were assessed on the MCQ once per memory. Although widely used by researchers as an assessment of the phenomenal characteristics of memories (e.g., D'Argembeau, Comblain & van der Linden, 2003; Destun & Kuiper, 1999), the psychometric properties of the MCQ have yet to be reported in the published literature.

Three items on the MCQ were used as memory criterion variables (i.e., question #8 [vividness]: 'overall vividness is': [from 1 = vague to 7 = very vivid]; question #9 [detail]: 'my memory for this event is': [from 1 = sketchy to 7 = very detailed]; question #33 [overall memory]: 'overall, I remember this event': [from 1 = hardly to 7 = very well]).

Design and Procedure

Interview

Trained forensic psychology graduate students, undergraduate students, and the first author conducted the interviews. Three of the interviewers were male and seven were female. Due to the breadth of the protocol, two weeks of training was necessary. The first step was to train the interviewers in the adult 'Step-wise' interview protocol (Yuille, 1990; for review, see Yuille, Marxsen & Cooper, 1999). This semi-structured interview is routinely used as an investigative tool for victims with allegations of sexual assault and domestic violence. Although there were no a priori reasons to expect the 'Step-wise' protocol could not be adapted for use with perpetrators of crime, this was one of the first studies to use the interview protocol on male incarcerated violent offenders. Using a funnel approach to questioning, up to three different memories for violence were elicited and exhausted for detail (see Cooper, 2005, for more information). In a non-leading fashion, participants were asked if they had perpetrated an act of instrumental violence. If they had,[1] they were asked to think about an experience and recall it; it was then exhausted for detail. The same procedure was completed for an act of reactive violence. Finally, in a non-suggestive manner, participants were asked if they had experienced a time in which they acted violently and had little or no memory for the event (i.e., lack of memory for violence). If they had, they were asked to think of an experience and recall it. As with the other two experiences, it was then exhausted for detail.

---

[1] As a group, the sample reported a variable yet entrenched history of violent acts (e.g., ranging from 1 to over 1,000). Although previous convictions were not recorded, the participants reported a mean of 138.44 ($SD = 702.41$) acts of instrumental violence and a mean of 98.42 ($SD = 416.08$) acts of reactive violence.

With the informed consent of the participants, the interviews were audiotaped to provide a verbatim account of the participants' memories. The verbatim accounts will be coded for future research, not for the purposes of the present research. At the outset of the interviews, the interviewers developed rapport with the participants, explained the scope of the study and the limits to confidentiality and received the participants' informed consent to participate. The interviewers then assessed the participants' demographic information (e.g., age, ethnic origin, nature of index offence, number of years incarcerated, history of drug and alcohol use). Following, the interviewers used the 'Step-wise' interview protocol to elicit the three different types of autobiographical experiences. The order of the memories was counter balanced to prevent an ordering effect of recall.

After each memory was elicited and exhausted for detail in a 'Step-wise' fashion, the interviewers assessed the participants' memories for state variables. The participants were asked to rate their emotional state (i.e., arousal and valence[2]) during each event in question using the Affect Grid (Russell et al., 1989). Each memory was then assessed regarding cognitive criteria such as vividness, detail, coherence, etc., using the MCQ (Johnson et al., 1988). Prior research with the MCQ and the Step-wise interview indicates memory assessed by both methods is significantly related (Griesel et al., 2005).

RESULTS

Types of Memories Provided

After each memory was provided, the interviewers applied a theme label (e.g., instrumental assault). After each interview, the author reviewed the theme label with each interviewer. There were no discrepancies between the interviewers and the author in this process. The theme labels for each memory resulted in the following categories. Although some of the following reflect behaviours that could be attributable to more than one category (e.g., a victim may have been stabbed during a sexual assault), it was felt that the following categories appropriately reflected the variability apparent in the participants' provided experiences. Statistical analyses were not conducted on these categories; they are presented to provide the reader with a flavour for the general types of experiences provided by the participants.

---

[2] Only valence was focused on for the purposes of the present chapter.

The memories for acts of instrumental violence (IV) provided by the participants were grouped into the following categories: assaults/fights (54.1%); robberies (19.7%); stabbings/shootings/murders (9%); sexual assaults (9%); and breaking and entering and home invasions involving IV (7.4%). Approximately 1% of the memories for acts of IV could not be grouped into these categories. The memories for acts of reactive violence (RV) provided by the participants were classified into the following categories: assaults/fights (79%); stabbings/shootings/murders (15.9%); and breaking and entering and robberies involving RV (1.4%). Approximately 4% of the memories for acts of RV could not be grouped into these categories. The lack of memory for violent experiences (LM) provided by the participants were grouped into the following categories: assaults/fights (67.1%); stabbings/shootings/murders (15.9%); sexual assaults (8.5%); and robberies involving violence (2.4%). Approximately 6% of the LM experiences could not be classified into these categories.

Memory for Violence

As a manipulation check in the larger study (Cooper, 2005), it was demonstrated that the LM experiences were recalled significantly poorer than both the acts of IV and RV. Thus, there was some indication that the participants understood what was asked of them (e.g., in terms of providing poorly recalled acts of violence). Analyses demonstrated that the LM experiences (i.e., 11.72 years old on average) were not significantly older in age than both the acts of IV (i.e., 11.42 years old on average) and RV (i.e., 11.99 years old on average) events, with no differences between the latter two events. Thus, any memory differences between events could not be directly due to the ages of the events.

Three repeated measures Analyses of Variances (ANOVAs) compared the MCQ memory criterion variables for acts of IV and RV. The main test of within-subject effects were significant for overall memory ($F[1, 115] = 8.97$, $p < .005$) and vividness ($F[1, 115] =$, $p < .05$) but not for detail ($F[1, 115] = 2.12$, $p > .10$). Thus, the acts of IV were recalled significantly better, in terms of overall memory and vividness but not detail, than acts of RV (see Table 3.1).

Other analyses examined participants' motivation (i.e., reactive versus instrumental) for committing their LM experiences. Fifty-five per cent of the sample provided such experiences. During data collection, the last 21 participants were asked whether their LM experiences were reactively or instrumentally motivated. As illustrated in Table 3.2 (participants' distinction), a Chi Square analysis indicated participants' LM experiences were significantly more likely

Table 3.1 Memory comparisons between IV and RV

	Instrumental Violence (IV)	Reactive Violence (RV)
MCQ 33 (Overall Memory)	5.89 (1.25)	5.46 (1.49) > IV, $p < 0.005$
MCQ 8 (Vividness)	5.51 (1.44)	5.18 (1.49) > IV, $p < 0.05$
MCQ 9 (Detail)	5.55 (1.40)	5.34 (1.37)

Table 3.2 Motivations for the LM experiences

	Instrumental	Reactive
Participants' Distinction	14% ($n = 3$)	86% ($n = 18$) > IV, $p < 0.01$
Coders' Distinction	24% ($n = 20$)	76% ($n = 62$) > IV, $p < 0.001$

to be reported as reactively than instrumentally motivated ($x^2[1] = 10.71$, $p < .01$).

Two trained coders examined the narratives of the 82 participants who provided LM experiences and coded such narratives (via transcription for the transcribed interviews or via audiotape for the non-transcribed interviews) for the instrumental–reactive distinction. There were no discrepancies between the coders. As shown in Table 3.2 (coders' distinction), Chi Square analysis indicated participants' LM experiences were significantly more likely to be reactively than instrumentally motivated ($x^2[1] = 21.52$, $p < .001$). In 18 out of the 21 cases, there was full agreement between participants' and coders' distinction. In two cases, participants indicated reactive motivations (i.e., for a robbery and subsequent assault; for forcible confinement and sexual assault) and such motivations were subsequently assessed to be instrumental in nature by the coders. In one case, both the participant and the coders deemed the experiences to be partially instrumentally and reactively motivated. In short, there was a high level of agreement between the participants' and coders' distinction of the motivation for the LM experiences.

Table 3.3 Correlations between valence and memory

	MCQ 8 (Vividness)	MCQ 9 (Detail)	MCQ 33 (Overall Memory)
Instrumental Violence (IV)	$r = 0.20$ $p < 0.05$	$r = 0.25$ $p < 0.01$	$r = 0.19$ $p < 0.05$
Reactive Violence (RV)	$r = 0.01$ $p > 0.50$	$r = 0.05$ $p > 0.50$	$r = 0.03$ $p > 0.50$

Valence

To examine potential valence differences between acts of IV and RV, a paired samples t-test was calculated on participants' responses to the valence dimension of the Affect Grid in terms of reports of valence during the main parts of these events. Participants reported significantly higher levels of positive valence regarding perpetrating IV ($X = 4.81$; $SD = 2.83$) in comparison to perpetrating RV ($X = 3.84$; $SD = 2.95$; $t[114] = 3.29$, $p < .005$).

Valence and Memory

To examine the association between valence and memory, bivariate Pearson two-tailed correlations were performed on participants' responses to the valence dimension of the Affect Grid concerning reports of valence during the main parts of each IV and RV experience and the MCQ memory criterion variables for each event. As Table 3.3 shows, participants' reports of valence during their acts of IV were significantly associated with their reports of memory vividness, detail, and overall memory. There was no significant association between valence and memory for RV.

DISCUSSION

Based on Hervé et al.'s (under review; Chapter 2 this volume) theory, Yuille, Cooper, Hervé and Hanson (2004) suggest, because the motivation to commit instrumental violence is, by definition, external (e.g., financial), a perpetrator of instrumental violence should focus on the event during the commission of such violence. Moreover, the preceding fantasy associated with such violence and/or the preceding planning or preparatory acts should have a positive effect on memory for the details of the event (Porter et al., 2001; Swihart et al., 1999). Thus, the instrumental nature of the violence should lead to relatively good memory for the details of the event. In contrast, due to the internal motivation of reactive violence (e.g., rage), a perpetrator of such violence should focus more on internal (e.g., their subjective state) than external sources. Accordingly, the perpetrator of reactive violence should have relatively poorer memory for the details of the event. Given that the present participants reported significantly higher levels of vividness and better overall memory for their instrumental acts of violence than their reactive acts of violence, these proposals were indirectly supported. Similarly, and consistent with the results of Taylor and Kopelman's (1984) research, the participants' lack of memory for violent experiences were significantly more likely to have been reactively motivated than instrumentally motivated. The prevalence rates for such types of experiences are also consistent with prior research (see Merckelbach & Christianson, Chapter 7 this volume; Porter, Woodworth & Doucette, Chapter 5 this volume; van Oorsouw & Cima, Chapter 8 this volume).

In addition to the precipitating nature of the violent events, other precipitating factors from Hervé et al.'s (under review; Chapter 2 this volume) theory impacted the participants' memories for their violent acts. In fact, one possible explanation for the poorer recall associated with reactively violent memories than instrumentally violent memories is valence. As reviewed earlier, extreme negative valence can have a debilitating effect on offenders' memory for violence (Bradford & Smith, 1979; Harry & Resnick, 1986; Hopwood & Snell, 1933; O'Connell, 1960). In the present investigation, the reactive acts of violence were experienced with significantly higher levels of negative valence than the instrumental acts of violence. As an example of negative valence and reactive violence, one participant was so angry during and subsequent to committing a reactive murder of his associate, he kicked the victim's dead body in a state of rage, yelling at him, asking why he provoked him. As Hervé et al.'s theory predicts, negative valence could lead to poor memory for violence, particularly in hypersensitive individuals who commit reactive violence. According to the Hervé et al., building upon the work of Mandler (1984) and Easterbrook (1959), the arousing nature of reactive violence could interact with a perpetrator's hypersensitivity to arousal, leading to a narrowed and disrupted focus of attention during an event. Issues related to arousal sensitivity aside, anecdotally, some support was found for the suggestion that negative valence could debilitate perception and thus memory. For example, one participant retrospectively described his affective state during the commission of a reactive murder as follows: 'when I started to lose my temper. . . it's kinda like my vision bubbled or something, it bubbled inside my eye. . . that's what it felt like, it felt like it bubbled from my vision. . . my vision was slightly distorted. . . that's how it gets when I'm really angry'. Similarly, another participant discussed part of his reactively motivated lack of memory for violence experience as follows: 'I mean when it's [violence] spur of the moment, right then and there, you know, who knows what happens. . . sometimes you do lose the memory. . . I'm not going to say I lost memory but sometimes anger gets in the way'. After some questioning, he went on to comment the following: 'because I was angry, and it's like when you are angry, you block things out, you don't care. . . anybody who threatens me or anyone close to me, that's it, I see red, I go after them and that's the way it is'. It is unclear whether the latter participant was reporting partial amnesia for violence or if he was claiming that he could not control himself of both. Issues of credibility aside for the moment, the point here is that the participant claimed that negative valence (i.e., anger) negatively affected his cognitive processing of the event.

These two aforementioned anecdotes arguably represent examples of the red out pattern of memory discussed earlier. Indeed, both involved reactive rage states that led to poor memory and both reactive violence and extreme negative valence are variables characteristic of red out experiences (Swihart et al., 1999). Interestingly, the latter participant actually described seeing the colour red, as did one of the batterers examined by Dutton (1995). Another participant from the present investigation provided a similar statement. As he was describing his poor memory for a reactive murder, he noted the following: '. . . that's when I started stabbing him, I can't remember if he lived or not. All I know is that, while I was going towards him, all I could see was red'. The interviewer then curiously stated the following, 'when you went to stab him, you mentioned that you saw red. Do you remember anything more about that?' The participant replied, '. . . when you're angry, you know, you don't see anything. Anything that makes sense anyways'. Unfortunately, for a number of reasons (e.g., the high rate of reported substance use during the acts of violence, low power), these apparent red out experiences contribute little beyond their anecdotal nature. Indeed, at present, the veracity of these reports of amnesia is unknown. It is, of course, possible that some participants malingered or somehow distorted their reports of amnesia. Jelicic and Merckelbach (Chapter 9 this volume) and Vrij and Granhag (Chapter 12 this volume) discuss a number of techniques that could be employed to assess crime-related amnesia in offenders. As expanded on later, we strongly recommend that an offender's eyewitness account be evaluated with a multi-modal approach employing, for example, statement-validity analyses.

Although negative valence appears to have negatively impacted some of the participants' memories of reactive violence, positive valence during acts of instrumental violence was associated with reports of better memory for such experiences. These findings support certain assumptions of the Hervé et al.'s theory. According to Hervé et al. (2003), an individual's affective response to an event should be positively associated with their memory for the event if the nature of the event is egosyntonic (e.g., experienced with positive valence; consistent with their world view), as opposed to egodystonic (e.g., experienced with negative valence; inconsistent with their world view), to the individual. In terms of the present participants' emotional responses to their provided events, the instrumental acts of violence were rated as significantly more positive in valence than the reactive acts of violence. Thus, the instrumental acts of violence were viewed as relatively egosyntonic to the participants and such an emotive response was positively related to their accounts of memory for such experiences. As an example of positive valence and good memory for instrumental violence, one participant with a particularly detailed account of his act of instrumental violence stated the following: 'I just kept stabbing, stabbing, stabbing. And I was laughing half the time I was doing this. I remember laughing at him. . . we started to beat the guy in the head with a hammer. And I'm sitting there holding this guy in place and we are both laughing our heads off. . . and we hear this funny noise like squishing, and we are all laughing hysterically at that'. In fact, the only negative affect displayed by this participant concerned the reality that the victim remained alive after his gruesome beating. In this vein, the participant stated the following, '. . . and I'm trying to convince them [his associates] to go back so I can finish the job. . . so I was kind of pissed off because I didn't get [kill] him'.

As this volume indicates, there are a number of other variables not touched on in the present chapter that affect eyewitness recall in offenders. For example, the results from the larger study on the present data (Cooper, 2005) suggest many of the present participants were psychopathic, a predisposing factor, and psychopathy had a facilitative effect on recall (see also Porter et al., Chapter 5 this volume). In terms of precipitating factors, state dissociation was shown to have a negative effect on memory. In regards to perpetuating factors, rehearsal was demonstrated to positively affect memory. Thus, as Hervé et al. (Chapter 2 this volume) suggest, a number of variables independently relate to recall. Clearly, assessors need to take a multidimensional approach to evaluating offenders' recall and the credibility of such. Issues related to credibility are discussed in more detail in the following section.

LIMITATIONS AND SUGGESTIONS FOR FUTURE RESEARCH

There were a number of limitations to the present study that deserve attention. The most obvious drawback is the fact that the veracity of the participants' memories is unknown. Although there was no *a priori* reason to expect most of the participants would deliberately distort their memories, the fact remains that deception and manipulation are cardinal components of a criminal lifestyle and, thus, the participants themselves. Psychopaths, in particular, are known for their tendency towards dissimulation and they may have consciously lied about some of their autobiographical experiences for no other reason than mere duping delight (Cooper & Yuille, 2006; Ekman, 1992; Peticlerc, Hervé, Hare & Spidel, 2000). Although it is likely at least some of the participants deliberately distorted their memories, it is doubtful whether this was a rampant problem. Save for duping delight, there were no strong reasons to expect most of the participants deliberately lied or withheld information. It was hoped the voluntary and confidential nature of the present investigation provided a context in which the participants could discuss their past experiences in a sincere fashion. Of course, whether they actually did so is an empirical question. In this regard, future plans for the present data set include assessing the credibility of the participants' narrative memories via Criterion Based Content Analysis (CBCA; Porter & Yuille, 1995, 1996; Vrij & Akehurst, 1998) and examining the veracity of some of their memories through a review of existing correctional file information and interviews with collaterals.

Related to the general issue of veracity of the memories is specific concern over the LM experiences. That is, we viewed the LM experiences as somewhat synonymous with dissociative amnesia. Although it is likely that at least some of the LM experiences are in fact bona fide examples of dissociative amnesia, it is impossible to make such diagnoses at the present time. Indeed, we would need to know more about such experiences in order to rule out organic (e.g., head trauma, substance use) precipitants and malingering (American Psychiatric Association, 2000).

Another limitation of the present investigation concerns the fact that central versus peripheral details of the participants' provided memories were not examined. In part, this issue was not investigated as the participants' narratives are in the process of being transcribed. After the transcription process is completed, the narratives will be coded for quality and quantity of detail using a procedure specifically developed for this purpose (Yuille et al., 1999). However, coding the narratives for central versus peripheral information will likely prove problematic. Although this can easily be done in analogue research (e.g., Loftus & Burns, 1982), the issue is far more complex in field research. Indeed, as Brown (2003) has stated, 'in a visually dynamic environment [such as the field] it is difficult to distinguish purely central and peripheral information. . . in a dynamic environment, information that could be defined as central one moment could also be defined as peripheral information at a later time, depending upon how eyewitnesses shift their attention over time' (p. 104). Although there will be difficulties, an attempt will be made to code the participants' memories for central versus peripheral information.

A final limitation concerns the instrumental–reactive dichotomy used in the present investigation. The reality is that many violent crimes often include both instrumental and reactive components. For example, a planned robbery may involve a reactive assault or murder, depending on how the victim(s) reacted to the event. For this reason, some researchers have used the term 'primarily instrumental' and 'primarily reactive' to refer to the principal act of violence and/or the motivation for such in a given situation (e.g., Woodworth & Porter, 2002). Although the flavour of the 'primarily instrumental–primarily reactive' dichotomy was used in the present investigation, for the sake of simplicity, the term primarily was not explicitly stated. Nevertheless, future plans for the present data set involve re-coding the participants' motivations (e.g., primarily instrumental–reactive vs primarily reactive–instrumental) and examining the impact of these more refined categorisations on memory. We also plan to examine the official record of some of the offences to assess the 'actual' reactive nature of the claimed reactive acts of violence. That is, it is possible that some participants created a reactive version of an act of violence that was, in fact, instrumental in nature.

IMPLICATIONS FOR THE CRIMINAL JUSTICE SYSTEM

The above noted limitations notwithstanding, the results of the present investigation have a number of implications for the criminal justice system. Of course, in light of the aforementioned limitations and the fact that much of the present research is novel, the following implications should be viewed cautiously until more research is conducted.

The present research has a few implications for the assessment of credibility. Broadly speaking, credibility assessments are conducted by many players in the criminal system tasked with evaluating the credibility of victims', witnesses', and perpetrators' accounts of crime, particularly violent crime (Memon, Vrij & Bull, 1998). For example, correctional psychologists routinely assess the credibility of incarcerated offenders' memories for their crimes in the context of conducting risk assessments for the National Parole Board. Further, not uncommonly, psychologists, testifying as expert witnesses, educate the triers of fact regarding issues related to credibility so the triers themselves can be in a better position to assess the credibility of an account of a given witness. To date, one of the most valid, reliable, and widely used techniques to assess credibility in these contexts is Statement Validity Analysis (SVA; Horowitz, 1991). As part of conducting SVA, clinicians are required to elicit a statement of the crime in question, via a semi-structured interview such as the Step-wise Interview (Yuille et al., 1999), as was done in the present investigation. After the narrative is exhausted for detail, CBCA is employed (Vrij, Akehurst, Soukara & Bull, 2002). This technique is primarily based on Udo Undeutsch's clinical-forensic experiences assessing the credibility of child witnesses' accounts of alleged crimes in Germany (Undeutsch, 1982; Vrij & Akehurst, 1998). Based on such experiences, he formulated the Undeutsch hypothesis, which suggests that qualitative and quantitative differences exist between individuals' memories of real events and memories of events not actually experienced (Porter & Yuille, 1995). CBCA has been used to explore qualitative and quantitative aspects of memory via an examination of a number of criteria (Steller & Koehnken, 1989). Some laboratory (Colwell, Hiscock & Memon, 2002; Porter & Yuille, 1996) and field research (Lamb et al., 1997) has shown that certain criteria, such as the amount of detail a witness can provide (i.e., an appropriate amount of detail), can reliably distinguish credible from non-credible accounts (for review, see Vrij & Akehurst, 1998; Yuille, 1988). Similarly, findings from the source monitoring literature consistently demonstrate memories of actual experiences have stronger phenomenal qualities (e.g., detail, vividness) than memories of imagined experiences (Johnson, Hashtroudi & Lindsay, 1993). Theories behind such research suggest: (a) it is extremely difficult to have a detailed narrative of a non-experienced event, as such details are not actually stored in memory (Porter & Yuille, 1995); and (b) deceptive accounts are accompanied by an increase in physiological arousal (e.g., anxiety), therefore increasing the possibility of detection (Colwell et al., 2002). Of course, if a witness practices his/her false account, such details will be available upon recall and research has shown that deceptors, trained in the use of CBCA, can fool evaluators, or at least obtain high CBCA scores resembling those of truth tellers (Vrij et al., 2002; Vrij, Akehurst,

Soukara & Bull, 2004; Vrij, Kneller & Mann, 2000). Such examples highlight the difficulties associated with the assessment of credibility.

The complexity of credibility assessment notwithstanding, based on the present findings, one should expect instrumental acts of violence to be better recalled than reactive acts of violence. Thus, during a risk assessment interview, for example, if an offender provides a detailed description of a reactive murder but claims dissociative amnesia for an instrumental physical assault, the institutional psychologist should have cause for concern. Of course, an appropriate amount of detail is only one CBCA criterion and CBCA is just one component of SVA. Such a technique should never be utilised in isolation. The more information the evaluator has (e.g., in terms of how memory works under different circumstances), the better position he/she will be in to assess the credibility of a given account of a crime. Indeed, as part of The Ekman Group: Training Division (PEG), an organisation that provides training on evaluating truthfulness, the present authors promote a multi-faceted approach to the assessment of truthfulness and credibility. In short, via active listening and observation, baseline information is collected and assessed. As many channels (e.g., face, voice, body, content of speech) as possible are actively examined and potential 'hot spots' (i.e., incongruence within and across channels; e.g., emotional 'leakage') are noted. For example, if a psychopathic offender claims that an instrumental act of violence he/she committed had a negative effect on him but a micro-expression (i.e., a very brief expression of emotion; Ekman, 2003) of happiness appears on his/her face as he/she is discussing the violence, the assessor would take a hypothesis testing approach to examine whether the offender was in fact being deceptive in regard to his/her account of his crime. This is a complex approach to evaluating truthfulness that should be viewed as a complement to the suggestions offered by Jelicic and Merckelbach (Chapter 9 this volume; e.g., the use of interviewing methods and tests of malingering) and Merckelbach and Christianson (Chapter 7 this volume; e.g., the use of and tests/scales of malingering) and Vrij and Granhag (Chapter 12 this volume; e.g., the use of specialised interviewing techniques).

Not only do psychologists directly assess credibility and educate the triers of fact about issues related to the credibility of memories, psychologists often discuss for the courts how memory works under different circumstances, particularly concerning instances of crime. As there has not been a great deal of research conducted on offenders' memories for their crimes, when the memory of an offender is an issue within a trial, expert psychologists, in an attempt to educate the triers of fact, often generalise the research on memory in victims and witnesses to the perpetrator context. Although it is logical to assume that many of the strong associations apparent in the victim and witness literature would hold true with perpetrators of crime, little research has addressed the validity of these generalisations. The present research was formulated, in part, to facilitate a larger knowledge base to which expert psychologists could draw from. For example, based on the present results, in conjunction with some of the past research and theorising on the topic, experts could discuss the fact that instrumental acts of violence are better recalled than reactive acts of violence and that the former type of violence is experienced with less negative valence than the latter.

CONCLUSION

In support of certain assumptions underlying Hervé et al.'s (Chapter 2 this volume) model of eyewitness memory, the present investigation demonstrated that a few memory influencing variables were associated with the participants' reported quality and quantity of their provided experiences. Specifically, the instrumentality of violence and the associated positive affect was shown to be positively related to reports of memory for perpetrated violence. These findings indicate situational (i.e., type of event) and individual difference variables (i.e., valence during events) affected the participants' accounts of their memories, thus providing a better understanding of the factors underlying the variable nature of eyewitness memory in offenders. As noted by Anderson, Cohen and Taylor (2000), 'the variability of personal memories is a relatively neglected aspect of autobiographical memory despite its obvious practical and theoretical importance. Practitioners in the fields of oral history or witness testimony need to take account of the existence and nature of variability and to understand the factors that influence it. Theories of representation and retrieval need to predict and explain variability of recall' (p. 452). As with the present investigation, future research on the subject should focus on how memories are affected by individual differences.

REFERENCES

American Psychiatric Association. (2000) *Diagnostic and statistical manual of mental disorders*, (4th ed, Test Revision), Washington, DC: Author.
Anderson, S.J., Cohen, G. & Taylor, S. (2000) Rewriting the past: Some factors affecting the variability of personal memories. *Applied Cognitive Psychology*, **14**(5), 435–54.

Berkowitz, L. (1983) The experience of anger as a parallel process in the display of impulsive, 'angry' aggression. In R.G. Green & E.I. Donnerstein (Eds), *Aggression: Theoretical and empirical views* (Vol. 1, pp. 103–34). New York: Academic Press.

Berkowitz, L. (1990) On the formation and regulation of anger and aggression: A cognitive-neoassociationistic analysis. *American Psychologist*, **45**(4), 494–503.

Bradford, J.W. & Smith, S.M. (1979) Amnesia and homicide: The Padola case and a study of thirty cases. *Bulletin of the American Academy of Psychiatry and Law*, **7**(3), 219–31.

Brown, J.B. (2003) Eyewitness memory for arousing events: Putting things into context. *Applied Cognitive Psychology*, **17**(1), 93–106.

Brown, S.L. & Forth, A.E. (1997) Psychopathy and sexual assault: Static factors, emotional precursors, and rapist subtypes. *Journal of Consulting and Clinical Psychology*, **65**(5), 848–57.

Bushman, B.J. & Anderson, C.A. (2001) Is it time to pull the plug on the hostile versus instrumental aggression dichotomy? *Psychological Review*, **108**(1), 273–9.

Chase, K.A., O'Leary, K.D., Heyman, R.E. (2001) Categorizing partner-violent men within the reactive–proactive typology model. *Journal of Consulting and Clinical Psychology*, **69**(3), 567–72.

Colwell, K., Hiscock, C.K. & Memon, A. (2002) Interviewing techniques and the assessment of statement credibility. *Applied Cognitive Psychology*, **16**(3), 287–300.

Cooper, B.S. (2005) *Memory for mayhem*. Unpublished Doctoral dissertation. University of British Columbia, Vancouver, British Columbia, Canada.

Cooper, B.S., Kennedy, M.A. & Yuille, J.C. (2004) Traumatic stress in prostitutes: A within-subject comparison of PTSD symptom levels across sexual and non-sexual traumatic experiences. *Journal of Trauma Practice*, **3**(1), 51–70.

Cooper, B.S. & Yuille, J.C. (2006). Psychopathy and deception. In H.F. Hervé'& J.C. Yuille (Eds), *The Psychopath: Theory, research and practice* (pp. 487–503). Mahwah, New Jersey: Lawrence Erlbaum Associates.

Cooper, B.S., Yuille, J.C. & Dar-Nimrod, I. (August, 2004) *Violent offenders' memories for instrumental and reactive violence*. Invited paper presented at the 28th International Congress of Psychology, Beijing, China.

Cornell, P.G., Warren, J., Hawk, G., Stafford, E., Oram, G. & Pine, D. (1996) Psychopathy in instrumental and reactive violent offenders. *Journal of Consulting and Clinical Psychology*, **64**(4), 783–90.

D'Argembeau, A., Comblain, C. & van der Linden, M. (2003) Phenomenal characteristics of autobiographical memories of positive, negative, and neutral events. *Applied Cognitive Psychology*, **17**(3), 281–94.

Darves-Bornoz, J. (1997) Rape-related psychotraumatic syndromes. *European Journal of Obstetrics & Gynecology and Reproductive Biology*, **71**(1), 59–65.

Destun, L.M. & Kuiper, N.A. (1999) Phenomenal characteristics associated with real and imagined events: The effects of event valence and absorption. *Applied Cognitive Psychology*, **13**(2), 175–86.

Dutton, D.G. (1995) *The batterer*. New York: Basic Books.

Easterbrook, J.A. (1959) The effect of emotion on cue utilization and the organization of behaviour. *Psychological Review* **66**(3), 183–201.

Ekman, P. (1992) *Telling lies: Clues to deceit in the marketplace, politics, and marriage*. New York: W. Norton.

Ekman, P. (2003) *Emotions revealed: Recognizing faces and feelings to improve communication and emotional life*. New York: Henry Holt and Company, LLC.

Griesel, D., Mancini, K., Daflos, S., Jones, M., Cooper, B.S. & Yuille, J.C. (March, 2005) *Reliability of self-reported quantity of detail in prostitutes' memories of sexual assaults*. Paper presented at the American Psychology and Law Society Convention, La Jolla, California.

Guttmacher, M.S. (1960) *The mind of the murderer*. New York: Farrar, Straus, & Cudahy.

Harry, B. & Resnick, P.J. (1986) Posttraumatic stress disorder in murderers. *Journal of Forensic Sciences*, **31**(2), 609–13.

Henkel, L.A., Franklin, N. & Johnson, M.K. (2000) Cross-modal source monitoring confusions between perceived and imagined events. *Journal of Experimental Psychology: Learning, Memory, and Cognition*, **26**(2), 321–35.

Hare, R.D. (1993) *Without conscience: The disturbing world of psychopaths among us*. New York: Pocket Books.

Hervé, H.F., Cooper, B.S. & Yuille, J.C. (June, 2002) *A biopsychosocial model of eyewitness memory*. Paper presented at the Canadian Psychological Association's Annual Convention, Vancouver, British Columbia.

Hervé, H.F., Cooper, B.S., Yuille, J.C. & Daylen (July, 2003) *The psychopathic eyewitness: Perspectives from a biopsychosocial model of eyewitness memory*. Paper presented at the Society for Applied Research on Memory and Cognition's (SARMAC) conference, Aberdeen, Scotland.

Hervé, H.F.M., Petticlerc, A.M. & Hare, R.D. (May, 1999) *Violence-related motivations in psychopathic and nonpsychopathic offenders: Egosyntonic and egodystonic motivations*. Poster presented at the Canadian Psychological Association's 60th Annual Convention, Halifax, Nova Scotia.

Hervé, H.F., Yuille, J.C. & Cooper, B.S. (under review). A biopsychosocial model of eyewitness memory.

Hopwood, J.S. & Snell, H.K. (1933) Amnesia in relation to crime. *Journal of Mental Science*, **79**, 27–41.

Horowitz, S.W. (1991) Empirical support for statement validity assessment. *Behavioral Assessment*, **13**, 293–313.

Hubbard, J.A., Dodge, K.A., Cillessen, A.H.N., Coie, J.D. & Schwartz, D. (2001) The dyadic nature of social information processing in boy's reactive and proactive aggression. *Journal of Personality and Social Psychology*, **80**(2), 268–80.

Johnson, M.K. (1988) Reality monitoring: An experimental phenomenological approach. *Journal of Experimental Psychology: General*, **117**(4), 390–4.

Johnson, M.K., Foley, M., Suengas, A. & Raye, C. (1988) Phenomenal characteristics of memories for perceived and imagined autobiographical events. *Journal of Experimental Psychology: General*, **117**(4), 371–6.

Johnson, M.K., Hashtroudi, S. & Lindsay, D.S. (1993) Source monitoring. *Psychological Bulletin*, **114**(1), 3–28.

Lamb, M.E., Sternberg, K.J., Esplin, P.W., Hershkowitz, I., Orbach, Y. & Hovav, M. (1997) Criterion-based content analysis: A field validation study *Child Abuse and Neglect*, **21**(3), 255–264.

Loftus, E.F. & Burns, T. (1982) Mental shock can produce retrograde amnesia. *Memory and Cognition*, **10**(4), 318–23.

Mandler, G. (1984) *Mind and body*. New York, NY: Norton.

Mather, M., Henkel, L.A. & Johnson, M. (1997) Evaluating characteristics of false memories: Remember/know judgements and memory characteristics questionnaire compared. *Memory and Cognition*, **25**(6), 826–37.

Mechanic, M.B., Resick, P.A. & Griffin, M.G. (1998) A comparison of normal forgetting, psychopathology, and information-processing models of reported amnesia for recent sexual trauma. *Journal of Consulting and Clinical Psychology*, **66**(6), 948–57.

Memon, A., Vrij, A. & Bull, R. (1998) *Psychology and law: Truthfulness, accuracy and credibility*. London: McGraw-Hill Publishing Company.

O'Connell, B.A. (1960) Amnesia and homicide: A study of 50 murderers. *British Journal of Delinquency*, **10**, 262–76.

Parwatikar, S.D., Holcomb, W.R. & Menninger, K.A. (1985) The detection of malingered amnesia in accused murderers. *Bulletin of the American Academy of Psychiatry and Law*, **13**(1), 97–103.

Peticlerc, A.M., Hervé, H.F., Hare, R.D. & Spidel, A. (June, 2000) *Psychopaths' reasons to deceive*. Poster presented at the Canadian Psychological Association's 61st annual convention.

Pollock, P.H. (1999) When the killer suffers: Post-traumatic stress reactions following homicide. *Legal and Criminological Psychology*, **4**(2), 185–202.

Porter, S., Birt, A.R., Yuille, J.C. & Hervé, H.F. (2001) Memory for murder: A psychological perspective on dissociative amnesia in legal contexts. *International Journal of Law and Psychiatry*, **24**(1), 23–42.

Porter, S. & Yuille, J.C. (1995) Credibility assessment of criminal suspects through statement analysis. *Psychology, Crime and Law*, **1**(4), 1–13.

Porter, S. & Yuille, J.C. (1996) The language of deceit: An investigation of the verbal clues to deception in the interrogation context. *Law & Human Behavior*, **20**(4), 443–58.

Porter, S. & Woodworth, M. (March, 2002) *An examination of the nature of sexual homicides as a function of psychopathy*. Paper presented at the American Psychology and Law Society's Biennial Conference, Austin, Texas.

Poulin, F. & Boivin, M. (2000) Reactive and proactive aggression: Evidence of a two-factor model. *Psychological Assessment*, **12**(2), 115–22.

Russell, J.A. (1980) A circumplex model of affect. *Journal of Personality and Social Psychology*, **39**(6), 1161–78.

Russell, J.A., Weiss, A. & Mendelsohn, G.A. (1989) Affect grid: A single-item scale of pleasure and arousal. *Journal of Personality and Social Psychology*, **57**(3), 493–502.

Salfati, C.G. (2000) The nature of expressiveness and instrumentality in homicide. *Homicide Studies*, **4**(3), 265–93.

Serin, R.C. (1991) Psychopathy and violence in criminals. *Journal of Interpersonal Violence*, **6**(4), 423–31.

Spitzer, C., Dudeck, M., Liss, H., Orlob, S., Gillner, M. & Freyberger, H.J. (2001) Post-traumatic stress disorder in forensic inpatients. *Journal of Forensic Psychiatry*, **12**(1), 63–77.

Steller, M. & Koehnken, G. (1989) Statement analysis: Credibility assessment of children's testimonies in sexual abuse cases. In D.C. Raskin (Ed.), *Psychological methods in criminal investigation and evidence* (pp. 217–45). New York: Springer Verlag.

Swihart, G., Yuille, J.C. & Porter, S. (1999) The role of state dependent memory in 'redouts.' *International Journal of Law and Psychiatry*, **125**(3–4), 199–212.

Taylor, P.J. & Kopelman, M.D. (1984) Amnesia for criminal offences. *Psychological Medicine*, **14**(3), 581–8.

Tweed, R.G. & Dutton, D.G. (1998) A comparison of impulsive and instrumental subgroups of batterers. *Violence & Victims*, **13**(3), 217–30.

Undeutsch, U. (1982) Statement reality analysis. In A. Trankell (Ed.), *Reconstructing the past: The role of psychologists in criminal trials*, (pp. 27–56), Kluwer: Deventer.

Vrij, A. & Akehurst, L. (1998) Verbal communication and credibility: Statement validity assessment. In A. Memon, A. Vrij & R. Bull (Eds), *Psychology and law: Truthfulness, accuracy and credibility* (pp. 3–26). London: McGraw-Hill Publishing Company.

Vrij, A., Akehurst, L., Soukara, S. & Bull, R. (2002) Will the truth come out? The effect of deception, age, status, coaching, and social skills on CBCA scores. *Law and Human Behavior*, **26**(3), 261–84.

Vrij, A., Akehurst, L., Soukara, S. & Bull, R. (2004) Let me inform you how to tell a convincing story: CBCA and reality monitoring scores as a function of age, coaching, and deception. *Canadian Journal of Behavioral Science*, **36**(2), 113–26.

Vrij, A., Kneller, W. & Mann, S. (2000) The effects of informing liars about criteria-based content analysis on their ability to deceive CBCA-raters. *Legal and Criminological Psychology*, **5**(1), 57–70.

Woodworth, M. & Porter, S. (2002) In cold blood: Characteristics of criminal homicides as a function of psychopathy. *Journal of Abnormal Psychology*, **111**(3), 436–45.

Yuille, J.C. (1988) The systematic assessment of children's testimony. *Canadian Psychology*, **29**(3), 247–62.

Yuille, J.C. (1990) *Adult 'step-wise' assault interview protocol*. Unpublished manuscript. University of British Columbia.

Yuille, J.C., Cooper, B.S., Hervé, H.F. & Hanson, I. (August, 2004) *Perpetrators' memories for violence: Perspectives from a biopsychosocial theory of eyewitness memory*. Invited paper presented at the International Congress of Psychology, Beijing, China.

Yuille, J.C., Daylen, J., Porter, S., Cooper, B.S. & Ghani, A. (1999) *A refined coding procedure for evaluating eyewitness accounts*. Unpublished manuscript. University of British Columbia.

Yuille, J.C., Marxsen, D. & Cooper, B.S. (1999) Training investigative interviewers: Adherence to the spirit, as well as to the letter. *International Journal of Law and Psychiatry*, **22**(3), 323–36.

CHAPTER 4

The Nature of Memories of Violent Crime among Young Offenders

CERI EVANS AND GILLIAN MEZEY

WHAT TYPES OF MEMORY DISTURBANCE DO VIOLENT OFFENDERS EXPERIENCE?

This chapter summarises some aspects of a cross-sectional study that aimed to describe the nature of memories of violent crime of young offenders and to investigate the risk factors for potential mechanisms that might underpin the development of different types of memory (Evans, 2004, 2006)[1].

There have been a number of studies of the *absence* of memory (i.e. amnesia) in perpetrators of crime over several decades but, overall, the existing body of research has significant scientific limitations, including methodological concerns about selection bias and measurement of dependent and independent variables (Bradford & Smith,

---

[1] Data included in this chapter has been accepted for journal publication.

Offenders' Memories of Violent Crimes. Edited by Sven Å. Christianson.
© 2007 John Wiley & Sons, Ltd.

1979; Evans, Mezey & Ehlers, submitted; Lynch & Bradford, 1980; Pope, Hudson, Bodkin & Oliva, 1998).

Studies of distressing memories relating to the commission of violence are, in contrast, part of a relatively more recent research effort. Most of these have focused on the presence of intrusive memories, as part of post-traumatic stress disorder (PTSD) in violent offenders detained in hospital settings. Some of these studies have measured PTSD arising from all causes in violent offenders (Gray et al., 2003; Kruppa, Hickey & Hubbard, 1995; Papanastassiou, Waldron, Boyle & Chesterman, 2004; Pollock, 1999; Spitzer et al., 2001). However, specific details of the nature of these memories are rarely provided and have not been systematically studied, even in victims of violence (Hackmann, Ehlers, Speckens & Clark, 2004).

WHAT ARE THE RISK FACTORS FOR MEMORY DISTURBANCE?

There has been little systematic empirical research into risk factors associated with amnesia in offender populations, although the evidence for some risk factors, e.g. alcohol intoxication (Bradford & Smith, 1979; O'Connell, 1960; Parwatikar, Holcomb & Menninger, 1985; Taylor & Kopelman, 1984) appears to be relatively consistent.

Several studies of amnesia for crime have suggested dissociation as the cause of amnesia (Hopwood & Snell, 1933; Taylor & Kopelman, 1984), but none of these studies include a measure of dissociation.

A more systematic approach has been adopted in studies of intrusive memories. It has been suggested that the overwhelming nature of traumatic events disrupts peri-traumatic cognitive processing which, in turn, results in a relatively disorganised and fragmented memory trace (Brewin, Dalgleish & Joseph, 1996; Ehlers & Clark, 2000; Horowitz, 1976; van der Kolk & Fisler, 1995). Problems in the way the trauma is encoded and laid down in memory are said to lead to the characteristics of intrusive memories and their typical pattern of retrieval (poor intentional recall, vivid unintentional re-experiencing and a 're-living' quality). Dissociation at the time of the event is thought to be particularly important (Ehlers, Mayou & Bryant, 1998; Halligan, Michael, Clark & Ehlers, 2003; Koopman, Classen & Speigel, 1994; Murray, Ehlers & Mayou, 2002; Shalev, Peri, Canetti & Schreiber, 1996), although it is unclear how this relates to other forms of cognitive processing that have been shown to influence memory (Roediger, 1990; Wheeler, 1997, 2000). Two further cognitive processing dimensions may be influential in determining whether or not people develop re-experiencing symptoms after trauma (Ehlers &

Clark, 2000; Ehlers, Hackmann & Michael, 2004a). First, autobiographical memory requires processing the event in a self-referent way (Wheeler, 1997), and therefore a *lack of self-referent processing* may lead to problems in remembering aspects of traumatic events (Ehlers & Clark, 2000; Ehlers, Hackmann & Michael, 2004b). Second, individuals who engage primarily in surface level, *data-driven processing* (i.e. processing sensory impressions and perceptual characteristics) during trauma are at greater risk of developing PTSD (and, by implication, intrusive memories) than those who engage in more in-depth, elaborative processing (Ehlers & Clark, 2000). These processes are thought to overlap in part with aspects of dissociation.

There is empirical evidence that excessively negative cognitive appraisals about the event are associated with the persistence of intrusive memories of trauma in victim samples (Clohessy & Ehlers, 1999; Dunmore, Clark & Ehlers, 1999, 2001; Ehlers, Clark et al., 1998; Steil & Ehlers, 2000) and can lead to poorer outcomes in victims (Dunmore et al., 1999, 2001). Little, if any, systematic research of this kind has been done on offender populations although it has been suggested that guilt in relation to an offence can be associated with the development of PTSD in offenders (McNally, 2003). In addition, there are parallels to be drawn between the appraisals of some offenders and those of victims, e.g. lack of control, sense of alienation and perceived physical threat, are similar to those described by victims (Alvarez-Conrad, Zoellner & Foa, 2001; Brewin & Holmes, 2003; Dunmore et al., 1999, 2001; Ehlers, Maercker & Boos, 2000; Foa, Tolin, Ehlers, Clark & Orsillo, 1999; Janoff-Bulman, 1992).

The following study was conducted to test the hypotheses that both amnesia and intrusive memories in violent offenders would be associated with different forms of disrupted cognitive processing and emotional factors at the time of the assault and cognitive appraisals preceding, during, and after the assault.

STUDY OF MEMORY DISTURBANCE IN YOUNG VIOLENT OFFENDERS

Using a cross-sectional design, we interviewed 100 violent young offenders who were imprisoned within the England and Wales Young Offender's Institution system, focusing on distressing intrusive memories and amnesia relating to the assault. All the participants had to have received a conviction for grievous bodily harm (GBH), attempted murder, manslaughter or murder. Ethical approval for the study was obtained from the Prison Health Research Ethics Committee (PHREC).

A broad range of measures was used in order to provide comprehensive data for analysis and included the following:

- **Participant characteristics**. Demographic, medical and forensic characteristics were assessed using a semi-structured interview (adapted from Dunmore et al., 1999, 2000). Previous traumatic experiences were also assessed. Characteristics of the offence were assessed using a semi-structured interview, which included questions related to legal, descriptive, medical, and situational aspects of the crime. Intelligence was measured by the Quick Test (Ammons & Ammons, 1962).
- **Intrusive memories**. The presence or absence of intrusive memories for the index offence was assessed using an adapted Intrusion Interview (Evans, Mezey, Ehlers & Clark, in press; Michael, Ehlers, Halligan & Clark, 2004), a semi-structured interview that covers occurrence, content, frequency, modalities and qualities of intrusive memories. Intrusive memories were defined as memories that (1) were part of what actually happened at the time, and (2) were recurrent, distressing and involuntarily triggered.
- **Symptoms of PTSD**. The PTSD Symptom Scale–Interview Version (PSS-I) was used to assess symptoms of PTSD as defined by DSM-IV (American Psychiatric Association, 1994) criteria. PTSD symptom severity was based on the total PSS-I score, used as a continuous measure.
- **Amnesia**. The presence or absence of amnesia for the index offence was assessed with Item 7 of the Clinician-Administered PTSD Scale (CAPS, [Blake et al., 1990]), as there is some empirical support for high interrater reliability using this approach (Mechanic, Resick & Griffin, 1998) and strong psychometric properties (Blake et al., 1995). The actual CAPS frequency and intensity items were used to operationally define amnesia, by dividing the sample into those participants who scored at least a 1 on frequency and 2 on intensity on CAPS Item 7 (Amnesia group) versus those whose scores fell below this threshold criterion (No Amnesia group).
- **Potential emotional and cognitive correlates of intrusions and amnesia**. *Emotions during the Assault*: Emotions during the assault were rated on a Likert-scale based on a questionnaire used in previous research on the victims of violent assaults (Dunmore et al., 1999). Factor analyses indicated six scales, including 'helplessness', 'anger', 'shame', 'fear', 'brave' and 'calm'. *Information Processing during the Assault*: The degree of dissociation experienced *during and immediately after* a traumatic event was measured using the *Peritraumatic Dissociative Experiences Questionnaire-Rater Version*

(PDEQ-R; Marmar, Weiss & Meltzer, 1997), a 10-item structured interview that comprises a variety of dissociative experiences including depersonalisation, derealisation, time distortion and
out-of-body experiences. A total dissociation score is generated by
summing the items. Two other scales were used which measured
aspects of information processing at the time of the offence were
used with empirical support from experimental psychology. The
Lack of Self-referent Processing Scale is an 8-item scale that has
been found to predict memory disorganisation and the development
of PTSD symptoms in survivors of assault and motor accidents
(Halligan et al., 2003; Rosario, Williams & Ehlers, in press) and has
good internal consistency (Halligan et al., 2003). The *Data-driven
Processing Scale* (Halligan et al., 2003; Michael, 2000) is an 8-item
scale that assesses the extent to which participants primarily engage
in surface level, perceptual processing during an assault (e.g. 'It was
just like a stream of unconnected impressions following each other').
The scale has been shown to have satisfactory-to-good internal
consistencies in patient and student populations (Michael, 2000), to
predict both narrative disorganisation and the development of PTSD
in prospective studies of motor vehicle accident victims (Murray
et al., 2002; Rosario et al., in press), and to predict the development
of analogue PTSD symptoms and disorganised narratives following
exposure to a distressing videotape (Halligan, Clark & Ehlers,
2002).

- **Memory disorganisation measures**. *Assault Narrative Task*:
Participants were asked to give an uninterrupted, detailed narrative of the assault, by recalling it as vividly, clearly, and in as much
detail as possible, while describing events in the order in which
they occurred. All narratives were tape-recorded. *Memory Disorganisation*: To check whether amnesia was related to wider deficits
with the autobiographical memory for the assault, narratives were
transcribed verbatim and scored for memory disorganisation (Foa,
Molnar & Cashman, 1995), as adapted by Halligan and colleagues
(Halligan et al., 2003). Narratives were divided into 'chunks' or
clauses containing 'only one thought, action, or speech utterance.'
A *Composite Memory Disorganisation Score* was calculated as a
standardised (z-transformed; this controlled for length of narrative)
score of *Repetitions* (Repeated clauses) plus *Disorganised Thoughts*
(expressions of uncertainty or confusion) minus *Organised Thoughts*
(clauses indicative of understanding, which was used as a reverse
measure of disorganisation). The rater also gave a global coherence rating, ranging from 1 ('not at all disorganised' – temporally
sequential with high amounts of detail relevant to the assault) to

10 ('extremely disorganised'), after reading each narrative and using a *Global Memory Disorganisation Rating Scale* for guidance. Inter-rater reliability was high for both measures.

- *Offender's perception of the assault*. Participant's perceptions of the assault in terms of their enduring attitudes and appraisals of the assault and its sequelae were rated on Likert scales using an extensive questionnaire. A broad range of cognitive appraisals were measured (all with $\alpha > 0.72$) including:

  - *Antisocial beliefs*: e.g. 'force or cunning is the best way to get things done';
  - *Social image damage*: e.g. 'The victim's actions caused me to lose face';
  - *Perceived control*: e.g. 'The situation never got out of hand';
  - *Victim status*: e.g. 'I was the victim in all of this';
  - *Perceived physical threat to the self*: e.g. 'During the assault I believed that I would be seriously injured';
  - *Negative view of self*: e.g. 'I am worthless';
  - *Alienation*: e.g. 'I feel isolated and set apart from others';
  - *Permanent change*: e.g. 'I have permanently changed for the worse';
  - *Negative impact on others*: e.g. 'What I did has caused other people to treat my family and friends badly';
  - *General appraisal of symptoms of the assault*: e.g. 'My reactions since the event show I must be losing my mind';
  - *Guilt*: e.g. 'I am constantly troubled by my conscience for the crime I committed' (this measure utilised four items with high 'guilt feeling attribution' loadings from the 'guilt attribution' subscale of the *Revised Gudjonsson Blame Attribution Inventory (BAI)* [Gudjonsson & Singh, 1989]).

The interviews and questionnaires were administered in a set sequence, typically requiring one-and-a-half to two hours to complete. Interviews were transcribed verbatim to facilitate analysis. In terms of data analysis, interrater reliability for presence or absence of intrusive memories was high. Both quantitative and qualitative analyses were undertaken, with the Interpretative Phenomenological Analysis (IPA) method (Smith, 1995; 1996) selected to carry out a detailed thematic analysis of the content and meaning of intrusive memories. Interrater reliability for both intrusive memory content and meaning was high.

THE MAIN FINDINGS

A very high compliance rate was achieved and all participants comp-leted the interview and questionnaires. The participants were an ethni-cally diverse group (with the majority being Caucasian), most of whom had poor educational and work records and low–normal intelligence. The majority had a previous conviction but had not been to prison before; of those who had, the majority had a conviction for violence. The average time between committing the offence and entering the study was just under two years. About one-third of the sample had killed their victim and one-quarter had been convicted of murder.

With respect to clinical variables, the majority of the group had expe-rienced a traumatic event, typically a violent one. Nearly the entire sample was free from previous subjective memory problems but about one-third reported a significant head injury in the past. The majority had no history of psychiatric involvement in the past, nor had they been referred for assessment since the offence. One-fifth of the group was alcohol dependent and the same proportion was dependent on illegal drugs. The level of alcohol intake and regular illegal drug use was high. The average number of post-traumatic symptoms, as measured by the PSS-I, was in the low range.

In terms of details of the offences, most of the assaults were of brief duration, unplanned and involved weapons. They were generally carried out with others, on strangers, during the hours of darkness and in public places, and in the context of alcohol and/or drug use.

The general characteristics of this sample of young offenders are consistent with those described in other cross sectional (Bailey, 1996; Busch, Zagar, Hughes, Arbit & Bussell, 1990; Cornell, Benedek & Benedek, 1987; Lewis, Lovely & Yeager, 1988; Toupin & Morissette, 1990; Zagar, Arbit, Sylvies, Busch & Hughes, 1990) and prospective longitudinal studies (Farrington, 1989) of young offenders.

What was the Nature of Intrusive Memories of Violent Offending?

Just under half of the participants reported intrusive memories of their violent offence, with several of the participants meeting diag-nostic criteria for symptoms of PTSD related to their own violent behaviour. Typically, those participants with intrusions reported that they experienced a small number of different intrusive memories that occurred only a few times each week, usually of brief duration of a few seconds. Nearly all the Intrusion group reported a sensory compo-nent to their intrusive memory, with a minority reporting either a feeling or thought component. The majority of participants reported visual images, with the most frequent sub-category a series of still visual images of the assault, although participants reported intrusive memory components including sounds, smells, tastes, and physical sensations. The intrusion characteristics that were significantly associated with a PTSD diagnosis were distress, 'here and now' quality, clarity, and vividness.

The majority of the participants identified their most distressing intrusive memory as the moment when the meaning of the event changed for the worse, for example the sight/smell of blood or the sight of the victim not moving, which then made them realise that they had hurt the victim more than intended.

Analysis of the *content* of intrusive memories of the offence yielded six categories of visual images, with the vast majority involving either the wounded victim or the actual assault itself, with a few participants reporting images of the weapon they used. Qualitative analysis of the *meaning* of intrusive memories yielded seven categories, with the main groupings centred on moral breaches, the victim not deserving the level of injury incurred, sudden realisation of the victim's level of injury during the assault, and shock or disbelief that they had acted so violently

The mean scores of the Intrusion group were significantly higher than the No-Intrusion group for feeling helpless and fearful at the time of the assault. The Intrusion group scored significantly higher on all three cognitive processing style measures, in accordance with the hypothesis that disrupted cognitive processing would be associated with the presence of intrusive memories. There were also significant positive associations between the PDEQ score and the Data-driven Processing score, between the PDEQ score and the Lack of Self-referent Processing score, and between the Data-driven Processing score and the Lack of Self-referent Processing score.

With respect to memory disorganisation, the mean Global Rating score and the mean Composite Memory Disorganisation score were significantly higher in the Intrusion group compared to the No-Intrusion group, indicating an association between disorganised memories and intrusive memories.

The mean score on Antisocial Beliefs was significantly *lower* in the Intrusion group than that of the No-Intrusion group, while the mean Negative View of Self, General Appraisal of Symptoms, and Guilt scores of the Intrusion group were significantly *higher* than those of the No-Intrusion group. The mean guilt appraisal score for participants in the Intrusion group was significantly higher than for participants in the No-Intrusion group, for participants who *did not* report strong feelings of helplessness or fear at the time of the assault.

Regression analysis showed that clinical measures (past psychiatric history and previous criminal offence) explained just under one-fifth of the variance of the presence of intrusive memories of the offence. Measures of emotional factors at the time of the offence (helplessness and fear), and cognitive processing and memory disorganisation both added double digit increases in the amount of variance explained. The cognitive appraisal measures explained a further one-fifth of the predicted variance, over and above the other clinical, emotional, memory and cognitive processing measures. In the final model, these factors combined explained almost two-thirds of the unique variance of the presence of intrusive memories.

What was the Nature of Amnesia for Violent Offending?

One-fifth of the sample was deemed to have amnesia for the assault, with all but one of these participants describing partial amnesia. There was a mixed picture in terms of the phenomenological nature of the memory gaps reported by participants:

- *Partial versus complete amnesia*: While the overwhelming majority of participants reported partial amnesia in relation to their offence, over three-quarters reported being able to remember more than half of the important features of the series of events. For example, although the majority of participants who claimed amnesia used a weapon in the assault, half of this group could not remember their weapon use at all.
- *Memories for events before and after the violence*: Every individual with amnesia was able to recall the events leading up to, or involving the start of violence. Most participants were able to describe in detail the immediate consequences of their violence, most notably in terms of the injuries caused to the victim. Only three participants reported amnesia that persisted *beyond* the assault. The overwhelming majority of the Amnesic group reported memory gaps lasting from a few seconds[2] to a few minutes.
- *The boundaries of memory gaps*: Over three-quarters of the Amnesia group reported a precise cut-off between what they could remember, and the gaps in their memory.
- *Number of memory gaps*: Although most participants described only one period of amnesia, over 40% described at least two periods of amnesia.

---

[2] Amnesia of only a few seconds duration was accepted only if it concerned a central aspect of the event that the participant was sure they should have been able to recall.

Analysis (using a MANOVA technique) of the information processing variables in terms of the presence or absence of amnesia showed significantly greater dissociation and lack of self-referent processing in the Amnesia group compared to the No-Amnesia group. For emotions during the assault, no significant group effect could be established and univariate analyses were therefore not undertaken. The participant's cognitions during the assault differed significantly between participants with and without amnesia and subsequent univariate analyses indicated that the Amnesia group was significantly more likely than the No-Amnesia group to perceive themselves as lacking control during the offence. There was also a significant group difference for Global Disorganisation Rating of the assault narrative.

Binary logistic regression analysis, with amnesia for the offence as the dependent variable showed that clinical measures (previous psychiatric history, current psychiatric medication, and ethnic origin) accounted for over one-fifth of the variance of amnesia for the offence. The variables entered in each further step including high alcohol intake, emotional ties to the victim, cognitive processing, and cognitive appraisals of the offence, each significantly improved the prediction. The final model explained over 40 % of the variance, with over 85 % of the participants being classified correctly in terms of their amnesia status.

WHAT WERE THE GENERAL CONCLUSIONS AND IMPLICATIONS?

This study systematically investigated both the nature of memories of violent crime including intrusive memories *and* the specific phenomenology of memory gaps, in a large sample of convicted violent offenders, using first-hand accounts from the perpetrators and clearly defined operational criteria.

Approaching half of the sample reported distressing intrusive memories of the offence even though the average time to interview approached two years after the offence, while one-fifth of the *same* sample reported amnesia. Partial amnesia, with good memory recall for the immediate antecedents of the assault, and the aftermath of the violence, was the most typical pattern in those reporting amnesia, whilst in contrast, complete amnesia was very uncommon. One explanation for the discrepancy between the findings of this study and previous studies, with regard the extent of reported amnesia for the offence, is the fact that, unlike previous studies, all the offenders in this study were post-conviction.

The hypothesis that intrusive memories would be associated with disrupted cognitive processing at the time of the assault, including dissociation, data-driven, and lack of self-referent processing, was also supported by the results of this study, with significant associations between all three measures of peri-traumatic cognitive processing and the severity of PTSD symptoms. Previous findings from assault victims, of an association between disrupted cognitive processing during an assault and the development of disorganised assault memories (Halligan et al., 2003) and between disorganised trauma memories and intrusive memories, were also replicated.

Although antisocial beliefs tended to be protective against the development of intrusive memories, some participants with antisocial beliefs did develop intrusive memories, for example if they felt that their particular victim had not deserved to be hurt, because of their age, gender, or because they felt they had done nothing wrong.

Consistent with previous studies (Taylor & Kopelman, 1984), having emotional ties with the victim was associated with amnesia for the offence. A further predicted, but new finding, was that perceived lack of control by the offender during the assault was associated with amnesia. It is recognised that perceived lack of control, is a key variable used to define psychological trauma in the victim literature (Janoff-Bulman, 1992), which suggests a possible link between trauma, perceived loss of control and amnesia for the event.

Theoretical Implications

There is now strong empirical evidence from research on victims that dissociative experiences arising in the course of a traumatic event (peri-traumatic dissociation), is predictive of the later development of PTSD (Ehlers, Mayou et al., 1998; Murray et al., 2002; Shalev et al., 1996). Our study demonstrated a similar association between peri-traumatic dissociation and intrusive memories in young violent offenders, as well as showing that data-driven and lack of self-referent processing were also associated with intrusive memories.

With respect to cognitive appraisals and associated emotional states, as Brewin and Holmes (2003) have pointed out, whereas some emotions are the direct result of what happens at the time of a trauma such as an assault, others depend on an element of cognitive appraisal *subsequent* to the trauma. The current data shows similar associations in perpetrators of violence, with high levels of guilt following the assault, associated with distressing intrusive memories of the assault, even in the absence of intense fear or helplessness at the time of the assault.

This suggests an alternative route to PTSD that may have special relevance for offenders (McNally, 2003).

This would also be consistent with the hypothesis that appraisals associated with persistent post-traumatic symptoms are linked, as they contribute to a *sense of serious current threat* (Ehlers & Clark, 2000), possibly exacerbated by dysfunctional, behavioural and cognitive strategies. The appraisals that were associated with intrusive memories in this study of perpetrators were mainly linked to a sense of current *internal* threat, for example a threat to one's self-view as an acceptable and worthwhile person, who would be able to achieve important life goals, such as achieving a career or having a family. The persistence of intrusions based on a sense of serious current threat (Ehlers & Clark, 2000) also makes conceptual sense of the cognitive factors that were found to have significant negative correlations with intrusive memories, namely antisocial core beliefs. Integrating an image of oneself as violent would arguably represent less of an internal threat to an individual who already either saw himself/herself as violent or who had been violent on a regular basis.

It has been argued that the fatal nature of an assault may be important in amnesia (Taylor & Kopelman, 1984). However, in this study the fatality of the assault in the current study did *not* differentiate between those who had intrusive memories or not, or for amnesia or not.

Clinical Implications

In terms of clinical management, it could be argued that, if the psychopathology of some perpetrators is so similar to that of victims following a violent assault, then they should be entitled to similar psychological interventions. It is possible that, in the long term, the effective treatment of symptoms such as increased irritability, hyperarousal and re-experiencing symptoms may help to reduce the risk of violent reoffending. However, the maintenance of distressing memories in violent offenders may, in itself, act as a deterrent against future reoffending and, moreover, some might argue against treatment on the basis that, unlike the 'innocent' victims of crime, the mental suffering of perpetrators is both expected and deserved.

Asking about intrusive memories provided rich clinical material relevant to risk assessment. Accounts of the meaning of intrusive memories provided valuable clinical information about their beliefs with respect to when violence was, and when it was not, justified. Even some perpetrators who, at face value, appeared to hold extreme antisocial attitudes, still developed intrusive memories of their crime.

One might speculate that those violent perpetrators who do not experience intrusive memories of their violent crime might pose greater future risk of violence, and may be less amenable to psychological interventions.

A direct implication of this study is to clarify the minimum requirement for history-taking by clinicians making medico-legal evaluations of cases involving claimed amnesia for crime. As much emphasis should be placed on establishing what memory is present, as for what memory is absent, in the clinical assessment of amnesia.

ACKNOWLEDGEMENTS

The authors wish to acknowledge and thank Professor Doctor Anke Ehlers and Professor David M. Clark, members of the study group for this research.

REFERENCES

Alvarez-Conrad, J., Zoellner, L.A. & Foa, E.B. (2001). Linguistic predictors of trauma pathology and physical health. *Applied Cognitive Psychology*, **15**, 159–170.

American Psychiatric Association. (1994). *Diagnostic and statistical manual of mental disorders* (4th ed.). Washington, DC: APA.

Ammons, R.B. & Ammons, C.H. (1962). *Quick test*. Missoula, MT: Psychological Test Specialists.

Bailey, S. (1996). Adolescents who murder. *Journal of Adolescence*, **19**, 19–39.

Blake, D.D., Weathers, F.W., Nagy, L.M., Kaloupek, D.G., Gusman, F.D. & Charney, D.S. (1995). The development of a clinician-administered PTSD scale. *Journal of Traumatic Stress*, **8**, 75–90.

Blake, D.D., Weathers, F.W., Nagy, L.M., Kaloupek, D.G., Klauminzer, G., Charney, D.S., et al. (1990). A clinician rating scale for assessing current and lifetime PTSD: The CAPS-1. *Behaviour Therapist*, **13**, 187–188.

Bradford, J.M. & Smith, S.S. (1979). Amnesia and homicide: The Padola case and a study of thirty cases. *Bulletin of the American Academy of Psychiatry and the Law*, **7**, 219–231.

Brewin, C., Dalgleish, T. & Joseph, S. (1996). A dual representation theory of posttraumatic stress disorder. *Psychological Review*, **103**, 670–686.

Brewin, C. & Holmes, E. (2003). Psychological theories of posttraumatic stress disorder. *Clinical Psychology Review*, **23**, 339–376.

Busch, K., Zagar, R., Hughes, J.R., Arbit, J. & Bussell, R.E. (1990). Adolescents who kill. *Journal of Clinical Psychology*, **46**, 472–485.

Clohessy, S. & Ehlers, A. (1999). PTSD symptoms, response to intrusive memories and coping in ambulance service workers. *British Journal of Clinical Psychology*, **38**, 251–265.

Cornell, D.G., Benedek, E.P. & Benedek, D.M. (1987). Characteristics of adolescents charged with homicide: Review of 72 cases. *Behavioural Sciences & the Law*, **5**, 11–23.

Dunmore, E., Clark, D.M. & Ehlers, A. (1999). Cognitive factors involved in the onset and maintenance of posttraumatic stress disorder (PTSD) after physical and sexual assault. *Behaviour Research and Therapy*, **37**, 809–829.

Dunmore, E., Clark, D.M. & Ehlers, A. (2001). A prospective investigation of the role of cognitive factors in persistent posttraumatic stress disorder (PTSD) after physical or sexual assault. *Behaviour Research and Therapy*, **39**, 1063–1084.

Ehlers, A. & Clark, D.M. (2000). A cognitive model of posttraumatic stress disorder. *Behaviour Research and Therapy*, **38**, 319–345.

Ehlers, A., Clark, D.M., Dunmore, E., Jaycox, L., Meadows, E. & Foa, E.B. (1998). Predicting the response to exposure treatment in PTSD: The role of mental defeat and alienation. *Journal of Traumatic Stress*, **11**, 457–471.

Ehlers, A., Hackmann, A. & Michael, T. (2004a). Intrusive reexperiencing in posttraumatic stress disorder: Phenomenology, theory and therapy. *Memory*, **12**, 403–415.

Ehlers, A., Hackmann, A. & Michael, T. (2004b). Intrusive re-experiencing in post-traumatic stress disorder: Phenomenology, theory, and therapy. *Memory*, **12**, 403–415.

Ehlers, A., Maercker, A. & Boos, A. (2000). Posttraumatic stress disorder following political imprisonment: The role of mental defeat, alienation, and permanent change. *Journal of Abnormal Psychology*, **109**, 45–55.

Ehlers, A., Mayou, R.A. & Bryant, B. (1998). Psychological predictors of chronic posttraumatic stress disorder after motor vehicle accidents. *Journal of Abnormal Psychology*, **107**, 508–519.

Evans, C. (2004). *The nature of memories of violent crime among young offenders*. University of London.

Evans, C. (2006). What violent offenders remember of their crime: empirical explorations. *The Australian and New Zealand Journal of Psychiatry*, **40**, 508–518.

Evans, C., Mezey, G. & Ehlers, A. (Submitted). Amnesia for violent crime among young offenders.

Evans, C., Mezey, G., Ehlers, A. & Clark, D.M. (In press). Intrusive memories and ruminations related to violent crime in young offenders: Phenomenological characteristics.

Farrington, D.P. (1989). Early predictors of adolescent aggression and adult violence. *Violence and Victims*, **4**, 79–113.

Foa, E.B., Molnar, C. & Cashman, L. (1995). Change in rape narratives during exposure therapy for posttraumatic stress disorder. *Journal of Traumatic Stress*, **8**, 675–690.

Foa, E.B., Tolin, D.F., Ehlers, A., Clark, D.M. & Orsillo, S.M. (1999). The Posttraumatic Cognitions Inventory (PTCI): Development and validation. *Psychological Assessment*, **11**, 303–314.

Gray, N.S., Carman, N., Rogers, P., MacCulloch, M.J., Hayward, P. & Snowden, R. (2003). Post-traumatic stress disorder caused in mentally disordered offenders by the committing of a serious violent or sexual offence. *The Journal of Forensic Psychiatry and Psychology*, **14**, 27–43.

Gudjonsson, G.H. & Singh, K.K. (1989). The Revised Gudjonsson Blame Attribution Inventory. *Personality and Individual Differences*, **10**, 66–70.

Hackmann, A., Ehlers, A., Speckens, A. & Clark, D.M. (2004). Characteristics and content of intrusive memories in PTSD and their changes with treatment. *Journal of Traumatic Stress*, **17**, 231–240.

Halligan, S.L., Clark, D.M. & Ehlers, A. (2002). Cognitive processing, memory, and the development of PTSD symptoms: Two experimental analogue studies. *Journal of Behavior Therapy and Experimental Psychology*, **33**, 73–89.

Halligan, S.L., Michael, T., Clark, D.M. & Ehlers, A. (2003). Posttraumatic stress disorder following assault: The role of cognitive processing, trauma memory and appraisals. *Journal of Consulting and Clinical Psychology*, **71**, 419–431.

Hopwood, J.S. & Snell, H.K. (1933). Amnesia in relation to crime. *Journal of Mental Science*, **79**, 27–41.

Horowitz, M.J. (1976). *Stress response syndromes* (1st ed.). New York: Jason Aronson.

Janoff-Bulman, R. (1992). *Shattered assumptions: Towards a new psychology of trauma*. New York: Free Press.

Koopman, C., Classen, C. & Speigel, D. (1994). Predictors of posttraumatic stress symptoms among survivors of the Oakland/Berkerly, Calif., firestorm. *American Journal of Psychiatry*, **151**, 888–894.

Kruppa, I., Hickey, N. & Hubbard, C. (1995). The prevalence of post traumatic stress disorder in a special hospital population of legal psychopaths. *Psychology, Crime and Law*, **2**, 131–141.

Lewis, D.O., Lovely, R. & Yeager, C. (1988). Intrinsic and environmental characteristics of juvenile murderers. *Journal of the American Academy of Child and Adolescent Psychiatry*, **27**, 582–587.

Lynch, B.E. & Bradford, J.M.W. (1980). Amnesia: Its detection by psychophysiological measures. *Bulletin of the American Academy of Psychiatry and the Law*, **8**, 288–297.

Marmar, C.R., Weiss, D.S. & Meltzer, T.J. (1997). The Peritraumatic Dissociative Experiences Questionnaire. In J.P. Wilson & T.M. Keane (Eds), *Assessing psychological trauma and PTSD*. New York: Guilford Press.

McNally, R.J. (2003). *Remembering trauma*. Cambridge, MA: The Belknap Press/Harvard University Press.

Mechanic, M., Resick, P.A. & Griffin, M.G. (1998). A comparison of normal forgetting, psychopathology, and information-processing models of reported amnesia of recent sexual trauma. *Journal of Consulting and Clinical Psychology*, **66**, 948–957.

Michael, T. (2000). *The nature of trauma memory and intrusive cognitions on posttraumatic stress disorder*. University of Oxford.

Michael, T., Ehlers, A., Halligan, S.L. & Clark, D.M. (2004). Unwanted memories of assault: What intrusion characteristics are associated with PTSD?, *Behaviour Research and Therapy*, **43**, 613–628.

Murray, J., Ehlers, A. & Mayou, R.A. (2002). Dissociation and posttraumatic stress disorder: Two prospective studies of motor vehicle accident survivors. *British Journal of Psychiatry*, **180**, 363–368.

O'Connell, A.A. (1960). Amnesia and homicide. *British Journal of Delinquency*, **10**, 262–276.

Papanastassiou, M., Waldron, G., Boyle, J. & Chesterman, L. (2004). Posttraumatic stress disorder in mentally ill perpetrators of homicide. *The Journal of Forensic Psychiatry and Psychology*, **15**, 66–75.

Parwatikar, S., Holcomb, W.R. & Menninger, K.A. (1985). The detection of malingered amnesia in accused murderers. *Bulletin of the American Academy of Psychiatry and the Law*, **13**, 97–103.

Pollock, P. (1999). When the killer suffers: Post-traumatic stress reactions following homicide. *Legal and Criminological Psychology*, **4**, 185–202.

Pope, H.G., Hudson, J.I., Bodkin, J.A. & Oliva, P. (1998). Questionable validity of 'dissociative amnesia' in trauma victims. Evidence from prospective studies. *British Journal of Psychiatry*, **172**, 210–215.

Roediger, H.L. (1990). Implicit memory. Retention without remembering. *American Psychologist*, **45**, 1043–1056.

Rosario, M., Williams, R. & Ehlers, A. (In press). Cognitive processing during motor vehicle accidents predicts posttraumatic stress disorder. *Submitted*.

Shalev, A.Y., Peri, T., Canetti, L. & Schreiber, S. (1996). Predictors of PTSD in injured trauma survivors: A prospective study. *American Journal of Psychiatry*, **153**, 219–225.

Smith, J.A. (1995). Semi-structured interviewing and qualitative analysis. In J.A. Smith, R. Harre & L.V. Langenhove (Eds), *Rethinking methods in psychology*. London: Sage.

Smith, J.A. (1996). Beyond the divide between cognition and discourse: Using interpretative phenomenological analysis in health psychology. *Psychology and Health*, **11**, 261–271.

Spitzer, C., Dudek, M., Liss, H., Orlob, S., Gillner, M. & Freyberger, H.J. (2001). Post-traumatic stress disorder in forensic inpatients. *Journal of Forensic Psychiatry*, **12**, 63–77.

Steil, R. & Ehlers, A. (2000). Dysfunctional meaning of posttraumatic intrusions in chronic PTSD. *Behaviour Research and Therapy*, **38**, 537–558.

Taylor, P.J. & Kopelman, M.D. (1984). Amnesia for criminal offences. *Psychological medicine*, **14**, 581–588.

Toupin, J. & Morissette, L. (1990). Juvenile homicide: A case control study. *Medicine and Law*, **9**, 986–994.

Van der Kolk, B.A. & Fisler, R. (1995). Dissociation and the fragmentary nature of traumatic memories: Overview and exploratory study. *Journal of Traumatic Stress*, **8**, 505–525.

Wheeler, M.A. (1997). Toward a theory of episodic memory: The frontal lobes and autonoetic consciousness. *Psychological Bulletin*, **121**, 331–354.

Wheeler, M.A. (2000). Episodic memory and autonoetic awareness. In *The Oxford handbook of memory*. Oxford: Oxford University Press.

Zagar, R., Arbit, J., Sylvies, R., Busch, K. & Hughes, J.R. (1990). Homicidal adolescents: A replication. *Psychological Reports*, **67**, 1235–1242.

CHAPTER 5

Memory for Murder: The Qualities and Credibility of Homicide Narratives by Perpetrators

STEPHEN PORTER, MICHAEL WOODWORTH AND NAOMI L. DOUCETTE

INTRODUCTION

Imagine being a juror in a trial concerning the strangulation murder of a woman in her home. Two weeks later, police arrest a suspect who is an acquaintance of the victim. The defendant – a 34-year-old man – was last seen in her company walking along the road to her home. From the time of his arrest, the defendant admitted that he spent the evening with the victim, but that he recalled almost nothing after she made disparaging comments about his family and an argument ensued. He claims to recall nothing after the argument until he read about her murder in the newspaper the next morning. Eyewitness evidence suggests that both the defendant and victim each had consumed two to three drinks earlier in the evening but likely were not

Offenders' Memories of Violent Crimes. Edited by Sven Å. Christianson.
© 2007 John Wiley & Sons, Ltd.

intoxicated. The evidence against the defendant is mainly circumstantial; there are no witnesses or physical evidence directly linking him to the crime. However, a psychologist has submitted a report to the court indicating that the defendant is a 'psychopath'. How would you decide on his guilt or innocence? Would you believe his story of amnesia? Would the amnesia be a factor in your decision of whether he was guilty of murder, or of whether the murder was first degree, second degree or manslaughter? Further, would the psychologist's assessment of psychopathy influence your decision? A potential variation on the above case would be that the defendant recalled killing the victim but claimed that it was in self-defence. How would you decide on the veracity of that claim in the absence of any other evidence?

Traditionally, almost all studies of crime narratives, or memory in forensic contexts more generally, focused on victims and witnesses. However, unlike other crimes of violence, the evidence following a homicide does not include victim testimony, and typically does not include eyewitness testimony. Even in the presence of physical or eyewitness evidence to establish culpability, the defendant's (or, following conviction, the 'perpetrator's') recollection of the events in question should be an important consideration for legal decision-making. For example, perpetrator amnesia is relevant to various legal constructs, including both competency to stand trial and criminal responsibility (for an overview see Porter, Birt, Yuille & Hervé, 2001). Further, the study of perpetrators offers an excellent opportunity for improving our understanding of the effects of extreme emotion on memory. Perpetrators of violence commonly report memory impairment for the violent act (see later section), and, especially murderers, refer to their actions as personally traumatic (e.g., Swihart, Yuille & Porter, 1999). In addition, the validity of claims of memory impairment in perpetrators can be relevant in treatment contexts (e.g., Porter et al., 2001). As such, we – like other authors in this text – have sought to complement the traditional approach to studying memory for crime in victims and witnesses by investigating perpetrator's memories for their violence.

The study of perpetrator memory offers both practical challenges and problems in data interpretation that we believe have dissuaded many applied memory researchers from conducting such research. Practical impediments with collecting any in-person data from incarcerated offenders include ethical concerns with a vulnerable population, problems in advertising the study, encouraging participation in the absence of monetary gain for participants (at least in Canada), a potential self-selection bias and the need for researchers to obtain security clearances. Research on murderers can be particularly challenging, with the competing requirements of minimising the presence of security staff during the research interview (to maintain anonymity/confidentiality) and ensuring the safety of interviewers. While we have found that these problems typically can be resolved with determination and innovation, a more complex issue with offenders that may be relatively trivial with victims or eyewitnesses pertains to the credibility and, thus, interpretation of the data collected during the research interviews. That is, it is possible that some perpetrators may choose to lie about their crime, even in a confidential research interview. While acknowledging that this possibility must be considered in drawing conclusions about the relation between emotion and memory, we look at it as an opportunity to yield valuable research findings that might improve deception detection in forensic contexts.

In this chapter, we provide an overview of what is known about the qualities of perpetrator memory for homicide, and describe our recent work that has focused directly on the credibility of offender accounts. Specifically, we have compared the crime narratives of homicide perpetrators with the official file descriptions of their crimes. As will be reviewed, we have found that some homicide perpetrators, namely psychopaths, are more likely than others to provide accounts of the crime that are distorted (often in subtle ways), even in a confidential research interview.

RECOLLECTIONS OF TRAUMATIC CRIMINAL EXPERIENCES: VICTIMS WITNESSES AND PERPETRATORS

The impact of trauma on memory has been the subject of a long-standing debate, with two main theoretical perspectives emerging. According to the *traumatic memory argument* (TMA), traumatic events result in memory impairment such that the recollections contain sensory/emotional images but lack a coherent verbal narrative (e.g., Herman, 1992; Kihlstrom, 1996). Conversely, the *trauma superiority argument* (TSA) asserts that trauma may enhance memory rather than impair it, resulting in vivid and coherent memories (Bernsten, 2001; Porter & Birt, 2001; Shobe & Kihlstrom, 1997). Because each of the witnesses, victims and perpetrators can experience trauma as a result of violent crime, the resolution of this controversy has great forensic relevance.

To date, most research has focused on trauma and memory in victims or witnesses (e.g., Peace & Porter, 2004a; Porter & Birt, 2001; Yuille & Cutshall, 1986) with relatively little attention to perpetrator memory. Based on work with victims and witnesses, there is increasing evidence for the validity of the TSA. For example, Terr (1979) investigated the memories of 25 children, 5–14 years of age, who had been kidnapped on a school bus, driven around for 11 hours, and then buried underground in a tractor-trailer. After 27 hours, part of the roof collapsed and the children dug their way to freedom. These children had intact and detailed memories of the incident after 13 months (Terr, 1979). In a follow-up study, Terr (1983) found that the children's memories for the event remained detailed four years later. In an investigation of the consistency of memory over a much longer period, Wagenaar and Groeneweg (1990) compared the memory reports of 78 World War II concentration camp survivors from the trial of Marinus De Rijke in the 1980s with statements given to Nuremberg investigators soon after the war. The survivors' often traumatic memories were accurate and detailed despite the passage of time. Specifically, the accounts of the camp, camp registration numbers, malicious treatment, daily routine, labour, housing and main guards were 'remarkably consistent' over four decades. Porter and Birt (2001) asked 306 adults to describe their most traumatic and their most positive experience. Although the traumatic memories (many concerning violent crime) were more detailed, both memory types were highly vivid and coherent. Further, trauma severity did not impair memory quality, despite a prediction of the TMA. Peace and Porter (2004a) conducted a prospective study of 59 community participants who had experienced a recent violent or non-violent trauma. They recalled both the traumatic and another emotional experience in interviews separated by three months. After three months, traumatic memories remained more vivid and consistent than other memories (and showed little major alteration or impairment), lending further support for the TSA. A later analysis by Peace and Porter (2004b) revealed that traumatic memories involving criminal victimisation were more consistently recalled over time than traumatic memories involving serious injuries or illness (Porter & Peace, 2006).

In one of the first field studies addressing eyewitness memory for a violent crime, Yuille and Cutshall (1986) examined the memories of 13 witnesses four to five months after they had witnessed a murder and attempted murder. Results indicated that the witnesses' memories were accurate, detailed and resistant to the effect of misinformation. Christianson and Hubinette (1993) examined witnesses' (victims' and bystanders') ability to recall post office robberies. Results indicated that recollections of details (actions, weapon, clothing) four to fifteen months after the crime were highly consistent with the initial reports to police. Overall, there is mounting evidence that both victims' and witnesses' memories of potentially traumatic events are relatively accurate for 'core' details and can be highly resistant to misinformation (e.g., Peace & Porter, 2004a; Wagenaar & Groeneweg, 1990; Yuille & Cutshall, 1986). On the other hand, peripheral details can become distorted or recalled in less detail due to a narrowing of attention with emotional stress (e.g., Burke, Heuer & Reisberg, 1992; Porter, Spencer & Birt, 2003).

Despite this typical pattern, in rare cases, people who experience violence forget part or all of the experience as a result of the psychological trauma. For example, Christianson and Nilsson (1984) reported a case study of a woman who developed amnesia after an assault and rape. This individual became extremely upset when taken back to the scene of the crime, despite that she did not explicitly recall what or where it had happened. This type of memory impairment is known as dissociative, functional or psychogenic amnesia. As described in the DSM-IV (APA, 1994), dissociative amnesia is characterised by an inability to recall important personal information in the absence of an organic pathology. In addition, the extent of the memory loss must be too great to be explained by ordinary forgetfulness. Of the several types of dissociative amnesia, the most common is *localised* amnesia (APA, 1994). This type is characterised by an inability to recall events occurring during a circumscribed period of time, which usually includes the first few hours following the traumatic event. Less common is selective amnesia, which is the failure to recall some, but not all, of the events during a circumscribed period of time. In general, dissociative amnesia can occur at the time of the traumatic experience and last from minutes to days (Bremner & Marmar, 1998; Schacter, Wang, Tulving & Freedman, 1982).

Researchers have found that perpetrators of violence frequently report such memory impairment for their crime (e.g., Kopelman, 1995; Porter et al., 2001; Schacter, 1986a), far more often than victims or witnesses. For example, estimates of self-reported amnesia in murderers range from 10% to 70% (Bradford & Smith, 1979; Cima, Nijman, Merckelbach, Kremer & Hollnack, 2004; Kopelman, 1987; Parwatikar, Holcomb & Menninger, 1985; Pyszora, Barker & Kopelman, 2003; Schacter, 1986a; Schacter, 1986b; Taylor & Kopelman, 1984). Further elaboration of perpetrator amnesia for crime can be found in Chapters 8 and 9, this volume.

Although claims of memory impairment by perpetrators may be genuine, other cases of reported perpetrator amnesia are almost certainly malingered. Perpetrators may make false claims of amnesia for a variety of reasons including an attempt to raise doubts about the degree of their involvement in the offence, to gain sympathy from others involved in the legal proceedings (e.g., judge/jury) or family members, to avoid having to lie outright about their involvement

(Porter et al., 2001; Porter & Yuille, 1995, 1996), or as a legal defence (e.g., insane automatism in Canada). For example, many defendants may claim amnesia to bring into question their criminal intention or *mens rea* (Swihart et al., 1999). Unfortunately, it is likely that such deception by perpetrators is often successful within the legal system. Numerous studies have demonstrated that both legal professionals and laypersons are poor at detecting deception, typically performing at around the level of chance (Vrij, 2000) or worse. For example, a sample of 32 Canadian parole officers performed significantly below chance at detecting deception in videotaped speakers (Porter, Woodworth & Birt, 2000). It appeared that a major factor in this poor performance was a reliance on erroneous cues to deception. Although this may come as a surprise to many judges, Justice Rooke of the Court of Alberta (1996) recognised the problem and stated (at a 1996 judicial conference) that judges are probably no better than laypersons in judging credibility. Lawyers may be no better at detecting lies. As well-known Canadian criminal lawyer Clayton Ruby observed, 'We're terrible. That's in part because people hear what they want to hear. You want to believe your client's version of events' (Dotto, 2004, p. 45).

DECEPTION BY AND MEMORY FUNCTION IN PSYCHOPATHIC PERPETRATORS

One subgroup of murderers who may be particularly prone to providing intentionally altered accounts of their homicides and also recalling them differently from other offenders is criminal psychopaths. Psychopaths, comprising about 15–25% of federally incarcerated inmates in most samples, long have been characterised as persistent liars (see Porter & Woodworth, 2006). For example, Cleckley (1976) viewed untruthfulness and insincerity as being important features of the disorder, an observation adopted by Hare (1991, 2003) in his development of the Psychopathy Checklist–Revised (PCL-R, 2003). Emotional factors have been implicated in psychopathic deception; anxiety and guilt are largely missing in the psychopath, facilitating the use of deception (e.g., Ekman, 2002; Lykken 1995). In contrast, some psychopaths may even experience 'duping delight' from success-fully deceiving others (e.g., Ekman, 1991, 2002; Porter et al., 2001). Despite these clinical observations, only a few empirical studies have addressed deception in psychopaths. Raskin and Hare (1978) examined the ability of incarcerated offenders to lie successfully during a poly-graph examination about a mock crime. They found that psychopaths were no more successful at lying than non-psychopaths, perhaps because of physiological arousal due to duping delight (as opposed to the anxiety experienced by other offenders). Studies addressing response to rehabilitation programmes provide indirect evidence for psychopathic deception in the treatment context. Seto and Barbaree (1999) found that offenders in a sex offender treatment programme who had received the most positive evaluations during treatment had high PCL-R scores and subsequently showed the highest re-offence rates. It is likely that psychopaths had 'put on a good show' during the programme through the proficient use of deception. On the other hand, given the research described above, Hare (2003) has suggested that while psychopaths may be no more adept than other offenders at deception, they are more likely to use deception than are other offenders. That is, they may simply be more likely to lie whether they are good actors or not.

In addition to their greater propensity for lying about their violent crimes, psychopaths also appear to have a profound emotional deficit that could influence the nature of their recall for their crimes. This emotional deficit is manifested as callousness, lack of remorse, lack of empathy and lack of anxiety. Research using a variety of paradigms has established the existence of the emotional deficit originally proposed by Cleckley (1976). For example, research has consistently demonstrated that psychopaths have a deficient startle reflex, considered to be a physiological correlate of both fear and anxiety (e.g., Levenston, Patrick, Bradley & Lang, 2000; Patrick, Bradley & Lang, 1993; Vanman, Mejia, Dawson, Schell & Raine, 2003). Patrick et al. (1993) examined the relationship between startle modification and psychopathy in a sample of 54 incarcerated offenders. While non-psychopaths showed an increase in the startle reflex during the presentation of negative stimuli, psychopaths displayed a similar startle reflex to both positive and negative stimuli. This emotional deficiency extends to the manner in which psychopaths process emotional language and sounds (e.g., Hervé, Hayes & Hare, 2003; Verona, Patrick, Curtin, Bradley & Lang, 2004). For example, Hervé et al. (2003) asked offender participants to sort a number of metaphorical statements on a continuum from very negative to very positive. Results indicated that psychopaths made significantly more sorting errors than non-psychopaths, despite being able to sufficiently understand the literal meaning of the metaphors. Hervé et al. (2003) concluded that psychopaths' emotional deficit translated to a decreased understanding of the emotional content of language. The results of a recent British study suggest that the emotional deficits observed in psychopaths may even extend to the commission of homicidal violence. Gray, Macculloch, Smith, Morris and Snowden

(2003) measured implicit beliefs about murder in psychopathic and non-psychopathic murderers, and psychopathic and non-psychopathic offenders who had committed other offences. The researchers used a modified Implicit Association Test (IAT), a test originally designed to implicitly assess an individual's negative views about others. The researchers presented participants with a word to which they had to respond by rating it either 'unpleasant' or 'pleasant' and either 'peaceful' or 'violent' by pressing the appropriate key on a computer. In some situations, the same response key was used for congruent words (e.g., words that were 'unpleasant' and 'violent'), and in others the same response key was used for incongruent words (e.g., words that were 'pleasant' and 'violent'). In general, individuals take longer to respond in the incongruent condition than the congruent condition. However, results indicated that psychopathic murderers did not display the same impairment in response time as non-psychopaths with an incongruent word presentation (pleasant and violent words). That is, they responded as if they did not associate violence with unpleasantness, and showed diminished negative reactions to violence compared with non-psychopathic murderers.

Other research demonstrated that the affective impairment associated with psychopathy extends to memory for emotional information. Research by Christianson, Forth, Hare, Strachan, Lidberg and Thorell (1996) found that psychopaths recalled both peripheral and central details from highly emotional scenes in a similar manner, while non-psychopaths were better able to recall the central and (generally most upsetting) details from the emotional scene (Christianson et al., 1996).

RECENT RESEARCH ON THE CREDIBILITY AND MEMORY QUALITIES OF PERPETRATORS' CRIME NARRATIVES

Until recently, no research had examined the *manner* in which homicide perpetrators describe their violence within their crime narratives. Yet, the manner in which a perpetrator describes the homicide can provide information that is relevant to understanding both his/her credibility and qualities of his/her memories.

Credibility of Perpetrator Accounts

The out of body experience started ah, shortly after my wife said 'I'm in control now'. It was just like... [a] blackout. And I had tunnel vision. It was like, ah slow motion. It was the start of... me having an out of body experience. I actually felt out of my body. It seemed very dark... darker than usual. Time seemed to slow down. We continued to struggle... down the stairway... [I] didn't see her face. I could see peripherally... and I had enough coherency... to know I was going down the stairwell... but [there] wasn't anything normal about it. I remember growling... I wasn't actually vocalizing that growl... but I was growling inside my head. I felt like I wasn't inside my head... it was almost as if another part of me was manipulating me. I was actually growling inside my head... and I felt like an animal almost. I wasn't aware... I was totally focused on what was in front of me and nothing else mattered. I remember choking her, but I don't remember seeing her face anymore... she wasn't a person anymore. I remember holding my wife while I picked up the knife. I remember picking up the knife over my head, and that's all I remember... from the point where I picked up the knife, it was black. I don't remember stabbing my wife. Apparently I stabbed her all over her body... I stabbed her 14 times.

The above account was given by a homicide offender who participated in a study by Porter and Woodworth (2006b) examining the qualities of the narratives of psychopaths and non-psychopaths concerning their homicides, relative to the official reports. The evaluation of a perpetrator's credibility or honesty includes an assessment of his/her self-reported description of the crime (Rogers & Cruise, 2000). In fact, the interview in which the perpetrator's account of the crime is collected is one of the most important evidence gathering tools during an investigation (e.g., Holmberg & Christianson, 2002). Additionally, reactive, spontaneous offences are often accompanied by a relatively light sentence, providing a motivation for some offenders to lie in their crime narratives. Subsequently, the manner in which an accused person discusses his/her crime and what he/she purports to remember about the incident, may have relevance when considering potential treatment and release options (e.g., Byrne, 2003). Considerations of credibility are especially relevant when the defendant is psychopathic. In the clinical literature, psychopaths long have been characterised as having a remarkable disregard for the truth (e.g., Cleckley, 1976; Hare, 1998; Meloy, 1988), to the extent that deceit often is regarded as a defining characteristic of the disorder. As described by Porter and Woodworth (2006b), there are several evolutionary, affective and social factors that may contribute to the prodigious use of deception seen among psychopathic individuals (e.g., Porter & Woodworth, 2006b).

Porter and Woodworth (2006) examined potential differences in the self-report and official descriptions of crimes by homicide offenders by using a coding scheme developed to examine the instrumentality/reactivity of a violent crime (Woodworth & Porter, 2002). This coding scheme was devised as a reliable measure of the level of instrumentality evidenced during a violent act by using a detailed official file-based description. However, this approach served as a foundation for a novel investigation of the credibility of psychopaths' own narratives in describing their criminal behaviour. Specifically, here the scheme was not only used to measure instrumentality from the official description, but to examine the instrumentality evidenced in the offender's own description. We hypothesised that psychopaths would be more likely than other offenders to 're-frame' the level of instrumentality that had been involved, in terms of minimising the degree of premeditation and exaggerating the victim's role in, and the spontaneity of, the offense. We also focused on another strategy that offenders may use to avoid acknowledging criminal culpability – leaving out key details of a crime, often referred to as 'deception by omission' (e.g., Ekman, 2002). It was predicted that psychopaths would be more likely than non-psychopaths to omit or alter the facts of their offence. For example, they may minimise or be reluctant to discuss sexual elements of the homicide (Warren, Hazelwood & Dietz, 1996). On the other hand, it is possible that psychopaths would be more likely than non-psychopaths to callously boast about their involvement in the offence, even to the point of exaggerating its instrumentality. Since all offenders in the sample had already been convicted (and were describing the offence in a confidential research interview), they would have little to gain by exaggerating the reactivity of the homicide.

The sample consisted of 50 convicted homicide offenders who were incarcerated in one of three correctional institutions in Atlantic Canada. Based on the above methodology, Porter and Woodworth (2006b) were able to compare the official and self-reported descriptions to investigate whether psychopaths were actually more likely than non-psychopaths to minimise the instrumentality (i.e., exaggerate the reactivity) of their crimes in a self-exculpating fashion. The results replicated previous research by Woodworth and Porter (2002) indicating that psychopaths were more likely to have committed instrumental (premeditated, goal-driven) homicides. However, this instrumentality difference disappeared when the offenders' narratives were examined. Psychopaths exaggerated the reactivity of their violence to the extent that it appeared as reactive as the violence carried out by the non-psychopaths. That is, psychopaths were more likely than other offenders to 're-frame' the level of instrumentality that had been involved, in terms of minimising the degree of planning/premeditation and exaggerating the victim's role in, and the spontaneity of, the offence. Although some non-psychopaths also exaggerated the reactivity of their offence, it was not to the same extent as the psycho-pathic offenders. Additionally, results revealed that the tendency to exaggerate the reactivity of the homicides was strongly related to the Factor 1 score on the PCL-R (Hare, 2003) that considers the interper-sonal and affective characteristics of psychopathy (e.g., shallow affect and lack of guilt). Such limited affect appeared to enable the psychopathic offender to discuss his homicide offence with cold disregard for the victim (casting blame for the crime on the deceased individual). As mentioned above, we also examined whether psychopaths were more likely to omit major details of the crime in their narratives. Such details were defined as any information that was crucial to understanding what occurred during the homicide (e.g., location, weapon use, sexual elements, extent of the violence, etc.). Results also indicated that psychopaths were more likely to omit major details of the offence. In summary, although murderers in general tend to exaggerate the reactivity or emotional intensity of the murder context, the pattern is stronger for psychopaths who also omit significant details or information from their stories. The applied implications for this research include highlighting the need to consider the concordance of the instrumentality of the official report and perpe-trator's self-report as a credibility assessment technique. A professional involved in interviews with suspects would certainly want to be aware of the need for increased scrutiny if they are obtaining the self-report of a psychopathic defendant. While the deceptive nature of psychopaths has long been acknowledged, Porter and Woodworth's (2006) findings suggest that psychopaths may try and stray from the truth in a subtle but self-serving manner. The above results might be useful in the offender treatment context. For example, an increasing concordance between the instrumentality of the official crime report and offender's report during treatment could be viewed as the offender's increased acceptance of responsibility for his/her crime.

The Qualities of Perpetrators' Memories for Homicide

Given the affective deficit associated with psychopathy (described previously), it seems unlikely that psychopathic murderers would expe-rience memory impairment of a dissociative or psychogenic origin (see Porter et al., 2001). As such, Woodworth, Porter, Cook, and Patenaude (2005) examined whether psychopathic murderers would be less likely to report experiences of amnesia or dissociation than non-psychopathic homicide offenders. The sample consisted of the same 50 homicide offenders from the credibility study discussed earlier. The authors were interested in examining whether the offenders would report any type of memory impairment before, during, or after their homicide offence. For coding purposes, 'before' and 'after' referred to events that did not include the actual murder, but were still considered to be an integral part of the homicide event. Memory impairment was classified into different categories considering the severity and type reported. These included 'partial' or 'patchy' amnesia, 'circumscribed' amnesia referring to a discrete period of complete forgetting within the homicide event, and generalised amnesia referring to a global amnesia including the entire homicide event. Dissociation was recorded if the offender reported any altered state of consciousness before, during, or after the homicide. Dissociation was further classified as either 'depersonalisation' or 'derealisation'. Depersonalisation was recorded if the offender reported a sense of detachment from himself/herself (e.g., one offender reported feeling as though he were a 'robot'; another example would be a report of feeling detached from himself and watching events unfold from a different vantage point in the room). Derealisation was recorded if the offender reported that the environment felt unreal, surreal, or dreamlike.

Our results demonstrated that nearly half (45.7%) of the murderers reported experiencing some type of memory impairment. Specifically, 23.9% of the offenders reported experiencing partial amnesia, 10.9% of the offenders reported circumscribed amnesia, and 10.9% of the offenders reported experiencing generalised amnesia. Further, 30.4% of the offenders reported a dissociative experience during the homicide. Specifically, 15.2% of the offenders reported an experience consistent with depersonalisation, 2.2% of the offenders reported an experience consistent with derealisation, and 13.0% of the offenders reported an experience consistent with both depersonalisation and derealisation. The mean score on the Dissociative Experiences Scale (DES; Bernstein & Putnam, 1986) was 17.4. Seven (13.5%) offenders scored above the suggested clinical cut-off of 30 for the presence of a potential dissociative disorder. Offenders who were experiencing a high level of dissociative symptomology exhibited less vivid and poorer memories for the homicide than other offenders. Dissociation also was positively correlated with periods of not remembering the event ($r = .36$) and the memory changing over time ($r = .34$).

Considering the possible role of psychopathy in the memory reports, 33.3% of the psychopathic offenders reported experiencing some type of memory impairment, compared to nearly half (48.6%) of the non-psychopathic offenders. Further only 11.1% of the psychopathic offenders reported experiencing some type of dissociative state in association with their offence, compared to 35.1% of the non-psychopathic offenders. However, these differences were non-significant, likely due to the small sample size. For example, the finding that 11.1% of the psychopaths experienced some type of dissociation means that only one of the nine psychopaths reported such an experience. Future studies with larger samples should be conducted to investigate whether such trends reflect true differences.

The results of the Porter and Woodworth (2006b) paper showed that psychopaths had committed significantly more instrumental offences. Research has demonstrated that the majority of offenders who report amnesia for criminal behaviour have committed non-premeditated murders (e.g., Kopelman, 1995; Taylor & Kopelman, 1984). In contrast, anecdotal evidence suggests that offenders who plan and premeditate their offence(s) tend to remember them vividly. As such, psychopaths may have superior memories for their violent crimes, as they are more likely to premeditate and fantasise about their crimes (see Porter et al., 2001).

Another line of research that would be useful in revealing the role of psychopathy in offender memory impairment could focus on *secondary* versus *primary* psychopathy. Primary, or fundamental, psychopathy is believed to largely stem from a polygenic or biological predisposition that hinders the development of affective bonds, and reflects the core underlying, innate deficit of the psychopathic personality. Alternatively, secondary psychopathy is thought to result largely from environmental factors in childhood. According to Porter (1996), secondary psychopaths have a capacity for empathetic responding, but it is 'turned off' with repeated disillusionment of the child through physical or sexual abuse or other mistreatments. Porter (1996) argued that a child who develops secondary psychopathy was born with the capacity to form a normal human affect, unlike a child with primary or fundamental psychopathy, who does not have this capacity as a result of their genetic predisposition. With secondary psychopathy, the profound affective deficit may result from an ability to detach oneself from their emotions as opposed to an inability to experience their emotions, as seen with fundamental psychopathy. In other words, it is not that the secondary psychopath cannot experience emotion, but rather that they would employ dissociative techniques during traumatic or psychologically difficult situations to avoid extreme emotional arousal. Poythress and Skeem (2006) explored Porter's hypothesis using a sample of 521 prison inmates. They tested whether dissociation symptoms mediated the relationship between child abuse and PCL-R scores. Child abuse correlated positively and directly to psychopathy and dissociation partially mediated the relationship. It would be useful to conduct future research investigating whether secondary psychopaths are more likely to experience some type of memory impairment (perhaps as a result of their proneness to dissociation) than other psychopaths.

Another important issue to consider is whether the offenders in the sample were providing honest accounts regarding potential memory impairment for their homicide. Considering the number of psychopaths (and, to a lesser degree, non-psychopaths) in the sample who exaggerated the reactivity of their offence, the credibility of the above self-reported memory impairment results must be interpreted with caution. Further, information pertaining to the homicide perpetrators' drug and alcohol use at the time of the homicide was available in the official file reports for most of the offenders. The potential influence of intoxicants on the perpetrators' memories for the incident was also a concern. However, results indicated that 53.8 % of the offenders who were under the influence of drugs or alcohol at the time of the homicide reported experiencing some type of amnesia, while 50.0 % of the offenders who were not under the influence at the time of the homicide reported experiencing some type of amnesia. Therefore, there was no significant relationship between intoxication and amnesia for the offence, suggesting that there were other factors that contributed to the memory impairment experienced (or at least reported) by the offenders in the sample. We suggest that future studies examine the level of suggestibility of the inmates to consider issues such as possible memory contamination. Further, more effort should be given to exploring various other factors that were not considered in the current study, and that may have contributed to the likelihood of the participants not providing credible memory accounts. For example, it was difficult to obtain information about the strength of external motivations for individual offenders to be dishonest in their self-reports.

FALSE CONFESSIONS TO MURDER

Adding further to the complexity of assessing the credibility of an individual's memory for a homicide offence is the phenomenon of false confessions, as outlined by Gudjonnson (Chapter 11 this volume). Typically, a false confession is revealed when the real perpetrator is found, if no crime was actually committed, or when other evidence (e.g., DNA) shows that the confessor clearly was innocent (Kassin & Gudjonsson, 2004). In one Canadian case, the body of Darrelle Exner, who had been raped, beaten and murdered, was found by one Kenneth Patton. During the course of the investigation the police questioned a 17-year-old boy and two of his friends, each of whom would eventually independently confess to the murder. However, all three confessions were determined to be false; DNA evidence established that the actual murderer was Kenneth Patton. Two of the three individuals who falsely confessed recounted detailed versions of how Exner was murdered that were inconsistent with the actual cause of death, while the third individual was unable to remember committing the offence (even though he 'confessed' to the murder of Exner) (see Wrightsman & Porter, 2006). Interviewed for the CBC documentary (*Disclosure*, 2003, January 28), Joel Labadie later stated 'I'm not even sure how to explain it, 'cause I'm not sure how it happened to me. All I know is for hours on end I said "No, I had nothing to do with it." Next thing you know I'm sitting here going 'Sure, why not? I did it.' More or less its [sic] like they kill your spirit or something'.

Given their highly selfish orientation, it may seem very unlikely that psychopaths would ever falsely confess to a crime. However, there are many cases to contradict this prediction. We believe that of the three main types of false confessions that have been identified (voluntary, compliant and internalised false confessions; Kassin, 1997; Kassin & Gudjonsson, 2004), psychopathic offenders are most likely to provide voluntary false confessions, and only when they are highly self-serving. For example, Henry Lee Lucas – a 'textbook psychopath' – became known as America's most prolific serial killer after a string of homicide confessions following his arrest in 1983. However, this claim since has been hotly contested after it was shown that numerous (perhaps hundreds) of his confessions clearly were implausible. He later recanted many of his confessions admitting that he wanted to improve his living conditions (he was, in fact, treated like a pseudo celebrity and often taken to restaurants and cafés by police investigators). Further, although he was sentenced to death, his cooperation with investigators in numerous investigations may have been an attempt to avoid the execution as long as possible (Cox, 1991).

Are police able to recognise false confessions? Recent research suggests not. Kassin, Meissner and Norwick (2005) had college students and police investigators view or listen to 10 offenders confessing to crimes. Half of the confessions were true and half were false (fabricated for the study). Students were more accurate than police in distinguishing true and false confessions, and accuracy rates were higher among those presented with the audiotaped versus the videotaped confessions. Further, police were more confident in their judgements despite their impaired performance.

CONCLUSION

A substantial amount of research on memory impairment has been conducted on victims or witnesses of traumatic events. In general, the evidence supports the trauma superiority argument, which posits that a traumatic incident may enhance someone's overall memory for an event. On the other hand, there is evidence that in rare cases, trauma can greatly impair memory to the point of psychogenic amnesia. Until recently, little research has been conducted on the crime narratives of the perpetrators of violent offences. Our programme of research has addressed both the credibility of murderers and the qualities of their memories concerning the homicide. We have demonstrated that murderers generally tend to minimise the instrumentality of their offence. That is, they tend to report that the crime was less premeditated and more provoked than indicated in the official report. Psychopathic offenders, known for their prodigious use of deception, exaggerate the reactivity of their crimes significantly more than other offenders. Psychopaths also omit central details from their crime narratives. Based on previous work and our recent work reported in this chapter, perpetrators of homicide report a substantial amount of memory impairment, including various forms of amnesia and dissociative experiences. As we reviewed earlier, some of these reports likely are sincere accounts. It is clear that homicide can be extremely traumatic for the perpetrator – assuming that he/she does not have the profound affective deficits associated with psychopathy – and this trauma can result in memory impairment in some cases. On the other hand, we provided tentative evidence to suggest that psychopaths may be less likely to experience any type of memory impairment, although larger samples are required to establish this pattern with greater confidence.

There is a great need for additional innovative research on perpetrators' memories for their crimes. As we have argued, such work has the potential to greatly advance our scientific knowledge concerning both deception and traumatic memory.

AUTHORS' NOTE

Please address all correspondence concerning this paper to Stephen Porter, Ph.D., Department of Psychology, Dalhousie University, Halifax, Nova Scotia, B3H 4J1, CANADA; telephone 902-494-6934; fax 902-494-6585; e-mail sbporter@dal.ca.

The authors would like to express appreciation to the Correctional Service of Canada for allowing and helping us to collect the data for this study. This research was graciously supported by grants to the first author from the Social Science and Humanities Research Council of Canada (SSHRC) and the Natural Sciences and Engineering Council of Canada (NSERC).

REFERENCES

American Psychiatric Association (1994) *Diagnostic and statistical manual of mental disorders* (4th ed.). Washington, DC: American Psychiatric Association.

Bernstein, E.M. & Putnam, F.W. (1986) Development, reliability, and validity, of a dissociation scale. *Journal of Nervous and Mental Disease*, **174**, 727–35.

Bernsten, D. (2001) Involuntary memories of emotional events: Do memories of trauma and extremely happy events differ? *Applied Cognitive Psychology*, **15**, 135–58.

Bradford, J.W. & Smith, S.M. (1979) Amnesia and homicide: The Padola case and a study of thirty cases. *Bulletin of the American Academy of Psychiatry and Law*, **7**, 219–31.

Bremner, J.D. & Marmar, C.R. (1998) *Trauma, memory and dissociation*. Washington, DC: American Psychiatric Press.

Burke, A., Heuer, F. & Reisberg, D. (1992) Remembering emotional events. *Memory and Cognition*, **20**, 277–90.

Byrne, M.K. (2003) Trauma reactions in the offender. *International Journal of Forensic Psychology*, **1**, 59–70.

Christianson, S.A., Forth, A.E., Hare, R.D., Strachan, C., Lidberg, L. & Thorell, L.H. (1996) Remembering details of emotional events: A comparison between psychopathic and nonpsychopathic offenders. *Personality and Individual Differences*, **20**, 437–43.

Christianson, S-A. & Hubinette, B. (1993) Hands up! A study of witnesses' emotional reactions and memories associated with bank robberies. *Applied Cognitive Psychology*, **7**, 365–79.

Christianson, S-A. & Nilsson, L.G. (1984) Functional amnesia as induced by psychological trauma. *Memory and Cognition*, **12**, 142–55.

Cima, M., Nijman, H., Merckelbach, H., Kremer, K. & Hollnack, S. (2004) Claims of crime-related amnesia in forensic patients. *International Journal of Law and Psychiatry*, **27**, 215–21.

Cleckley, H. (1976) *The mask of sanity* (5th ed.). St Louis, MO: Mosby.

Cox, M. (1991) *The confessions of Henry Lee Lucas*. New York: Pocket Books.

Disclosure (2003, January 28) *Inside the interrogation room: The Darrelle Exner murder*. Retrieved August 7, 2004, from the Canadian Broadcasting Corporation Web site: http://www.cbc.ca/disclosure/archives/030128_confess/murder_print.html.

Dotto, L. (2004) Liar liar. *National Magazine*, **13**, 44–9.

Ekman, P. (1991) *Telling lies: Clues to deceit in the marketplace, politics and marriage*. New York, NY: Norton.

Ekman, P. (2002) *Telling lies: Clues to deceit in the marketplace, politics and marriage* (2nd ed.). New York, NY: Norton.

Gray, N.S., Macculloch, M.J., Smith, J., Morris, M. & Snowden, R.J. (2003) Violence viewed by psychopathic murderers: Adapting a revealing test may expose those psychopaths who are most likely to kill. *Nature*, **423**, 497–8.

Hare, R.D. (1991) *The Hare Psychopathy Checklist-Revised*. Toronto, Ontario: Multi-Health Systems, Inc.

Hare, R.D. (1998) Psychopathy and its nature: Implications for mental health and criminal justice systems. In T. Millon, E. Simonsen, M. Birkert-Smith & R.D. Davis (Eds). *Psychopathy: Antisocial criminal and violent behavior* (pp. 188–212). New York: The Guilford Press.

Hare, R.D. (2003) *The Hare Psychopathy Checklist-Revised* (2nd ed.). Toronto, Ontario: Multi-Health Systems, Inc.

Herman, J.L. (1992) *Trauma and memory*. New York, NY: Basic Books.

Hervé, H.F., Hayes, P.J. & Hare, R.D. (2003) Psychopathy and sensitivity to the emotional polarity of metaphysical statements. *Personality and Individual Differences*, **35**, 1497–1507.

Holmberg, U. & Christianson, S.A. (2002) Murderers' and sexual offenders' experiences of police interviews and their inclination to admit or deny crimes. *Behavioral Sciences and the Law*, **20**, 31–45.

Kassin, S.M (1997) The psychology of confession evidence. *American Psychologist*, **52**, 221–33.

Kassin, S.M. & Gudjonsson, G.H. (2004) The psychology of confessions: A review of the literature and issues. *Psychological Science in the Public Interest*, **5**, 33–67.

Kassin, S.M., Meissner, C.A. & Norwick, R.J. (2005) 'I'd know a false confession if I saw one': A comparative study of college students and police investigators. *Law and Human Behavior*, **29**, 211–27.

Kihlstrom, J.F. (1996) The trauma-memory argument and recovered memory therapy. In K. Pezdek & W.P. Banks (Eds), *The recovered memory/false memory debate* (pp. 297–311). San Diego, CA: Academic Press.

Kopelman, M.D. (1987). Crime and amnesia: A review. *Behavioral Sciences & the Law*, **5**, 323–42.

Kopelman, M.D. (1995) The assessment of psychogenic amnesia. In A.D. Baddeley, B.A. Wilson & F.N. Watts (Eds.), *Handbook of memory disorders* (pp. 427–48). Chichester: John Wiley & Sons, Ltd.

Levenston, G.K., Patrick, C.J., Bradley, M.M. & Lang, P.J. (2000) The psychopath as observer: Emotion and attention in picture processing. *Journal of Abnormal Psychology*, **109**, 373–85.

Lykken, D.T. (1995) *The antisocial personalities*. Hillsdale, NJ: Lawrence Erlbaum Associates.

Meloy, J.R. (1988) *The psychopathic mind: Origins, dynamics, and treatments*. Northvale, NJ: Jason Aronson, Inc.

Parwatikar, S.D., Holcomb, W.R. & Menninger, K.A. II. (1985) The detection of malingered amnesia in accused murderers. *Bulletin of the American Academy of Psychiatry and Law*, **13**, 97–103.

Patrick, C.J., Bradley, M.M. & Lang, P.J. (1993) Emotion in the criminal psychopath: Startle reflex modulation. *Journal of Abnormal Psychology*, **102**, 82–92.

Peace, K.A. & Porter, S. (2004a) A longitudinal investigation of the reliability of memories for trauma and other emotional experiences. *Applied Cognitive Psychology*, **18**, 1143–59.

Peace, K.A. & Porter, S. (2004b) Tales of trauma: Symptom profiles and memory consistency across a diverse range of traumatic experiences. Paper presented at the 65th Annual Convention of the Canadian Psychological Association (CPA), St. John's, NFLD, Canada.

Porter, S. (1996) Without conscience or without *active* conscience?: The etiology of psychopathy revisited. *Aggression and Violent Behavior*, **1**, 179–89.

Porter, S. & Birt, A.R. (2001) Is traumatic memory special? A comparison of traumatic memory characteristics with memory for other emotional life experiences. *Applied Cognitive Psychology*, **15**, 101–17.

Porter, S., Birt, A.R., Yuille, J.C. & Hervé, H.F. (2001) Memory for murder: A psychological perspective on dissociative amnesia in legal contexts. *International Journal of Law and Psychiatry*, **24**, 23–42.

Porter, S. & Peace, K.A. (2006, in press) The scars of memory: A prospective longitudinal investigation of the consistency of traumatic memories in childhood. *Psychological Science*.

Porter, S., Spencer, L. & Birt, A. (2003) Blinded by emotion? Effect of the emotionality of a scene on susceptibility to false memories. *Canadian Journal of Behavioural Science*, **35**, 165–75.

Porter, S. & Woodworth, M. (2006a) Patterns of violent behaviour in the criminal psychopath. In C. Patrick (Ed.), *Handbook of psychopathy* (pp. 481–94). New York, NY: Guilford Press.

Porter, S. & Woodworth, M. (2006b, submitted for publication) 'I'm sorry I did it . . . But he started it': A comparison of the official and self-reported homicide descriptions of psychopaths and non-psychopaths. *Law and Human Behavior*.

Porter, S., Woodworth, M. & Birt, A.R. (2000) Truth, lies, and videotape: An investigation of the ability of federal parole officers to detect deception. *Law and Human Behavior*, **24**, 643–58.

Porter, S. & Yuille, J.C. (1995) Credibility assessment of criminal suspects through statement analysis. *Psychology, Crime, and Law*, **1**, 319–31.

Porter, S. & Yuille, J.C. (1996) The language of deceit: An investigation of the verbal clues to deception in the interrogation context. *Law and Human Behavior*, **20**, 443–58.

Poythress, N.G. & Skeem, J.L. (2006) Disaggregating psychopathy: Where and how to look for subtypes. In C. Patrick (Ed.), *Handbook of psychopathy*. New York: The Guilford Press.

Pyszora, N.M., Barker, A.F. & Kopelman, M.D. (2003) Amnesia for criminal offences: A study of life sentence prisoners. *The Journal of Forensic Psychiatry & Psychology*, **14**, 475–90.

Raskin, D.C. & Hare, R.D. (1978) Psychopathy and detection of deception in a prison population. *Psychophysiology*, **15**, 126–36.

Rogers, R. & Cruise, K.R. (2000) Malingering and deception among psychopaths. In C.B. Gacano (Ed.), *The clinical and forensic assessment of psychopathy: A practitioner's guide* (pp. 269–84). Mahwah, NJ: Lawrence Erlbaum Associates, Inc.

Rooke, A. Justice. (1996, March 20). Assessing credibility in arbitrations and in court: A difficult task for judge, jury or arbitrator. Presentation to the Canadian Bar Association. Edmonton, AB.

Schacter, D.L. (1986a) Amnesia and crime: How much do we really know? *American Psychologist*, **41**, 286–95.

Schacter, D.L. (1986b) On the relation between genuine and simulated amnesia. *Behavioral Sciences & the Law*, **4**, 47–64.

Schacter, D.I., Wang, P.L., Tulving, E. & Freedman, M. (1982) Functional retrograde amnesia: A qualitative case study. *Neuropsychologia*, **20**, 523–32.

Seto, M.C. & Barbaree, H.E. (1999) Psychopathy, treatment behavior, and sex offender recidivism. *Journal of Interpersonal Violence*, **14**, 1235–48.

Shobe, K.K. & Kihlstrom, J.F. (1997) Is traumatic memory special? *Current Directions in Psychological Science*, **6**, 70–4.

Swihart, G., Yuille, J.C. & Porter, S. (1999) The role of state-dependent memory in 'red-outs.' *International Journal of Law and Psychiatry*, **22**, 199–212.

Taylor, P.J. & Kopelman, M.D. (1984) Amnesia for criminal offences. *Psychological Medicine*, **14**, 581–8.

Terr, I.C. (1979) Children of Chowchilla: A study of psychic trauma. *The Psychoanalytical Study of the Child*, **34**, 547–623.

Terr, I.C. (1983) Chowchilla revisited: The effects of psychic trauma four years after a school bus kidnapping. *American Journal of Psychiatry*, **140**, 1543–50.

Vanman, E.J., Mejia, V.Y., Dawson, M.E., Schell, A.M. & Raine, A. (2003) Modifications of the startle reflex in a community sample: Do one or two dimensions of psychopathy underlie emotional processing? *Personality and Individual Differences*, **35**, 2007–21.

Verona, E., Patrick, C.J., Curtin, J.J., Bradley, M.M. & Lang, P.J. (2004) Psychopathy and physiological response to evocative sounds. *Journal of Abnormal Psychology*, **113**, 99–108.

Vrij, A. (2000) *Detecting lies and deceit: The psychology of lying and its implications for professional practice*. Chichester: John Wiley & Sons, Ltd

Wagenaar, W.A. & Groeneweg, J. (1990) The memory of concentration camp survivors. *Applied Cognitive Psychology*, **4**, 77–87.

Warren, J.I., Hazelwood, R.R. & Dietz, P.E. (1996) The sexually sadistic serial killer. *Journal of Forensic Sciences*, **41**, 970–4.

Woodworth, M. & Porter, S. (2002) In cold blood: Characteristics of criminal homicides as a function of psychopathy. *Journal of Abnormal Psychology*, **111**, 436–45.

Woodworth, M., Porter, S., Cook, B. & Patenaude (2005) *An investigation of memory impairment in psychopathic and non-psychopathic homicide offenders*. Manuscript in preparation.

Wrightsman, L. & Porter, S. (2006) *Forensic psychology, First Canadian edition*. Ontario, Canada: Thomson Nelson.

Yuille, J.C. & Cutshall, J.L. (1986) A case study of eyewitness memory for a crime. *Journal of Applied Psychology*, **71**, 291–301.

Part 2
Evaluating Offenders' Memories

CHAPTER 6

Neuroimaging and Crime

HANS J. MARKOWITSCH AND ELKE KALBE

INTRODUCTION

Is there a neural basis for criminal behaviour? More precisely, are there neural constitutions with which, under certain circumstances, aggressive or criminal behaviour occurs more likely than with other brain networks? Advances in research in this area has a long legacy, which is not only interesting from a theoretical point of view but – given that neural abnormalities may point to some form of illness – is of utmost relevance for the discussion about the responsibility of criminals for their acts of crime. On the other hand, it is known that brain abnormalities (or deviances from the normal appearance) need not necessarily result in definite, unidirectional changes.

Consequently, the topic regarding the correlation between crime and possible neural constituents represents an expanding and important research field of modern cognitive neuroscience (Cauffman, Steinberg & Piquero, 2005). The recent appearance of modern neuroimaging techniques allows scientists to study cerebral structures and their functioning noninvasively in healthy subjects as well as morphological and functional abnormalities in sick people – or people showing abnormal traits, for example criminal behaviour.

Offenders' Memories of Violent Crimes. Edited by Sven Å. Christianson.
© 2007 John Wiley & Sons, Ltd.

This chapter reviews achievements in the field of neuroimaging and crime. After a short historical review we will summarise modern attempts to relate structure and function with respect to personality dimensions and, more specifically, criminal or antisocial behaviour.

THE HISTORY

There is a long, and in many respects disappointing, tradition to researching the relationship between certain brain features and the tendency to commit crimes. This tradition started in a more general context with the advent of Gall's 'phrenology', which became popular all over the globe from Europe to Asia and Australia (cf. Gall, 1825; Markowitsch, 1992). Gall viewed the brain as a complex machine producing behaviour, thoughts and emotions. He and Spurzheim assumed that intellectual abilities and personality features are inter-individually varying and are distributed accordingly in 'faculties' on the cerebral cortex. The prominence of these faculties may be visible in cranial bumps on the outer surface of the head. The faculties included positive and negative traits, among them 'destructiveness' and 'combativeness'. The widespread and influential belief in phrenology diminished only with painstaking studies of the brain, its morphology and its functions, which commenced during the last three decades of the 19th century (Markowitsch, 1992).

In those more 'modern' times, scientists also studied the anatomy of criminals – body, skull and brain (Benedikt, 1879; see Markowitsch, 1992 for further references). Benedikt (1879) concluded that 'the brains of criminals show deviations from the normal type and that the criminals might be considered as an anthropological variation of its species or at least of the cultured races' (p. 110). Publishing in a journal on psychiatry, psychology and forensic medicine, Meynert in 1867 (cited in Markowitsch, 1992) measured the total and the partial weights of the brains of those who died in the Vienna lunatic asylum in the year 1866 and related the outcome to gender, age and insanity.

Criminological debates on nature–nurture relationships were influences by Italian scientists such as Enrico Ferri and Cesare Lombroso. Lombroso believed that about 40 % of criminals were born as such and could be identified by specific body features. He therefore suggested detaining them for life. Ferri (1896) opposed the views of his teacher Lombroso (1876). He proposed that crime is the product of the character of the criminal *plus* the conditions of society existing in the moment of his or her crime. Consequently, Ferri denied the existence of a free will and of personal guilt.

This work was embedded in the general ideas of scientists of that time that it might be possible to find correlations between exceptional intellectual capacities and the weight, size or morphology of the brain. Marshall (1892/1893; cited in Markowitsch, 1992), for example, provided comparisons of brain weights for 15 outstanding individuals and Retzius, a famous Swedish physiologist, devoted many years of his life to measuring the brains of, for example, a prominent astronomer, a female mathematician, a physicist, a statesman and a physiologist (cf. references in Markowitsch, 1992). Other scientists of this time similarly studied the brains of prominent historians, chemists or painters (see Ch. 2 in Markowitsch, 1992). Matiegka (1902; cited in Markowitsch, 1992), a member of the Bohemian Science Society, was quite careful in his comparisons, listing 15 factors that might influence brain weight. His principal conclusion (summarised in a table in *Science*) was that there is an increase in brain weight from day-labourers to tradeworkers and businessmen to scholars, physicians, and other persons of higher mental abilities. Other scientists collected information on up to more than 100 brains to support their idea that exceptional persons have exceptional brains (Markowitsch, 1992) and did not refrain from statements such as the following: 'The brain of a first-class genius like Friedrich Gauss is as far removed from that of the savage bushman as that of the latter from the brain of the nearest related ape' (Spitzka, 1907, p. 226).

This work diminished after the turn of the 20th century. Initially, at that time, scientists still tried to explain contradictory findings of large brains in mentally poor individuals by commenting, for instance: 'who would equalize the functionless brain mass of a lunatic with the active brain mass of mentally distinguished persons' (Matiegka, 1902, p. 30; cited in Markowitsch, 1992). Thereafter, however, there were only very few attempts to relate brain morphology to intellectual capacity, among them Vogt's (1929; cited in Markowitsch, 1992) study of I. Lenin's brain and Harvey's study of Albert Einstein's brain (e.g., Anderson & Harvey, 1996; Witelson et al., 1999).

MODERN BASES FOR ATTEMPTS TO RELATE STRUCTURE AND FUNCTION WITH RESPECT TO PERSONALITY DIMENSIONS

The revival of relating structure and function in human beings in general, and in criminals in particular, came from various sources: research on brain plasticity in humans and animals, the appearance of structural and functional imaging methods, various findings on morphological and physiological abnormalities in psychiatric patients, and findings on brain differences in male vs female and in heterosexual vs homosexual human beings.

Research on plasticity revealed that the environment shapes our brain to a major extent and that even short periods of training or lack of training find their expression in the waxing or waning of neuronal connections, synaptic and dendritic growth or retraction (Kolb & Whishaw, 1998; McEwen, 1999; Trupp, 2003). Structural and functional imaging methods allowed studying the human brain in vivo, both with respect to its detailed morphology and with respect to changes induced by perception, mental thinking, memorising, etc. (e.g., Markowitsch et al., 2000b; Reinhold et al., 2006; Stern & Silbersweig, 2001). The imaging methods revolutionised brain research, both with respect to clinical applications and basic investigations. They brought major new insights into possible brain bases of psychiatric illnesses. Current psychiatric journals are full of evidence on structural and functional abnormalities in psychiatric patient groups compared to normals. These include morphological changes (smaller, missing, or altered gyrification, more or less dense packing of neurons, specific types of neurons, altered glia-neuron ratios, different appearance of cortical columns, smaller or larger cortical thickness, changes in connectivity) in certain brain regions such as prefrontal, temporal and limbic, and partly also subcortical and parietal areas of the brain. On the functional level, there may be reductions in glucose metabolism, altered binding for specific transmitters, increased or decreased levels of brain hormones, such as stress hormones. The finding of such changes holds true for patients with schizophrenia (e.g., Byne et al., 2001; Freedman, 1999), major depression (e.g., Hickie et al., 2005; Videbech & Ravnkilde, 2004), autism (e.g., Luna et al., 2002), attention hyperactivity disorders (Sowell et al., 2003), posttraumatic stress disorder (Driessen et al., 2004; Winter & Irle, 2004), mnestic block syndrome (Markowitsch et al., 1998, 2000a) and other diseases.

Finally, similar research, and also reports from the animal literature and post mortem studies, revealed that the brains of men – known to have higher potentials of aggression – and women differ in a number of features (e.g., Courten-Myers, 1999; Luders et al., 2004) such as weight, size and cortical neuronal density (bigger/higher in men) as well as size of the posterior corpus callosum and neuropil/neuronal processes (bigger/increased in women). Similarly, brain differences in hetero- and homosexual subjects have been described (e.g., LeVay, 1993; Maddox, 1991; Matsumoto, 2000; Swaab et al., 1992). These were noted in particular in the sexually dimorphic nucleus (nucleus interstitialis striae terminalis) and in other hypothalamic nuclei that are much smaller in homosexual compared to heterosexual men, so that it is comparable in size to that of heterosexual women. And even in the morphology and size of fingers and finger digits significant differences were observed between homosexual and heterosexual men (e.g., Hall & Kimura, 1994).

FRONTAL LOBES, TEMPORAL LOBES AND THE AMYGDALA

Early evidence that brain damage can alter the personality came from the 'famous' patient Phineas Gage – the so-called crowbar case (Damasio et al., 1994). Harlow gave two reports on the case (1848, 1869; cited in Markowitsch, 1992) and Bigelow (1850; cited in Markowitsch, 1992), on the man whose maxillary bone was pierced by an iron rod of over one metre in length and roughly 6 kg in weight, which passed behind the left eye, through the frontal lobe, and exited at the beginning of the right upper cranium. Harlow (1848) described the man as 'Phineas P. Gage, a foreman, engaged in building the road, 25 years of age, of middle stature, vigorous physical organization, temperate habits, and. . . of considerable energy of character' (p. 20; cited in Markowitsch, 1992).

While the accident caused no physical disablement (aside from the loss of the left eye) and no deterioration of movement and speech, learning and memory abilities and intelligence in the conventional sense, his personality had changed. Harlow (1869, p. 13) stated, 'the equilibrium or balance, so to speak, between his intellectual faculty and animal propensities' had been destroyed in that he had become irreverent and capricious, he had lost respect for the social conventions, offended people with his abundant profanity and had lost his sense of responsibility. With an opening of the skull of about 8 cm in diameter the patient's state (who was initially conscious) worsened at first and he lay in a semi-comatose condition for more than two weeks, but then improved during the next month, regaining a good physical condition. His personality, however, had changed radically so that his friends said that he was 'no longer Gage' (Harlow, 1869, p. 14). In the years following the accident he worked in a livery stable and then in Chile 'to establish a line of coaches at Valparaiso' (p. 14), where he remained for nearly eight years, before returning to the United States. He died after several epileptic fits.

This case demonstrated that after substantial damage of the prefrontal cortex a person can still survive for years, engage in responsible work and therefore appear to be functioning on only a slightly subnormal intellectual level; nonetheless it seems that the case description remained largely unknown for a considerable time and/or was regarded as atypical. It did show that the frontal lobes were – in accordance with the observations of many scientists at the turn of the century – not directly involved in sensory or motor acts and could be lost to a substantial degree without being vital for life to the subject. On the other hand, the case of Phineas Gage also revealed that frontal lobe damage may result in personality changes and especially the loss of foresight and persistence in following through ideas or intentions. In Harlow's (1869, p. 13) words: 'The equilibrium or balance, so to speak, between his intellectual faculties and animal propensities, seems to have been destroyed. He is fitful, irreverent, indulging at times in the grossest profanity (which was not previously his custom), manifesting but little deference for his fellows, impatient of restraint or advice when it conflicts with his desires, at times pertinaciously obstinate, yet capricious and vacillating, devising many plans of future operation, which are no sooner arranged than they are abandoned in turn for others appearing more feasible. A child in his intellectual capacity and manifestations, he has the animal passions of a strong man'.

Similar evaluations of the consequences of frontal lobe damage were given by Welt (1888) and Halpern (1930) (both cited in Markowitsch, 1992). Fanny Halpern stated that prefrontal damage makes man more similar to animals with respect to attitude and movements and Eleonore Welt, one of the first female medical doctors, gave detailed descriptions of character changes after frontal lobe damage. The first case she described was that of a 37-year-old Swiss craftsman who fell from the fourth floor of a house and received damage to the left frontal lobe. She gave a very clear, detailed description of changes in the character of this patient. Prior to the trauma he had been a cheerful, relaxed man of good humour, but afterwards he became very critical and annoying to his co-patients. For, when the professor of the clinic urged him to behave himself and told him that he received good meals and the best wine in the hospital, the patient answered that the other patients and the hospital staff were at fault and, concerning the wines, that he was used to drinking Chateau Laffite and other French wines but not the sour stuff provided in the clinic. Welt added further case descriptions; she noted that character changes in different patients might go from better to worse, or vice versa, someone who was originally taciturn might develop a lively, merry and alert character. Her report is of value because of the detailed tables she gave on roughly 50 cases taken from older literature (dating from 1819) in which frontal lobe damage was accompanied by character changes. From comparing locations she concluded that changes in character most likely followed damage to the (right) medial orbital surface of the frontal lobes.

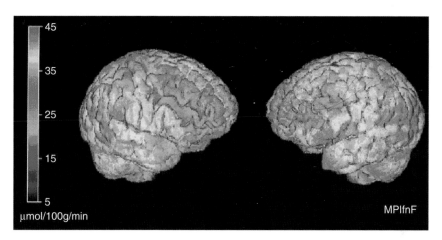

Colour plate Figure 6.1 Dynamic functional brain imaging in a patient with degenerative frontal lobe damage and major personality changes (Kessler et al., 1999, Degenerative prefrontal damage in a young adult: Static and dynamic imaging and neuropsychological correlates. *Neurocase*, **5**, 173–9. Reproduced by permission from Psychology Press. http://www.psypress.co.uk/journals.asp.)

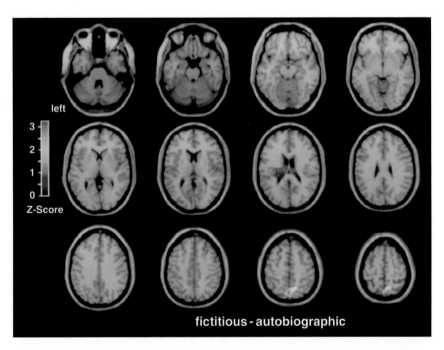

left

3
2
1
0
Z-Score

fictitious - autobiographic

Colour plate Figure 6.2 Functional imaging in normal subjects during the comparisons 'retrieving autobiographic events versus lies (autobiographic-fictitious)' and vice versa 'retrieving lies versus autobiographic events (fictitious-autobiographic)'. Note that for the first comparison (true events) the right amygala and the right temporo-frontal region showed activations together with some further frontomedial and left temporal spots, while for the second comparisons (lies) only a posterior region (precuneus) was activated. This region has been termed the mind's eye as it is important for mental imagery – a process certainly necessary when trying to reproduce invented situations. The first part of the figure (autobiographic-fictitious) is reprinted from Markowitsch, H.J., Thiel, A., Reinkemeier, M., Kessler, J., Koyuncu, A. & Heiss, W.-D. (2000b). Right amygdala and temporofrontal activation during autobiographic, but not during fictitious, memory retrieval. *Behavioural Neurology*, **12**, 181–90, with permission from IOS Press.

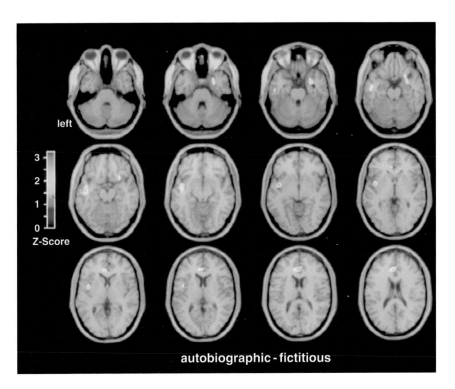

Colour plate Figure 6.2 (Continued)

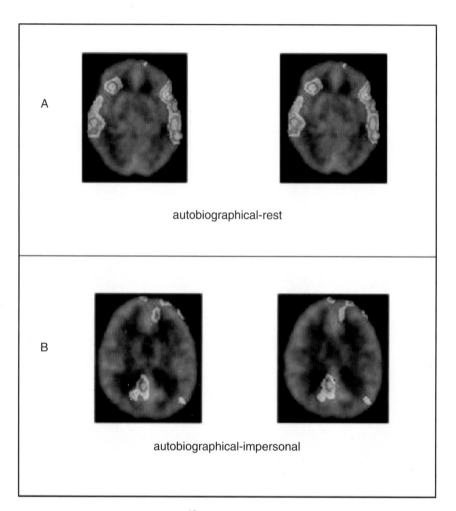

Colour plate Figure 6.3 $H_2{}^{15}O$ PET images of the brain of patient AA who had murdered her children in an extended suicide. A): Increased left lateralised frontal and temporal brain activation patterns when listening to autobiographical episodes compared to a rest condition. B): Marked activation in the right precuneus when listening to autobiographical episodes compared to a condition in which episodes of another person were presened. (After Kalbe et al., in preparation)

A detailed behavioural and anatomical analysis of a 39-year-old woman, who developed personality changes (including religious delusions) after massive prefrontal degeneration, can also be found in Voegelin (1897; cited in Markowitsch, 1992), and the case of a young soldier with basal prefrontal damage and bizarre social behaviour was given by Knörlein (1865; cited in Markowitsch, 1992).

It is of major interest that these old reports pointed to a relation between – especially right-hemispheric – orbitofrontal damage and changes in personality dimensions. Flechsig (1896a) considered them responsible for the control of drives, and that as prefrontal regions developed only later ontogenetically, he regarded animals and human infants with their underdeveloped prefrontal cortex merely as 'Affectwesen' ('affective creatures'). At the same time, Bianchi (1895; cited in Markowitsch, 1992) in Italy wrote that frontal lobe damage 'disaggegrate[s] the personality, and incapacitates for serializing and synthesizing groups of representations' (p. 522). The relation between the control of higher emotions and the orbitofrontal cortex was later reinstated by Kleist (1934) on the basis of his experience with short and shrapnel wounded veterans (Figure 6.1).

Shortly after Kleist's publication, Edgar Moniz (re-)introduced psychosurgery to alter a patient's personality to the positive. (In 1891, the Swiss psychiatrist Gottlieb Burckhardt [cited in Markowitsch, 1992] had performed psychosurgery on four of his patients.) Based on hearing about the findings on 'Becky' and 'Lucy', two chimpanzees with frontal lobe removal, Moniz decided to destroy portions of the prefrontal cortex of his psychiatric patients in order to make them more adapted. He thought that inhibitory activity of the frontal lobes disturbed an equilibrium in the brains of his patients. Therefore, in his first operation, he injected alcohol into the human subcortical white matter, but thereafter used a leucotome to cut away portions of the prefrontal cortex (Moniz, 1936). Various versions of lobectomy (removal of tissue) and lobotomy (separating frontal from posterior tissue by cutting) were performed between the end of 1930s and the 1960s with more than 50,000 surgeries in the initial wave in the United States (Markowitsch, 1992). Indeed, numerous reports appeared praising the advantage of this method in curing psychotic patients and in creating normal citizens again. The popularity of the method soon led to its application for all kinds of so-called deviant behaviour – from schizophrenia over tics and neuroses to criminal behaviour (Valenstein, 1973, 1980). While benefits cannot be denied for certain cases, this radical treatment is no longer regarded as ethically tolerable and has declined with the advent of psychopharmaca.

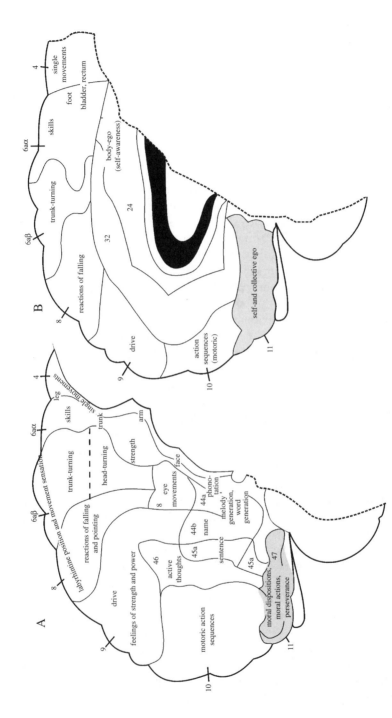

Figure 6.1 Kleist's (1934) map of (A) the lateral and (B) medial human cerebral cortex; based on his experiences with World War I veterans with traumatic brain damage. The map is based on Brodmann's (1914) cytoarchitectonic map

Personality changes nevertheless are still commonly observed after frontal lobe damage. We ourselves had a 27-year old patient who came to our attention because her mother observed some personality changes in her – she stored garbage instead of suitcases in the car and failed to go outside with her dog (Kessler et al., 1999; Markow-itsch & Kessler, 2000). While she had been a well-educated student, she never managed to establish long-term relationships with respect to her professional or social life. Initially, her brain appeared normal when investigated with static functional magnetic resonance imaging (MRI) (Figure 6.2) while an [18F] fluorodeoxyglucose position emission tomography demonstrated a reduced prefrontal metabolism that was especially prominent in the right orbitofrontal region (colour plate Figure 6.1). Though her disease progressed quickly to a stage where the neural correlates were visible with static MRI (Fig. 6.3), she all the time remained rather indifferent and relaxed with respect to her condition. She died four years after her first neurological examination.

These case reports reveal that specific regions within the human brain – the prefrontal cortex in particular – are in control of personality

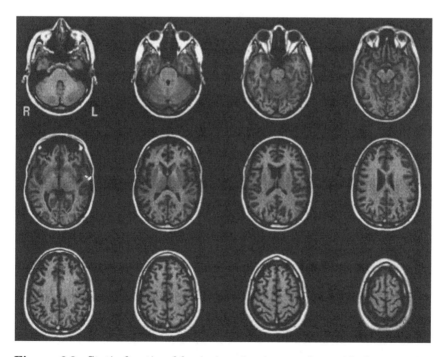

Figure 6.2 Static functional brain imaging in a patient with degenerative frontal lobe damage and major personality changes (Figure 6.1 of Markowitsch & Kessler, 2000; Springer Press)

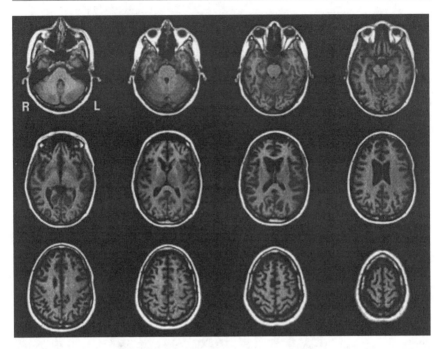

Figure 6.3   Static functional brain imaging in a patient with degenerative frontal lobe damage and major personality changes (Figure 6.2 of Markowitsch & Kessler, 2000; Springer Press)

dimensions relating to the self and the self-perspective (Keenan, Wheeler, Gallup, & Pascual-Leone, 2000; Vogeley & Fink, 2003), with moral judgements and affect (Kleist, 1934; Stuss, Gallup & Alexander, 2001), and with 'theory of mind' functions (Bird et al., 2004; Shallice, 2001). To have a 'theory of mind' implies to be able to feel how other persons might feel and think (Calarge, Andreasen, & O'Leary, 2003), an ability that appears only late in childhood (Perner & Dienes, 2003) and that is thought to be impaired in criminals and individuals with antisocial behaviour (Dolan & Fullam, 2004).

Another structure, implicated in many of these functions is the amygdala, a large telencephalic nucleus situated in the temporal lobe in front of the hippocampus. This structure receives preprocessed information from all sensory modalities and evaluates it with respect to its biological and social significance (Markowitsch, 1998/99). Patients with damage to the amygdala (Fig. 6.4) consequently have problems in affect evaluation and in combining or synchronising memory and affect (Markowitsch et al., 1994; Siebert, Markowitsch & Bartel, 2003). Damage to the amygdala similarly has been reported to result in deficits in theory of mind functions (Fine, Lumsden & Blair,

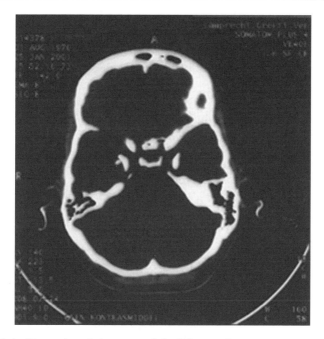

Figure 6.4 Example of the amygdaloid brain damage of a patient with Urbach-Wiethe disease (cf. Siebert et al., 2003).

2001; Shaw et al., 2004) and the amygdala and the orbitofrontal cortex interact to a major degree in evaluating emotions (Driessen et al., 2004), a finding that is reinforced by the existence of a major fibre pathway – the uncinate fascicle – interconnecting the orbitofrontal and anterior temporal regions (within which the amygdala is situated). The uncinate fascicle has been found to be about one-third larger in the right compared to the left hemisphere (Highley et al., 2002), which underlines the importance of especially the right hemisphere in emotive interpretation (Schore, 2002).

It should also be noted that there is a vast literature on prefrontal, temporal and other brain changes in patients with psychotic disturbances, especially schizophrenia (Pierri, Volk, Auh, Sampson & Lewis, 2001; Woodruff et al., 1997) and that there is major evidence for theory of mind changes in these patients (Frith, 2004).

THE BRAINS OF CRIMINALS AND INDIVIDUALS WITH ANTISOCIAL BEHAVIOUR

In light of this evidence scientists were interested in studying the brains of individuals with a criminal or antisocial history directly. And indeed, there is accumulating evidence for brain abnormalities – especially in the frontal lobes, and secondarily in fronto-temporal/limbic structures – in these groups (Bassarath, 2001; Blake, Pincus & Buckner, 1995). (The limbic system is an agglomerate of various brain structures – from the cerebral cortex to the brain stem – that are implicated largely in emotional behaviour and in emotion-memory processing; Markowitsch, 1999a, 1999b.)

In a few incidences direct relations could be established in that way as with the appearance of brain damage subjects changed from a normal family father to a criminal paedophilic (Burns & Swerdlow, 2003), or, vice versa, that a criminal convict after hemorrhagic brain damage changed into an obsessive artist (Giles, 2004). Interestingly, related to the tumour patient of Burns and Swerdlow, Sullivan had in 1911 described two criminals with tumours in their frontal lobes (cited in Markowitsch, 1992).

The groups of subjects investigated nowadays include severe criminals (murderers), on the one hand, and patients with a forensic-psychiatric background, on the other. Raine did a number of studies in which he used glucose positron emission tomography (PET) in order to study functional brain abnormalities in murderers (Raine et al., 1998a; 1998b). He found that affective murderers show a reduced prefrontal metabolism. Raine (2001) found with morphological studies a prefrontal thinning in patients with antisocial personality disorder, together with a reduced prefrontal grey matter volume (Raine et al., 2000) and corpus callosum abnormalities (Raine et al., 2003). The corpus callosum constitutes the major pathway interconnecting the two cerebral cortical hemispheres. As the two hemispheres serve different functions – the left one being usually responsible for language functions and detailed analyses, and the right one more for the control of emotions and for more general, *Gestalt*-like analyses – a proper interaction between the two is of major importance for an integrated personality (Zaidel & Iacobini, 2003). Crow (1998) even proposed the idea that schizophrenia might be a transcallosal misconnection syndrome, and Gazzaniga (2000) asked whether the corpus callosum might make men humane. Other authors discussed relations between prefrontal and limbic system dysfunctions or abnormalities and psychopathic or antisocial behaviour as well (Bower & Price, 2001; Cauffman et al., 2005; Kiehl et al., 2001).

While all studies point to relations between neurological or physiological variables and criminal behaviour, little seems to be known with regard to possible gender or cultural differences. The recent study of Cauffman et al. (2005), for example, compared offenders and non-offenders of both sexes and of various ethnicities, but found only a minor evidence for temperance differences (e.g., impulse control, aggression suppression) in the way that there was a tendency for the temperance difference to be greater for female offenders vs nonoffenders compared to male offenders as opposed to non-offenders.

Anneliese Pontius pointed out that antisocial behaviour or aggressive offences such as homicide can be a possible consequence of epileptic seizures – a phenomenon that she termed 'limbic psychotic trigger reaction' (Pontius, 1996; 2003). It is conceptualised as a fleeting de novo psychosis that is caused by a specific subtype of seizure, a 'simple' partial seizure activity in limbic portions of the brain and interferes with volition and the 'sense of self', but preserves memory for the acts. Seen in this way, murder for these cases might be an act of automatism, triggered by their temporarily changed brain condition (namely, seizure activity that disturbs, blurs or changes the person's will, insight, foresight and self-control). In Pontius' (2003, p. 547) words: 'The acts are nonvolitional, unplanned, nonintended, motiveless, purposeless, and out-of-character, ranging from socially bizarrely inappropriate behaviour to homicide'. Pontius also suggested that the frontal lobe system is not yet properly matured in juvenile delinquents (Pontius & Ruttiger, 1976), or is dysfunctional otherwise (Pontius & Yudowitz, 1980).

The maturation of the frontal lobes has been a major issue since the 19th century when Flechsig (1896b) found that the prefrontal cortex maturates much later than most of the other cortex regions (Gibson, 1991; Huttenlocher, 1994). (Maturation meaning that the axons [fibers] of the nerve cells are properly shielded in order to propagate electrical activity more accurately and faster than without them.) While many cortex regions are mature at birth, some need months to years more and portions of the prefrontal cortex may be completely matured only in the third decade of life (Nagy, Westerberg & Klingberg, 2004). As the prefrontal cortex is also most vulnerable to age-related changes, both anatomically (Raz et al., 1997) and on the behavioural level (Rossi et al., 2004), this speaks all the more for a relation between deviant behaviour and frontal brain functioning. And it implies that these cortical regions especially need proper environmental stimulation for their maturation.

All these results concerning the brains of criminals and individuals with antisocial behaviour elicited by morphological and functional brain imaging studies speak for direct interactions between brain and environment, as mentioned above. It appears to be a natural consequence that the brains of criminals may deviate in a number of features from those of non-criminals and that these deviations have an impact on behaviour. When future research is able to reveal the validity and reliability of such brain features, they may be used in a predictive way. That is, at least with certain likeliness, inferences might be drawn.

FUNCTIONAL IMAGING STUDIES DEMONSTRATING THE POSSIBILITY TO INFER UNDERLYING THOUGHTS FROM IMAGING PATTERNS

In a number of functional imaging studies we asked normal subjects, largely university students, to tell us significant episodes from their past life (Fink et al., 1996; Markowitsch, Fink, Thöne, Kessler & Heiss, 1997a; Markowitsch, Vandekerckhove, Lanfermann & Russ, 2003; Piefke, Weiss, Zilles, Markowitsch & Fink, 2003; Vandekerckhove, Markowitsch, Mertens & Wörmann, 2005). In these studies we found that remembered episodes from decades ago activated other brain regions rather than episodes from the more recent past (Piefke et al., 2003), that emotionally, positively valued episodes activated medial orbitofrontal regions, while negatively valued ones activated lateral orbitofrontal areas, and that the right fronto-temporal lobes are particularly active when individuals retrieve emotional episodes with ease (Fink et al., 1996).

In order to find out whether persons who due to psychogenic amnesia or psychogenic fugue conditions fail to retrieve their autobiographic past show different brain activations, we applied functional imaging techniques – single photon emissioned computed tomography (SPECT), glucose and water PET and functional magnetic resonance imaging (fMRI) – in addition to performing a number of neuropsychological tests. Generally, we found that a number of these patients did indeed show deviances in their brain activation patterns, which confirm that memory blocks have a correlate in the brain (Driessen et al., 2004; Fujiwara et al., 2004, in press; Markowitsch, 1999c, 1999d, 2003a; Markowitsch et al., 1997b, 1998, 2000a). We assume that these brain changes – usually reduced metabolic states in fronto-temporal regions of the right hemisphere or reductions in memory processing limbic brain areas – are due to a major increase in stress hormones (glucocorticoids) in the brain. It is known that glucocorticoids have their major reception sites in anterior temporal lobes (amygdala, hippocampus), and consequently those brain regions undertake the analysing and synthesising of cognitive and emotive aspects of information.

As an example, we will describe the case of a patient who came to our attention because of a persistent retrograde amnesia after a fugue condition. That is, he had lost access to his biography due to a psychic stress or trauma condition and had left his home and travelled by bike several hundreds of kilometres without knowing who he was or why he did this. After several days he arrived in a big city where he entered a university psychiatric clinic. His condition remained unchanged for more than one year (we lost contact with him after that time). The patient had had a poor childhood. His mother would have preferred a daughter and put him into female clothes for the first five years of his life. Later, she frequently told him that he would ruin their restaurant and would be unable to lead a successful life. He had spontaneously 'escaped' from his life situation before the present fugue, but had not lost his identity at those occasions. The patient was of above average intelligence and had good anterograde memory abilities (i.e., he could acquire new information long term). After the fugue he changed his life habits and manifested other somatic changes (e.g., he gained 15 kg of body weight within a short time, lost his allergy and asthma, changed his profession and no longer wanted to drive or ride cars because of their speed).

The patient did not reveal any brain abnormalities under static ('morphological') MRI or when recording EEGs. However, after an ^{15}O-PET activation study where a comparison was made of his brain activity when monitored for imagery of sentences containing autobiographic events and those containing biographic events from somebody else, it was revealed that he processed both kinds of information in a similar way and different from normals (Fink et al., 1996). As Figure 6.5 reveals, activations were mainly observed in his left anterior hemisphere, which is more indicative of processing neutral than personal emotional memories (Kroll, Markowitsch, Knight & von Cramon, 1997; Markowitsch, Calabrese, Neufeld, Gehlen & Durwen, 1999); vice versa, normal control subjects showed brain activations predominantly in their right hemisphere.

As subsequently carried out by others (Ganis, Kosslyn, Stose, Thompson & Yurgelun-Todd, 2003; Kozel & Padgett, 2004; Spence et al., 2001), we investigated brain correlates of lying vs telling the truth (Markowitsch et al., 2000b). In order to do so we asked normal students to tell us specific episodes of their biography (as, e.g. in Fink et al., 1996) and, on the other hand, to invent episodes in a normal way whilst autobiographical material was retrieved. For example, a student mentioned that after finishing high school, he flew with his girl friend to Australia. In Melbourne they rented a car and went via Ayers Rock to the Kakadu National Park where they had a flat tyre. For us as outsiders it could not be determined which stories were true and which not. When comparing brain activations it became, however, easy to distinguish these two types of stories: The true stories activated the right hemispheric amygdala, the right temporo-frontal junction areas and further cortical regions; the fictitious stories, on the other hand, only resulted in an activation in the posterior medial – the precuneus – region of the brain (colour plate Figure 6.2). The precuneus has been termed the mind's eye as it is most consistently activated during mental imagery and this probably reflected the subjects' main task while thinking about events which might have happened, but in fact had not happened.

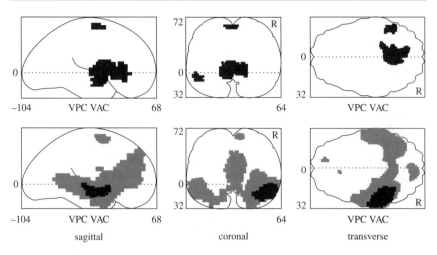

sagittal   coronal   transverse

Figure 6.5 Schematic illustration of differently activated brain regions during imagination and recall of events from one's own past (Markowitsch et al., 1997a). The brain is shown as a so-called glass brain, that is schematically in three levels – sagittal (as if translucent from posterior to anterior, activations of both hemispheres integrated), frontal (as if divided between the ears), and horizontal (as if cut through roughly on the level of eyes and ears) so that activations are reduced to two dimensions, but can be mentally reconstructed into three. Dark areas represent activated regions. The patient with psychogenic amnesia manifested brain activations largely in the left frontal hemisphere when being confronted with his own past (top three sections). Such an activation otherwise occurs when someone is confronted with neutral information, stemming from a third person, unknown to him or her. Normal subjects usually manifest largely right-hemispheric activations in this situation (bottom three sections)

CRIME-RELATED BRAIN ACTIVATIONS

These findings from imaging studies demonstrates the possibility to infer underlying thoughts from activation patterns, and brings us to discuss brain activations of subjects who had committed crimes or who were involved in court situations. In one such situation, we had to determine whether a witness was telling the truth or not. As we have mentioned previously, brain damage to right-hemispheric fronto-temporal regions impairs autobiographical memory retrieval, while brain damage to the left-hemispheric counterparts is more closely associated with impairments in recalling world knowledge. These different anatomico-behavioural relations hold also for other forms of memory. We currently distinguish five long-term memory systems – all of which are processed by different brain networks and all of which may be selectively disturbed (Figure 6.6). The most complex of these

LONG-TERM MEMORY SYSTEMS

PROCEDURAL MEMORY	PRIMING	PERCEPTUAL MEMORY	SEMANTIC MEMORY	EPISODIC MEMORY
Procedural memory stands for mechanical or motor-related skills.	**Priming** means a higher probability of recognizing previously perceived information.	**Perceptual memory** refers to the recognition of stimuli and is related to familiarity judgements.	**Semantic memory** is oriented to the present and represents general context-free facts.	The **episodic memory system** is a past-oriented memory system, allowing mental time-travel through autonoetic awareness.

H_2O=water
$a^2+b^2=c^2$
Paris = capital of France

RELEVANT BRAIN STRUCTURES

	PROCEDURAL MEMORY	PRIMING	PERCEPTUAL MEMORY	SEMANTIC MEMORY	EPISODIC MEMORY
Encoding and consolidation	Basal ganglia, motor-related areas	Primary and association cortex	Posterior sensory cortex	Cerebral cortex, limbic structures	Limbic system, prefrontal cortex
Storage	Basal ganglia, motor-related areas	Primary and association cortex	Posterior sensory cortex	Cerebral cortex (mainly association areas)	Cerebral cortex (mainly association areas), limbic regions
Retrieval	Basal ganglia, motor-related areas	Primary and association cortex	Posterior sensory cortex	Frontotemporal cortex (left)	Frontotemporal cortex (right), limbic regions

Figure 6.6 The five long-term memory systems

memory systems is the episodic-autobiographical memory system that combines and synchronises cognitive and affective aspects of information. Due to this function it is the most vulnerable among the memory systems and the one recruiting most diverse structures in the brain. The episodic memory system is always context-embedded and allows mental time travelling. It requires the differentiating between self and others and to reflect on one's own position in the world (including, of course, the social environment). Next to it, the semantic memory has to be named, which represents context-free facts. Still on the conscious (noetic) level is the perceptual memory system, which allows to identify objects on the basis of their individual features and to distinguish them from related objects. All three systems are sometimes also named explicit memory systems and are thereby distinguished from the other two, the implicit ones. These are the priming and the procedural memory systems. Priming information allows the establishment of a trace in the brain, which, however, exists on a subconscious level. Similarly, procedural information is processed subconsciously – usually the information represented in this system has some relation to motoric actions: driving a car, riding a bike, swimming, skating, playing piano or cards, for example. Once acquired, we process and retrieve this information automatically – without conscious reflection. On the contrary, conscious reflection requires momentary deliberation for the quick and accurate processing of such information. As an example, consider driving a car with a gear-shifting system: what would you need to do first when you want to shift from the second into the third gear? The correct response is to remove the right foot from the gas pedal; many people, however, due to the automaticity of the gear-shifting process, would respond: first, press the clutch pedal.

A person telling the truth should engage his or her episodic memory system, requiring both emotional and cognitive synchronisation. From the brain's point of view, if a witness tells the truth, there should be prefronto-temporal activations, if he or she fakes, there should be activations largely confined to the precuneus region (Markowitsch et al., 2000b). We tested this with an eyewitness to a murder who herself had been severely wounded by the murderer. In addition to performing fMRI while she was confronted with episodes of the murder, we tested her with a broad battery of tests, including those on memory functions, emotions, personality traits, attention and concentration, etc. (cf. Markowitsch, 2003a). Specifically with respect to possible lying, we used tests on confabulatory tendencies (especially of importance as she had some frontal brain damage), and on faking (e.g., the TOMM-test; Tombaugh, 1996). All in all, we found that she responded reliably, never attempted to confabulate and that her brain activations corresponded to those of the normals, retrieving autobiographical episodes.

In another study, we tested brain activations in a patient suffering from a psychogenic fugue condition. This man did not remember anything of his personal past (autobiography), though he was largely normal with respect to his fact (semantic) memory and with respect to his social behaviour (Markowitsch et al., 1997a). Functional brain imaging demonstrated that – when confronted with events from his personal past – his brain activations were largely left-hemispheric in areas typical for retrieval of semantic information, while control subjects in the same paradigm manifested right-hemispheric activations known to be relevant for autobiographical memory retrieval. These findings indicated that the patient treated personal episodic information in a neutral or 'semantic' way. This case was subsequently discussed by a professor of law under the heading of 'Personal identity and the limits of criminal responsibility' (Merkel, 1999).

While our patient had no criminal background, the question of criminal responsibility is of particular relevance when criminals deny remembering their act of crime (Davis & O'Donohue, 2004; Eccleston & Ward, 2004; Tsai, Morsbach & Loftus, 2004). Our results from patients with enduring conditions of dissociative amnesia (Fujiwara et al., 2004, 2006) indicate that these patients indeed change their personality considerably – from Saul to Paul, so to say. The patient just discussed lost his conditions of allergy and asthma, no longer wanted to drive cars (considering them to be too speedy), changed his profession, gained weight, etc. As these patients have to reference to their past, it is clear that even long-standing personality traits may become altered. This implies that the law system has to determine how to treat these, in a way, 'new' persons.

Furthermore, functional imaging results of the kind just mentioned prove that a patient is not lying, but indeed does not have access to his personal past. Vice versa – and we have done this in a court case – functional imaging methods may be used to prove that a witness is telling the truth (or at least what he or she believes to be the truth). Therefore, this research has a number of implications for the treatment of both witnesses and defendants.

Homicide and Functional Neuroimaging

Severe autobiographical memory deficits were evidenced, both on the behavioural and the neural level in a woman we called AA (Kalbe et al., in preparation) who had killed two of her children in an act of 'extended suicide'. At the age of 47, two years prior to our examination, AA had been admitted to a forensic clinic after having killed two of her three children by first sedating and then drowning them. An attempted suicide failed. According to the court experts she had been suffering from an affective disorder in the form of a long lasting severe depressive episode with psychotic symptoms (F 32.3 according to ICD-10) and was thus found not guilty by reason of insanity. AA's prominent psychotic symptom had spread over years and was still present at the time of our examination. It consisted of the delusion that she and her children suffered from a genetic defect that resulted in the inability to feel emotions and to communicate with other people. (When she first spoke to one of the authors, HJM, she suggested to be tested for Urbach-Wiethe disease, a condition frequently leading to bilateral amygdala calcification and, as a consequence, to emotional flattening. As HJM had done investigations on these patients [Markowitsch et al., 1994; Siebert et al., 2003], she contacted him.) As a consequence, she thought that her life and those of her children were senseless, and was convinced about the justification of her children's death.

Our neuropsychological examination revealed a within or above average performance in all cognitive domains (intelligence, attention, speed of information processing, executive functions, anterograde memory and also remote memory for non-personal facts), except autobiographical memory. She could remember some autobiographical facts but was especially deficient in remembering autobiographical episodes with a temporal gradient towards the present. She reported her inability to visualise these memories and that remembering them did not arouse any emotional involvement. Furthermore, while basic emotional processing (such as inferring people's emotions from their facial expressions) were mostly unaffected, dysfunctions were observed in 'theory of mind' tasks testing the ability to infer other people's thoughts, intentions and beliefs – a function that has been linked to autobiographical memory (Corcoran & Frith, 2003; Markowitsch, 2003b). Malingering was not addressed with any specific neuropsychological test instrument. However, AA's neuropsychological profile did not give any hints of a tendency to simulate test performance.

To study possible neural correlates of her emotional autobiographical memory impairments, we conducted an $H_2{}^{15}O$ PET. During the scan, AA was confronted with verbally presented episodes of her own biography (without referring to the offence) and, in another condition, matched episodes of another person's biography, following principally the paradigm used by Fink et al. (1996). When contrasting the autobiographical to a rest condition, we found an increased left-lateralised frontal and temporal brain activation pattern – a result that is in contrast to Fink et al.'s observation of a right-lateralised network of mainly frontal and temporal activations, but which is in conformity to corresponding left-hemispheric activations in a patient suffering from psychogenic amnesia (fugue) (Markowitsch et al., 1997a; cf. above). Furthermore, AA exhibited a marked activation in the right precuneus when listening to her own biography compared to listening to another person's episodes (see colour plate Figure 6.3). We concluded that while the activation in the precuneus, which has been found to be part of a network for self-referential processing (e.g. Kjaer et al., 2002; Uddin et al., 2005), suggested some effort to access information concerning herself, the missing right-lateralised temporofrontal activation in listening to autobiographical data seemed to reflect AA's lack of affective processing concerning her own biography, which was also seen on the behavioural level.

CONCLUSIONS

Brain correlates of criminal behaviour become of increasing importance with the advent of sophisticated technologies that allow a refined analysis of brain states during mental processing. In the near future it is very likely that brain imaging will be routinely used in cases of doubt or in order to confirm suspicious facts. While the limits of these methods should not be neglected, they at least will be of important influence in proving an individual's innocence. Brain imaging nowadays is applied in a number of fields, where until a few years ago no one thought about its applicability (e.g., neuroeconomics; Glimcher & Rustichini, 2004). While legal systems are more conservative, they nevertheless cannot close their eyes with respect to the advances of modern neuroscience.

There is, at present, already substantial – though mainly correlative – evidence that certain morphological and metabolic abnormalities appear with regularity in individuals with a criminal background. As, however, some of these changes appear also in persons not committing criminal acts, there is (as yet) no strict one-to-one relationship between neural and behavioural deviations. Data are usually collected post hoc. We therefore need longitudinal studies with high numbers of subjects in risk of performing criminal acts and should perform functional imaging on them repeatedly over time. Headlines, such as 'Brain imaging ready to detect terrorists, say neuroscientists' (*Nature*, Vol. 437, 22 September 2005) are still beyond solid evidence, nevertheless, the potential of functional brain imaging should not be underestimated.

With respect to relations between abnormal states and brain findings the available evidence is already more promising. We can describe – even with quantitative precision when using glucose PET

(Markowitsch et al., 2000a) – whether the brain of an individual works in the normal range, is reduced in glucose activation over widespread regions, or in particular, in memory processing regions. Using fMRI, sophisticated paradigms can, with considerable certainty, reveal whether a person is lying overtly or believes in his or her words. Brain imaging may consequently be a method of choice that is superior to lie detectors that measure electrodermal, and therefore peripheral, activity. Even morphological abnormalities, detectable with conventional MRI, may become suggestive of deviant behaviour as Yang et al. (2005) showed with respect to liars.

Neuroscience revealed that brain and environment are interwoven: The outside world leaves continuous imprints on the nervous system and the condition of the nervous system widens or restricts our perception and interpretation of our surroundings. Consequently – and this cannot be emphasised enough – a healthy, friendly and trustful environment during childhood and youth is the best protector against the development of criminal behaviour later in life. Vice versa, it has to be acknowledged that many offenders become so due to adverse social circumstances in their past life. Not only the legal system, but society in general, has to adjust its reactions towards offenders in the light of these dependences.

REFERENCES

Anderson, B. & Harvey, T. (1996) Alterations in cortical thickness and neuronal density in the frontal cortex of Albert Einstein. *Neuroscience Letters*, **210**, 161–4.

Bassarath, L. (2001) Neuroimaging studies of antisocial behaviour. *Canadian Journal of Psychiatry*, **46**, 728–32.

Benedikt, M. (1879) *Anatomische Studien an Verbrecher-Gehirnen* [Anatomical studies on the brains of criminals]. Wien: Wilhelm Braumüller.

Bird, C.M., Castelli, F., Malik, O., Frith, U. & Husain, M. (2004) The impact of extensive medial frontal lobe damage on 'Theory of mind' and cognition. *Brain*, **127**, 914–28.

Blake, P.Y., Pincus, J.H. & Buckner, C. (1995) Neurologic abnormalities in murderers. *Neurology*, **45**, 1641–7.

Bower, M.C. & Price, B.H. (2001) Neuropsychiatry of frontal lobe dysfunction in violent and criminal behaviour: A critical review. *Journal of Neurology, Neurosurgery & Psychiatry*, **71**, 720–6.

Brodmann, K. (1909) *Vergleichende Lokalisationslehre der Grosshirnrinde in ihren Prinzipien dargestellt auf Grund des Zellenbaues* [Comparative study of the localization in the cerebral cortex, demonstrated in its principles on the basis of cytoarchitecture]. Leipzig: Barth.

Brodmann, K. (1914) Physiologie des Gehirns. In P. von Bruns (Hrsg.), *Neue deutsche Chirurgie* (Bd. 11, Tl. 1) (pp. 85–426). Stuttgart: Enke.

Burns, J.M. & Swerdlow, R.H. (2003) Right orbitofrontal tumor with pedophilia symptom and constructional apraxia sign. *Archives of Neurology*, **60**, 437–40.

Byne, W., Buchsbaum, M.S., Kemether, E., Hazlett, E.A., Shinwari, A., Mitropoulou, V. & Siever, L.J. (2001) Magnetic resonance imaging of the thalamic mediodorsal nucleus and pulvinar in schizophrenia and schizotypal personality disorder. *Archives of General Psychiatry* **58**, 133–40.

Calarge, C., Andreasen, N.C. & O'Leary, D.S. (2003) Visualizing how one brain understands another: a PET study of theory of mind. *American Journal of Psychiatry* **160**, 1954–64.

Cauffman, E., Steinberg, L. & Piquero, A.R. (2005) Psychological, neuropsychological and physiological correlates of serious antisocial behaviour in adolescence: The role of self-control. *Criminology*, **43**, 133–76.

Corcoran, R. & Frith, C.D. (2003) Autobiographical memory and theory of mind: Evidence of a relationship in schizophrenia. *Psychological Medicine*, **33**, 897–905.

Courten-Myers, G. (1999) The human cerebral cortex: Gender differences in structure and function. *Journal of Neuropathology and Experimental Neurology*, **58**, 217–26.

Crow, T.J. (1998) Schizophrenia as a transcallosal misconnection syndrome. *Schizophrenia Research*, **30**, 11–114.

Damasio, H., Grabowski, T., Frank, R., Galaburda, A.M. & Damasio, A.R. (1994) The return of Phineas Gage: Clues about the brain from the skull of a famous patient. *Science*, **264**, 1102–5.

Davis, D. & O'Donohue, W.T. (2004) The road to perdition: Extreme influence tactics in the interrogation room. In O'Donohue & E.R. Levensky (Eds), *Handbook of forensic psychology* (pp. 897–996). Amsterdam: Elsevier.

Dolan, M. & Fullam, R. (2004) Theory of mind and mentalizing ability in antisocial personality disorders with and without psychopathy. *Psychological Medicine*, **34**, 1093–1102.

Driessen, M., Beblo, T., Mertens, M., Piefke, M., Rullkötter, N., Silva Saveedra, A., Reddemann, L., Rau, H., Markowitsch, H.J., Wulff, H., Lange, W. & Woermann, F.G. (2004) Different fMRI activation patterns of traumatic memory in borderline personality disorder with and without additional posttraumatic stress disorder. *Biological Psychiatry*, **55**, 603–11.

Eccleston, L. & Ward, T. (2004) Assessment of dangerously and criminal responsibility. In O'Donohue & E.R. Levensky (Eds), *Handbook of forensic psychology* (pp. 85–101). Amsterdam: Elsevier.

Ferri, E. (1896) *Das Verbrechen als soziale Erscheinung* [Crime as a social phenomenon]. (transl. by H. Kurella). Leipzig: Wigand.

Fine, C., Lumsden, J. & Blair, R.J.R. (2001) Dissociation between 'theory of mind' and executive functions in a patient with early left amygdala damage. *Brain*, **124**, 287–98.

Fink, G.R., Markowitsch, H.J., Reinkemeier, M., Bruckbauer, T., Kessler, J. & Heiss, W.-D. (1996) Cerebral representation of one's own past: Neural networks involved in autobiographical memory. *Journal of Neuroscience*, **16**, 4275–82.

Flechsig, P. (1896a) *Gehirn und Seele*. Leipzig: Veit.

Flechsig, P. (1896b) *Die Lokalisation der geistigen Vorgänge, insbesondere der Sinnesempfindungen des Menschen*. Leipzig: Veit & Comp.

Freedman, R. (1999) Schizophrenia as a neuronal illness. *Biological Psychiatry*, **46**, 587–8.

Frith, C.D. (2004) Schizophrenia and theory of mind. *Psychological Medicine*, **34**, 385–9.

Fujiwara, E., Piefke, M., Lux, S., Fink, G.R., Kessler, J., Kracht, L., Diebel, A., Netz, J. & Markowitsch, H.J. (2004). Brain correlates of functional retrograde amnesia in three patients. *Brain and Cognition*, **54**, 135–6.

Fujiwara, E., Brand, M., Kracht, L., Kessler, J., Diebel, A., Netz, J. & Markowitsch, H.J. (in press). Functional retrograde amnesia: A multiple case study. *Cortex*.

Gall, F.J. (1825) *Sur les fonctions du cerveau et sur celles de chacune de ses parties* [On the functions of the brain and on some of its parts]. (6 vols). Paris: Baillière.

Ganis, G., Kosslyn, S.M., Stose, S., Thompson, W.L. & Yurgelun-Todd, D.A. (2003) Neural correlates of different types of deception: An fMRI investigation. *Cerebral Cortex*, **13**, 830–6.

Gazzaniga, M.S. (2000) Cerebral specialization and interhemisperic communication. Does the corpus callosum enable the human condition? *Brain*, **123**, 1293–1326.

Gibson, K.R. (1991) Myelination and behavioral development: A comparative perspective of neoteny, altriciality and intelligence. In K.R. Gibson & A.C. Peterson (Eds), *Brain maturation and cognitive development: Comparative and cross-cultural perspectives* (pp. 29–64). New York: Aldine de Gruyter.

Giles, J. (2004) Change of mind. A brain haemorrhage turned an ex-convict into an obsessive artist. *Nature*, **430**, 14.

Glimcher, P.W. & Rustichini, A. (2004) Neuroeconomics: The consilience of brain and decision. *Science*, **306**, 447–52.

Hall, J.A.Y. & Kimura, D. (1994) Dermatoglyphic asymmetry and sexual orientation in men. *Behavioral Neuroscience*, **108**, 1203–1206.

Hickie, I., Naismith, S., Ward, P.B., Turner, K., Scott, E., Mitchell, P., Wilhelm, K. & Parker, G. (2005) Reduced hippocampal volumes and memory loss in patients with early- and late-onset depression. *British Journal of Psychiatry*, **186**, 197–202.

Highley, J.R., Walker, M.A., Esiri, M.M., Crow, T.J. & Harrison, P.J. (2002) Asymmetry of the uncinate fasciculus: A post-mortem study of normal subjects and patients with schizophrenia. *Cerebral Cortex*, **12**, 1218–24.

Huttenlocher, P.R. (1994) Synaptogenesis in human cerebral cortex. In G. Dawson & K.W. Fischer (Eds), *Human behavior and the developing brain* (pp. 137–52). New York: The Guilford Press.

Kessler, J., Markowitsch, H.J., Ghaemi, M., Rudolf, J., Weniger, G.H. & Heiss, W.-D. (1999) Degenerative prefrontal damage in a young adult: Static and dynamic imaging and neuropsychological correlates. *Neurocase*, **5**, 173–9.

Keenan, J.P., Wheeler, M., Gallup, Jr. G.G. & Pascual-Leone, A. (2000) Self-recognition and the right prefrontal cortex. *Trends in Cognitive Sciences*, **4**, 338–44.

Kiehl, K.A., Smith, A.M., Hare, R.D., Mendrek, A., Forster, B.B., Brink, J. & Liddle, P.F. (2001) Limbic abnormalities in affective processing by criminal psychopaths as revealed by functional magnetic resonance imaging. *Biological Psychiatry*, **50**, 677–684.

Kjaer, T.W., Nowak, M. & Lou, H.C. (2002) Reflective self-awareness and conscious states: PET evidence for a common midline parietofrontal core. *Neuroimage*, **17**, 1080–6.

Kleist, K. (1934) *Gehirnpathologie. Vornehmlich auf Grund der Kriegserfahrungen* [Brain pathology. Based on war experiences]. Leipzig: Barth.

Kolb, B. & Whishaw, I.Q. (1998) Brain plasticity and behavior. *Annual Reviews of Psychology*, **49**, 43–64.

Kozel, F.A. & Padgett, T.M. (2004) A replication study of the neural correlates of deception. *Behavioral Neuroscience*, **118**, 852–6.

Kroll, N., Markowitsch, H.J., Knight, R. & von Cramon, D.Y. (1997) Retrieval of old memories–the temporo-frontal hypothesis. *Brain*, **120**, 1377–99.

LeVay, S. (1993) *The sexual brain*. Cambridge, MA: MIT Press.

Lombroso, C. (1876) *L'Uomo delinquente in rapporto all'antropologia, alla giurisprudenza et alle discipline carcerarie*. Milano: Hoepli. (German transl.: *Der Verbrecher in anthropologischer, ärztlicher und juristischer Beziehung*. Bd. 1. Hamburg: Richter, 1887, Bd. 2 Hamburg: Richter, 1890).

Luders, E., Narr, K.L., Thompson, P.M., Rex, D.E., Jäncke, L., Steinmetz, H. & Toga, A.W. (2004) Gender differences in cortical complexity. *Nature Neuroscience*, **7**, 799–800.

Luna, B., Minshew, N.J., Garver, K.E., Lazar, N.A., Thulborn, K.R., Eddy, W.F. & Sweeney, J.A. (2002) Neocortical system abnormalities in autism. An fMRI study of spatial working memory. *Neurology*, **59**, 834–40.

Maddox, J. (1991) Is homosexuality hard-wired? *Nature*, **353**, 13.

Markowitsch, H.J. (1992) *Intellectual functions and the brain. An historical perspective*. Toronto: Hogrefe & Huber Publs.

Markowitsch, H.J. (1998/99) Differential contribution of the right and left amygdala to affective information processing. *Behavioural Neurology*, **11**, 233–44.

Markowitsch, H.J. (1999a) Limbic system. In R. Wilson & F. Keil (Eds), *The MIT encyclopedia of the cognitive sciences* (pp. 472–5). Cambridge, MA: MIT Press.

Markowitsch, H.J. (1999b) *Gestalt* view of the limbic system and the Papez circuit–another approach on unity and diversity of brain structures and functions. *Behavioral and Brain Sciences*, **22**, 459–60.

Markowitsch, H.J. (1999c) Functional neuroimaging correlates of functional amnesia. *Memory*, **7**, 561–83.

Markowitsch, H.J. (1999d) Neuroimaging and mechanisms of brain function in psychiatric disorders. *Current Opinion in Psychiatry*, **12**, 331–7.

Markowitsch, H.J. (2003a) Memory: Disturbances and therapy. In T. Brandt, L. Caplan, J. Dichgans, H.C. Diener & C. Kennard (Eds), *Neurological disorders; Course and treatment* (2nd ed., pp. 287–302). San Diego: Academic Press.

Markowitsch, H.J. (2003b) Autonoëtic consciousness. In A.S. David & T. Kircher (Eds), *The self in neuroscience and psychiatry* (pp. 180–96). Cambridge: Cambridge University Press.

Markowitsch, H.J., Calabrese, P., Neufeld, H., Gehlen, W. & Durwen, H.F. (1999) Retrograde amnesia for famous events and faces after left fronto-temporal brain damage. *Cortex*, **35**, 243–52.

Markowitsch, H.J., Calabrese, P., Würker, M. Durwen, H.F., Kessler, J., Babinsky, R., Brechtelsbauer, D., Heuser, L. & Gehlen, W. (1994) The amygdala's contribution to memory–A PET-study on two patients with Urbach-Wiethe disease. *NeuroReport*, **5**, 1349–52.

Markowitsch, H.J., Fink, G.R., Thöne, A.I.M., Kessler, J. & Heiss, W.-D. (1997a) Persistent psychogenic amnesia with a PET-proven organic basis. *Cognitive Neuropsychiatry*, **2**, 135–58.

Markowitsch, H.J. & Kessler, J. (2000) Massive impairment in executive functions: The case of a patient with severe degeneration of the prefrontal cortex. *Experimental Brain Research*, **133**, 94–102.

Markowitsch, H.J., Kessler, J., van der Ven, C., Weber-Luxenburger, G. & Heiss, W.-D. (1998) Psychic trauma causing grossly reduced brain metabolism and cognitive deterioration. *Neuropsychologia*, **36**, 77–82.

Markowitsch, H.J., Kessler, J., Weber-Luxenburger, G., van der Ven, C. & Heiss, W.-D. (2000a) Neuroimaging and behavioral correlates of recovery from 'mnestic block syndrome' and other cognitive deteriorations. *Neuropsychiatry, Neuropsychology, and Behavioral Neurology*, **13**, 60–6.

Markowitsch, H.J., Thiel, A., Kessler, J., von Stockhausen, H.-M. & Heiss, W.-D. (1997b) Ecphorizing semi-conscious episodic information via the right temporopolar cortex–a PET study. *Neurocase*, **3**, 445–9.

Markowitsch, H.J., Thiel, A., Reinkemeier, M., Kessler, J., Koyuncu, A. & Heiss, W.-D. (2000b) Right amygdalar and temporofrontal activation during autobiographic, but not during fictitious memory retrieval. *Behavioural Neurology*, **12**, 181–90.

Markowitsch, H.J., Vandekerckhove, M.M.P., Lanfermann, H. & Russ, M.O. (2003) Engagement of lateral and medial prefrontal areas in the ecphory of sad and happy autobiographical memories. *Cortex*, **39**, 643–65.

Matsumoto A. (Ed.) (2000) *Sexual differentiation of the brain*. Boca Raton: CRC Press.

McEwen, B.S. (1999) Stress and hippocampal plasticity. *Annual Review of Neuroscience*, **22**, 105–22.

Merkel R. (1999) Personale Identität und die Grenzen strafrechtlicher Zurechnung. *Juristen Zeitung*, **10**, 502–11.

Moniz, E. (1936) *Tentatives opèratoires dans le traitement des certaines psychoses* [Tentative surgery for the treatment of certain psychoses]. Paris: Masson.

Nagy, Z., Westerberg, H. & Klingberg, T. (2004) Maturation of white matter is associated with the development of cognitive functions during childhood. *Journal of Cognitive Neuroscience*, **16**, 1227–33.

Perner, J. & Dienes, Z. (2003) Developmental aspects of consciousness: How much theory of mind do you need to be consciously aware? *Consciousness and Cognition*, **12**, 63–82.

Piefke, M., Weiss, P.H., Zilles, K., Markowitsch, H.J. & Fink, G.R. (2003) Differential remoteness and emotional tone modulate the neural correlates of autobiographical memory. *Brain*, **126**, 850–68.

Pierri, J.N., Volk, C.L.E., Auh, S., Sampson, A. & Lewis, D.A. (2001) Decreased somal size of deep layer 3 pyramidal neurons in the prefrontal cortex of subjects with schizophrenia. *Archives of General Psychiatry*, **58**, 466–73.

Pontius, A.A. (1996) Forensic significance of the limbic psychotic trigger reaction. *Bulletin of the American Academy of Psychiatry and the Law*, **24**, 125–34.

Pontius, A.A. (2003) From volitional action to automatized homicide: Changing levels of self and consciousness during partial limbic seizures. *Aggression and Violent Behavior*, **8**, 547–61.

Pontius, A.A. & Ruttiger, K. (1976) Frontal lobe system maturational lag in juvenile delinquents shown in narratives test. *Adolescence*, **11**, 509–18.

Pontius, A.A. & Yudowitz, B.S. (1980) Frontal lobe system dysfunction in some criminal actions as shown in the narratives test. *Journal of Nervous and Mental Disease*, **168**, 111–17.

Raine, A. (2001) Is prefrontal cortex thinning specific for antisocial personality disorder? *Archives of General Psychiatry*, **58**, 402–3.

Raine, A., Lencz, T., Bihrle, S., LaCasse, L. & Colletti, P. (2000) Reduced prefrontal gray matter volume and reduced autonomic activity in antisocial personality disorder. *Archives of General Psychiatry*, **57**, 119–27.

Raine, A., Lencz, T., Taylor, K., Hellige, J.B., Bihrle, S., Lacasse, L., Lee, M., Ishikawa, S. & Colletti, P. (2003) Corpus callosum abnormalities in psychopathic antisocial individuals. *Archives of General Psychiatry*, **60**, 1134–42.

Raine, A., Meloy, J.R., Bihrle, S., Stoddard, J., LaCasse, L. & Buchsbaum, M.S. (1998a) Reduced prefrontal and increased subcortical brain functioning assessed using positron emission tomography in predatory and affective murderers. *Behavioral Sciences and the Law*, **16**, 319–32.

Raine, A., Stoddard, J., Bihrle, S. & Buchsbaum, M. (1998b) Prefrontal glucose in murderers lacking psychosocial deprivation. *Neuropsychiatry, Neuropsychology, and Behavioral Neurology*, **11**, 1–7.

Raz, N., Gunning, F.M., Head, D., Dupuis, J.H., McQuain, J.M., Briggs, S.D., Thornton, A.E., Loken, W.J. & Acker, J.D. (1997) Selective aging of human cerebral cortex observed in vivo: Differential vulnerability of the prefrontal grey matter. *Cerebral Cortex*, **7**, 268–82.

Reinhold, N., Kühnel, S., Brand, M. & Markowitsch, H.J. (2006). Functional imaging in memory and memory disturbances. *Current Medical Imaging Reviews*, **2**, 35–57.

Rossi, S., Miniassi, C., Pasqualetti, P., Babiloni, C., Rossigni, P.M. & Cappa, S.F. (2004) Age-related functional changes of prefrontal cortex in long-term memory: A repetitive transcranial magnetic stimulation study. *Journal of Neuroscience*, **24**, 7939–44.

Schore, A.N. (2002) Dysregulation of the right brain: A fundamental mechanism of traumatic attachment and the psychopathogenesis of posttraumatic stress disorder. *Australian and New Zealand Journal of Psychiatry*, **36**, 9–30.

Shallice, T. (2001) 'Theory of mind' and the prefrontal cortex. *Brain*, **124**, 247–8.

Shaw, P., Lawrence, E.J., Radbourne, C., Bramham, J., Polkey, C.E. & David, A.S. (2004) The impact of early and late damage to the human amygdala on 'theory of mind' reasoning. *Brain*, **127**, 1535–48.

Siebert, M., Markowitsch, H.J. & Bartel, P. (2003) Amygdala, affect, and cognition: Evidence from ten patients with Urbach-Wiethe disease. *Brain*, **126**, 2627–37.

Sowell, E.R., Thompson, P.M., Welcome, S.E., Henkenius, A.L., Toga, A.W. & Peterson, B.S. (2003) Cortical abnormalities in children and adolescents with attention deficit hyperactivity disorder. *Lancet*, **362**, 1699–1707.

Spence, S.A., Farrow, T.F.D., Herford, A.E., Wilkinson, I.D., Zheng, Y. & Woodruff, P.W.R. (2001) Behavioural and functional anatomical correlates of deception in humans. *NeuroReport*, **12**, 2849–53.

Spitzka, E. (1907) A study of the brains of six eminent scientists and scholars belonging to the American Anthropometric Society, together with a description of the skull of Professor E.D. Cope. *Transactions of the American Philosophical Society (New series)*, **21**, 175–308.

Stern, E. & Silbersweig, D.A. (2001) Advances in functional neuroimaging methodology for the study of brain systems underlying human neuropsychological function and dysfunction. *Journal of Clinical and Experimental Neuropsychology*, **23**, 3–18.

Stuss, D.T., Gallup, Jr G.G. & Alexander, M.P. (2001) The frontal lobes are necessary for 'theory of mind'. *Brain*, **124**, 279–86.

Swaab, D.F., Gooren, L.J.G. & Hofman, M.A. (1992) The human hypothalamus in relation to gender and sexual orientation. *Progress in Brain Research*, **93**, 205–19.

Tombaugh, T.N. (1996) *Test of memory malingering (TOMM)*. New York: Multi Health Systems.

Trupp, M.S. (2003) The mind and the brain: Neuroplasticity and the power of mental force. *Journal of Nervous and Mental Disease*, **191**, 765–6.

Tsai, A.C., Morsbach, S.K. & Loftus, E.F. (2004) In search of recovered memories. In O'Donohue & E.R. Levensky (Eds), *Handbook of forensic psychology* (pp. 555–77). Amsterdam: Elsevier.

Uddin, L.Q., Kaplan, J.T., Molnar-Szakacs, I., Zaidel, E. & Iacoboni, M. (2005) Self-face recognition activates a frontoparietal 'mirror' network in the right hemisphere: An event-related fMRI study. *Neuroimage*, **25**, 926–35.

Valenstein, E.S. (1973) *Brain control: A critical examination of brain stimulation and psychosurgery*. New York: John Wiley & Sons, Inc.

Valenstein, E.S. (Ed.) (1980) *The psychosurgery debate. Scientific, legal, and ethical perspectives*. San Francisco: W.H. Freeman.

Vandekerckhove, M.M.P., Markowitsch, H.J., Mertens, M. & Wörmann, F. (2005). Bi-hemispheric engagement in the retrieval of autobiographical episodes. *Behavioural Neurology*, **16**, 203–10.

Videbech, P. & Ravnkilde, B. (2004) Hippocampal volume and depression: a meta-analysis of MRI studies. *American Journal of Psychiatry*, **161**, 1957–66.

Vogeley, K. & Fink, G.R. (2003) Neural correlates of the first-person-perspective. *Trends in Cognitive Sciences*, **7**, 38–42.

Winter, H. & Irle, E. (2004) Hippocampal volume in adult burn patients with and without posttraumatic stress disorder. *American Journal of Psychiatry*, **161**, 2194–2200.

Witelson, S.F., Kigar, D.L. & Harvey, T. (1999) The exceptional brain of Albert Einstein. *Lancet*, **353**, 2149–53.

Woodruff, P.W.R., Wright, I.C., Shuriquie, N., Russouw, H., Rushe, T., Howard, R.J., Graves, M., Bullmore, E.T. & Murray, R.M. (1997) Structural brain abnormalities in male schizophrenics reflect fronto-temporal dissociation. *Psychological Medicine*, **27**, 1257–66.

Yang, Y., Raine, A., Lencz, T., Bihrle, S., Lacasse, L. & Colletti, P. (2005) Prefrontal white matter in pathological liars. *British Journal of Psychiatry*, **187**, 320–5.

Zaidel, E. & Iacoboni, M. (Eds) (2003) *The parallel brain. The cognitive neuroscience of the corpus callosum*. Cambridge, MA: MIT Press.

CHAPTER 7

Amnesia for Homicide as a Form of Malingering

HARALD MERCKELBACH AND SVEN Å. CHRISTIANSON

A RELATIONSHIP BREAKDOWN TURNED DEADLY

For about 18 months, Ferdinand, 27, and Jane, 22, had had a very problematic relationship. Then, during the first weeks of 2003, Jane decided to put an end to it. Ferdinand said he felt angry and depressed about their relationship breakdown. He phoned and e-mailed Jane, who stayed at her parents, but she didn't want to talk to him. On 20 February 2003, Ferdinand went to the house where Jane and her parents lived. Later, Ferdinand would say to the police that he went there to return a kitchen knife that Jane once gave him as a birthday present. Ferdinand rang at the door and Jane's father answered it. He refused to let Ferdinand in. They started an argument, during which Jane's father allegedly laughed in an arrogant manner. At least that is what Ferdinand said when he was interrogated by the police. Ferdinand got angry – angrier than he had ever been before. He stabbed the father across his neck and body. The father died from the stab wounds. Ferdinand fled the scene and after two days of wandering around he turned himself in to the police.

During the interrogations, Ferdinand told the police that he was unable to remember what had happened precisely. He said that he

Offenders' Memories of Violent Crimes.   Edited by Sven Å. Christianson.
© 2007 John Wiley & Sons, Ltd.

recalled how he went to the house and how the father had laughed. He also vaguely recalled that he had tried to beat the father. And next, there was a 'blackout'. The first normal thought occurred to him 24 hours later.

Ferdinand was charged with murder, and during the investigations, the court ordered a psychiatric evaluation. Two psychiatrists interviewed Ferdinand during four sessions. In their 31-page report to the court, they concluded that Ferdinand had reacted with an acute dissociative state to the father's arrogant laughing. More specifically, the psychiatrists opined that Ferdinand had a narcissistic personality structure and that against the background of the relationship breakdown, the father's laughing had triggered an overwhelming rage in him. Also, the experts stressed that as a child, Ferdinand had been physically abused by his father. This is what Ferdinand told the psychiatrists about his youth: 'During one of the abuse incidents, I said to my father that he should not beat my mother. My father looked at me and laughed'. The psychiatrists advised the court to consider that Ferdinand had completely lost control over his behaviour and that this resulted in the stabbing. During the court proceedings, the psychiatrists took the witness stand and said: 'In our report, we conclude that the defendant suffered from acute dissociation and lack of control during the incident. We have based our conclusions on the facts as related by the defendant, which show that he suffered from amnesia for the crime'. Furthermore, the experts informed the court about the following rule: 'the more a defendant has specific memories about an incident, the more this defendant was fully aware of what happened during the incident, and the less likely it is that he suffered from lack of control'. For reasons to be explained below, the court found the conclusions of the psychiatric experts not fully convincing. However, citing the psychiatrists' expert testimony about Ferdinand's rage and his narcissistic personality, the court ruled that this was a case of reduced criminal liability. Thus, Ferdinand was convicted of manslaughter rather than murder and sentenced to eight years in prison.

CRIME-RELATED AMNESIA IN A HISTORICAL PERSPECTIVE

The story of Ferdinand is a real[1] and fairly prototypical case of what has been termed crime-related amnesia (Christianson & Merckelbach, 2004). Crime-related amnesia refers to a claim raised by defendants

---

[1] More specifically, the case was tried by the superior court of 's Hertogenbosch. The case number is LJN: AR 4567.

or convicted perpetrators that they cannot remember essential details of the crime they have committed or even of their entire life including the crime. The phenomenon is not new. For example, the German neurologist Liepmann (2002, p. 635) remarked in his 1910 paper on a Korsakow case of amnesia: 'This year, I have had the opportunity to observe no fewer than five defendants who claim to have lost their memory of many years of their lives. Understandably, these statements are met with a certain degree of mistrust'.

Even before the turn of the century, there had been, especially in France, high-publicity cases in which murderers claimed to be amnestic for their crimes. A fine example is the famous l'affaire Valroff (1893), in which a butler murdered his Lordship. Interestingly, the details of such cases reflected the preoccupations of contemporary French psychiatry. Thus, in the Valroff case, the defendant said that he was somnambulistic and under the influence of a hypnotic trance when he committed his murder (Ellenberger, 1970). Much the same is true for our era, although in our times, it is Hollywood that shapes the notions laypeople have about amnesia. In an impressive article, Baxendale (2004) catalogued the various movies in which amnesia appears: from 'Les Dimanches de Ville d'Avray' (1962), in which a fighter pilot developed amnesia after having killed a child, to 'The Eternal Sunshine of the Spotless Mind' (2004), in which the leading character tries to erase his memories of a failed relationship by undergoing a procedure that roughly resembles transcranial magnetic stimulation. To be sure, the influence of cinematographic pathology on how psychiatric symptoms are expressed has been amply documented. Cases in point are involuntary visual images known as flashbacks, which are considered to be a key symptom of post-traumatic stress disorder (PTSD). Jones, Hodgins Vermaas, McCartney, Beech and colleagues (2003) showed, on the basis of archival data, that flashbacks were extremely rare in cohorts of stressed soldiers up to World War II. It was only in the more recent cohorts that the symptom began to surface. The authors link this to 'the mass production of affordable television sets in the 1950s and 1960s and the subsequent introduction of video recorders' (Jones et al., 2003, p. 162). Apparently, traumatised soldiers use the video playback metaphor to describe their intrusive recollections. Meanwhile, static and technical metaphors to describe memory phenomena are not limited to traumatised soldiers. Both psychology undergraduates and licensed psychotherapists tend to think that metaphors such as the computer or the video-apparatus provide appropriate descriptions of memory (Merckelbach & Wessel, 1998). When taken to its logical conclusion, this type of metaphor not only allows for exact photocopies of reality (e.g., flashbacks), but also

for complete memory erasion (e.g., amnesia) due to technical failures (e.g., a psychological blow) or calculated manipulation (e.g.,
repression).

As Baxendale (2004) showed, the Hollywood portrayal of amnesia
is often highly misleading. Here, the video erase metaphor leads
scriptwriters to assume that certain events have the potential to erase
autobiographical memories in a highly precise way with sharp limits
for beginning and end of the amnesia, for example, from 11 p.m. to 12
a.m. However, this type of movie amnesia bears little resemblance to
amnesia as it is seen in the clinic. To the forensic expert, amnesia at
the movies is a blessing in disguise: it seduces criminals who want to
feign amnesia to come up with a description of their memory problems
that is not very plausible (see also Chapter 9 by Jelicic & Merckelbach
in this volume).

WHY FEIGN AMNESIA?

Like Liepmann (2002), some clinicians are very skeptical about the
possibility for criminals to develop a genuine amnesia for their crime.
For example, forensic psychologist Centor (1982, p. 240) wrote: 'My own
experience, during a period of over 11 years in a forensic unit, failed
to confirm even one case of psychogenic amnesia in the absence of a
psychotic episode, brain damage, or acute brain syndrome'. Likewise,
Ornish (2001, p. 27) wrote about dissociative amnesia that 'it is reminiscent of the defense suggested in the Steve Martin joke: Just tell the
judge that you forgot it was against the law to rob a bank. Self-serving
amnesia purportedly due to dissociation with a sharply defined onset
and termination, especially in the absence of any major psychiatric
disorder or alcohol intoxication, should be highly suspect'. And writing
about sexual offenders, Marshall, Serran, Marshall and Fernandez
(2005, p. 32) said: 'our clinical interactions with these amnesic sexual
offenders suggested to us that most (if not all) of them had deliberately
adopted this stance rather than having a genuine case of amnesia'.

So what about the Ferdinand case? Unfortunately, the psychiatrists
did not read all the depositions that the police obtained from various
witnesses. Had they done so, they would have seen that there was one
witness who had provided critical collateral information about Ferdinand. This witness was a friend of Ferdinand's. The friend told the
police that he had a meeting with Ferdinand the day after Jane's father
was stabbed to death. The friend stated that Ferdinand had told him
the following about the tragic incident: 'Somehow, Jane's father saw
the knife. Ferdinand said that the father's facial expression became

fearful. The father retreated and hid behind his daughter. Ferdinand told that he followed him with the intention to teach him a lesson, to show that there was nothing to laugh about. Ferdinand described that he had then stabbed the father. I asked him how many times he had stabbed. Ferdinand answered that he had stabbed several times'. Obviously, this is not an eyewitness describing his conversation with an amnestic criminal. There can, in other words, be little doubt that Ferdinand feigned his amnesia.[2]

But why should defendants like Ferdinand try to feign amnesia for their crimes in the first place? There are three related motives. To begin with, claiming amnesia allows you to exploit your right to remain silent in an elegant way. A defendant would make an uncooperative impression if he were to say to his police interrogators: 'I'm not talking to you guys. I've got the right to remain silent and I'm going to use that right'. Saying, instead, that you would like to help the police, but that you can't remember is a smarter solution. In Ornish's (2001, p. 27) words, when feigning amnesia 'the defendant can testify in his own defence while evading answering cross-examination questions about his criminal behavior because of his purported inability to remember due to amnesia while dissociated'.

Second, claiming amnesia elicits what might be termed a psychiatric expert cascade. Thus, if a defendant says he can't remember committing a crime, chances are fairly high that the police, prosecutor or judge will order a psychiatric evaluation of the defendant. In an unpublished study, we gave a case vignette similar to Ferdinand's to 108 law students and lawyers. The large majority of the respondents (i.e., 74%) felt that a court would be well-advised to have the amnestic defendant examined by a psychiatrist (Merckelbach, Cima & Nijman, 2002). The point is that judicial decision-makers lack expert knowledge about human memory and at the same time, they are concerned that they might overlook an important disease from which the defendant is suffering. And while it is true that 'no court has found a defendant incompetent to stand trial solely because of amnesia' (Parwatikar, Holcomb & Menninger, 1985, p. 202), it is also the case that psychiatric experts have a pathology bias. The tendency of such experts to conclude that normal individuals are brain damaged or abnormal has been well-documented. Wedding and Faust (1989, p. 241) summarise the relevant literature as follows: 'Across a series of studies examining the accuracy of clinicians, normal individuals have been misdiagnosed as brain

---

[2] One is reminded of the words of Leo Tolstoy (1869) who, in his 'Kreuzer Sonata', wrote this about defendants like Ferdinand: 'When people say they don't remember what they do in a fit a fury, it is rubbish, falsehood'. See also Wagenaar and Crombag (2005).

damaged in about one out of every three cases'. In the case of Ferdinand, it eventually became clear that his amnesia was feigned, but at that point, psychiatrists had already examined him and concluded that he suffered from a narcissistic personality disorder, which the court considered as a mitigating factor. A study by Pyszora, Barker and Kopelman (2003) further underlines this point. In their sample of 207 criminals who had been sentenced to life imprisonment, 59 (29 %) individuals claimed or had claimed to be amnestic for their crime. Those with amnesia claims more often had a psychiatric report prepared pre-trial and more often had undergone CT or MRI examination (see below) than those without amnesia claims. On a related note, those with amnesia claims more often used the defence of diminished responsibility or lack of intent during trial than did those without amnesia claims, who more often relied on an alibi defense.

Third, even when defendants are eventually convicted, claiming amnesia confers an advantage: it allows them to avoid painful memories of the crime and it gives them an excuse not to speak about their crimes with social workers or therapists (Marshall et al., 2005). Indeed, from this perspective, amnesia claims are a risk factor for recidivism. Christianson and Merckelbach (2004) briefly address several cases in which amnesia claims were associated with re-offending. Data collected by Cima, Nijman, Merckelbach, Kremer and Hollnack (2004, p. 220) showed that, in their sample of 308 forensic male patients, claims of amnesia were typical among older patients with a long criminal career. This led the authors to conclude that 'such claims are the product of a learning process. Thus, it may well be that those who are familiar with the penal system have experienced the advantage of claiming amnesia' (Cima et al., 2004, p. 220).

RED-OUTS AND DISSOCIATIVE AMNESIA

That those who claim amnesia for their crime feign a memory disorder is one possible interpretation of the phenomenon. Researchers differ in the extent to which they believe that this interpretation may account for all or a large majority of crime-related amnesia cases. For example, Pyszora and co-workers (2003) found that only a small minority (7 %) of prisoners claiming amnesia denied their offence. In fact, denial was significantly less likely in these prisoners than in control prisoners (7 % versus 37 %, respectively). The authors wrote: 'We would argue that this provides evidence against the commonly held assumption by police, the legal profession, prison staff, and clinicians that a claim of amnesia is used as an easy way of denying the offence or responsibility of it' (Pyszora et al., 2003, p. 487). A similar line of reasoning can be found in Kopelman (1995, p. 435), who opines that many crime-related amnesias are authentic because in such cases, it is often the defendant himself who reports the crime to the police. As Kopelman (1995, p. 435) states: 'This makes an account of amnesia as simulation to avoid punishment seem less plausible'. However, the argument is not as compelling as it may seem at first sight. Consider the case of Ferdinand: there was an abundance of technical and eyewitness evidence pointing to him as the murderer. For him, it would have made no sense to deny that he killed the father of his ex-girlfriend. In his situation, it was far better to tell the dissociative amnesia story, so as to set into motion the psychiatric expert cascade. There is no empirical evidence showing that claims of crime-related amnesia are typical for cases such as Ferdinand's, i.e., cases in which the technical evidence against the defendant is overwhelming. Yet, there are indirect indications from Pyszora et al.'s (2003) study, in which alibi evidence was found to be significantly less likely in amnesia than in control cases.

A second interpretation of crime-related amnesia is that it is a genuine memory deficit resulting from the stress and extreme emotions that perpetrators experience when they commit a crime (e.g., Arboleda-Florez, 2002). The idea here is that an intense provocation (i.e., a 'psychological blow') caused the defendant to act like an automaton and that he committed his crime in this automatic (i.e., unconscious and/or uncontrollable) state. Closely related to this interpretation is the notion that perpetrators of violent crimes may be traumatised by their own actions and that, through repression or related mechanisms (e.g., dissociation), they later find it difficult to retrieve memories of the crime. Consider Ferdinand's case. If there had not been the eyewitness testimony of his friend implying that Ferdinand remembered the details of the crime, we – as the psychiatrists did in this case – would have focused on Ferdinand's self-report about the extreme rage that he felt when his father provoked him by laughing arrogantly. Ferdinand said that he had never felt such an intense rage before, and this description is reminiscent of what Swihart, Yuille and Porter (1999) have dubbed 'red-outs', i.e., episodes of explosive aggression during which the individual is said to lose control and for which he/she later claims to be amnestic. In this context, authors commonly use the terms functional or dissociative amnesia to stress that the amnesia claim is authentic and has a psychological causation (e.g., Porter, Birt, Yuille & Hervé, 2001). Again, the idea behind this term is long-standing in forensic psychiatry. For example, in what seems to be the first systematic empirical study on amnesia and crime, Hopwood and Snell (1933) examined the cases of 100 prisoners who had claimed amnesia during their trials. The authors argued that amnesia claims were typically raised in highly emotional murder cases and that the large majority of them (78%) were bona fide, in the sense that they were the result of repression or dissociation. A similar view is echoed in a study by Grierson (1936, p. 369), who stated about repression: 'this mental mechanism is most frequently met with in cases of serious crime. The extent of the amnesia from repression varies; it may cover the crime only, but more frequently it extends to periods before and since that experience'.

There are, however, more recent theoretical assumptions that bear relevance to dissociative amnesia in offenders and the way in which extreme emotions may affect memory encoding. Horowitz (1978) argued that unassimilated traumatic experiences are stored in a special kind of 'active memory', which has an intrinsic tendency to repeat the representation of contents. Only when the individual develops a new mental 'schema' for understanding what has happened is the trauma resolved. Other researchers claim that traumatic memories lack verbal narrative and context and that they are encoded in the form of vivid sensations and images. For example, some neuroimaging studies of trauma patients have suggested that Broca's area, responsible for translating personal experiences into communicable language, is inactivated (Rauch, van der Kolk, Fisler, Alpert, Orr, Savage, Fischman, Jenike & Pitman, 1996; see also Chapter 6 in this volume). Furthermore, van der Kolk (1988) argued that in states of high sympathetic nervous system arousal, the linguistic encoding of memory is inactivated and the central nervous system reverts to the sensory and iconic forms of memory that predominate in early life. Thus, when imagery and bodily sensations become dominant and in the absence of verbal narrative, traumatic memories resemble the memories of young children. In this context, Payne, Nadel, Britton and Jacobs (2004) argued that traumatic stress impairs the function of the hippocampus and the formation of memories. This causes stressful events to be encoded in a 'fragmented' manner. 'At the same time, emotion works (via the amygdala) to promote memory for the gist of an event, leading to well-encoded memories for the thematic content of an emotion event. . . ' (Payne et al., 2004, p. 44). Along similar lines, Buchanan and Adolphs (2004) emphasised the role of the amygdala in the enhancement of memory for emotional events, during the period of memory consolidation as well as during retrieval of emotional memories.

There are still other perspectives that reiterate the point that crime-related amnesia might be a genuine condition resulting from an avoidant style of coping with the extreme emotions involved in committing a crime. For example, in his scholarly review, Moskowitz (2004,

p. 35) remarks that 'although some amnesia claims are undoubtedly simulated, it appears unlikely that the majority are'. Evidence for this position comes from two sources. To begin with, studies suggest that prevalence rates of post-traumatic stress disorder (PTSD) symptoms in homicide perpetrators are probably higher than has previously been thought (e.g., Pollock, 1999). The large majority of homicide perpetrators suffering from PTSD (95%) have been involved in reactive (i.e., provoked and unpremeditated aggression) rather than instrumental (i.e., goal-directed) violence and the condition is rare, if not absent in perpetrators who have psychopathic traits and who have been involved in instrumental violence (Pollock, 1999).[3] In keeping with this, Christianson and von Vogelsang (2003) found, in their study on homicide cases, that crime-related amnesia claims were more typical for reactive homicide cases (56%) than for instrumental homicide cases (30%). Another line of research providing tentative evidence for the concept of dissociative amnesia concerns studies examining the prevalence of dissociative symptoms in criminal and forensic samples. There is growing evidence that these samples exhibit heightened levels of dissociative symptoms (e.g., derealisation experiences; see review by Moskowitz, 2004). For example, Spitzer, Liss, Dudeck, Orlob and co-workers (2003) found, in their group of 57 forensic patients incarcerated for violent crimes, sexual crimes, or arson, that 25% had clinically raised scores on the Dissociative Experiences Scale (Bernstein & Putnam, 1986; DES). In a similar vein, Cima, Merckelbach, Klein, Schellbach-Matties and Kremer (2001) noted extremely high DES scores in their sample of 30 forensic patients. However, Cima and co-workers also documented that these heightened DES scores were related to abnormal frontal functioning rather than traumatic experiences. This is consistent with a study by McLeod, Byrne and Aitken (2004), who found that male prisoners' raised levels of dissociative symptoms were not related to the violence of their crimes.

While from a clinical stance red-outs or functional/dissociative amnesia does have some intuitive appeal, these concepts seem to fly in the face of well-established memory principles. For the perpetrator,

---

[3] We address the issue of PTSD in criminal populations because one symptom of PTSD is thought to be the inability to remember important aspects of the trauma. On the other hand, Collins and Bailey (1990) demonstrated in their study that prison inmates suffering from PTSD report symptoms like nightmares, hypervigilance and insomnia, but not amnesia. Clearly, the precise connection between PTSD and claims of crime-related amnesia deserves further study. Note, however, that so far, studies have been unable to document a connection between dissociative or PTSD symptoms and claims of complete amnesia for crimes (McLeod et al., 2004; Rivard, Dietz, Martell & Widawski, 2002).

a violent crime is (1) an act, (2) that is carried out by the perpetrator himself, and (3) that, at least in cases of reactive violence,
the perpetrator feels remorseful about later. Against this background,
crime-related amnesia is an unlikely outcome, given that an extensive body of memory literature shows that (1) people remember acts
better than other types of information (e.g., words; action-superiority
effect; Engelkamp & Zimmer, 1994), (2) people remember their own
acts far better than acts they only have witnessed (self-reference effect;
Symons & Johnson, 1997), and (3) people have recurrent thoughts
about memories they try to suppress because they feel ashamed about
them (white-bear effect; Wegner, Schneider, Carter & White, 1987).[4]

Another finding that is difficult to reconcile with the idea of dissociative amnesia is that this phenomenon appears to be rare in people who
have been the victims of evidently traumatising events (e.g., concentration camps; Merckelbach, Dekkers, Wessel & Roefs, 2003a, 2003b;
Yehuda, Elkin, Binder-Brynes, Kahana, Southwick, Schmeidler &
Giller, 1996). On a related note, eyewitnesses to extreme violence only
rarely report that they are amnesic for the events they have witnessed
(Porter et al., 2001). These considerations have led various authors
to be critical about the assumption that dissociative amnesia is a
prevalent phenomenon among traumatised individuals. In fact, some
(e.g., McNally, 2003, p. 157) have gone so far as to conclude that 'the
notion that the mind protects itself by repressing or dissociating memories of trauma rendering them inaccessible to awareness, is a piece of
psychiatric folklore devoid of convincing empirical support'.

ORGANIC AMNESIA

A third interpretation of claims of crime-related amnesia is that they
are genuine and originate from structural or transient brain damage.
Here, the amnesia is the acute manifestation of brain dysfunction and,
therefore, it is known as organic amnesia. An example would be the
Canadian case of *Bleta v the Queen* (1964), in which a victim first hit the
perpetrator on his head, who as a result sustained concussive injury.
During the immediate post-injury phase, the perpetrator killed the

---

[4] Some authors have argued that even from a psychodynamic point of view, func-
tional/dissociative amnesia is an improbable outcome. For example, Arboleda-Florez
(2002, p. 573) concludes: 'Psychoanalytic unconscious acts, however, take place when
the individual is fully conscious and is capable of registering and retaining the memory
for the event: he knows the what, but fails to grasp the why. For legal purposes,
psychoanalytic unconscious acts do not qualify as automatisms'.

victim. Evidence shows that in cases such as these, there is a serious probability that perpetrators acted in a state of dazed consciousness and afterwards suffer from an authentic amnesia for their violent behaviour (McCrory, 2001). It should be added, though, that in acute concussion cases, dazed consciousness and agitated behaviour resolves within 20–30 minutes post-injury. Thus, logically, the amnesia can only pertain to this relatively short time frame.[5]

When a defendant performs criminal actions without conscious knowledge, he or she is said to be in state of automatism. The notion of automatism dates back to the 19th century, when British neurologist Huglings Jackson used it to describe the bizarre behaviour of patients with temporal lobe epilepsy (Kalant, 1996). In Anglo-Saxon law systems, it is common to make a distinction between two types of automatisms. One type is sane automatism, in which an external force (e.g., a severe blow to the head; injection with insulin) leads to confusion and lack of full behavioural control. The other type is insane automatism, in which an internal factor (e.g., cerebral tumor, an epileptic seizure) has these consequences (e.g., Arboleda-Florez, 2002). As Fenwick (1993) has pointed out, the distinction between sane and insane automatisms does not always make medical sense. For example, both legal and medical authors strongly differ as to whether sleepwalking violence is a form of sane or insane automatism (see also Cartwright, 2004). From a legal point of view, the distinction does matter, because a perpetrator found not guilty due to sane automatism walks free from court, whereas a verdict of not guilty due to insane automatism often results in mandatory referral to a secure hospital. However, medical and legal scholars do seem to agree that a crime committed during a state of automatism – e.g., during sleepwalking, an epileptic seizure, hypoglycemia, concussion – is difficult to remember later on.[6] That is, whenever structural or transient brain dysfunctions create a condition of automatism, organic amnesia will ensue.

---

[5] The issue of acute post-injury states during which an illegal act is performed for which the defendant later claims amnesia figures in a number of cases of Australian footballers who had to appear before disciplinary tribunals (McCrory, 2001). One celebrated case (2004) is that of St. Kilda tagger Steven Baker, who pleaded guilty to striking the Tigers' Kane Johnson in an off-the-ball incident. While Baker pleaded guilty, he told the tribunal he had no memory of the incident even though he said he could remember the lead-up to the incident. Video footage of the incident showed Baker run several metres to strike Johnson on the eye, while also revealing that Johnson had pushed Baker to the ground from behind just moments before the strike occurred.

[6] Many authors address the issue of alcohol or drug intoxication in the context of automatisms. Here, we do not deal with this complex legal issue. Suffice it to say that a crime-related amnesia claim on the basis of an alcohol blackout is not as plausible as it may seem. See Chapter 8 this volume for a discussion of alcohol blackouts.

The difficulties associated with an alleged defense of automatism and a defendant's claim of amnesia are exemplified in the following case. NN, a 40-year-old man, was at a nightclub in Malmö, Sweden, together with a female friend. They had both consumed some alcoholic beverages during the evening, and NN was tipsy. Another man and his friend had approached NN a few times during the course of the evening. They were provocative, and the third time they came to NN's table they attacked him. He received several blows to the head and tried to defend himself, but was struck on the forehead with an object and collapsed to the floor. NN was under threats from a criminal gang and feared for his life. Because of these threats, he was carrying a loaded pistol. After being struck to the ground, he immediately got up and pulled his gun. The man who had struck him fled, and NN followed him, shooting after him at every opportunity until the weapon was empty. The man died as a result of his bullet wounds (in the turmoil, NN also shot and seriously injured one of his own friends), and NN, who was picked up by the police minutes after the shooting, was charged with murder. He did not try to escape and he was completely unaware of what had happened or what he had done. His memory function improved when he was at the police station, but at that time, he had no real recollection of what happened immediately before, during and after the shooting. Later, NN remembered brief fragments from outside the nightclub and when he was arrested.

The medical history of NN showed that he had suffered head trauma at several times in his life, with resultant effects on memory and symptoms of epilepsy. Thus, there were reasons to suspect that the amnesia and behaviour displayed by NN in connection with the criminal event may have a neuropsychiatric basis. Due to with a single-vehicle accident in 1987, NN became disoriented and amnesic (memory loss). There were suspicions of intracranial bleeding/skull injury and epilepsy, but adequate assessment and treatment did not occur because NN left the hospital. Ten years later, in 1997, NN sought medical care for muscle spasms and in 1999, an epileptic seizure was triggered in connection with playing a home-video game; this resulted in memory loss. An EEG test was conducted in 2001, after NN's repeated attempts to receive help with memory disturbances and headaches. Note that repeated episodes of memory loss or 'blackouts' are one of the primary clinical symptoms of brain injury. The neuropsychological assessment conducted on NN also showed certain symptoms of neuropsychological dysfunction, thus indicating possible problems associated with brain injury. Thus, it is fully conceivable that a blow to the head or extreme stress could have triggered epileptogenic activity in NN, at the same time as he performed appropriate motoric actions, but in the absence of conscious control over these actions, such that the attack on him was followed by marked anterograde amnesia. In clinical contexts, this type of epileptic attack has been established in patients using deep electrodes tapping the amygdala and hippocampus and has also been observed in association with fits of rage and violence. Additional factors that may have aggravated effects on NN's memory are that he, besides receiving a blow to the head and possibly experiencing epileptic activity, was also under the influence of alcohol, benzodiazepines and anabolic steroids. These substances in combination have significant deleterious effects on memorial ability. Thus, two crucial questions arise: is the case of NN a reliable example of organic amnesia and did the defendant NN have the mental state required for a criminal conviction?

Depending on the precise type of underlying brain dysfunction, the various features – e.g., length and intensity – of organic amnesia vary, but in general, they have been well-described in the literature. For example, retrograde amnesia (i.e., memory loss pertaining to the period before the head trauma) as a result of severe head trauma will gradually resolve, thereby following a pattern that is known as Ribot's law (Haber & Haber, 1998), after the 19th century French memory expert Theodule Ribot. According to this law, older memories return sooner in the weeks following the head trauma than do more recent memories, and eventually the amnesia will largely disappear and be limited to the traumatic event itself and the few seconds that preceded it. A defendant who claims severe retrograde amnesia as a result of brain trauma, but whose memory recovery does not follow Ribot's law, should be approached with respectful skepticism (Christianson & Merckelbach, 2004). As another example, in less severe cases of brain injury, there might be a post-traumatic amnesia pertaining to the period immediately after the brain trauma. However, when a defendant who sustained a mild concussion claims a post-traumatic amnesia extending over several hours, the possibility of malingering should be seriously considered (McCrory, 2001). Or consider an automatic defence on the basis of hypoglycemia: the mere fact that a defendant suffers from diabetes is insufficient to back up such a defence, as a recent meta-analysis showed that this condition is associated with only mild cognitive deficits, among which memory problems are not the most prominent (Brands, Biessels, de Haan, Kappelle & Kessels, 2005). Admittedly, in rare instances, complete anterograde amnesia might be associated with acute hypoglycemia (Strachan, Deary, Ewing & Frier, 2000), but in such cases coma is likely to occur, which is not the best condition for committing a crime.[7]

Organic amnesia requires that the defendant be currently suffering or has been suffering from a brain dysfunction. Even when this can be shown to be the case, the causal relationships between brain dysfunction, the criminal act and subsequent amnesia need not be obvious. A fine illustration is provided by the case of *R. v Chhoa* (1998), in which the defendant was accused of having been involved in a fatal automobile accident. Chhoa claimed to be amnestic for his role in the accident and this claim was in itself plausible. However, it was unclear whether his amnesia was the result of a head injury that he had sustained during a fight that took place immediately before the accident or whether it was the result of the automobile accident per se. In the first case, there would have been room for an interpretation by which concussion led to an automatic state, which in turn led to reckless driving. In the latter case, the most plausible interpretation would be that the accused was fully functional and therefore responsible when his car crashed into a bridge abutment, leading to the death of two of his friends (Arboleda-Florez, 2002).

In the case of NN, the degree and character of his memory loss suggest organic amnesia. NN displayed limited retrograde amnesia, but pronounced anterograde amnesia, which can be observed in cases of cranial trauma and epileptic attacks. The fact that NN showed islands/fragments of memory, some – though limited – recovery of detailed information and that he had a history of memory loss suggests that his amnesia was genuine. Moreover, given that NN, in the aftermath of the violence perpetrated by him, did not try to hide his crime or flee from the scene of the crime and was not conscious of his violent actions, but instead directed attention to his own injuries, is in accordance with a state of disorientation following an epileptic seizure. Accordingly, the defence argued for a state of insane (epileptic) automatism, and that his amnesia was relevant in showing that the defendant did not know what he was doing as a result of neurological disease. In court, the second author supported the possibility that NN had a genuine amnesia and committed his crime in a state of automatism caused by a subclinical seizure (a possibility that had been ignored in the psychiatric evaluation of NN). The appellate court, however, ruled that NN was conscious of his actions, that he acted

---

[7] An illustrative case is *R. v Quick* (1973), in which the defendant, a diabetic, visited his ex-girlfriend's new boyfriend. While there, he felt unwell. He took a mixture of sugar and water, but ate nothing. Ten minutes later the defendant struck the victim on the head with an iron bar. The defendant later claimed to have been unable to control his actions because he had been hypoglycemic. Quick also claimed amnesia for the incident. See Arboleda-Florez (2002) for more recent cases.

highly rationally and on the basis of definite goals, e.g., '... in that he carried a loaded pistol, followed and shot his antagonist... in that almost all shots fired hit the antagonist'. NN was convicted of murder and sentenced to 10 years in prison.

Turning back to the case of Ferdinand, with which we began this chapter, there was no indication that he suffered from a concussion, epileptic seizure, hypoglycemia or sleepwalking episode when he stabbed his ex-girlfriend's father. Nor had he consumed alcohol or drugs. Ferdinand himself used a video metaphor to describe how he reacted to what he considered to be the starting point of his amnesia, viz. the father's arrogant laughing: 'it was as if someone pushed the fader button; from that moment on, I heard nothing'.

EVALUATING AND TESTING

In the case of Ferdinand, the expert psychiatrists were quick to assume that Ferdinand's amnesia was a dissociative reaction to a psychological blow, the blow being the arrogant laughing of the father. Curiously enough, the experts did not ask themselves whether it was reasonable to assume that the arrogant laughing could qualify as a psychological blow to someone like Ferdinand. Ferdinand was very well trained in Thai fighting and, as a matter of fact, he had won the Dutch Thai boxing champions league for three consecutive years. It is difficult to see how an arrogant laugh could produce a severe psychological blow to someone with this background. One is reminded of Rosen's (2004) critical discussion of how, in clinical practice, concepts like psychological trauma and stress have been expanded and trivialised so as to accommodate relatively minor troubles. In a thoughtful review, McSherry (2004) summarises data showing that the provocation defence is generally raised by men who kill others in the context of a relationship breakdown. This author suggests that the doctrine of provocation is predominantly used to excuse male anger and violence against women and their families. What all this implies is that in Ferdinand's case – as in many Dutch court cases in which amnesia claims surface – the expert psychiatrists were not sensitive to other interpretations of his amnesia claim. This is also shown by their expert testimony before court, which communicated the message that amnesia points to automatism during the crime. Many authors have explained why this proposition is logically flawed: 'whereas there is no automatism without amnesia, not every case of amnesia amounts to automatism' (Arbodela-Florez, 2002, p. 573; see also Kalant, 1996; Yeo, 2002).[8]

That the expert psychiatrists in the case of Ferdinand ignored the possibility that his amnesia claim might originate from other factors than a dissociative reaction (e.g., malingering) is further evinced by the lack of thorough neuropsychological testing in this case. As part of the psychiatric evaluation, Ferdinand was given an intelligence test and a couple of simple self-report scales, but there was no formal testing of his tendency to produce bizarre or unlikely symptoms. Over the past ten years or so, neuropsychology has made great progress in developing valid tests to detect malingering and insufficient effort (see for a review, Larrabee, 2005; see also Chapter 9 by Jelicic & Merckelbach in this volume). Therefore, we agree with Denney and Wynkoop (2000, pp. 810, 811), who in their review concluded that 'the need to assess malingering in all forensic evaluations cannot be overstated . . . ' and 'failure to address malingering in forensic neuropsychological evaluations could reflect an inadequate, even incompetent evaluation'.

The failure to address the issue of malingering in Ferdinand's case might reflect the expert psychiatrists' assumption that the base rate of malingering is zero. This assumption was, and to some extent still is, an opinion that is fashionable in clinical quarters (e.g., Gerson, 2002). However, the available statistics indicate that, in the criminal arena, malingering of cognitive deficits such as amnesia is anything but rare. Thus, for example, in their survey of 131 neuropsychological experts, Mittenberg, Patton, Canyock and Condit (2002) found that their respondents estimated the base rate of malingering in criminal cases referred to them to be in the range of 11–20 %. Likewise, Frederick and Denney (1998) estimated the base rate of malingering – including feigned amnesia – in a sample of 893 defendants referred for pre-trial evaluation to be in the order of 12 %. Additionally, there are good reasons to believe that even trained forensic experts miss 50 % of malingerers when they exclusively rely on patients' self-reports and have no access to the outcomes of appropriate psychological tests (Rosen & Phillips, 2004; Rubenzer, 2004).

---

[8] To complicate matters even further, some authors (Yeo, 2002) have argued that an impaired consciousness and/or a memory deficit is not essential for a state of automatism to exist. By this view, lack of control rather than lack of consciousness is the defining feature of automatism. The problem with this approach, however, is that it assumes that normal human beings are permanently in full control of their behaviour. As McSherry (2004) points out, the voluntary–involuntary dichotomy common in the legal context is foreign to psychological thinking. After all, most psychologists agree that 'human behavior is the result of rule-following by our automatic brains . . . A key feature of these rules is that they operate, for the most part, outside of our conscious awareness. That is to say, we follow the rules without really thinking about it, or more to the point, without choosing to' (Waldbauer & Gazzaniga, 2001, p. 363).

Admittedly, the prevalence rates cited above pertain to malingering in general. We do not know what the true prevalence of feigned amnesia in the criminal arena is and we will never know, simply because it is impossible to establish with sufficient accuracy the ground truth. As Faust (1995, p. 255) said: 'Doctor each time you've been fooled, you don't know it, do you?'. But what we do know from several experimental simulation studies is that when normal participants are instructed to play the role of a murderer who is confronted with abundant evidence during interrogation, the most frequently chosen strategy of these participants is to claim amnesia for the criminal act and to attribute it to an internal force (i.e., an alternate personality) that they cannot control (Spanos, Weekes & Bertrand, 1986; Rabinowitz, 1989). We also know that offenders are highly motivated to forget their offences. When convicted homicide and sexual offenders serving their sentences in Swedish prisons were asked whether they had ever felt that they truly wanted to forget the crime event, 53 % of the homicide offenders and 35 % of the sexual offenders answered in the affirmative (Christianson, Holmberg, Bylin & Engelberg, 2006). When asked about their estimation of how often offenders generally deliberately feign loss of memory for the crime in order to avoid conviction, only 2 % of the homicide offenders thought that perpetrators of this type of crime never feign memory loss to some degree (see also next section).

PSYCHOPATHY

Clearly, people differ in their ability to feign a disorder. Porter and co-workers (2001) argued that false claims of amnesia might be especially prominent in the group of psychopathic perpetrators. After all, malingering amnesia is a form of deception and deception is a hallmark feature of psychopathy.[9] Furthermore, due to their emotional deficiency, psychopaths are immune to intensive emotional stress and so genuine dissociative amnesia is an unlikely outcome in psychopathic offenders.

In an unpublished study, a sample of 37 male prison inmates were asked what they thought about the plausibility of crime-related

---

[9] It must be acknowledged, though, that empirical support for the psychopathy-malingering connection is mixed. For example, relying on a small sample of prison inmates, Poythress, Edens and Watkins (2001) found no significant correlation between a psychopathy scale and scores on instruments measuring the tendency to exaggerate or fabricate symptoms. On the other hand, there is evidence that people with psychopathic personality features exhibit an increased willingness to engage in feigning and deception across a broad range of forensic contexts (Edens, Buffington & Tomicic, 2000).

amnesia claims and whether they themselves had amnesia for their crimes.[10] The inmates were also asked to fill out the Revised Gudjonsson Blame Attribution Inventory (Gudjonsson, 1984), a measure that explores to what extent individuals feel remorseful about their crime and whether they have a tendency to attribute it to external or internal factors. The large majority (70%) of the inmates had committed violent or sexual crimes. Interestingly, while 23 out of 37 (62%) inmates knew someone who claimed amnesia for his crime, only seven inmates (19%) believed that these claims were bona fide. On the other hand, 10 inmates (27%) said that they themselves had genuine amnesia for the crime for which they had been sentenced to jail. This is an interesting asymmetry: inmates are more skeptical towards others raising amnesia claims than they appear to be when they themselves raise such claims. Of course, this could be the result of a lack of self-knowledge, but another possibility is that the asymmetry reflects psychopathic individuals' familiarity with their own and others' deceptive strategies. Interestingly, a robust correlation was found ($r = -0.52$) between the tendency to claim amnesia and a lack of remorse about the crime. All in all, this shows that in crime-related amnesia cases, experts are well-advised to include formal tests of psychopathy, precisely because 'reports of dissociative amnesia from psychopathic offenders are very likely to be fabricated' (Porter et al., 2001, p. 37).

What about Ferdinand? In his case, the court-appointed experts not only failed to include tasks and tests to assess malingering, but they also overlooked the possibility of employing standard psychopathy measures (e.g., the Hare Psychopathy Checklist-Revised; Hare, 1998). In Ferdinand's case, it would have been informative to use psychopathy measures, if only because the experts were unanimous in their impression that Ferdinand was a charming, intelligent and articulate person. Also, the experts knew that Ferdinand had lied to them about his criminal record: Ferdinand said that he had one previous conviction when, in fact, the official documentation showed that he had at least four previous convictions. Similarly, Ferdinand told different stories about why he had gone to the house of his ex-girlfriend's parents. To his friend, he admitted that he wanted to intimidate the parents and their daughter. To the experts, he said that, initially, he wanted to return the knife to show his ex-girlfriend that 'she need not be afraid of me'. Finally, during the court proceedings, the judge noted that the defendant 'seems to be more concerned with his own future than

---

[10] These data come from an unpublished M.Sc. thesis (Schrijen, 2001).

he is with the grief and pain of the family'. Ferdinand's pattern of behaviour is consistent with key features of the psychopathic personality, notably superficial charm, manipulative behaviour and lack of remorse. To be sure, it is only with specialised testing that one could have determined with sufficient confidence whether Ferdinand was a psychopath. But even in the absence of such tests, it is difficult to understand why the psychiatric experts accepted Ferdinand's stories about his amnesia, the knife and his unhappy childhood at face value. Again, given his behavioural characteristics, the experts should have taken the possibility into account that Ferdinand fabricated a story to cover up his premeditation and to invoke something that, at least according to Hollywood standards, looks like a psychological blow – the father's arrogant laughing reminding him of his own abusive father. Ferdinand's narrative might be a good example of how psychopaths 're-frame' the level of instrumentality of their crimes by minimising the degree of premeditation and exaggerating the victim's role in, and the spontaneity of, the offense (see Porter et al., Chapter 5 this volume).

BRAIN AND MIND WORDS

In what is probably one of the most thorough reviews on the issue, Kopelman (2000) reminds us that the three types of amnesia – malingered, dissociative and organic – can best be seen as end-points along a continuum rather than as highly discrete categories. Accordingly, this author emphasises the overlap and dynamics that might occur between the amnesia types. An example would be the individual who previously experienced a transient organic amnesia as the result of head injury and who subsequently, when faced with a social dilemma, draws upon this experience to simulate amnesia. Kopelman's point bears strong relevance to the issue of crime-related amnesia. For example, a recurrent finding in the literature on crime-related amnesia is that offenders who raise amnesia claims more often have substance abuse problems than do offenders who do not make such claims (e.g., Cima et al., 2004; Hopwood & Snell, 1933; Pyszora et al., 2003). One interpretation of this is that offenders claiming amnesia are familiar with memory problems due to intoxication and use this experience strategically when confronted with the forensic evidence against them. Ferdinand's career as a Thai boxer is not without significance in this context. Studies show that severe head injuries leading to knock out are quite common in amateur and professional Thai boxers (Gartland, Malik & Lovell, 2001). Thus, there can be little doubt that Ferdinand was familiar with the phenomenon of knock out.

Pyszora et al. (2003) noted that prison inmates who had claimed amnesia for their crimes were more likely to have had CT or MRI scans performed than were those who had not made such claims (the proportions were 11% and 2%, respectively). With MRI facilities now being widely available, we may expect that in the years to come brain scanning will be a standard procedure in crime-related amnesia cases.[11] While some authors are enthusiastic about this development, arguing that 'brain words can be more precise than mind words' (Fenwick, 1993), we feel that it is of some concern. Plainly, coloured PET or MRI scans have a seductive power in the courtroom (Kulynych, 1996), because they purportedly present a direct picture of the brain. However, these are, in fact, highly reconstructive images, depending on a series of technical steps each of which can be manipulated (Reeves, Mills, Billick & Brodie, 2003).

Assume, for example, that Ferdinand's lawyers had found a radiology department willing to make some scan images of Ferdinand's brain with the department's MRI machine. Giving his Thai boxing background, chances are good that the experts would have found frontal abnormalities, bilateral parietal decrements, ventricular enlargements and so on, because every brain that is scanned shows some form of 'irregularity'. But, then, the question arises of how such brain words may shed light on the issue of whether Ferdinand was unaware of or not responsible for killing his ex-girlfriend's father. On the basis of current scientific knowledge, we would argue that scanning evidence has limited evidentiary value in amnesia cases. We concur with Reeves et al. (2003, p. 94) who argued that 'to date, a functional deviation shown by imaging has never been causally associated with an isolated, complex behavior (including, but not limited to, assault, rape, and murder)'.[12] In other words, it would be a huge forensic leap of faith to argue, on the basis of a deviant imaging picture, that a defendant must have an authentic amnesia. Clearly, one of the greatest problems in this regard is that 'the most common cause of

---

[11] For example, Ornish (2001) describes how one psychiatry department's scanning machine was financed by running the machine for lawyers who sought expert testimony about the brains of their clients.

[12] We do not deny that the literature offers exciting ideas about the neurobiological basis of crime-related amnesia. For example, Evans and Claycomb (1999) found, in their EEG study on six patients with dissociative amnesia for their violent behaviour, that the patients exhibited heightened alpha power at the frontal sites. The authors speculate that this EEG pattern reflects susceptibility to trance states. As is true of many such studies, the empirical merits of this speculation are, as yet, unknown: controlled studies including various reference groups (e.g., nonviolent participants) have not been conducted.

brain atrophy is staying alive (aging)' (Lees-Haley, Green, Rohling, Fox & Allen, 2003, p. 589).

WHAT CAN BE LEARNED?

Let us first point out that not everything went wrong in Ferdinand's case. For example, the psychiatrists did not use diazepam or a related drug to reactivate Ferdinand's memories of the crime. While this strategy is recommended by some clinicians as a safe intervention for memory retrieval in amnestic patients (Ballew, Yasser Morgan & Lippmann, 2003), it is useless at best and dangerous at worst.[13] In his review, Piper (1993) concluded that truth serum drugs have a memory-distorting effect, eliciting confabulations and fantasies in people with memory complaints (see, for an example, Glisky, Ryan, Reminger, Hardt, Hayes & Hupbach, 2004). This is not to say that therapeutic interventions to 'recover' memories in offenders claiming amnesia should never be used. As a matter of fact, such interventions might be important in sensitising offenders to treatment. Marshall and co-workers (2005) proposed a series of face-saving techniques and found that these techniques produced a miraculous recovery of amnesia in the large majority (73%) of offenders claiming amnesia.

Having said this, experts who have to evaluate claims of crime-related amnesia can learn the following lessons from the obvious errors made in Ferdinand's case as well as in the case of NN:

(1) Experts should ensure that they have access to the complete record of the defendant. In particular, third-party eyewitness testimonies about the defendant's behaviour before and after the crime might be informative.
(2) Experts should have access to collateral sources that might provide them with crucial information about the defendant's background.
(3) Experts should not take the defendant's self-report about his memory complaints at face value. That is, psychological testing of memory functioning is essential.
(4) Experts should routinely use appropriate tests and tools to evaluate the possibility of malingering.
(5) Experts are well advised to consider the medical records of the defendant critically and to ask themselves whether the amnesia

---

[13] Much the same holds, of course, for hypnosis. See Kebbell and Wagstaff (1998).

claim is consistent with well-established facts about organic amnesia (e.g., time frames, Ribot's law).

(6) Experts should not use PET, MRI or EEG data as a starting point for a forensic leap of faith.

REFERENCES

Arboleda-Florez, J. (2002) On automatism. *Current Opinion in Psychiatry*, **15**, 569–76.

Ballew, L., Yasser Morgan, E. & Lippmann, S. (2003) Intravenous diazepam for dissociative disorder: Memory lost and found. *Psychosomatics*, **44**, 346–7.

Baxendale, S. (2004) Memories aren't made of this: Amnesia at the movies. *British Medical Journal*, **329**, 1480–3.

Bernstein, E.M. & Putnam, F.W. (1986) Development, reliability, and validity of a dissociation scale. *Journal of Nervous and Mental Disease*, **174**, 727–735.

Brands, A.M.A., Biessels, G.J., de Haan, E.H.F., Kappelle, L.J. & Kessels, R.P.C. (2005) The effect of type 1 diabetes on cognitive performance: A meta-analysis. *Diabetes Care*, **28**, 726–35.

Buchanan, T.W. & Adolphs, R. (2004) The neuroanatomy of emotional memory in humans. In D. Reisberg & P. Hertel (Ed.), *Memory and emotion. Series in affective science* (pp. 42–75). Oxford: Oxford University Press.

Cartwright, R. (2004) Sleepwalking violence; A sleep disorder, a legal dilemma, and a psychological challenge. *American Journal of Psychiatry*, **161**, 1149–58.

Centor, A. (1982) Criminals and amnesia: Comment on Bower. *American Psychologist*, **37**, 240.

Christianson, S.Å., Holmberg, U., Bylin, S. & Engelberg, E. (2006) *Homicide and sexual offenders' motivation to forget their crimes*. Unpublished manuscript.

Christianson, S.Å. & Merckelbach, H. (2004) Crime-related amnesia as a form of deception. In P.A. Granhag & L.A. Strömwall (Eds), *The detection of deception in forensic contexts* (pp. 195–225). Cambridge: Cambridge University Press.

Christianson, S.Å. & von Vogelsang, E. (2006) *Reactive and instrumental homicide offenders who claim amnesia for their crime*. Unpublished manuscript.

Cima, M., Merckelbach, H., Klein, B., Schellbach-Matties, R. & Kremer, K. (2001) Frontal lobe dysfunctions, dissociation, and trauma self-reports in forensic psychiatric patients. *Journal of Nervous and Mental Disease*, **189**, 188–90.

Cima, M., Nijman, H., Merckelbach, H., Kremer, K. & Hollnack, S. (2004) Claims of crime-related amnesia in forensic patients. *International Journal of Law and Psychiatry*, **27**, 215–21.

Collins, J.J. & Bailey, S.L. (1990) Traumatic stress disorder and violent behavior. *Journal of Traumatic Stress*, **3**, 203–20.

Denney, R.L. & Wynkoop, T.F. (2000) Clinical neuropsychology in the criminal forensic setting. *Journal of Head Trauma Rehabilitation*, **15**, 804–28.

Edens, J.F., Buffington, J.K. & Tomicic, T.L. (2000) An investigation of the relationship between psychopathic traits and malingering on the psychopathic personality inventory. *Assessment*, **7**, 281–96.

Ellenberger, H. (1970) *The discovery of the unconscious.* New York: Basic Books.

Engelkamp, J. & Zimmer, H.D. (1994) *Human memory.* Seattle: Hogrefe.

Evans, J.R. & Claycomb, S. (1999) Abnormal QEEG patterns associated with dissociation and violence. *Journal of Neurotherapy*, **4**, 21–7.

Faust, D. (1995) The detection of deception. In M.I. Weintraub (Ed.), *Malingering and conversion reactions. Neurological clinics vol. 13* (pp. 255–65). Philadelphia: Saunders.

Fenwick, P. (1993) Brain, mind, and behaviour: Some medico-legal aspects. *British Journal of Psychiatry*, **163**, 565–73.

Frederick, R.I. & Denney, R.L. (1998) Minding your p's and q's when using forced-choice recognition tests. *Clinical Neuropsychologist*, **28**, 193–205.

Gartland, S., Malik, M.H.A. & Lovell, M.E. (2001) Injury and injury rates in Muay Thai kick boxing. *British Journal of Sports Medicine*, **35**, 308–13.

Gerson, A. (2002) Beyond DSM-IV: A meta-review of the literature on malingering. *American Journal of Forensic Psychology*, **20**, 57–69.

Glisky, E.L., Ryan, L., Reminger, S., Hardt, O., Hayes, S.M. & Hupbach, A. (2004) A case of psychogenic fugue: I understand aber ich verstehe nichts. *Neuropsychologia*, **42**, 1132–47.

Grierson, H.A. (1936) Memory and its disorders in relation to crime. *Journal of Mental Science*, **82**, 360–7.

Gudjonsson, G.H. (1984) A new scale of interrogative suggestibility. *Personality and Individual Differences*, **5**, 303–314.

Haber, L. & Haber, R.N. (1998) Criteria for the admissibility of eyewitness testimony of long past events. *Psychology, Public Policy, and Law*, **4**, 1135–59.

Hare, R.D. (1998) The Hare PCL-R: Some issues concerning its use and misuse. *Legal and Criminological Psychology*, **3**, 99–119.

Hopwood, J.S. & Snell, H.K. (1933) Amnesia in relation to crime. *Journal of Mental Science*, **79**, 27–41.

Horowitz, M.J. (1979) Psychological response to serious life events. In V. Hamilton & D.M. Warburton (Eds), *Human stress and cognition* (pp. 235–263). Northvale NJ: Jason Aronson.

Jones, E., Hodgins Vermaas, R., McCartney, H., Beech, C., Palmer, I., Hyams, K. & Wessely, S. (2003) Flashbacks and post-traumatic stress disorder: The genesis of a 20th century diagnosis. *British Journal of Psychiatry*, **182**, 158–63.

Kalant, H. (1996) Intoxicated automatism: Legal concept vs. scientific evidence. *Contemporary Drug Problems*, **23**, 631–48.

Kebbell, M.R. & Wagstaff, G.F. (1998) Hypnotic interviewing: The best way to interview the eyewitness? *Behavioral Sciences and the Law*, **16**, 115–29.

Kopelman, M.D. (1995) The assessment of psychogenic amnesia. In A.D Baddeley, B.A. Wilson & F.N. Watts (Eds), *Handbook of memory disorders* (pp. 427–48). New York: John Wiley & Sons, Inc.

Kopelman, M.D. (2000) Focal retrograde amnesia and the attribution of causality: An exceptionally critical review. *Cognitive Neuropsychology*, **17**, 585–621.

Kulynych, J. (1996) Brain, mind, and criminal behavior: Neuroimages as scientific evidence. *Jurimetrics Journal*, **36**, 235–44.

Larrabee, G.J. (2005) *Forensic neuropsychology: A scientific approach.* Oxford: Oxford University Press.

Lees-Haley, P.R., Green, P., Rohling, M.L., Fox, D.D. & Allen, L.M. (2003) The lesion(s) in traumatic brain injury: Implications for clinical neuropsychology. *Archives of Clinical Neuropsychology*, **18**, 585–94.

Liepmann, H. (2002/1910) Contribution to the understanding of the amnesic symptom complex. *Cortex*, **38**, 635–9.

Marshall, W.L., Serran, G., Marshall, L.E. & Fernandez, Y.M. (2005) Recovering memories of the offense in 'amnesic' sexual offenders. *Sexual Abuse: A Journal of Research and Treatment*, **17**, 31–8.

McCrory, P. (2001) The medicolegal aspects of automatism in mild head injury. *British Journal of Sports Medicine*, **35**, 288–96.

McLeod, H.J., Byrne, M.K. & Aitken, R. (2004) Automatism and dissociation: Disturbances of consciousness and volition from a psychological perspective. *International Journal of Law and Psychiatry*, **27**, 471–87.

McNally, R.J. (2003) *Remembering trauma*. Cambridge, MA: Harvard University Press.

McSherry, B. (2004) Criminal responsibility, fleeting states of mental impairment, and the power of self-control. *International Journal of Law and Psychiatry*, **27**, 445–57.

Merckelbach, H., Cima, M. & Nijman, H. (2002) Daders met geheugenverlies [Offenders with memory loss]. In P.J. van Koppen, D.J. Hessing, H. Merckelbach & H. Crombag (Eds), *Het recht van binnen: Psychologie van het recht*. [The law inside: The psychology of law] (pp. 667–85). Deventer: Kluwer.

Merckelbach, H., Dekkers, Th., Wessel, I. & Roefs, A. (2003a) Dissociative symptoms and amnesia in Dutch concentration camp survivors. *Comprehensive Psychiatry*, **44**, 65–9.

Merckelbach, H., Dekkers, Th., Wessel, I. & Roefs, A. (2003b) Amnesia, flashbacks, nightmares, and dissociation in aging concentration camp survivors. *Behaviour Research and Therapy*, **41**, 351–60.

Merckelbach, H. & Wessel, I. (1998) Assumptions of students and psychotherapists about memory. *Psychological Reports*, **82**, 763–70.

Mittenberg, W., Patton, C., Canyock, E.M. & Condit, D.C. (2002) Base rates of malingering and symptom exaggeration. *Journal of Clinical and Experimental Neuropsychology*, **24**, 1094–1102.

Moskowitz, A. (2004) Dissociation and violence: A review of the literature. *Trauma, Violence & Abuse*, **5**, 21–46.

Ornish, S.A. (2001) A blizzard of lies: Bogus psychiatric defenses. *American Journal of Forensic Psychiatry*, **22**, 19–30.

Parwatikar, S.D., Holcomb, W.R. & Menninger, K.A. (1985) The detection of malingered amnesia in accused murderers. *Bulletin of the American Academy of Psychiatry and Law*, **13**, 97–103.

Payne, J.D., Nadel, L., Britton, W.B. & Jacobs, W.J. (2004) The biopsychology of trauma and memory. In D. Reisberg, & P. Hertel (Eds), *Memory and emotion. Series in affective science* (pp. 42–75). Oxford: Oxford University Press.

Piper, A. (1993) Truth serum and recovered memories of sexual abuse: A review of the evidence. *Journal of Psychiatry and Law*, **21**, 447–471.

Pollock, Ph.H. (1999) When the killer suffers: Post-traumatic stress reactions following homicide. *Legal and Criminological Psychology*, **4**, 185–202.

Porter, S., Birt, A.R., Yuille, J.C. & Herve, H.F. (2001) Memory for murder: A psychological perspective on dissociative amnesia in legal contexts. *International Journal of Law and Psychiatry*, **24**, 23–42.

Poythress, N.G., Edens, J.F. & Watkins, M.M. (2001) The relationship between psychopathic personality features and malingering symptoms of major mental illness. *Law and Human Behavior*, **25**, 567–82.

Pyszora, N.M., Barker, A.F. & Kopelman, M.D. (2003) Amnesia for criminal offences: A study of life sentence prisoners. *Journal of Forensic Psychiatry & Psychology*, **14**, 475–490.

Rabinowitz, F.E. (1989) Creating the multiple personality: An experiential demonstration for an undergraduate abnormal psychology class. *Teaching of Psychology*, **16**, 69–71.

Rauch, S., van der Kolk, B.A., Fisler, R., Alpert, N.M., Orr, S.P., Savage, C.R., Fischman, A.J., Jenike, M.A. & Pitman, R.K. (1996) A symptom provocation study of posttraumatic stress disorder using positron emission tomography and script-driven imagery. *Archives of General Psychiatry*, **53**, 380–7.

Reeves, D., Mills, M.J., Billick, S.B. & Brodie, J.D. (2003) Limitations of brain imaging in forensic psychiatry. *Journal of the American Academy of Psychiatry and the Law*, **31**, 89–96.

Rivard, J.M., Dietz, P., Martell, D. & Widawski, M. (2002) Acute disssociative responses in law enforcement officers involved in critical shooting incidents: The clinical and forensic implications. *Journal of Forensic Sciences*, **47**, 1–8.

Rosen, G.M. (2004) Malingering and the PTSD data base. In G.M. Rosen (Eds), *Posttraumatic stress disorder: Issues and controversies* (pp. 85–99). Chichester: John Wiley & Sons, Ltd.

Rosen, G.M. & Phillips, W.R. (2004) A cautionary lesson from simulated patients. *Journal of the American Academy of Psychiatry and the Law*, **32**, 132–3.

Rubenzer, S. (2004) Malingering, incompetence to stand trial, insanity, and mental retardation. *The Texas Prosecutor*, **6**, 17–23.

Schrijen, D.D. (2001) *De relatie tussen amnesie en misdaad: De rol van persoonlijkheid*. [The relationship between amnesia and crime: The role of personality]. Unpublished M. Sc. thesis, Maastricht University.

Spanos, N.P., Weekes, J.R. & Bertrand, L.D. (1986) Multiple personality: A social psychological perspective. *Journal of Abnormal Psychology*, **94**, 362–76.

Spitzer, C., Liss, H., Dudeck, M., Orlob, S., Gillner, M., Hamm, A. & Freyberger, H.J. (2003) Dissociative experiences and disorders in forensic patients. *International Journal of Law and Psychiatry*, **26**, 281–8.

Strachan, M.W., Deary, I.J., Ewing, F.M. & Frier, B.M. (2000) Recovery of cognitive function and mood after severe hypoglycemia in adults with insulin-treated diabetes. *Diabetes Care*, **23**, 305–12.

Swihart, G., Yuille, J. & Porter, S. (1999) The role of state-dependent memory in red-outs. *International Journal of Law and Psychiatry*, **22**, 199–212.

Symons, C.S. & Johnson, B.T. (1997) The self-reference effect in memory: A meta-analysis. *Psychological Bulletin*, **121**, 371–94.

Van der Kolk, B.A. (1988) The trauma spectrum: The interaction of biological and social events in the genesis of the trauma response. *Journal of Traumatic Stress*, **1**, 273–90.

Wagenaar, W.A. & Crombag, H.F.M. (2005) *The popular policeman and other cases: Psychological perspectives on legal evidence*. Amsterdam: Amsterdam University Press.

Waldbauer, J.R. & Gazzaniga, M.S. (2001) The divergence of neuroscience and law. *Jurimetrics Journal*, **41**, 357–64.

Wedding, D. & Faust, D. (1989) Clinical judgment and decision making in neuropsychology. *Archives of Clinical Neuropsychology*, **4**, 233–65.

Wegner, D.M., Schneider, D.J., Carter, S.R. & White, T.L. (1987) Paradoxical effects of thought suppression. *Journal of Personality and Social Psychology*, **53**, 5–13.

Yehuda, R., Elkin, A., Binder-Brynes, K., Kahana, B., Southwick, S.M., Schmeidler, J. & Giller, E.L. (1996) Dissociation in aging Holocaust survivors. *American Journal of Psychiatry*, **153**, 935–40.

Yeo, S. (2002) Clarifying automatism. *International Journal of Law and Psychiatry*, **25**, 445–458.

CHAPTER 8

The Role of Malingering and Expectations in Claims of Crime-related Amnesia

KIM VAN OORSOUW AND MAAIKE CIMA

This chapter focuses on crime-related amnesia as a form of malingering, on the one hand, and the influence of expectations on such claims, on the other. Crime-related amnesia is reported by approximately 25 to 40 % of violent offenders (Guttmacher, 1955; Leitch, 1948; O'Connell, 1960; Taylor & Kopelman, 1984; Kopelman, 1995). In only a handful of these cases, brain dysfunctions (i.e., organic amnesia) accounted for the memory loss. Many times, amnesia is feigned for strategic purposes. There are reasons to believe that those who use an amnesia claim as a strategy to minimize responsibility are characterised by a typical personality profile. These personality characteristics and the role of extreme levels of stress or intoxication in claims of crime-related amnesia will be discussed in this chapter. Although it is possible that genuine amnesia for crimes occurs as a result of extreme emotional arousal or intoxication, some of our recent studies show that blaming amnesia on such factors could also be a form of

Offenders' Memories of Violent Crimes.   Edited by Sven Å. Christianson.
© 2007 John Wiley & Sons, Ltd.

faking bad (Cima, 2003). Another important aspect of claims of crime-related amnesia are expectations about ones own memory. The research presented in this chapter shows that expectations about memory can affect memory performance. Several case-studies in which we tested the veracity of amnesia claims, and in which we explicitly manipulated expectations in forensic patients claiming amnesia are discussed. It appears that typical personality characteristics, expectations and malingering are factors that are closely related when it comes to claims of crime-related amnesia.

SIMULATED AMNESIA

According to some authors, the most common form of amnesia in the legal domain is simulated amnesia (Cima, Merckelbach, Nijman, Knauer & Hollnack, 2002; Sadoff, 1974; Schacter, 1986). One obvious motive for offenders to feign amnesia is to avoid or reduce punishment (Parwatikar, Holcomb & Menninger, 1985). An historic example is the case of the Collegno amnesic (see for an elaborate description, Zago, Sartori & Scarlato, 2004). In 1926, a man was admitted to the Collegno alsylum in Turin, Italy. He was taken there by the police who arrested him for trying to steal a copper vase from a tomb in a cemetery. The man claimed to have no autobiographical memories. After his picture appeared in the newspaper one year later, a Mrs Canella identified him as her lost husband, Professor Canella, who had disappeared during the war in 1916. The Collegno amnesic continued his life as Professor Canella, with the additional advantage that his wife's family was very rich. However, when another woman claimed that the Collegno amnesic was her husband Mario Bruneri, a man who was wanted for fraud, a new investigation started. It turned out that the Collegno amnesic had feigned his amnesia. He was, indeed, Mario Bruneri. By feigning amnesia, he did not only escape from being convicted for robbery and fraud, but also became a very rich man thanks to the Canella widow, who for her own reasons claimed to be his wife.

As this anecdote illustrates, crime-related amnesia may be used as a strategy when people think that this diminishes their criminal responsibility. On a related note, we tested the influence of certain situations (e.g., prison vs pre-trial) on amnesia claims. We demonstrated that inmates who were not yet incarcerated (pre-trial) significantly more often claimed amnesia for their crime than did inmates who were already convicted (see Table 8.1). These

Table 8.1 Influence of the situation on crime-related amnesia claims ($n = 34$)

	Amnesic patients ($n = 14$)	Control patients ($n = 20$)
Pre-trial $n = 12$	$n = 9$ (75%)	$n = 3$ (25%)
Prison $n = 22$	$n = 5$ (23%)	$n = 17$ (77%)

Notes: $\chi^2(1) = 8.76$; $p < 0.05$ (d = 0, 45).

findings support the idea of malingering as being a strategy. Sometimes, claimed amnesia prevents defendants from fully participating in their defence. For instance, Rudolf Hess claimed to be amnesic for his Third Reich period at the start of the 'Nuremberg' trials. A group of prominent psychiatrists examined Hess and concluded that his amnesia was genuine. When it became clear to Hess that the amnesic role conferred a disadvantage in the sense that one cannot respond to allegations, he suddenly announced during one of the trial sessions that he had fooled the psychiatrists and feigned his amnesia (Gilbert, 1971; for a somewhat different interpretation see Picknett, Prince & Prioir, 2001). Despite this, claims of crime-related amnesia may also serve the defendant well in the sense that he/she will not be held fully responsible for the criminal act. Although claims of crime-related amnesia do not necessarily imply that the crime came about unconsciously or automatically (Kalant, 1996), the German Bundesgerichtshof argued that 'a verified amnesia for the criminal act – alone or in combination with other factors – is a sign of an emotionally based disorder of consciousness' (BGH 4 Str 207/87; see Barbey, 1990). In this sense the strategy of claiming amnesia may serve offenders well until their incarceration. However, once they are in prison or in a forensic hospital it obstructs the beneficial effects of intervention. Recalling crime-related memories in therapy is necessary for patients to work through their offence and come to terms with their criminal act. Not recalling these acts prevents the development of offence pathways and the learning of relapse prevention strategies (Marshall, Serran, Marshall & Fernandez, 2005). Despite the beneficial effects of remembering crime-details in terms of therapeutic progress and prospects of early parole, talking extensively about their crimes is something that forensic patients would rather prevent in order to make their stay in the forensic clinic much more comfortable. Especially when guilt and shame are involved (e.g., in sexual offenders), talking about the crime can be rather uncomfortable. In such cases, feigning amnesia becomes an attractive tool.

That feigning amnesia does not only obstruct therapeutic progress but also undermines memory for the crime, has been demonstrated by several laboratory studies (Christianson & Bylin, 1999; van Oorsouw & Merckelbach, 2004; 2006). Van Oorsouw and Merckelbach (2004, in press) instructed participants to feign amnesia after committing a mock crime (i.e., hit and rob a dummy in a bar). In order to encourage participants to feign amnesia in a more elaborate way than just saying 'I can't remember' or 'I was not there', they were told that a witness saw them near the bar. One week later all participants were instructed to tell the truth. Compared to participants who were instructed to tell the truth from the start, participants who first feigned amnesia were eventually less complete and made more commission errors while describing the crime events (see Table 8.2).

Table 8.2 Mean proportion of correctly reported free-recall information, proportion of omissions and number of commissions of participants in the simulating ($n = 21$, $n = 27$, respectively in the two studies) and honestly responding ($n = 20$, $n = 30$ respectively in the two studies) condition during the first (T1) and second (T2) test occasion. Standard deviations appear between parentheses

	Simulating participants		Honestly responding controls	
Van Oorsouw & Merckelbach (2004)	T1	T2	T1	T2
Proportions correct	0.09 (0.07)[a]	0.25 (0.10)[c]	0.29 (0.10)	0.32 (0.08)[b,c]
Proportion omissions	0.91 (0.05)[a]	0.75 (0.11)[c]	0.71 (0.14)	0.68 (0.08)[b,c]
Number of commissions	11.5 (5.2)[a]	4.7 (3.9)[c]	1.1 (1.5)	3.5 (2.3)[c]
	Simulating participants		Honestly responding controls	
Van Oorsouw & Merckelbach (2006)	T1	T2	T1	T2
Proportions correct	0.11 (0.09)[a]	0.49 (0.11)[c]	0.57 (0.16)	0.57 (0.11)[b]
Proportion omissions	0.89 (0.09)[a]	0.51 (0.11)[c]	0.43 (0.16)	0.43 (0.11)[b]
Number of commissions	7.89 (5.35)[a]	2.37 (2.13)[c]	0.70 (1.08)	1.20 (0.99)[b,c]

Notes: a= $p < 0.05$ between groups at T1
b= $p < 0.05$ between groups at T2
c= $p < 0.05$ within groups between T1 and T2

In the van Oorsouw and Merckelbach (2006) study, free-recall narratives of the simulating participants were evaluated. Adhering to the instructions, the majority of the simulators (85%) pretended to have some type of memory loss and made up an alternative story. Seventeen per cent claimed to have had an alcohol blackout, while 11% pretended to have witnessed the crime and to have been hit on the head themselves (i.e., claimed organic amnesia). Four per cent completely denied being involved in the crime. The other participants did not use any particular excuse and described the events as if they had problems remembering what happened. In most narratives peripheral details like the environment, their reasons for being in the bar, and the people in the bar were described, while details about the crime (assault and robbery) were omitted. Interestingly, all participants stated that they had been *in* the bar at the day of the crime (e.g., having drinks, playing pool) and created stories that contained mixtures of lies (e.g., 'when I came back from the toilet the bartender was lying on the floor', or, 'three men came into the bar. Suddenly I heard a loud noise and someone was throwing water at me. The next moment I was outside and went home') and claims about memory problems (e.g., 'I asked the bar tender for a bicycle-pump because I had a flat tire, the next thing I remember is that I woke up at home with a headache' or 'I was sitting at the bar and all of a sudden everything became hazy and I decided to leave. This happened to me before and it scares me'). Apparently, suspects find it difficult to remain silent, especially when they are confronted with evidence against them, and feel the need to come up with a statement (see also Kassin, 2005). Our results show that once defendants start fabricating statements about their memory loss, genuine memory for the crime is undermined and valuable crime-related information may get lost.

PERSONALITY CHARACTERISTICS

Surprisingly, few studies have looked at the personality characteristics of individuals claiming amnesia for their crimes. In an early study, O'Connell (1960) suggested that low intelligence is related to claims of amnesia. He argued that because of its simplicity, claims of amnesia might constitute an attractive defence manoeuvre for those with low intelligence. Parwatikar et al. (1985) argued that depressive symptoms often accompany amnesia for crime. Taylor and Kopelman (1984) reported a similar finding, but these authors remind us of the possibility that in some cases, depression might be a reaction to the crime. In one of the most systematic studies to date, Gudjonsson, Hannesdottir and Petursson (1999) administered individual difference measures to criminals who claimed amnesia for their violent offences and a control group. These authors found that amnesic offenders scored relatively high on introversion and low on impulsivity. However, O'Connell (1960) and Parwatikar et al. (1985) found that hysterical personality characteristics are rather prevalent among offenders claiming amnesia. To the extent that hysteria implies extraverted and impulsive behaviour, this finding is difficult to reconcile with the results reported by Gudjonsson and associates. In addition, Cooper (2005) found that individuals who claimed amnesia for their violent crimes had higher neuroticism scores on the Big Five Inventory-44S (BFI-44S; John & Srivastava, 1999) than individuals who did not claim amnesia. This is in line with O'Connell's (1960) findings given that neuroticism was an underlying component of the hysterical personality disorder in the DSM-II (Sigmund, Barnett & Mundt, 1998). Another prominent feature of hysterical personality is manipulative behaviour, which is also an important aspect of psychopathy. In the words of Porter, Birt, Yuille and Hervé (2001, p. 36): 'Psychopaths use a high degree of manipulation, deception, and malingering relative to other offenders and would be likely to use a false claim of amnesia if any personal gains were anticipated'. Some traits (e.g., low intelligence, hysteria) that have been found to be typical for offenders claiming amnesia fit nicely with a malingering interpretation, while other traits (e.g., depression, introversion, low impulsivity) ascribed to this group seem to be more consistent with the idea that the highly emotional nature of a crime may cause memory dysfunction. Although research has resulted in conflicting findings about the personality characteristics of criminals who claim amnesia, there is consensus about two issues. First, as alluded to earlier, it is a well-established fact that claims of amnesia more often pertain to violent crimes than to non-violent crimes (e.g., Taylor & Kopelman, 1984). Second, crime-related amnesia is often associated with alcohol and/or drug intoxication during the crime (e.g., Gudjonsson et al., 1999). The role of alcohol in claims of crime-related amnesia will be discussed later.

To the extent that claims of crime-related amnesia are a form of feigning, one would expect that they are raised by individuals who have relatively low IQs, psychopathic features, impulsivity manifesting itself in poor executive (i.e., frontal lobe) functions and heightened scores on malingering scales. A study by Cima, Merckelbach, Hollnack and Knauer (2003) investigated whether such a constellation of features is typical for psychiatric prison inmates who claim amnesia. In this study, all of the forensic patients had been involved in legal proceedings by which extensive and detailed patient records were

Table 8.3   Mean (SDs) IQ levels, frequency (%) of APD (antisocial personality disorder), mean (SDs) PCL-SV (Psychopathy Checklist-Screening Version) scores, BIS-10 (Barrett Impulsiveness Scale-10) scores, BADS (Behavioural Assessment of Dysexecutive Syndrome) scores, and SIMS (Structured Inventory of Malingered Symptomatology) scores of amnesic ($n = 17$) and control ($n = 45$) patients

	Amnesic patients ($n = 17$)	Control patients ($n = 45$)
Total IQ*	78.5 (10.4)	90.8 (19.5)
APD*	12.0 (71%)	21.0 (47%)
Total PCL-SV	13.3 (4.0)	13.1 (3.8)
Total BIS-10	73.5 (10.9)	72.0 (12.9)
Total BADS*	6.1 (2.6)	8.3 (3.2)
SIMS > 16*	53%	18%

Notes: * = $p \leq 0.05$, two-tailed.

available. The main results of this study are shown in Table 8.3. As can be seen, a considerable minority (27%) of the forensic patients claimed amnesia for their offences. In line with previous studies (Kopelman, 1995; Taylor & Kopelman, 1984), claims of amnesia were found to be fairly typical for those who had committed violent crimes. Also, patients claiming amnesia had lower IQ scores and were more often diagnosed with antisocial personality disorder (APD) than controls. Furthermore, patients claiming amnesia showed executive dysfunctions and more frequently scored above the cut-off on a malingering scale (SIMS, Smith & Burger, 1997) compared to controls. This is reminiscent of a previous study (Cima, Merckelbach, Klein, Schellbach-Matties & Kremer, 2001), which showed that poor executive functions go hand in hand with self-reports of dissociative symptomatology. However, in contrast to what may be expected based on Porter et al.'s (2001) suggestions no differences were found in levels of psychopathy between offenders claiming amnesia and those who did not, as measured by the Psychopathy Checklist-Screening Version (PCL-SV; Hart, Cox & Hare, 1996). One possible explanation for not finding a link between psychopathy and amnesia in the sample of Cima and colleagues (2003) could be that the patients suffered from genuine memory loss. However, this is not very plausible given the raised SIMS scores found in those who claimed amnesia (see Table 8.3), indicating that it is more likely that amnesia was feigned in the high scorers. Another possibility is that malingered amnesia is different from the more subtle types of manipulative behaviour found among psychopathic individuals. Thus, it may well be that malingered amnesia is more typical for those with relatively low IQ scores, while other and more subtle forms of deception are typical for psychopathic individuals with relatively normal or above normal IQ. Interestingly, a study by Poythress, Edens and Watkins (2001) also failed to find a link between psychopathic personality features and straightforward malingering. Clearly, the precise links between types of malingering, IQ and psychopathy warrant systematic investigation. By and large, when offenders claim amnesia, the following scenario demands serious attention: Because of their low intelligence, and lack of executive control, these individuals engage in violent behaviour and later try to avoid responsibility by claiming amnesia (Cima et al., 2003).

STRESS AND EMOTIONS

According to Kopelman (1995) punishment reduction or avoiding responsibility are not the main motives for feigning memory problems. He pointed out that even though criminals claim amnesia, they often report their crimes to the police. This would argue against the view of amnesia claims in terms of malingering. Kopelman assumes that extreme emotions, which often accompany a criminal act, may cause genuine dissociative (i.e., psychogenic) amnesia for the crime (see also Chapter 3 of this volume; Swihart, Yuille & Porter, 1999). Although this explanation of extreme stress leading to dissociative amnesia may sound plausible, it is at odds with studies showing that most eyewitnesses (or victims) of extreme violence have accurate rather than impaired memory for the events (for a review, see Porter et al., 2001). Yet, another point difficult to reconcile with the stress-dissociation account is that survivors of WW II concentration camps rarely report amnesia for their horrifying experiences in these camps (Kuch & Cox, 1992; Merckelbach, Dekkers, Wessel & Roefs, 2003; Wagenaar & Groeneweg, 1990).

A recent study which examined the stress-dissociation hypothesis was conducted in substantial samples ($N = 308$) from German and Dutch forensic hospitals (Cima, Nijman, Merckelbach, Kremer & Hollnack, 2004). If extreme levels of stress were to be related to crime-related amnesia, one would expect that such claims are typically found among those who committed violent and emotional crimes. However, it appeared that there was no support for the stress-dissociation hypothesis of crime-related amnesia. That is, in contrast to previous studies (Kopelman, 1995; O'Connell, 1960; Taylor & Kopelman, 1984), claims of amnesia were not more prevalent among patients who had committed more serious emotional crimes like homicide. This again emphasises that claims of dissociative amnesia for crimes should be treated with caution, and that the possibility of malingering should be considered. In other words, even when extreme stress or emotions accompany a criminal act (as with homicide crimes), this does not necessarily imply that a claim of amnesia for that crime is genuine or a form of dissociative amnesia. One limitation of the Cima et al. (2003) study was that violent crimes like homicide were categorised as an emotional and thus highly stressful crime. Although this may be the case in the more reactive crimes, this does not necessarily have to be true in the instrumental ones (see also Chapters 1 and 3 of this volume).

INTOXICATION AND CLAIMS OF CRIME-RELATED AMNESIA

A number of authors have suggested that excessive alcohol or drug use may contribute to (dissociative) amnesia for a crime (Eich, Weingartner, Stillman & Gillin, 1975; Fillmore, Vogel-Sprott & Gavrilescu, 1999; Goodwin, 1995; Goodwin, Crane & Guze, 1969; Kopelman, 1987; Swihart, et al., 1999). According to DSM-IV, alcohol-induced amnesia should be distinguished from dissociative amnesia since it is not a psychological blow, but a substance that is responsible for the memory loss. However, this only holds true when it can be objectively demonstrated that the amount of alcohol consumed has reached levels at which an alcohol blackout might be clinically possible, and malingering can be ruled out. In cases where memory loss for a crime is attributed to alcohol intoxication, the veracity of these claims cannot always be tested. Simulation of memory loss as a strategic function should thus be considered in claims of alcohol amnesia.

Severe intoxication may lead to storage problems. According to the state-dependent memory theory (Bower, 1981), the context of encoding and retrieval of information should be the same. Theoretically, when crime-memories are encoded during an exceptional state (e.g., extreme agitation and/or intoxication), subsequent retrieval of these memories will be difficult or even impossible as long as the original state is not reproduced. By this view, memories encoded during intoxication cannot be retrieved when blood alcohol levels have returned to normal and hence, amnesia would occur.

Some authors argue that Sirhan Sirhan, who murdered Robert Kennedy represents a good example of someone suffering from state-dependent amnesia. Sirhan claimed that he could not remember murdering Kennedy because he was in an agitated state during the murder. When he was hypnotised and brought back into that state, he suddenly remembered details of the murder (Swihart et al., 1999).[1] However, the state-dependent memory hypothesis of amnesia for crimes is not based on solid evidence. Wolf (1980) showed that inducing a state of intoxication in murderers who claimed amnesia did not lead to a return or recovery of crime memories. In Wolf's study, five Alaskan natives with no prior history of violence committed murder while intoxicated. They claimed they could not recall the murder, but indicated to have been vaguely aware that the killings took place. In a controlled hospital condition, and while monitoring blood alcohol levels, affective state and EEG, Wolf attempted to regain the same level of intoxication the killers had while committing their crimes. Although the men became more and more angry and experienced violent feelings, none of them remembered the homicides (Moskowitz, 2004). Kalant (1996, p. 368) drew attention to another shortcoming of state-dependency accounts by arguing that 'the typical action of alcohol on the brain . . . is to progressively decrease all types of nerve cell activity, including those involved in coordinated movements and those involved in consciousness and memory, more or less *in parallel*' (our italics). Thus, it is highly unlikely that an alcohol-intoxicated person engages in complex criminal behaviour, but has no memory of this behaviour.

In the United States and Canada, alcohol blackouts are sometimes associated with loss of criminal intent or automatic behaviour (Crombag, 2002; Kalant, 1996). This link received much attention in Canada when the Supreme Court in the case of *Deviault v R.*, decided that the defendant, who had no memory of his crime due to alcohol intoxication, should be acquitted. This decision was based on a testimony that linked automatism to blackout. In the Netherlands, such an acquittal would be inconceivable because of the ruling 'culpa in causa' doctrine. According to this doctrine, the suspect is expected to know the consequences of excessive alcohol use, and should thus be held fully responsible for his behaviour while under influence. Although alcohol impairs short-term memory, which may lead to a problem storing unlawful deeds, remote memory remains intact (Critchlow, 1986; Goodwin, 1995; White, 2000). This means that during an event for which the person later experiences a blackout, he/she should be perfectly able to retrieve rules of conduct, and be aware that what he/she is about to do is wrong.

Irrespective of the research and theoretical speculations discussed above, many lay people assume that alcohol releases inhibitions and makes people less responsible for their behaviour (Critchlow,

---

[1] It later appeared that Sirhan had feigned his amnesia (Moldea, 1995).

1986). For example, van Oorsouw, Merckelbach, Ravelli, Nijman and Mekking-Pompen (2004) investigated whether alcohol blackouts are indeed a frequently occurring phenomenon or are merely used as an excuse to minimise criminal responsibility. In two surveys they investigated the prevalence of alcohol blackouts for criminally relevant behaviour by asking people from the general population about their experiences with blackouts for criminally relevant behaviour. The first survey ($n = 256$) only focused on participants' own experiences with alcohol blackouts. The second ($n = 100$) asked about blackouts they had witnessed in a friend or relative. In both surveys, blackouts were frequently reported for oneself and others (67 % and 76 %, respectively). Blackouts pertained to criminally relevant behaviour in 15 % and 33 % in the first and second survey, respectively. These results show that alcoholic blackouts are frequently reported in the general population. However, they are less frequently reported for criminally relevant behaviour. In another study, van Oorsouw and colleagues (2004) compared blood-alcohol concentrations for people who did and did not claim blackouts when stopped in a traffic-control for suspicious driving behaviour or for causing an accident. In the traffic-control study, blackouts were reported less frequently (14 %). Interestingly, in this study, blackouts were only reported when persons had been involved in an accident (85 %), indicating that they may serve a strategic purpose.[2] Moreover, their blood-alcohol levels did not differ from persons not claiming amnesia. Both were 180 mg/100 ml. When asked whether they had ever experienced an alcohol blackout before, this question was answered affirmatively by only 15 % of the participants. It should be noted that this question was asked by a psychiatrist who had to decide about participants' driving competency and return of licence. In this context, failing to report previous blackout experience may also have served a strategic goal. Thus, although alcoholic blackouts are frequently reported outside the court, both the denial and the claim of blackouts may have face-saving purposes (van Oorsouw et al., 2004).

The studies discussed above suggest that claiming an alcoholic blackout may serve citizens from the general population well in order to evade responsibility for their behaviour. Cima and colleagues (2004) investigated the relation between alcohol and substance abuse and claims of amnesia in a sample of psychiatric inmates. If alcoholic blackouts for criminal behaviour occur frequently, one would anticipate that a diagnosis of alcohol or substance abuse would be rather common

---

[2] None of the drivers were injured on the head, which excludes the possibility of genuine organic amnesia.

among those who claim amnesia for their offence. However, only a small minority of the cases actually had a history of alcohol or drug abuse, indicating that patients who blame their memory loss on an intoxicated state may be trying to evade responsibility by doing so.

EXPECTATIONS

In the previous sections we distinguished between malingered amnesia, genuine amnesia and alcohol amnesia. The latter type of amnesia could be genuine (i.e., organic), feigned (i.e., simulated) or dissociative. This distinction is different from the classical types of amnesia in which they are classified as either organic (e.g., blow to the head, intoxication), or dissociative (e.g., stress or dissociation). Later on, malingered amnesia was added to this classification. Kopelman (2000, p. 608) already argued that the different forms of amnesia may not be so easily distinguished and 'form endpoints along a continuum rather than discrete categories'. A previous experience with organic amnesia may become the basis of simulation, and people may come to believe in their memory loss or role-playing. International Classification of Diseases (ICD-10; WHO, 1992) lists dissociative amnesia along with other pseudo-neurological disorders (e.g., paralysis, pseudo-seizures), and calls it dissociative conversion disorders (Holmes, Brown, Mansell, Fearon, Hunter et al., 2005). Such conversion symptoms can be directly removed by hypnotic suggestion (Holmes et al., 2005), indicating that expectancies or beliefs may underlie the symptoms. Thus, similar to the belief of being paralysed in a typical conversion disorder, one can believe to have lost one's memory when, in fact there is no objective medical reason for this belief (see also Jureidini, 2004). Several studies have suggested that expectations about memory loss may underlie claims of amnesia. For example, according to Ponds and colleagues (2000), pessimistic expectations about memory in the elderly (i.e., fear of dementia) negatively affect their daily cognitive functioning, when in fact their objective performance is not different from younger people. To a similar extent, Winkielman, Schwarz and Belli (1998) have shown that the retrieval of many childhood memories paradoxically induces the belief that memory for childhood is poor (see also Belli, Winkielman, Read, Schwarz & Lynn, 1998). In their study, participants assessed their memory for childhood as inferior after successfully recalling many (12) childhood memories, to that of participants who recalled only few (4) childhood memories. It is suggested that the perceived difficulty of retrieving many childhood memories is responsible for the belief that one has few childhood memories. In addition, van Oorsouw and Merckelbach (submitted) showed that pessimistic beliefs about memory can affect autobiographical memory performance negatively. In their study, participants were administered an Autobiographical Memory Task (AMT; Williams & Broadbent 1986) after the retrieval of either few or many childhood memories. Similar to the Winkielman (1998) study, their participants rated their childhood memory as inferior after the retrieval of many, as compared to few, childhood memories. However, they also performed more poorly on the subsequent AMT. That is, they had more problems retrieving specific cue related autobiographical memories. According to van Oorsouw and Merckelbach, this lack of specificity was related to the pessimistic beliefs participants had about their (general) memory.

That expectations play a role in memory performance has also been demonstrated by the use of placebos. Assefi and Garry (2003) showed that the mere suggestion to subjects that they had consumed alcohol, when in fact is was plain tonic, made them more susceptible to misleading information. On a related note, Kvavilashvili and Ellis (1999) demonstrated that subjects who received a placebo, but were told that it was a memory-impairing substance, performed less well on a memory test compared to control subjects. In a more recent study, the role of such expectations on memory for an emotional film-fragment was tested (van Oorsouw and Merckelbach, in press). The fragment contained an emotional scene of the movie 'American History X'. The scene is about a neo-Nazi who shoots and kills three African-American men who are trying to steal his car. The most horrific part of the scene is when the neo-Nazi orders one of the men to open his mouth on the curb and kicks him on the back of his head. After watching the video fragment, participants were given a placebo capsule in combination with either the story that it would enhance or the story that it would impair their memory for the film-fragment. Compared to the memory-impairing placebo group and controls who received no placebo, participants who received a memory-enhancing placebo significantly recalled 10 % more details of the film fragment. Participants who had received an allegedly memory-impairing placebo did not recall fewer details of the fragment than controls. They did, however, make more distortion errors (i.e., minor changes in the details of the story). For example, instead of recalling that the shooter had a swastika tattooed on his chest, the tattoo was said to be on his arm. Thus, the expectation that memory would improve as a result of this memory-improving drug, positively affected memory performance. The expectation that a drug would impair memory did not decrease the proportion of correctly recalled information but did induce more distortion errors.

EXPECTATIONS IN OFFENDERS CLAIMING AMNESIA: TWO CASES

Since memory-enhancing placebos could improve memory, a further study of Van Oorsouw, Cima, Merckelbach and Kortleven (2006) administered placebos to two psychiatric inmates who claimed to have no memory of the crime they committed. The offenders were told that the treatment would restore crime-related memories. If the amnesia claimed by the offender was expectancy based (i.e., he convinced himself that his amnesia is genuine), then changing these expectations using a memory-enhancing placebo could perhaps resolve the amnesia. Another scenario could be that the amnesia was feigned. In order to overcome the possibility of feigned amnesia, questionnaires that assess the tendency to malinger were administered. The questionnaires we used were the Structured Inventory of Malingered Symptomatology (SIMS; Smith & Burger, 1997) and the Symptom Validity Test (SVT; Denney, 1996; Frederick, Carter & Powel, 1995). The SIMS is a self-report 75-item instrument that measures the tendency to feign bizarre psychiatric symptoms and/or cognitive impairments like low intelligence and amnesia. The SVT is a forced-choice procedure in which the defendant or forensic patient has to answer questions regarding their crime choosing from two equally plausible alternatives of which only one is correct. Someone performing below chance level is suspected of malingering (see also Chapter 10 of this volume for a more detailed explanation of SIMS and SVT).

It should be noted that feigned amnesia does not necessarily annul beneficial placebo effects. When the offender wants to give up his/her role of claiming amnesia (e.g. for the benefits of treatment and early parole) a placebo might also be 'effective' for resolving feigned amnesia. To assess offenders' personality and tendency to behave supernormal, the Psychopathic Personality Inventory (PPI; Lilienfeld & Andrews, 1996), and Supernormality Scale-Revised (SS-R; Cima et al., 2003) were administered. Supernormality refers to the tendency to systematically deny the presence of common symptoms (e.g., intrusive thoughts). It differs from defensiveness, in that supernormality is not just denial of psychiatric symptoms, but it also refers to the tendency to deny the presence of common symptoms. It differs from social desirability in that supernormality does not only depend on the social context. Moreover, supernormality implies more than just exhibiting a tendency to endorse 'normal' answer options. For example, it is quite common for healthy people to report that they have experienced, at least at some occasions, intrusions (i.e., 'normal obsessions'; Rachman & de Silva, 1978), rituals (i.e., 'normal compulsions'; Muris, Merckelbach & Clavan, 1997), worrisome thoughts (i.e., 'normal worries'; Clark & Claybourn, 1997), and mild persecutory delusions (Fenigstein & Vanable, 1992). Persons with a tendency to produce social desirable answers would not necessarily deny common, but slightly deviant human experiences. The SS-R differs from existing lie or social desirability scales questionnaires in that it intends to tap specifically denial of common psychological symptoms (Cima et al., 2003). To assess whether the placebo would be effective, both before and after the treatment, memory for the crime was tested using the SVT. Since our forensic patients were tested long after they had committed the crime, the usefulness of the SVT as a tool to detect malingering was minimal (see Chapter 10 of this volume). For that reason, in the present study SVT was mainly used to test offender's recollection of crime-related details and changes in that recollection after treatment.

The first forensic patient we tested, a 28-year-old man who was incarcerated for armed robbery and assault, stayed in a forensic institution in Germany. For this offender the placebo treatment turned out to be ineffective. His performance on the SVT did not improve after the placebo. Since this offender had knowledge about his crime from reading his files, and thus knew the correct answers to most of our SVT questions, the SVT could not be employed as a tool to detect malingering. However, in order to measure changes in the offender's memory as an effect of the placebo treatment, we asked for each question whether he 'remembered' the correct answer or 'knew' the correct answer from reading it in the files. If the amnesia was based on expectations, one would expect a shift from 'know' on the first SVT, to 'remember' on the second. Thus, since our offender had crime knowledge from reading his files and hence objective memory could not be measured by absolute performance on SVT, a shift from 'know' to 'remember' was the only objective measure of memory improvement. Both before and after the placebo was administered, the offender claimed that he 'knew' the correct alternative from reading it in the files. Interestingly, he also claimed to 'know' things from the files that were actually not in the files. For example, on the question 'Where was the cash register?' (a) in the office; (b) behind the front desk, he answered that it was in the office and that he 'knew' this from the files. Although we do not know the answer to this question, neither could the offender because the information was not in the files. This is rather suspicious. Furthermore, scores on the amnesia subscale of the SIMS revealed that this offender deliberately feigned memory problems. In addition, his low scores on SS-R suggested that he tried to perform healthier (e.g., supernormal) than control subjects would. Furthermore, his high scores on the PPI suggest that this offender possessed psychopathic personality traits. Scores on these three tests described a person with psychopathic traits who is trying to behave supernormal in order to leave the clinic as soon as possible. In addition, his scores on the amnesia scale of the SIMS suggested that his memory problems were most likely feigned. The fact that this offender displayed high levels of psychopathic traits fits previous research that has shown that psychopathic (mostly instrumental) offenders have more detailed memories of their offence and less often report lack of memories (Cooper, 2005; see also Chapter 3 of this volume). Thus, in this case a claim of amnesia is more likely to be malingered.

The second forensic patient, a 40-year-old man staying in a forensic clinic in Belgium for attempted murder, claimed to be only partially amnesic for the crime he committed. Since we did not know exactly which part he claimed amnesia for, we again asked for 'remember' or 'know' responses for each SVT-question. On a questionnaire asking about his expectations about memory loss, this offender expressed strong beliefs about the reality of crime-related amnesia. He also claimed to have prior experience with memory loss from a blow to the head when he was a child. In addition, he was very pessimistic about the quality of his memory. For this offender, the placebo treatment appeared to be partially successful in that his memory for the crime, as measured with SVT, improved. That is, after the treatment he reported to remember details about stabbing his victim, which he said he could not remember or only 'knew' on the first SVT. Thus, although he almost obtained the maximal score on both SVTs, he shifted from 'know' to 'remember' on three questions that concerned the stabbing and the victim. The pattern of responding on the SIMS, SS-R and PPI was normal, indicating that he did not feign psychiatric symptoms, did not want to behave supernormal and had no psychopathic personality characteristics. Since the PPI also contains three validity scales intended to measure impression measurement, malingering, careless or random responding and difficulty comprehending the items or instructions, it is very unlikely that someone scoring low on this questionnaire is faking. This offender's pronounced expectations about crime-related amnesia, and his previous experience with organic memory loss may have contributed to his amnesia claim.

To recapitulate, memory enhancing placebos may be successful when forensic patients claim amnesia with no apparent organic source. Their success is, however, dependent on the type of memory loss (e.g., simulated or bona fide). Additional instruments measuring the tendency to simulate psychiatric symptoms and an assessment of personality traits that are known to be related to simulation are informative in this type of patient-directed research.

TWO CASES OF CRIME-RELATED AMNESIA

In addition to what we already knew, the two cases presented in the previous section show that the Symptom Validity Test can only be effective to detect malingerers when the offender has not read his files and, thus, has no second-hand knowledge of crime-related details that are used to compile the SVT questions. The following two cases illustrate that when these demands are met, the SVT can be highly effective for forensic experts to detect genuine amnesia or expose an amnesia imposter.

Case 1[3] is about a middle-aged man (44 years), incarcerated for murdering a 16-year-old girl, who claimed to have complete amnesia for the crime. He was diagnosed with antisocial personality disorder (APD; American Psychological Association (APA), 1994) and also suffered from epilepsy. The offender claimed that his memory problems were the result of his epilepsy. However, as his seizures had declined over the years, forensic experts suspected that the offender malingered his crime-related amnesia. This clinical judgement was based on decreasing seizure activity and a kind of 'feeling' that the offender often lied. However, no tests were performed to evaluate his memory loss in more detail. In this case, a SVT was used to do just that. We developed 15 questions. Examples were: (1) Did the offender use a pistol? (a) Yes; (b) No*); (2) Was the victim a girl? (a) Yes*; (b) No).[4] The offender correctly answered seven out of 15 questions ($z = 0.516$; one tailed $p = 0.30$).[5] Although it is still possible that he feigned amnesia, these results suggest that he suffered from an organic amnesia related to his epilepsy.

In the second case,[6] the SVT was administered to a 33-year-old man who was convicted of arson. He had diagnoses of pyromania and APD (APA, 1994). The offender was incarcerated for burning down

---

[3] This vignette is based on a real case.

[4] * is the correct answer.

[5] $Z = [(x \pm 0.5) - NP]/\sqrt{NPQ}$: where Z is the test statistic, x is the number of correct responses, N is the number of items administered, P is the probability of a correct discrimination given no true ability (0.50), and Q represents $1-p$.

[6] This vignette is based on a real case.

his landlord's house. He claimed that his memory loss for the crime was due to excessive alcohol use. Because of his amnesia, the court reasoned that he must have committed his crime unconsciously and unintentionally. It was assumed that an alcohol blackout could have led to the development of a limited amnesia, which, in turn, was taken as evidence that he could not be held fully responsible for his crime. However, an alcohol blackout is an organic form of amnesia resulting from excessive alcohol use within a very short time span. In other words, consuming 5 glasses of whisky or 20 glasses of beer within four hours, may lead to an alcohol blackout (Goodwin, 1995). In the case of the arsonist, there was no indication that he had consumed such an amount of alcohol. In this case, we were able to develop 25 questions based on file information. Examples were: (1) Where was the garage? (a) Next to the house; (b) Behind the house*; (2) How was the garage set on fire? (a) Using a lighter*; (b) Using matches). [7] In this case, the offender correctly answered six of 25 questions ($z = -2.40$; one tailed $p < 0.008$). Such a performance would only occur less than eight times out of 1,000 by chance alone. Given these SVT results and the absence of any evidence that the man had consumed enormous amounts of alcohol prior to the crime, strongly suggests that the offender feigned his amnesia.

As three out of the four cases presented in this and the preceding section demonstrate, feigning amnesia is a frequently occurring phenomenon not only at pre-trial but also among forensic patients. Claims of amnesia are common for violent, low-intelligent offenders who try to evade responsibility by claiming amnesia, and seem to be a strategy used to avoid painful discussions about crime details during therapy sessions. A malingering interpretation of amnesia claims would predict that such claims are typical for recidivists who have learned that claiming amnesia provides them with an opportunity to avoid discussions about their criminal career. Indeed, a recent study of Cima and colleagues (2004) has shown that the most pronounced difference between offenders claiming amnesia and controls was that the former were older and had more prior convictions (i.e., experience). Thus, it may well be that offenders who were familiar with the penal system have had more opportunities to experience the advantages of claiming (partial) amnesia for their crime. More generally, if crime-related amnesia is, indeed, part of a conscious strategy to minimise responsibility, recidivism rates might also be higher for criminals with such claims. In other words, the fact that amnesia claims were especially prevalent among recidivists and related to length of criminal career, indicates that such claims are often the product of a

---

[7] * is the correct answer

learning process. Thus, the association between crime-related amnesia and prior convictions suggests that it might be worthwhile for future studies to examine more systematically whether and to what extent amnesia serves as a predictor of criminal recidivism.

CONCLUSION

When a defendant or forensic inpatient claims crime-related amnesia, the amnesia could be genuine (i.e., dissociative or organic), based on expectations, but also malingered. The studies discussed in this chapter have shown that there are a number of factors that should be taken into account before a claim of amnesia is taken seriously. First of all, it appears that simulating amnesia is a popular strategy to minimise responsibility for a crime and has substantial prevalence rates. Secondly, it appears that offenders with certain characteristics like low IQ and poor executive functions are more likely to feign amnesia, which could be taken into account when assessing the credibility of an amnesia claim. Also, it was demonstrated that severe emotional arousal and alcohol intoxication should not be easily accepted as evidence for genuine amnesia. In the latter case, measuring blood alcohol concentrations could help decide whether an alcohol blackout would be clinically possible. Furthermore, some evidence has been found that expectations about memory could play a role in claims of amnesia and that manipulating these expectations could affect memory for the event. These last findings demonstrate that perhaps the different types of amnesia cannot be strictly separated. A previous experience with organic amnesia, strong beliefs or expectations about memory loss for emotional events as well as an experience with alcohol blackouts, are factors that may contribute to an offender's strategy to simulate amnesia. What has been a conscious strategy in first instance could lead to an unconscious belief about being amnesic for the crime. Kopelman's (2000) statement that the classifications of amnesia form endpoints on a continuum and do not necessarily form discrete categories seems to be quite applicable to crime-related amnesia and should be taken into consideration. Fortunately, there are tools like SIMS and SVT available to evaluate whether an amnesia claim is likely to be malingered or not. Chapter 11 will discuss more tools to test claims of amnesia. By using these tools in combination with an assessment of a defendant's personality, and his beliefs or expectations about memory loss, we should come close to determining whether an amnesia claim is bona fide.

REFERENCES

American Psychiatric Association. (1994) *Diagnostic and statistical manual of mental disorders* (4th ed.). Washington, DC: APA.

Assefi, S.L. & Garry, M. (2003) Absolute (R) memory distortions: Alcohol placebos influence the misinformation effect. *Psychological Science*, **14**, 77–80.

Barbey, I. (1990) Postdeliktische Erinnerungsstörungen: Ergebnisse einer retrospektiven Erhebung. *Blutalkohol*, **27**, 241–59.

Belli, R.F, Winkielman, P., Read, J.D., Schwarz, N. & Lynn, S.J. (1998) Recalling more childhood events leads to judgments of poorer memory: Implications for the recovered/false memory debate. *Psychonomic Bulletin and Review*, **5**, 318–23.

Bower, G.H. (1981) Mood and memory. *American Psychologist*, **36**, 129–48.

Christianson, S.-Å. & Bylin, S. (1999) Does simulating amnesia mediate genuine forgetting for a crime event? *Applied Cognitive Psychology*, **13**, 495–511.

Cima, M.J. (2003) *Faking good, bad, and ugly. Malingering in forensic psychiatric inpatients*. Landgraaf: Groeneveldt BV.

Cima, M., Merckelbach, H., Hollnack, S., Butt, C., Kremer, K., Schellbach-Matties, R. & Muris, P. (2003) The other side of malingering: Supernormality. *Clinical Neuropsychologist*, **17**, 235–43.

Cima, M., Merckelbach, H., Klein, B., Schellbach-Matties, R. & Kremer, K. (2001) Frontal lobe dysfunctions, dissociation, and trauma self-reports in forensic psychiatric patients. *Journal of Nervous and Mental Disease*, **189**, 188–90.

Cima, M., Merckelbach, H., Hollnack, S. & Knauer, E. (2003) Characteristics of psychiatric prison inmates who claim amnesia. *Personality and Individual Differences*, **35**, 373–80.

Cima, M., Merckelbach, H., Nijman, H., Knauer, E. & Hollnack, S. (2002) I can't remember your honour: Offenders who claim amnesia. *German Journal of Psychiatry*, **5**, 24–34.

Cima, M., Nijman, H., Merckelbach, M., Kremer, K. & Hollnack, S. (2004) Claims of crime-related amnesia in forensic patients. *International Journal of Law and Psychiatry*, **27**, 215–21.

Clark, D.A. & Claybourn, M. (1997) Process characteristics of worry and obsessive intrusive thoughts. *Behaviour Research and Therapy*, **35**, 1139–41.

Cooper, B.S. (2005) *Memory for mayhem*. Unpublished Doctoral dissertation. University of British Columbia, Vancouver, BC.

Critchlow, B. (1986). The powers of John Barleycorn: Beliefs about the effects of alcohol on social behavior. *American Psychologist*, **41**, 751–64.

Crombag, H.F.M. (2002) Over opzet en schuld [About intention and guilt]. In P.J. v. Koppen, D.J. Hessing, H.L.G.J. Merckelbach & H.F.M. Crombag (Eds) *Het recht van binnen*. [Law from the inside] (pp. 737–60). Deventer: Kluwer.

Denney, R.L. (1996) Symptom validity testing of remote memory in a criminal forensic setting. *Archives of Clinical Neuropsychology*, **11**, 589–603.

Eich, J.E., Weingartner, H., Stillman, R.C. & Gillin, J.C. (1975) State-dependent accessibility of retrieval cues in the retention of a categorized list. *Journal of Verbal Learning and Verbal Behavior*, **14**, 408–17.

Fenigstein, A. & Vanable, P. (1992) Persecutory ideation and self-consciousness. *Journal of Personality and Social Psychology*, **62**, 124–38.

Fillmore, M.T., Vogel-Sprott, M. & Gavrilescu, D. (1999) Alcohol effects on intentional behavior: Dissociating controlled and automatic influences. *Experimental Clinical Psychopharmacology*, **7**, 372–8.

Frederick, R.I., Carter, M. & Powel, J. (1995) Adapting symptom validity testing to evaluate suspicious complaints of amnesia in medicolegal evaluations. *Bulletin of the American Academy of Psychiatry and the Law*, **23**, 227–33.

Gilbert, G.M. (1971) *Nürnberger Tagebuch: Gespräche der Angeklagten mit dem Gerichts-psychologen*. Frankfurt am Main: Fischer.

Goodwin, D.W. (1995) Alcohol amnesia. *Addiction*, **90**, 315–17.

Goodwin, D.W., Crane, J.B. & Guze, S.B. (1969) Phenomenological aspects of the alcoholic 'blackout'. *British Journal of Psychiatry*, **115**, 1033–38.

Gudjonsson, G.H., Hannesdottir, K. & Petursson, H. (1999) The relationship between amnesia and crime: The role of personality. *Personality and Individual Differences*, **26**, 505–10.

Guttmacher, M.S. (1955) *Psychiatry and the law*. New York: Grune & Stratton.

Hart, S.D., Cox, D.N. & Hare, R.D. (1996) *Manual of the Screening Version of Psychopathy Checklist Revised (PCL-R: SV)*. Toronto, ON: Multi-Health Systems.

Holmes, E.A., Brown, R.J., Mansell, W., Fearon, R.P., Hunter, E.C.M., Frasquilho, F. & Oakley, D.A. (2005) *Clinical Psychology Review*, **25**, 1–23.

John, O. & Srivastava, S. (1999) The Big Five trait taxonomy: History, measurement and theoretical perspectives. In L. Pervin & O. John (Eds), *Handbook of personality* (2nd ed.), (pp. 102–38). New York Press: Guilford.

Jureidini, J. (2004). Does dissociation offer a useful explanation for psychopathology. *Psychopathology*, **37**(6), 259–65.

Kalant, H. (1996) Intoxicated automatism: Legal concept vs. scientific evidence. *Contemporary Drug Problems*, **23**, 631–48.

Kassin, S.M. (2005) On the psychology of confessions: Does innocence put innocents at risk? *American Psychologist*, **4**, 215–28.

Kopelman, M.D. (1995) The assessment of psychogenic amnesia. In A.D. Baddely, B.A. Wilson & F.N. Watts (Eds), *Handbook of memory disorders* (pp. 427–48). Chichester: John Wiley & Sons, Ltd.

Kopelman, M.D. (1987) Amnesia: Organic and psychogenic. *British Journal of Psychiatry*, **150**, 428–42.

Kopelman, M.D. (2000) Focal retrograde amnesia and the attribution of causality: An exceptionally critical review. *Cognitive Neuropsychology*, **17**, 585–621.

Kuch, K. & Cox, B.J. (1992) Symptoms of PTSD in 124 survivors of the Holocaust. *American Journal of Psychiatry*, **149**, 337–40.

Kvavilashvili, L. & Ellis, J.A. (1999) The effect of positive and negative placebos on human memory performances. *Memory*, **7**, 421–37.

Leitch, A. (1948) Notes on amnesia in crime for the general practioner. *The Medical Press*, **26**, 459–63.

Lilienfeld, S.O. & Andrews, B.P. (1996) Development and preliminary validation of a self-report measure of psychopathic personality traits in a noncriminal populations. *Journal of Personality Assessment*, **66**, 488–524.

Marshall, W.L., Serran, G, Marshall, W.E., & Fernandez, Y.M. (2005) Recovering memories of the offense in 'amnesic' sexual offenders. *Sexual Abuse: A Journal of Research and Treatment*, **17**, 31–8.

Merckelbach, H., Dekkers, T.H., Wessel, I. & Roefs, A. (2003) Amnesia, flashbacks, nightmares, and dissociation in aging concentration camp survivors. *Behaviour Research and Therapy*, **41**, 351–60.

Moldea, D.E. (1995) *The killing of Robert F. Kennedy: An investigation of motive, means, and opportunity.* New York: Norton.

Moskowitz, A. (2004) Dissociation and violence: A review of the literature. *Trauma, Violence & Abuse,* **5**, 21–46.

Muris, P., Merckelbach, H. & Clavan, M. (1997) Abnormal and normal compulsions. *Behaviour Research and Therapy,* **35**, 249–52.

O'Connell, M. (1960) Amnesia and homicide. *British Journal of Delinquency,* **10**, 262–76.

Oorsouw, K. Van & Merckelbach, H. (2004) Feigning amnesia undermines memory for a mock crime. *Applied Cognitive Psychology,* **18**, 505–18.

Oorsouw, K. Van & Merckelbach, H. (2006). Simulating amnesia and memories of a mock crime. *Psychology, Crime and Law,* **12**, 261–71.

Oorsouw, K. Van, Merckelbach, H., Ravelli, D., Nijman, H. & Mekking-Pompen, I. (2004) Alcoholic blackout for criminally relevant behavior. *Journal of the American Academy of Psychiatry and the Law,* **32**, 364–70.

Oorsouw, K. Van & Merckelbach, H. (submitted). Remembering causes amnesia: The paradoxical effect of remembering.

Oorsouw, K. Van & Merckelbach, H. (in press). Expectations and memory: A placebo study.

Oorsouw, K. Van, Cima, M., Merckelbach, H. & Kortleven, S. (2006). Placebo's, verwachtingen en daderamnesie: Twee gevalsstudies. [Placebo, expectations and crime-related amnesia: Two case-studies], *The American Journal of Psychiatry, Directive Therapy,* **26**, 126–40.

Picknett, L., Prince, C. & Prioir, S. (2001) *Double standards: The Rudolf Hess Cover-Up.* London: Little, Brown & Company.

Ponds, R.W.H.M., Van Boxtel, M.P.J. & Jolles, J. (2000) Age-related changes in subjective cognitve functioning. *Educational Gerontology,* **26**, 67–81.

Parwatikar, S.D., Holcomb, W.R. & Menninger, K.A. (1985) The detection of malingered amnesia in accused murderers. *Bulletin of the American Academy of Psychiatry and the Law,* **13**, 97–103.

Porter, S., Birt, A.R., Yuille, J.C. & Hervé, H.F. (2001) Memory for murder: A psychological perspective on dissociative amnesia in legal contexts. *International Journal of Law and Psychiatry,* **24**, 23–42.

Poythress, N.G., Edens, J.F. & Watkins, M.M. (2001) The relationship between psychopathic personality features and malingering symptoms of major mental illness. *Law and Human Behavior,* **25**, 567–82.

Rachman, S. & de Silva, P. (1978) Abnormal and normal obsessions. *Behaviour Research and Therapy,* **16**, 233–48.

Sadoff, R.L. (1974) Evaluation of Amnesia in criminal-legal situations. *Journal of Forensic Sciences,* **19**, 98–101.

Schacter, D.L. (1986) Amnesia and crime: How much do we really know? *American Psychologist,* **41**, 286–95.

Sigmund, D., Barnett, W. & Mundt, C. (1998) The hysterical personality disorder: A phenomenological approach. *Psychopathology,* **31**, 311–30.

Smith, G.P. & Burger, G.K. (1997) Detection of malingering: Validation of the Structured Inventory of Malingered Symptomatology (SIMS). *Journal of American Academic Psychiatry and the Law,* **25**, 183–9.

Swihart, G., Yuille, J. & Porter, S. (1999) The role of state-dependent memory in 'red-outs'. *International Journal of Law and Psychiatry,* **22**, 199–212.

Taylor, P.J. & Kopelman, M.D. (1984) Amnesia for criminal offences. *Psychological Medicine,* **14**, 581–8.

Wagenaar, W.A. & Groeneweg, J. (1990) The memory of concentration camp survivors. *Applied Cognitive Psychology*, **4**(2), 77–87.

Winkielman, P., Schwarz, N. & Belli, R.F. (1998) The role of ease of retrieval and attribution in memory judgments: Judging your memory as worse despite recalling more events. *Psychological Science*, **9**, 124–6.

White, A.M., Matthews, D.B. & Best, P.J. (2000) Ethanol, memory, and hippocampal function: A review of recent findings. *Hippocampus*, **10**, 88–93.

Williams, J.M. & Broadbent, K. (1986) Autobiographical memory in suicide attempters. *Journal of Abnormal Psychology.*, **95**, 144–9.

Wolf, A.S. (1980) Homicide and blackouts in Alaskan natives. *Journal of Studies on Alcohol*, **2**, 456–62.

WHO (1992) *The ICD-10 classification of mental and behavioral disorders: Clinical descriptions and diagnosis guidelines.* Geneva, NY: World Health Organization.

Zago, S., Sartori, G. & Scarlato, G. (2004) Malingering and retrograde amnesia: The historic case of the collegno amnesic. *Cortex*, **40**, 519–32.

CHAPTER 9

Evaluating the Authenticity of Crime-related Amnesia

Marko Jelicic and Harald Merckelbach

Offenders who have committed serious crimes frequently claim amnesia for their offences. There is reason to believe that many of them are feigning their memory loss (Christianson & Merckelbach, 2004). The aim of this chapter is to discuss methods that can be used to evaluate the authenticity of crime-related amnesia. First, the frequency of crime-related amnesia and explanations for memory loss in offenders will be described. Next, we will focus on the different strategies that have been proposed to determine the veracity of crime-related amnesia. These methods are critically evaluated. In our view, two methods to detect feigning of crime-related amnesia may have a place in forensic assessments.

BACKGROUND

On a regular basis, practitioners in the field of forensic psychiatry and psychology are confronted with offenders who claim to have no memory for their criminal acts. Indeed, the scientific literature shows that such claims of crime-related amnesia are by no means rare. Taylor and Kopelman (1984) interviewed 34 murderers and observed that

---

Offenders' Memories of Violent Crimes. Edited by Sven Å. Christianson.
© 2007 John Wiley & Sons, Ltd.

9 (26%) of them reported memory loss for their offence. Moreover, a study examining the psychiatric reports on 64 men convicted for homicide or other violent crimes found that 21 (32%) offenders claimed crime-related amnesia (Gudjonsson, Petursson, Skulason & Sigurdarddottir, 1989). A recent retrospective study based on case-notes of 207 individuals sentenced to life imprisonment demonstrated that 60 (29%) of them indicated memory loss for their crime (Pyszora, Barker & Kopelman, 2003). Thus, as a rule of thumb, one could say that about 20 to 30% of individuals who commit violent crimes report amnesia for their offences. Although claims of crime-related amnesia are common in violent offenders, such claims are sometimes also raised by individuals charged with non-violent offences such as fraud (e.g., Kopelman, Green, Guinan, Lewis & Stanhope, 1994). The incidence of crime-related amnesia in minor offences, however, is unknown.

There are different ways to explain memory loss for criminal offences. Some crimes, particularly violent offences, are committed by individuals who are intoxicated by alcohol and/or drugs (e.g., Bourget & Bradford, 1995; Bradford & Smith, 1979). Intoxication may undermine the ability to encode and consolidate crucial events in memory (Kopelman, 2002). Diabetic offenders suffering from hypoglycaemia (Lancet, 1978) and offenders who sustained mild head injury just prior to a criminal act (McCrory, 2001) may also fail to store pertinent events in memory. Clearly, crime-related details that are poorly encoded and/or consolidated due to brain dysfunctions may be difficult to retrieve from memory. This type of memory loss can be regarded as a form of organic amnesia (Cima, Merckelbach, Nijman, Knauer & Hollnack, 2002). A second explanation emphasises the notion that many violent crimes are committed during extreme rage, anger or another altered state (e.g., psychosis). Some authors contend that during a radical emotional state or in a state of altered consciousness, information is stored in an exceptional context (Porter, Birt, Yuille & Hervé, 2001). When an offender later has returned to a more calm, relaxed or normal state and tries to retrieve crime-related memories, these memories would – due to the discrepancy between the storage and retrieval phase – be largely inaccessible. This type of memory loss is often referred to as dissociative amnesia (Cima, et al., 2002). Dissociative amnesia for crimes of passion has also been termed 'red-outs' (Swihart, Yuille & Porter, 1999). A third explanation pertains to failures in meta-memory. Christianson and Merckelbach (2004) recently suggested that some offenders may truly believe that they are amnesic while in fact they are not. There is some experimental evidence for this notion. In a few studies, undergraduate students were asked to commit a mock crime. Next, they were presented with the instruction to simulate amnesia for this event or did not receive any instructions. When, one week later, simulators were asked to give up their role as amnesic, they were outperformed by the controls on a test of memory for details of the mock crime (Christianson & Bylin, 1999; van Oorsouw & Merckelbach, 2004; see also Chapter 8 of this volume). Christianson and Merckelbach (2004) speculated that offenders who initially played the role of an amnesic person may have strong expectations that they will perform poorly on a subsequent memory test. A fourth explanation is that offenders may feign crime-related amnesia in order to obstruct police investigation and/or reduce responsibility for their acts (Cima et al., 2002). In contrast with the previous explanation for memory loss in offenders, this explanation contends that offenders are deliberately simulating their memory problems. A famous historical example of feigned amnesia is that of Rudolf Hess, who at the start of the Nuremberg trials, claimed to have no recollections of his personal and political activities during the Third Reich period. Several prominent psychiatrists examined Hess and they all declared that his amnesia was genuine. When, after some time, Hess realised that he could not respond to the allegations because of his poor memory, he stated suddenly during one of the trial sessions that he had simulated his amnesia (Gilbert, 1947).

THE REALITY OF MALINGERED CRIME-RELATED AMNESIA

In our view, it would be naïve to assume that malingering of crime-related amnesia is limited to isolated cases such as the Rudolf Hess example. In fact, several authors have warned that, especially when there is overwhelming evidence that an individual did commit the acts for which he or she is charged, offenders often engage in feigning amnesia (e.g., Centor, 1982; Cima et al., 2002; Ornish, 2001).

Research on the prevalence of simulated amnesia is scarce. In an older study, it was suggested that about 20 % of offenders with 'no recollections' of their criminal acts are feigning their memory loss (Hopwood & Snell, 1933). There is, however, reason to believe that the true rate of feigning in this population is much higher, in the sense that many individuals who claim to have crime-related amnesia because of intoxication or extreme emotions are actually simulating their memory loss. To start with, while laboratory studies demonstrate that discrepancies in mood or state between the acquisition and test phase do lead to impaired recollection of stimuli presented to participants, it hardly ever results in complete amnesia for these stimuli (Eich, 1989). Secondly, a bulk of research has shown that self-performed actions are better remembered than information presented to participants (see Nilsson, 2000, for an overview). Given that violent crimes, almost by definition, involve motor activity, this would mean that such acts would be difficult to forget. Thirdly, most victims or eyewitnesses of violent crimes do not report memory loss for pertinent events. Rivard, Dietz, Martell and Widawski (2002) studied acute dissociative responses in 115 police officers who were involved in critical shooting incidents. Although some of these officers reported a degree of memory impairment for details of the incident, there were no reports of amnesia for the entire event. In a similar vein, Yuille and Cutshall (1986) analysed eyewitness memory in 21 witnesses of a serious shooting incident. Most witnesses were highly accurate in their accounts, and this continued to be the case several months after the incident. Interestingly, witnesses who reported high stress levels during the shooting had better memory for events than those who indicated moderate levels of stress. Fourthly, Christianson, Bylin and Holmberg (2003) asked 83 convicted homicide and sexual offenders how often offenders generally feign loss of memory for the crime in order to avoid conviction. Only 2% of the homicide offenders thought that perpetrators of this type of crime never feign memory loss to some degree. Finally, Cima, Merckelbach, Hollnack and Knauer (2003) noted that more than half of psychiatric prison inmates who claimed crime-related amnesia scored above the cut-off of a self-report instrument taping the tendency to feign rare and bizarre cognitive and psychiatric symptoms (e.g., the Structured Inventory of Malingered Symptomatology; SIMS; Smith, 1997; Smith & Burger, 1997) against 18% of psychiatric prison inmates who did not claim crime-related amnesia.

Kopelman (2002; Pujol & Kopelman, 2003) has warned that not all claims of crime-related amnesia should be regarded as feigned amnesia. He pointed out that offenders who indicate that they cannot remember their criminal acts sometimes report their crimes to the police or fail to take measures to avoid their capture. According to Kopelman, this makes an account of amnesia as simulation to obstruct police investigation and/or to reduce self-responsibility for their behaviour less plausible. In our opinion, this argument is not very strong. An offender who knows that there is abundant evidence against him or her, may turn him or herself in and claim amnesia in order to make a sympathetic impression on judges or a jury (see Ornish, 2001, for a similar argument; see also Chapter 7 of this volume).

ASSESSING CLAIMS OF CRIME-RELATED AMNESIA

In the Netherlands, forensic experts usually investigate claims of crime-related amnesia by interviewing the offender. The following case serves as an illustration (Merckelbach & Jelicic, 2005; Wagenaar & Crombag, 2005).

In August 2001, in a town called Assen, a man was having an argument with his wife. The woman wanted a divorce and accused her husband of sexually abusing their daughter. The man later would say that upon hearing this accusation, his ears began to tingle and his vision became blurred. When the man recovered consciousness, his wife was lying dead on the ground and he was sitting next to her with his hands loosely around her neck. During the trial, the man said he could not remember anything from the strangulation. Two psychiatrists and a clinical psychologist were asked to assess the defendant's claim of amnesia. Based on interviews with the defendant, the three 'experts' agreed that his amnesia was authentic. One psychiatrist said '. . . basically, there is evidence of a primitive, animal-like reaction. When someone is feeling threatened, such reactions are elicited immediately, for a large part outside conscious control. By and large, it is reflexive behaviour serving as a defence mechanism. Apparently, the offender was engaged in such a reflexive (fight) reaction. He cannot remember what had happened, except for some quiet weeping from a distance. In psychiatric terms, the man was suffering from an acute dissociative reaction'. Although none of the experts had looked meticulously at the quality of his amnesia, the court ruled, on the basis of their reports about dissociative amnesia, that the defendant was not responsible for the crime. The defendant was therefore acquitted.

Most authors agree that a psychiatric interview alone is insufficient to assess claims of crime-related amnesia (Christianson & Merckelbach, 2004; see also Chapter 7 of this volume). In addition to interviewing the defendant, four strategies to test the veracity of crime-related amnesia have been proposed in the literature. To begin with, certain characteristics of the amnesia and/or the defendant can be used as clues to distinguish true from feigned amnesia. Administering standard malinger questionnaires or tests to the defendant is a second procedure to evaluate the authenticity of the alleged memory loss. Such tests or questionnaires are commonly used in forensic neuropsychology to detect feigning of memory loss due to alleged head injury. A third way to assess the authenticity of the amnesia is to subject the defendant to special symptom validity tests (SVT). SVT consists of a forced-choice procedure in which the offender's knowledge of the crime is tested by means of a series of questions relating to the crime and the crime scene. A fourth strategy to test claims of amnesia is a form of lie detection known as the Guilty Knowledge Test (GKT).

Below we describe the four strategies that have been proposed to evaluate the authenticity of crime-related amnesia are described below. The rationale and usefulness of these methods are critically evaluated.

CHARACTERISTICS OF THE AMNESIA AND THE DEFENDANT

It has been suggested that the characteristics of the amnesia might be helpful in distinguishing true from feigned amnesia for criminal acts. Power (1977) noted that, in patients with mental disorders, periods of amnesia are usually gradual and blurred in onset and termination. In his view, an amnesic episode of sudden onset and termination is suggestive of feigned memory loss. Moreover, in true amnesia, patients usually have 'islands of memory'. That is, they do not suffer from complete memory loss, but are able to remember fragments of the events that took place during the amnesic episode (Whitty & Zangwill, 1997). A patchy amnesia, in which some features of the crime are recalled, would suggest a genuine loss of memory, while absolute amnesia would be indicative of malingering (Bradford & Smith, 1979). Also, the period of amnesia is usually variable in true memory disordered patients. Especially in people with mild head injury there is shrinkage of amnesia. This pattern of memory recovery is such that old memories return before more recent memories, a pattern first described by the 19th-century French psychologist Theodule Ribot (Haber & Haber, 1998) and therefore known as Ribot's Law. According to Schacter (1986a), feeling-of-knowing ratings may also be helpful in distinguishing true from feigned amnesia. Feeling of knowing refers to a subjective conviction that one could retrieve information from memory if one were given some useful hints or cues. Schacter (1986b) conducted a series of experiments showing that participants who were asked to simulate amnesia had substantially lower feeling-of-knowing ratings than honest responders who were given a difficult memory task leading to some degree of induced amnesia. Possibly, simulators provided lower feeling-of-knowing ratings because they had the inaccurate idea that true forgetfulness goes along with low feeling-of-knowing ratings. Although Schacter's suggestions may prove useful, Porter et al. (2001) stated that they remain untested in defendants and should be considered tentative. In more general terms, however, it is true that when asked how they would fake a severe memory problem, naïve participants come up with strategies that, from a scientific point of view, make little sense. That is, malingerers often have a strong preference for over-the-top portrayal of their memory loss. Not only do they have erroneous views of the demarcations and completeness of the lost memory episodes, they sometimes also claim amnesia for personal identity, past knowledge, family and friends. These exotic claims might also go along with slow response times, hesitations, confusion, and repetition of questions, compared to patients with genuine organic amnesia (Hall & Poirier, 2001; Iverson, 1995).

A number of authors have argued that characteristics of the defendant and his or her crime may provide clues concerning the authenticity of the amnesia. Swihart et al. (1999) discussed two reasons why psychopathic offenders who claim crime-related amnesia are probably feigning their memory loss. First, given that deceptive behaviour is one of the core features of psychopathy, it is likely that psychopathic offenders who claim amnesia simulate memory loss. To illustrate this point, Swihart et al. quoted Hare (1993) who noted that 'memory loss, amnesia, blackouts, multiple personality, and temporary insanity crop up constantly in interrogations of psychopaths' (p. 43). In addition, Swihart et al. (1999) argued that psychopathic offenders would be more likely to remember details of an offence because they typically commit their crimes in a relatively calm state. Psychopaths have a flat affect and a low level of emotional reactivity. Thus, in this group of offenders, it is unlikely that discrepancies exist between encoding of crime details and retrieval of this information. Hence, there is little ground for suspecting that state-dependent effects may create memory difficulties in psychopaths. Using polygraphy, Lynch and Bradford (1980) found that 63 % of offenders with psychopathic features were being deceptive in their amnesia, compared to 50 % in those without personality disorders or other psychopathology. In cases of premeditated crime, claims of amnesia for criminal acts should also be treated with scepticism (Porter et al., 2001; Power, 1977). It is well documented that elaborative processing and rehearsal enhances memory (Brown & Craik, 2000). If anything, premeditation and planning should facilitate memory for a crime. This would especially be the case for sexual murderers who plan to commit serial offences. They often engage in fantasying about sexual molesting and killing certain victims, sometimes for years before the initial homicide takes place (Holmes & Holmes, 1998). Both the rehearsal of these fantasies and the actual murder will lead to firmly consolidated memories for criminal acts (Porter et al., 2001).

In evaluating the authenticity of crime-related amnesia, it would not be wise to solely use features of the memory loss and/or the defendant.

Possibly, some defendants engage in feigning memory loss because they, at one time in their lives, have experienced genuine amnesia as a result of e.g. mild head injury, or because one of their relatives or friends once sustained amnesia (cf. Kopelman, Green, Guinan, Lewis & Stanhope, 1994). Also, it might be easy for an informed lawyer to 'coach' an offender to behave in a way that is typical for real amnesic patients (Schacter, 1986a).

STANDARD MALINGER QUESTIONNAIRES AND TESTS

Another strategy for evaluating the authenticity of crime-related amnesia would be to administer questionnaires and tests that measure the degree to which a defendant displays a tendency to feign symptoms. One such instrument is the Structured Inventory of Malingered Symptomatology (SIMS; Smith, 1997; Smith & Burger, 1997). The SIMS is a self-report measure designed to screen for malingering of psychiatric symptoms and/or cognitive impairment. It consists of 75 yes/no items pertaining to malingering in five different areas including amnesia. The SIMS is based on the idea that malingerers do not know how genuine symptoms manifest themselves. As a result, they tend to endorse atypical and bizarre symptoms that seem to be related to the condition they are feigning. Examples of items from the amnesia subscale are 'Recently I've noticed that my memory is getting so bad that there have been entire days I cannot recall' and 'At times I've been unable to remember the names or faces of close relatives so that they seem like complete strangers'. Scores on the 75 items are summed to obtain a total SIMS score. A score exceeding the cut-off of 16 is considered indicative of malingering (Rogers, Hinds & Sewell, 1996). Studies in which college students were instructed to feign psychopathology or cognitive impairments have supported the usefulness of the SIMS for detecting feigning (Edens, Otto & Dwyer, 1999; Merckelbach & Smith, 2003; Rogers et al., 1996). These simulation studies demonstrate that the SIMS has high sensitivity, specificity, hit rate, positive predictive power (PPP) and negative predictive power (NPP). The PPP pertains to the probability that someone with a score exceeding the cut-off on the SIMS is indeed a malingerer, the NPP to the probability that someone with a score below the cut off is a non-malingerer. Lewis, Simcox, and Berry (2002) showed that the SIMS also has diagnostic accuracy in defendants who underwent insanity evaluations. That is, the SIMS was able to differentiate between defendants who were classified as malingerers (based on a structured interview) and those who were considered honest responders. Cima et al. (2003) studied psychiatric prison inmates with and without amnesia for their criminal acts. They noted that more than 50 % of the inmates who claimed memory loss scored above the SIMS cut-off, against 18 % of those who did not claim crime-related amnesia. For completeness sake, it should be noted here that there are other self-report scales that capatalise on the tendency of malingerers to endorse atypical or bizarre symptoms. One well-established self-report is, of course, the Minnesota Multiphasic Personality Inventory (MMPI). There are studies in which the MMPI was administered to patients with improbable memory problems (e.g., Greiffenstein, Gola & Baker, 1995), but these suggest that domain-specific (e.g., memory) measures are better in detecting malingering than global validity scales of the MMPI. Another alternative for the SIMS and the MMPI validity scales is the Wildman Symptom Check-list (Wildman & Wildman, 1999), which lists 60 clinically unbelievable symptoms and preferences. Unfortunately, there are no data about the accuracy of this checklist in detecting false claims of memory loss.

Some offenders say they cannot remember details of their criminal acts because they suffer from poor memory due to a neurological or psychiatric disorder (cf. Brand, Rubinsky & Lassen, 1985; Denney, 1996). In these cases, the use of methods designed to detect malingering of a general memory deficit might be an option. These methods were developed in forensic neuropsychology to identify feigning of memory problems after alleged whiplash or traumatic brain injury (Denney & Wynkoop, 2000). The idea behind these methods is that malingerers do not know that true memory-impaired patients perform poorly on free-recall tests, but exhibit relatively normal performance on recognition tests. Recall performance relies on strategic, effortful processes, while recognition is based on more passive processes. Both traditional memory measures and special malinger tests can be used to detect simulating memory dysfunction. Brandt et al. (1985) administered a standard memory test to healthy participants, patients with head injury or Huntington's disease, and a murderer with crime-related amnesia. They presented the participants with a list of 20 words. When asked to freely recall the study words, control participants outperformed the patients and the offender. On a subsequent two-alternative, forced recognition test, however, the offender performed worse than controls and patients. In fact, his performance was below chance level (4 out of 20 previously presented target words). Although it is difficult to compare one murderer with groups of patients and healthy controls, it seems that standard recognition tests might, at least in some cases, be useful to detect feigned crime-related amnesia. Much the same is true for memory tests that tap memory performance in an indirect or implicit way (Roediger, 1990). A fine example can be found in Horton, Smith, Barghout and Connolly (1992). These authors presented honest and simulating participants with a list of words. Next, participants were given a word-fragment completion task of which half the items (e.g., _ I _ _ AMO _) referred to the study words (e.g., CINNAMON). Participants who simulated memory problems completed fewer items than control participants. In more technical terms: controls, but not simulators exhibited a priming effect. Priming refers to an improvement in performance attributable to a past event, regardless of whether a participant is able to remember that experience (Roediger, 1990). The finding that simulators exhibit impaired priming is important because it is well known that priming effects are fully preserved in patients with amnesic syndromes (Parkin & Leng, 1993).

Dedicated malinger tests such as the Test of Memory Malingering (TOMM; Tombaugh, 1996) may also be helpful in identifying simulated memory impairments in offenders who claim to have memory loss for their criminal acts. The TOMM is a recognition test consisting of two learning trials and an optional retention trial. During each learning trial, the individual is presented with 50 line drawings of common objects, followed by a forced choice task in which he or she must select the previously presented drawings from new drawings. Feedback is given after each item. The retention trial, given 15 minutes after the last learning trial, consists of the forced choice task only. A score of less than 45 on the second learning trial or the retention trial is considered indicative of malingering. Research has shown that the TOMM demonstrates adequate classification accuracy in discriminating between individuals with genuine memory dysfunction and those who simulate memory problems (Vallabhajosula & van Gorp, 2001). To our knowledge, the TOMM has not yet been used in research on crime-related amnesia. However, two studies have employed the TOMM to evaluate feigning of memory impairment in forensic patients who underwent competency to stand trial (CST) evaluations. Weinborn, Orr, Woods, Conover and Feix (2003) found that more inpatients admitted for CST evaluations (36%) scored below the TOMM cut-off relative to patients admitted for other reasons (6%). Delain, Stafford and Ben-Porath (2003) studied 64 patients who underwent evaluations for a variety of forensic referral questions (including CST and criminal responsibility), and reported that 29 patients (45%) had scores below the TOMM cut-off. Most of these patients also exhibited other signs of malingering, such as an uncooperative attitude and a diagnosis of antisocial personality disorder. Hence, the TOMM appears to have some validity in detecting feigning of memory dysfunction in forensic patients. With these considerations in mind, we think that it is a useful tool for evaluating claims of crime-related amnesia, especially in defendants who say they suffer from forgetfulness due to a neurological or psychiatric disorder.

Apart from the TOMM, there are other psychometrically sound instruments to detect feigning of general memory impairment. Well researched candidates are the Amsterdam Short-Term Memory Test (Schmand, Lindeboom, Schagen, Heijt, Koene & Hamburger, 1998) and the Word Memory Test (WMT; Green, Iverson & Allen, 1999). Research indicates that these tests vary in their sensitivity, such that, for example, the WMT detects three times more malingering than the TOMM (Gervais, Rohling, Green & Ford, 2004).

One limitation of standard malinger questionnaires and tests is that they provide the forensic psychiatrist or psychologist with only indirect information regarding the authenticity of crime-related amnesia. That is, in many criminal cases the problem is not so much a general or global amnesia claim, but rather an amnesia claim that specifically focuses on the crime. In such cases, Symptom Validity Testing might be considered in addition to the methods we discussed above.

SYMPTOM VALIDITY TESTING

Symptom Validity Testing (SVT) procedures were originally developed to detect malingering of deafness (Pankratz, 1979) and cognitive dysfunction (Binder & Pankratz, 1987). More recently, SVT has been applied as a tool for assessing the veracity of memory loss in offenders who claim to have no recollections of the crimes they committed (Denney, 1996; Frederick, Carter & Powel, 1995). Briefly, SVT consists of a forced choice procedure in which offenders are asked a series of questions about details of the crime and/or the crime scene. For each question, the offender must choose between two equally plausible answers one of which is correct and the other is incorrect. Genuine amnesia for a crime should result in random performance on the SVT. That is, true memory loss will result in approximately 50% of the answers being correctly answered. Below chance performance – the incorrect answer is chosen significantly more often than the correct answer – indicates deliberate avoidance of correct answers, and, hence, intact memory for the crime. SVT is based on binomial statistics, which has the clear advantage that memory performance can be quantified. Thus, one can determine the exact probability that someone with genuine amnesia answers only 7 of 25 true/false questions correctly. According to binomial statistics, this probability is less than

5 % (Siegel & Castellan, 1988). Thus, below chance performance on a SVT procedure provides strong evidence for feigned memory loss for criminal acts.

Denney (1996) successfully applied SVT in three criminal cases in which offenders claimed memory loss for their crimes. In one of these cases, a bank robber said he could not remember anything from the robbery because he was suffering from forgetfulness due to a neurological condition. Denney drafted 29 questions using information from investigative reports. Each of these questions included the correct answer and a reasonably plausible alternative. Examples of the questions were 'What was the robber wearing? A. Dress or B. Pants', 'What type of hat did he wear? A. Felt or B. Straw', and 'What was to be used to carry the money? A. Purse or B. Paper bag'. The offender correctly answered only 7 of 29 questions ($z = -2.6$, one-tailed; $p < 0.005$). Based on his performance on the SVT and the incongruence between the severity of the memory loss he claimed and his sound neurological condition, it was concluded that this offender had simulated his crime-related amnesia. Note that Cima (2003), Frederick et al. (1995) and Rosen and Powel (2003) also applied SVT successfully in cases of offenders who claimed to have no recollections of their criminal acts.

One could argue that some educated offenders who simulate memory loss will readily understand the rationale behind SVT. Hence, they might realise that, in order to defeat the SVT, they will need to answer half the answers correctly and the other half incorrectly. With this in mind, Merckelbach, Hauer and Rassin (2002) studied the efficacy of SVT in educated people with some understanding of statistics. Twenty undergraduate students were instructed to steal an envelope containing money from an empty bar. Subsequently, they were asked to feign memory loss for this mock crime. The students were then given a SVT containing 15 true/false questions about the crime and the crime scene. The questions had two equally plausible answers. Examples of the questions were 'What amount of money was in the envelope? A. $ 10.00 or B. $ 20.00' and 'Is there a pool table in the bar? A. Yes or B. No'. About half of the students (53 %) gave less than four correct answers and were successfully identified as malingerers. The others performed at chance level and thus seemed able to feign amnesia in a convincing way. Interestingly, post-experimental interviews showed that only a few participants had some idea of the rationale behind the SVT. These results were replicated in follow-up studies with different mock crimes and other research samples (Jelicic, Merckelbach & van Bergen, 2004a; 2004b). Given that around 50 % of undergraduates are unable to defeat the SVT, the efficacy of SVT in detecting feigning should be considerably better with less-educated offenders simulating amnesia. This would especially be the case when the SVT consists of large number of items. With 30 items or more, responding in a random fashion would be an ardous job, due our limited working memory capacity (cf. Baddeley, 1986). Note that there is also a statistical test to determine whether SVT scores at chance level were given in a truly random order (Cliffe, 1992). A discussion of this 'runs'-test would fall beyond the scope of this chapter, but we will summarise the basic principle behind it. Suppose an offender is subjected to a 30-items SVT. If the offender gives correct answers to the first 15 questions and wrong answers to the remaining questions, his or her SVT score would be perfectly at chance level. However, since too few 'runs' – only two in this case – have been made, the offender would still be classified as a malingerer.

SVT does not require any special technical facilities. Paper, pencil and elementary knowledge of statistics are all that is needed. However, one does need to have investigative reports from which a series of questions about the crime and crime scene can be drawn (Denney, 1996). Also, in a proper SVT procedure, the offender should be the only person with intimate knowledge about the crime. When newspapers or other media have described the crime in some detail, or when police detectives or solicitors reveal details of the crime, an offender might claim amnesia and at the same time legitimise an above-chance level performance on the SVT by referring to the media, police detectives or solicitors. Furthermore, it is essential that the correct and incorrect alternatives are first evaluated by a panel of naïve participants. When this panel judges the incorrect alternatives as more plausible than the correct ones, it is possible that a truly amnesic patient performs below chance level. Apart from the above-mentioned considerations, SVT procedures do not suffer from any drawbacks. Denney and Wynkoop (2000, p. 816) wrote about their experiences with the SVT in court: 'On most occasions, judges understood and accepted the statistical principles involved. Although a novel use of SVT, the procedure meets scientific admissibility factors outlined by the US Supreme Court in *Daubert v Merrill Dow Pharmaceuticals* by incorporating hypothesis testing, having a known error rate, and having been subjected to peer review in the publication process'.

GUILTY KNOWLEDGE TEST

A defendant who feigns amnesia is lying about his involvement in the crime. As a matter of fact, when you are guilty, there is only a subtle difference between saying 'I have no memories of that murder' and saying 'I didn't commit that murder'. Thus, it is not too farfetched to consider the use of lie detection methods in evaluating claims of crime-related amnesia. Of course, lie detection has a bad scientific reputation. Yet, as Ben-Shakhar, Bar-Hillel and Kremnitzer (2002) pointed out, a lie detection technique that is based on sound and well-established principles does exist. This technique is known as the Guilty Knowledge Test (GKT; Lykken, 1998). The aim of this technique is the detection of intimate knowledge that the defendant denies to possess rather than the detection of lies. Basically, it consists of a series of questions followed by five alternatives. An example would be: 'Did you enter the house in which the murder took place through (1) the garage; (2) the patio; (3) a basement window; (4) the front door or (5) a second story window?' Typically, electrodermal (i.e., sweat gland activity) reactions from the hand palms are recorded while the defendant listens to the alternatives. As electrodermal activity is sensitive to emotionally provocative and familiar stimuli, guilty defendants who feign amnesia, but not others (i.e., guilty defendants with genuine amnesia or innocent people) will react with a heightened electrodermal response to the correct alternative (Allen & Iacono, 2001). The GKT closely resembles the SVT in that error rates can be calculated a priori. Thus, the probability that a guilty defendant with bona fide amnesia reacts with heightened responses to all three correct alternatives in a three-item GKT with five alternatives is $0.2 \times 0.2 \times 0.2. = 0.008$. Because error rates are known and peer-reviewed studies have found the GKT to be able to detect around 80 % of guilty subjects, Ben-Shakar and colleagues (2002) opined that this technique should be admissible in court.

One limitation of the traditional GKT technique is that it heavily depends on so-called autonomic responses, notably electrodermal reactions, that are known to be reduced in psychopaths (Lorber, 2004). Thus, its sensitivity might be compromised in this particular group. More recent versions of the GKT employed Event-Related brain Potentials (ERPs) that can be derived from the ElectroEncephaloGram (EEG). More specifically, these studies looked at whether ERP components that are a reflection of recognition memory can be used as a tool to detect malingering of amnesia (Allen & Iacono, 2001; Rosenfeld, Ellwanger & Sweet, 1995). For example, Rosenfeld and co-workers had participants malinger amnesia for autobiographical facts (birth date, mother's name, etc). Next, these facts along with other facts were presented to the participants while ERPs were measured. On the basis of the ERP magnitudes, the authors were able to detect 77 % of the cases in which participants falsely denied having memories of the target facts. ERPs provide a direct window to brain activity and accordingly, they might provide a more sensitive measure than elec-trodermal reactivity in psychopaths. However, while ERPs hold great promise as a tool for evaluating amnesia claims, more research is needed to determine the precise detection rates of this technique.

Apart from their detection rates, lie detection methods have another quality that may make them attractive to experts evaluating claims of crime-related amnesia. Lie detection machines look impressive and when confronted with a high-tech device that is said to measure honesty, defendants may give up their attempts to feign amnesia. This bogus-pipeline effect has been described in detail in the literature and rests on the manipulative power of lie detection devices. However, Cross and Saxe (2001, p. 201) warned that lie detection 'may lose some of its manipulative effect the more it is used. A placebo can func-tion, but over time, the manipulated subjects may realize that it has little power'.

CONCLUSIONS

There are different strategies for forensic psychiatrists and psychol-ogists to evaluate the authenticity of crime-related amnesia claims. In our view, SVT and standard malinger tests are useful methods to detect feigned memory loss. In cases where only the offender has knowledge of the crime and crime scene, it would be worthwhile to subject the defendant to an SVT procedure. SVT provides hard statis-tical evidence for feigned amnesia in case the defendant performs below chance level. Meanwhile, SVT is a challenge test. Below chance perfor-mance indicates malingering, but chance performance does not show that the amnesia is genuine. The defendant might be clever and knowl-edgeable that random performance is the preferred outcome on this test. If SVT is impossible to realise, or if the defendant is performing at chance level on this test, one could use standard malinger question-naires to determine the defendant's tendency to endorse bizarre items about memory loss. The scores on such instruments should, however, be interpreted with caution: they provide only indirect evidence as to whether the defendant is feigning his crime-related amnesia. Scores indicative of malingering in conjunction with other indices of feigned amnesia, may be suggestive of simulated loss of memory for criminal acts. Evaluating the characteristics of the amnesia and/or the offender and his or her crime without additional testing is, in our opinion, not to be recommended. Offenders who are simulating their memory loss may do so in a rather convincing way (Schacter, 1986a). Finally, for clinical use a GKT might be informative. However, given that only few studies directly looked at GKT and feigned amnesia, more research is needed before GKT evidence can be brought in court.

REFERENCES

Allen, J.J.B. & Iacono, W.G. (2001) Assessing the validity of amnesia in dissociative identity disorder: A dilemma for the DSM and the courts. *Psychology, Public Policy*, **7**, 311–44.

Baddeley, A. (1986) *Working memory*. Oxford: Oxford University Press.

Ben-Shakhar, G., Bara-Hillel, M. & Kremnitzer, M. (2002) Trial by polygraph: Reconsidering the use of the guilty knowledge technique in court. *Law and Human Behavior*, **26**, 527–41.

Binder, L.M. & Pankratz, L. (1987) Neuropsychological evidence of a factitious memory complaint. *Journal of Clinical and Experimental Neuropsychology*, **9**, 167–71.

Bourget, D. & Bradford, J.M.W. (1995) Sex offenders who claim amnesia for their alleged offense. *Bulletin of the American Academy of Psychiatry and the Law*, **23**, 299–307.

Bradford, J.W. & Smith, S.M. (1979) Amnesia and homicide: The Padola case and a study of thirty cases. *Bulletin of the American Academy of Psychiatry and the Law*, **7**, 219–31.

Brandt, J., Rubinsky, E. & Lassen, G. (1985) Uncovering malingered amnesia. *Annals of the New York Academy of Sciences*, **44**, 502–3.

Brown, S.C. & Craik, F.I.M. (2000) Encoding and retrieval of information. In E. Tulving & F.I.M. Craik (Eds), *The Oxford handbook of memory* (pp. 93–107). New York: Oxford University Press.

Centor, A. (1982) Criminals and amnesia: Comment on Bower. *American Psychologist*, **37**, 240.

Christianson, S.-Å. & Bylin, S. (1999) Does simulating amnesia mediate genuine forgetting for a crime event? *Applied Cognitive Psychology*, **13**, 495–511.

Christianson, S.-Å., Bylin, S. & Holmberg, U. (2003) Homicide and sexual offenders' view of crime-related amnesia. Unpublished manuscript.

Christianson, S.-Å. & Merckelbach, H. (2004) Crime-related amnesia as a form of deception. In P.A. Granhag & L.A. Strömwall (Eds), *The detection of deception in forensic contexts* (pp. 195–225). Cambridge: Cambridge University Press.

Cima, M. (2003) *Faking good, bad, and ugly: Malingering in forensic psychiatric inpatients*. Ph.D. Thesis Maastricht University.

Cima, M., Merckelbach, H., Hollnack, S. & Knauer, E. (2003) Characteristics of psychiatric prison inmates who claim amnesia. *Personality and Individual Differences*, **35**, 373–80.

Cima, M., Merckelbach, H., Nijman, H., Knauer, E. & Hollnack, S. (2002) I can't remember your honor: Offenders who claim amnesia. *German Journal of Psychiatry*, **5**, 24–34.

Cliffe, M.J. (1992) Symptom-validity testing of feigned sensory or memory deficits: A further elaboration for subjects who understand the rationale. *British Journal of Clinical Psychology*, **31**, 207–9.

Cross, Th.P. & Saxe, L. (2001) Polygraph testing and sexual abuse: The lure of the magic lasso. *Child Maltreatment*, **6**, 195–206.

Delain, S.L., Stafford, K.P. & Ben-Porath, Y.S. (2003) Use of the TOMM in a criminal court forensic assessment setting. *Assessment*, **10**, 370–81.

Denney, R.L. (1996) Symptom validity testing of remote memory in a criminal forensic setting. *Archives of Clinical Neuropsychology*, **11**, 589–603.

Denney, R.L. & Wynkoop, T.F. (2000) Clinical neuropsychology in the criminal forensic setting. *Journal of Head Trauma Rehabilitation*, **15**, 804–28.

Edens, J.F., Otto, R.K. & Dwyer, T. (1999) Utility of the Structured Inventory of Malingered Symptomatology in identifying persons motivated to malinger psychopathology. *Journal of the American Academy of Psychiatry and the Law*, **27**, 387–96.

Eich, E. (1989) Theoretical issues in state dependent memory. In H.L. Roediger III & F.I.M. Craik (Eds), *Varieties of memory and consciousness: Essays in honour of Endel Tulving* (pp. 331–54). Hillsdale, NJ: Lawrence Erlbaum.

Frederick, R.I., Carter, M. & Powel, J. (1995) Adapting symptom validity testing to evaluate suspicious complaints of amnesia in medicolegal evaluations. *Bulletin of the American Academy of Psychiatry and the Law*, **23**, 227–33.

Gervais, R.O., Rohling, M.L., Green, P. & Ford, W. (2004) A comparison of the WMT, CARB, and TOMM failure rates in non-head injury disability claimants. *Archives of Clinical Neuropsychology*, **19**, 475–87.

Gilbert, G.M. (1947) *Nuremberg diary*. New York: Straus & Cudaty.

Green, P., Iverson, G.L. & Allen, L.M. (1999) Detecting malingering in head injury litigation with the Word Memory test. *Brain Injury*, **13**, 813–19.

Greiffenstein, M.F., Gola, T. & Baker, W.J. (1995) MMPI-2 validity scales versus domain specific measures in detection of factitious brain injury. *Clinical Neuropsychologist*, **9**, 230–40.

Gudjonsson, G.H. Petursson, H., Skulason, S. & Sigurdardottir, H. (1989) Psychiatric evidence: A study of psychological issues. *Acta Psychiatrica Scandinavia*, **80**, 165–9.

Haber, L. & Haber, R.N. (1998) Criteria for the admissibility of eyewitness testimony of long past events. *Psychology, Public Policy, and Law*, **4**, 1135–59.

Hall, H.V. & Poirier, J.G. (2001) *Detecting malingering and deception: Forensic distortion analysis*. Boca Raton: CRC.

Hare, R.D. (1993) *Without conscience: The disturbing world of the psychopaths among us*. New York: Simon & Schuster.

Holmes, R.M. & Holmes, S.T. (1998) *Serial murder*. Thousand Oaks, CA: Sage.

Hopwood, J.S. & Snell, H.K. (1933) Amnesia in relation to crime. *Journal of Mental Science*, **79**, 27–41.

Horton, K.D., Smith, S.A., Barghout, N.K. & Connolly, D.A. (1992) The use of indirect memory tests to assess malingered amnesia: A study of metamemory. *Journal of Experimental Psychology: General*, **121**, 326–51.

Iverson, G.L. (1995) Qualitative aspects of malingered memory deficits. *Brain Injury*, **9**, 35–40.

Jelicic, M., Merckelbach, H. & van Bergen, S. (2004a) Symptom validity testing of feigned amnesia for a mock crime. *Archives of Clinical Neuropsychology*, **19**, 525–31.

Jelicic, M., Merckelbach, H. & van Bergen, S. (2004b) Symptom validity testing of feigned crime-related amnesia: A simulation study. *Journal of Credibility Assessment and Witness Psychology*, **5**, 1–8.

Kopelman, M.D. (2002) Psychogenic amnesia. In: A.D. Baddeley, M.D. Kopelman & B.A. Wilson (Eds), *Handbook of memory disorders*, 2nd ed. (pp. 451–71). Chichester: John Wiley & Sons, Ltd.

Kopelman, M.D., Green, R.E.A., Guinan, E.M., Lewis, P.D.R. & Stanhope, N. (1994) The case of the amnestic intelligence officer. *Psychological Medicine*, **24**, 1037–45.

Lancet (1978) Editorial: Factitious hypoglycaemia. *Lancet*, **I**, 1293.

Lewis, J.L., Simcox, A.M. & Berry, D.T.R. (2002) Screening for feigned psychiatric symptoms in a forensic sample by using the MMPI-2 and the Structured Inventory of Malingered Symptomatology. *Psychological Assessment*, **14**, 170–6.

Lorber, M.F. (2004) Psychophysiology of aggression, psychopathy, and conduct problems: A meta-analysis. *Psychological Bulletin*, **130**, 531–52.

Lykken, D.T. (1998) *A tremor in the blood*. Reading: Perseus Publishing.

Lynch, B.E. & Bradford, J. (1980) Amnesia: Detection by psychophysiological measures. *American Academy of Psychiatry and the Law*, **8**, 288–97.

McCrory, P. (2001) The medicolegal aspects of automatism in mild head injury. *British Journal of Sports Medicine*, **35**, 288–96.

Merckelbach, H., Hauer, B. & Rassin, E. (2002) Symptom validity testing of feigned dissociative amnesia: A simulation study. *Psychology, Crime, and Law*, **8**, 311–18.

Merckelbach, H. & Jelicic, M. (2005) *Hoe een CIA-agent zijn geheugen hervond en andere waargebeurde verhalen [How a CIA agent recovered his memories and other true stories]*. Amsterdam: Contact.

Merckelbach, H. & Smith G.P. (2003) Diagnostic accuracy of the Structured Inventory of Malingered Symptomatology (SIMS) in detecting instructed malingering. *Archives of Clinical Neuropsychology*, **18**, 145–52.

Nilsson, L.G. (2000) Remembering actions and words. In E. Tulving & F.I.M. Craik (Eds), *Oxford handbook of memory* (pp. 137–48). New York: Oxford University Press.

Ornish, S.A. (2001) A blizzard of lies: Bogus psychiatric defenses. *American Journal of Forensic Psychiatry*, **22**, 19–30.

Pankratz, L. (1979) Symptom validity testing and symptom retraining: Procedures for the assessment and treatment of functional sensory deficits. *Journal of Consulting and Clinical Psychology*, **47**, 409–10.

Parkin, A.J. & Leng, N.R.C. (1993) *Neuropsychology of the amnesic syndrome*. Hove: Lawrence Erlbaum.

Porter, S., Birt, A.R., Yuille, J.C. & Hervé, H.F. (2001) Memory for murder: A psychological perspective on dissociative amnesia in legal contexts. *International Journal of Law and Psychiatry*, **24**, 23–42.

Power, D.J. (1977) Memory, identification and crime. *Medicine, Science, and the Law*, **17**, 132–9.

Pujol, M. & Kopelman, M.D. (2003). Psychogenic amnesia. *Practical Neurology*, **3**, 292–9.

Pyszora, N.M., Barker, A.F. & Kopelman, M.D. (2003) Amnesia for criminal offences: A study of life sentence prisoners. *Journal of Forensic Psychiatry & Psychology*, **14**, 475–90.

Rivard, J.M., Dietz, P., Martell, D. & Widawski, M. (2002) Acute dissociative responses in law enforcement officers involved in critical shooting incidents: The clinical and forensic implications. *Journal of Forensic Science*, **47**, 1093–1100.

Roediger, H.L. (1990) Implicit memory: Retention without remembering. *American Psychologist*, **45**, 1043–56.

Rogers, R., Hinds, J.D. & Sewell, K.W. (1996) Feigning psychopathology among adolescent offenders: Validation of the SIRS, MMPI-A, and SIMS. *Journal of Personality Assessment*, **67**, 244–57.

Rosen, G.M. & Powel, J.E. (2003) Use of a symptom validity test in the forensic assessment of posttraumatic stress disorder. *Journal of Anxiety Disorders*, **17**, 361–7.

Rosenfeld, J.P., Ellwanger, J. & Sweet, J. (1995) Detecting simulated amnesia with event-related brain potentials. *International Journal of Psychophysiology*, **19**, 1–11.

Schacter, D.L. (1986a) Amnesia and crime: How much do we really know? *American Psychologist*, **41**, 286–95.

Schacter, D.L. (1986b) Feeling-of-knowing ratings distinguish between genuine and simulated forgetting. *Journal of Experimental Psychology: Learning, Memory, and Cognition*, **9**, 39–54.

Schmand, B., Lindeboom, J., Schagen, S., Heijt, R., Koene, T. & Hamburger, H.L. (1998) Cognitive complaints in patients after whiplash injury: The impact of malingering. *Journal of Neurology, Neurosurgery and Psychiatry*, **64**, 339–343.

Siegel, S. & Castellan, N.J. (1988) *Nonparametric statistics for the behavioral sciences*. New York: McGraw-Hill.

Smith, G.P. (1997) Assessment of malingering with self-report instruments. In R. Rogers (Ed.), *Clinical assessment of malingering and deception* (pp. 351–70). New York: Guilford.

Smith, G.P. & Burger, G.K. (1997) Detection of malingering: Validation of the Structured Inventory of Malingered Symptomatology (SIMS). *Journal of the American Academy of Psychiatry and the Law*, **25**, 180–9.

Swihart, G., Yuille, J. & Porter, S. (1999) The role of state-dependent memory in 'red-outs'. *International Journal of Law and Psychiatry*, **22**, 199–212.

Taylor, P.J. & Kopelman, M.D. (1984) Amnesia for criminal offenses. *Psychological Medicine*, **14**, 581–8.

Tombaugh, T.N. (1996) *Test of Memory Malingering (TOMM)*. New York: Multi-Health Systems.

Vallabhajosula, B. & van Gorp, W.G. (2001) Post-Daubert admissibility of scientific evidence on malingering of cognitive deficits. *Journal of the American Academy of Psychiatry and the Law*, **29**, 207–15.

Van Oorsouw, K. & Merckelbach, H. (2004) Feigning undermines memory for a mock crime. *Applied Cognitive Psychology*, **18**, 505–18.

Wagenaar, W.A. & Crombag, H. (2005) *The popular policeman and other cases: Psychological perspectives on legal evidence*. Amsterdam: Amsterdam University Press.

Weinborn, M., Orr, T., Woods, S.P., Conover, E. & Feix, J. (2003) A validation of the Test of Memory Malingering in a forensic psychiatric setting. *Journal of Clinical and Experimental Neuropsychology*, **25**, 979–90.

Whitty, C.W.M. & Zangwill, O.L. (1977) Traumatic amnesia. In: C.W.M. Whitty & O.L. Zangwill (Eds), *Amnesia* 2nd ed. (pp. 118–35). London: Butterworths.

Wildman, R.W. & Wildman, R.W. (1999) The detection of malingering. *Psychological Reports*, **84**, 386–88.

Yuille, J.C. & Cutshall, J.L. (1986) A case study of eyewitness memory of a crime. *Journal of Applied Psychology*, **71**, 291–301.

Part 3
Interviewing Offenders

CHAPTER 10

Interviewing Suspects of Crime

CAROLE HILL AND AMINA MEMON

INTRODUCTION

In order to solve criminal investigations it is essential that police officers gather as much information and evidence as possible so that they can determine how and why the crime occurred, and who committed the crime. One of the most valuable tools used by police officers when gathering evidence in criminal investigations is the investigative interview. This is particularly so when other forms of evidence against a suspect are weak or non-existent. The amount of research conducted into the quality of investigative interviews in Britain has been substantial. Importantly, this research has resulted in the production of guidelines regarding investigative interviewing, training for investigators as well as influencing legal policies in Britain (e.g. Clarke & Milne, 2001; Home Office, 1985, 2001; Home Office, Youth Justice and Criminal Evidence Act, 1999; Scottish Executive, 2003).

With regards to the investigative interviewing of suspects, the techniques used during the interview phase of an investigation have changed markedly over the last century. This chapter will review these changes in interview techniques and will focus in particular on current interviewing practices in Britain and America. The chapter will also review research examining investigator bias, a presumption

Offenders' Memories of Violent Crimes. Edited by Sven Å. Christianson.
© 2007 John Wiley & Sons, Ltd.

that a suspect is guilty and how this can impact on the subsequent investigation.

INTERROGATION MANUALS

'Third degree' techniques, where admissions of guilt and self-incriminating information are extracted using physical violence or by inflicting mental suffering, were widely utilised in America during the early 1900s. According to Munsterberg (1908/1923) torture and threats were used all over the world for thousands of years as a means of getting people to confess. In his book Munsterberg described the 'third degree' with reference to dazzling lights, cold water hoses and secret blows. In the early part of the last century police interview tactics were characterised by coercion, which ranged from direct physical violence, such as beating the suspect with a baseball bat or burning the suspect with red hot pokers, to more psychological techniques such as keeping the suspect in solitary confinement for days/weeks or depriving the suspect of food and sleep for days at a time (for a detailed review of third degree practices see Leo, 2004). The 1940s and 1950s saw the publication of the first police interrogation manuals in America. These manuals condemned the widespread use of 'third degree' interrogation practices and instead recommended the use of more subtle methods to elicit confessions. It was believed that this change in interviewing practices would eradicate coercive and unethical police interviews as well as the occurrence of miscarriages of justice due to false confessions. Although the use of third degree tactics has drastically declined over the past century, there is evidence to indicate that the new interrogation methods recommended in these manuals can still result in miscarriages of justice as a result of false confessions (Bedau & Radelet, 1987; Brandon & Davies, 1973; Drizin & Leo, 2004; Gudjonsson, 2003; Leo & Ofshe, 1998).

One of the most influential manuals is *Criminal Interrogation and Confessions* by Inbau, Reid, Buckley and Jayne (2001). The main assumption behind this manual is that guilty suspects will be reluctant to confess to a crime, unless they have been caught in the act, and that they therefore need to be persuaded to confess through the use of techniques designed to break down their resistance. Inbau et al. (2001) describe a nine-step method for breaking down the resistance of reluctant suspects and making them confess. This method is known widely as the 'Reid Technique'.

In the first step of the Reid Technique (Direct Positive Confrontation) the investigator directly confronts the suspect with a statement indicating that he is absolutely certain of the suspect's guilt. The authors also recommend that investigators take an evidence folder, or a simulation of one, into the interview room with them in order to lead the suspect to believe that the folder contains 'information and material of incriminating significance', even if it does not. The investigator also provides the suspect with a perceived benefit for telling the truth (i.e. identifying a motive or the circumstances surrounding the offence).

In Step 2 (Theme Development) the investigator offers the suspect a 'moral excuse' for having committed the offence or minimises the moral implications of such behaviour. These themes or moral excuses are developed in order to provide the suspect with a face-saving excuse for committing the offence, thus increasing the probability that the suspect will confess. Examples of suggested themes that can be developed include indicating that others might have behaved in the same manner under similar circumstances and sympathising with the suspect by condemning others such as the victim or accomplice. Alternatively, the investigator can exaggerate the nature and seriousness of the offence, enabling a guilty suspect to feel that the offence he has committed is not as serious, and therefore making the suspect more likely to confess.

The third step (Handling Denials) involves the investigator preventing the suspect from engaging in denials. This is achieved by persistently interrupting any denials by telling the suspect to listen to what the investigator has to say. The authors recommend this technique because the more a guilty suspect denies his involvement, the less likely he will be to confess later. Instead the investigator should aim to return the suspect to the theme developed in Step 2.

Step 4 (Overcoming Objections) is designed to overcome the excuses or reasons given by the suspect as to why he could not/would not have committed the crime. In this step it is recommended that the investigator turn the objection round and use it as a reason why the suspect should tell the truth as well as to develop the theme from Step 2. The authors state that when the suspect's objections have been handled properly the suspect may become uncertain and start to withdraw from the interrogation. If this is the case then Step 5 is recommended.

The fifth step (Keeping the Suspect's Attention) is recommended when the suspect is no longer interacting with the investigator either verbally or mentally and appears to be withdrawing from the interrogation and ignoring the investigator's theme. Techniques for keeping the suspect's attention include the investigator moving his seat closer to the suspect, increasing attempts to establish/maintain eye contact or the use of visual aids such as physical evidence. After re-establishing rapport with the suspect, the authors assume that a guilty suspect will have become reticent and quiet because his denials and objections are not being listened to. The next step is Step 6.

In Step 6 (Handling the Suspect's Passive Mood) the investigator must recognise the passive mood and deal with this. In order to deal with a passive mood it is recommended that the investigator focus on one specific theme/moral excuse and continue to develop it, whilst at the same time appealing to the suspect's sense of decency and honour. The authors note that the investigator must continue to be understanding and sympathetic whilst urging the suspect to tell the truth. Once the suspect shows physical signs of resignation Step 7 should be utilised.

During Step 7 (Presenting the Alternative Question) an alternative question is put to the suspect. The alternative question is normally the end result of the theme development and is designed to get the suspect to admit to the lesser alternative, rather than an alternative that shows the suspect in a worse light. Basically this involves the suspect being pressured to choose between two alternatives, both of which result in an incriminating admission (e.g. 'Did you plan to keep that money all along, or did you only borrow it with the plan of paying it back?').

Once a suspect has chosen an alternative, and thus made a self-incriminating admission, the investigator moves on to Step 8 (Bringing the Suspect into the Conversation). This involves engaging the suspect in the conversation in order to develop a full confession and obtain details of the offence orally from the suspect.

Finally, Step 9 (The Written Confession) involves converting the oral confession into a written confession. The authors highlight that it is important to obtain the written confession as soon as possible after it is made so that the suspect does not have time to reflect on the interrogation and retract the confession. The Reid manual also suggests that the written confession can be used to create an illusion of credibility. For example, interrogators are asked to deliberately make minor mistakes such as spelling the suspect's name incorrectly or inaccurately recording some other personal details (Inbau et al., 2001). The aim is to get the suspect to spot the error, to correct it and to write their initials beside it. This is believed to create an illusion that the written confession is credible and genuine and make it more difficult for the suspect to distance themselves from the statement later on. Another tactic that is recommended to investigators in order to increase the authenticity of a statement is to insert irrelevant details about the suspect's personal history that is only known to them, such as the name of their first school (Inbau et al., 2001).

Kassin and McNall (1991) have identified two general approaches to interrogation in Inbau et al.'s (2001) manual, both designed to elicit confessions. The first approach, termed 'maximisation', is where the investigator attempts to intimidate and scare the suspect into confessing. Techniques that can be used to achieve this include making false claims about evidence against the suspect and exaggerating the seriousness of the offence. The second approach has been called 'minimisation'. This approach attempts to lull the suspect into a false sense of security using various techniques such as blaming the victim or an accomplice, playing down the seriousness of the charges, offering sympathy or face-saving excuses and by referring to extenuating circumstances. Explicit promises of leniency or threats of punishment are not admissible in court. However, research evidence indicates that minimisation techniques, which are admissible in court, communicate an implicit promise that suspect's will be treated with leniency if they confess. Similarly, maximisation techniques (also admissible in court) were found to communicate a threat of punishment via pragmatic implication (Kassin & McNall, 1991). In addition, recent research indicates that the use of such minimisation techniques, and their inherent inference of leniency, has led college students to falsely confess within the laboratory environment (Russano, et al. 2005; for a review of this research see Gudjonsson, Chapter 11, this volume).

Despite the risks associated with the interrogation techniques described, Inbau et al. (2001) argue that 'it must be remembered that none of the steps is apt to make an innocent person confess and that all the steps are legally as well as morally justifiable' (p. 212). One of the reasons for their stance is that they recommend that prior to the formal interrogation, described above, suspects be interviewed informally. This informal interview preferably takes place in a non-custodial setting, where suspects do not have to be informed of their rights, and is non-accusatory in nature. The main purpose of the interview is to develop rapport with the suspect and to conduct a 'Behaviour Analysis Interview'. The Behaviour Analysis Interview is a set of pre-interrogation questions designed to evoke certain behaviours in the suspect from which their guilt or innocence can be determined. Suspects, who answer a certain number of these questions in what is perceived to be a deceptive manner, should be treated as guilty and formally interrogated using the Reid Technique. Suggested questions for the Behaviour Analysis Interview range from general questions (i.e. 'What do you think should happen to the person who committed the crime?') to specific questions (i.e. 'Would you be willing to take a polygraph?'). Therefore formal interrogations, according to the manual, should only be commenced when the investigator is definite or reasonably certain of the suspect's guilt. However, unless there is evidence such as witness reports or physical evidence, this assumes that investigators are able to detect deception through the use of the Behaviour Analysis Interview.

Over the years researchers have consistently demonstrated that people (including professional lie catchers) rarely perform better than chance when trying to detect deception and that training has a limited and inconsistent impact on the ability to detect deception (for reviews see Granhag & Stromwell, 2004; Memon, Vrij & Bull, 2003; Vrij, 2000; see also Vrij & Granhag, Chapter 12, this volume). In addition, Vrij, Mann and Fisher (2005) have recently conducted the first empirical test of the Behaviour Analysis Interview. They found that the verbal and non-verbal behaviours considered by Inbau et al. (2001) to be indicative of deception (e.g. being unhelpful in response to questions and showing nervous behaviours such as performing grooming behaviours) were in fact more typical of truth tellers. Thus, if judgements on whether to formally interrogate are based on inaccurate behavioural indicators of deception, there is a considerable risk that innocent people will be perceived as deceptive or guilty and formally interrogated using the coercive and manipulative interviewing techniques described above.

Narchet, Coffman, Russano and Meissner (2005) have recently analysed the types of interrogation techniques recommended by 11 modern-day interrogation manuals, including Inbau et al.'s. They found that 100 % of the manuals advocated minimisation techniques, with 82 % suggesting that investigators blame the victim and 64 % suggesting that the investigator offer face-saving excuses to the suspect. In addition, 82 % of these manuals were found to recommend maximisation techniques with 73 % of them suggesting the use of false evidence and 54 % advocating that the investigator play the co-accused off against one another. An important point to note is that only 36 % of the manuals warned investigators about the possibility that someone may confess to a crime that they are innocent of. The high percentage of interrogation manuals recommending the use of such coercive techniques, and the lack of warnings about their potential dangers, is particularly concerning given that researchers have demonstrated that some of these interviewing techniques can result in the elicitation of false confessions (for a review of this research see Chapter 11, this volume).

Whilst it is clear that coercive and manipulative interrogation techniques are being recommended to investigators through interrogation manuals, it is not entirely clear how often these are being used in practice. The following sections will review studies of police practice in Britain and America.

POLICE PRACTICE IN BRITAIN

The introduction of the Police and Criminal Evidence Act 1984 (PACE) was a major development in police interviewing practices in England and Wales. One of the requirements of the Act was that police interviews with suspects be recorded on audiotape. The recording of interviews was introduced to ensure that the rights of suspects were safeguarded during interviews. However, recording also allows false allegations made by suspects about the way they were interviewed to be exposed, as it ensures a factually accurate record of the interview. Special protections for vulnerable suspects, for example those who are mentally ill, mentally handicapped or juveniles, were also introduced. Vulnerable suspects must have an 'appropriate adult' present to offer them special assistance i.e. to ensure that they understand what is going on, the questions they are asked and the consequences of any statements they make. An appropriate adult is a responsible adult who can be a relative or professional. Despite the progress made by the introduction of PACE and the accompanying guidelines about interview procedure, there was no specific training for officers in the interviewing techniques they should be using (see Milne and Bull, 1999 for a review).

Prior to the introduction of PACE two studies were carried out to examine the interview techniques that were being used by police officers in England. These two studies came to quite different conclusions as to the coerciveness of the tactics used by police officers. Softley (1980) observed the interviews of 218 suspects. In 60% of the interviews at least one persuasive interviewing tactic was used to encourage a suspect to part with information. The most common tactic observed, involved the interviewer pointing out contradictions in the suspect's account. This was observed in 22% of the interviews. In 13% of the interviews the police stressed the overwhelming evidence against the suspect, which made denial seem pointless. In 15% of the interviews the police appeared to bluff or hint that other evidence would be forthcoming. The police minimised the seriousness of the offence or the suspect's part in it in about 6% of the interviews and in about 7% of the interviews the police hinted at the possibility of a longer detention unless the suspect cooperated. Softley (1980) concluded that overall police practice was fair to the suspect. However, Irving's (1980) research paints a different picture.

Over a six-month period Irving (1980) observed the interviews of 60 suspects in Brighton Police Station in England and recorded the tactics used by interrogators. This study was carried out in 1979. Police were observed to use persuasive and manipulative interrogation tactics in about two-thirds of the cases. More than one type of tactic was commonly used within interviews and each type of tactic was sometimes used more than once with each suspect. The type of tactics observed were subtly telling the suspect that it was futile to deny their guilt (e.g. pretending they had more information to link the suspect to the crime than they did), minimising the seriousness of the offence and advising suspects that it was in their best interests to confess. The conclusion made by Irving (1980) was that the police commonly used manipulative and persuasive interrogation techniques, which were similar to the techniques, recommended in American police interrogation manuals (Irving & McKenzie, 1989).

In order to measure the effectiveness of PACE a further two studies were carried out by Irving and McKenzie (1989) after the implementation of PACE. Both these studies were replications of Irving's (1980) study. The two studies were carried out in 1986 and 1987, the only difference between the two being that the later study focused on more serious cases. The results of the 1986 study indicated that there had been a dramatic fall in the number of manipulative and persuasive tactics used by detectives at Brighton police station. The number of tactics used was 42 in 68 cases, compared to 165 tactics in 60 cases in the original study. It was concluded that this fall in the number of tactics used by the police was almost certainly due to the implementation of PACE, although other factors could not be conclusively ruled out. However, in the third study, conducted in 1987, the number of tactics used increased to 88 in 68 cases. In addition, the proportion of suspects for whom some tactic was used fell from 73 % in 1979 to 57 % in 1986 before rising to 62 % in 1987. This rise may have been due to the fact that suspects were being interviewed about more serious offences in the 1987 study, which would be consistent with Leo's (1996) findings that more tactics are used as crime seriousness increases. Interestingly, Irving and McKenzie (1989) reported that the proportion of interviews that contained an admission or a confession by the suspect did not change dramatically following the introduction of audio recording suspect interviews. However, this may have been due to the fact that there was sufficiently strong evidence against the suspect so that a confession was not needed to secure a prosecution, although this is at odds with the findings described in the next section.

A number of similar studies have been carried out since the implementation of PACE. One of these studies reported by Moston,

Stephenson and Williamson in 1992 noted that in cases where there was strong evidence against the suspect there was a tendency for interviewers to use accusatorial strategies of questioning. This involved the suspect being confronted with the accusation against them at the very beginning of questioning. Information gathering strategies, characterised by the asking of 'open' questions were typical in cases where there was minimal evidence against the suspect. However, Moston et al. point out that this strategy was largely dictated by the fact that there was no evidence available to confront the suspect with. This differs from Leo's (1996) research where he found that more interrogation tactics were used when the evidence was weak. Baldwin (1992) examined 600 interviews recorded between 1989 and 1990. Thirty-six per cent of the interviews were assessed as unsatisfactory. He identified the main weaknesses as lack of preparation, general ineptitude, poor technique, an assumption of guilt, unduly repetitive, persistent or laboured questioning, failure to establish relevant facts and the exertion of too much pressure.

The previous studies discussed have looked at the interviewing of adult suspects. The following study by Evans and Webb (1993) appears to be the only study that has specifically looked at the interviewing strategies police use with juvenile suspects. Evans and Webb (1993) examined a random selection of 60 tape-recorded interviews from all police divisions in Merseyside. The selection of tapes included a cross-section of criminal offences. The interviews were conducted in 1990 under the provisions of PACE. Both male and female suspects, ranging in age from 10 to 16 years old, were interviewed. The results indicated that approximately half of all the questioning involved counter-productive questions (e.g. leading questions, multiple questions, option questions and statements) and risky questions (closed yes/no questions). Evans and Webb (1993) also found that younger children (10–13 year olds) had more statements made to them and had fewer questions asked of them compared to older children (14–16 year olds). No differences in questioning style between male and female juvenile suspects were reported. This is clearly an area where further research is needed.

Although Irving and McKenzie (1989) found that the use of persuasive interviewing techniques had fallen since the implementation of PACE it is clear from the studies discussed above that they were still being used at times. One case example is that of Stephen Miller who was convicted of murder in 1989 after confessing to the crime. Miller was arrested and interviewed after the implementation of PACE. The police interviewed him on 19 occasions over a period of five days. Fortunately, the hostile, intimidating and oppressive interviewing techniques used in this case were recorded on audiotapes, which were used as evidence in his appeal and resulted in his conviction being overturned (Gudjonsson, 2003). It is not really surprising that persuasive and manipulative police interviewing techniques continued to be used as British police officers did not start to receive national training in interviewing techniques until 1993 when the 'National Package on Investigative Interview Training' commenced. This five-day training course is based on the PEACE model of interviewing (Planning and preparation, Engage and explain, Account, Closure and Evaluation) and emphasises that the aim of the interview is to search for the truth. The aim of this course is to train all operational police officers in England and Wales to interview suspects, victims and witnesses to a reasonable level of interviewing skills. The two primary techniques taught in this training package are: Conversation Management and the Cognitive Interview. The Cognitive Interview is a technique for use with cooperative interviewees, typically witnesses who are not suspects (Fisher, Brennan & McCauley, 2002). Conversation Management provides the interviewer with a framework through which they can effectively manage a conversation (for an in depth review of these two techniques see Milne & Bull, 1999).

Since the implementation of the national PEACE training a number of studies have examined the police interview techniques that are being used during interviews with suspects. However, these studies did not explicitly evaluate the effectiveness of the PEACE training. For example, Bull and Cherryman (1995) examined 69 audiotape-recorded interviews, which were rated by four independent raters on 29 characteristics. Six skills were identified as missing from the interviews. These were the development of rapport, the use of pauses and silences, open-mindedness, flexibility, empathy/compassion and the avoidance of the use of leading questions. The authors did not state how many of these officers had received interview training and in particular training in the PEACE model of interviewing. Pearse and Gudjonsson (1996) have analysed police interview tapes from suspects at two police stations in England. They found that the introduction of allegations against the suspect (74 % of cases) and challenging a lie or an inconsistency in statements (20 % of cases) were the most common persuasive tactics used. Various other types of challenge such as emphasising the seriousness of the offence and psychological manipulation were present in less than 8 % of cases. They further found that open-ended questions were used in 98 % of the interviews, although 73 % of interviews also contained leading questions. Again it is not clear how many of the interviews observed were carried out by officers trained in the PEACE model of interviewing.

McGurk, Carr and McGurk (1993) carried out an evaluation of the impact of PEACE training on interview performance prior to the training being implemented across England and Wales. They found that the training improved both the knowledge and skill of the interviewers, compared to a control group who received no training. Additionally, they found that this benefit was retained six months later. Recently Clarke and Milne (2001) have carried out a national evaluation of the PEACE training package. They noted that although initial evaluation of the PEACE training was positive, subsequent research appeared to be demonstrating that training was not having much of an effect on interviewer skills.

In their 2001 study, Clarke and Milne examined 177 interviews conducted with suspects. Two-thirds of the interviewers had been trained in the PEACE model and one-third had not received this training. Although they found few statistically significant differences between trained and untrained officers, the authors concluded that there is some evidence that PEACE interviewing skills have been transferred into interviews with suspects. However, they noted that this appeared to relate more to the legal requirements rather than communication skills or the structured development of a suspect's account. In addition, 10% of the interviews observed were highlighted as possibly breaching PACE. The reasons identified for these possible breaches were oppressive behaviour including instances of undue pressure, bullying and continual challenge. There was also concern over the suspect's mental health and legal issues such as failure to caution a suspect.

Surprisingly, Clarke and Milne (2001) found that fewer PEACE interviewing skills were observed in interviews with witnesses and victims compared to interviews with suspects. Overall, few interviewers made an effort to engage with the witness and there was little evidence of any interviewing taking place at all. Most officers seem preoccupied with getting a statement from the witness and asking closed questions. There were no significant differences between those officers trained in PEACE and those who were not trained. As Clarke and Milne (2001) themselves point out, although not all of the participants in this study had been PEACE trained the majority of them had heard about the training and thus had exposure to PEACE.

A similar investigative interviewing training package has been introduced in Scotland and is delivered by the Scottish Police College (Scottish Investigators Guide). The investigative interviewing model taught by the college is based on the mnemonic PRICE: Planning and preparation, Rapport building, Information gathering, Confirming the content and Evaluate and action. During the training course officers are informed that the aim of a suspect interview is to accumulate information and to search for the truth. Even though officers have reasonable grounds for suspecting that the individual has committed an offence (or they would not be interviewed as a suspect), they are taught to remain open to the possibility that the suspect is innocent. Officers are also asked to bear in mind that some suspects may occasionally confess to a crime that they have not committed. The authors are not aware of any studies examining actual police practices in Scotland or of research examining the effectiveness of the PRICE training.

The introduction of guidelines on interviewing suspects, along with training in investigative interviewing, appear to be having an overall positive effect on the quality of suspect interviews in England and Wales. However, there is certainly room for further improvement in the quality of suspect interviews.

POLICE PRACTICE IN AMERICA

In comparison to the research that has been conducted into police interviews in Britain, there have been very few studies regarding police practice in America. One of the most recent studies was conducted by Leo in 1996. Leo (1996) observed the interrogations of 182 suspects in three American police departments in order to identify the most common strategies used. Each interrogation was coded for 25 potential interrogation techniques. It was found that police investigators generally began the interrogation by confronting the suspect with evidence suggesting his guilt, whether this was genuine (85%) or false (30%). They then tended to undermine the suspects' denials (43%) whilst identifying contradictions is the suspect's account (42%). Other tactics observed were appealing to the suspect's self-interest (88%), offering moral justifications/psychological excuses for committing the offence (34%), using praise or flattery (30%), minimising the moral seriousness of the offence (22%), appealing to the importance of cooperation with legal authorities (37%), appealing to the investigator's expertise/authority (29%), or appealing to the suspect's conscience (22%).

Leo (1996) reported that police investigators tended to use several tactics within an interrogation, with 5.6 tactics being used on average per interrogation. He found that the only variables in his sample that were significantly related to confessions were the number of tactics used by the police investigators and the length of the interrogation. He also found that police investigators were significantly more likely to increase the use interrogation tactics as crime seriousness increased, as well as in cases where the strength of evidence prior to the interrogation was weak. Thus with more serious offences, the interrogations tended to last longer, with more tactics being used, and the suspect was more likely to make a confession. Four tactics in particular were found to be significantly related to obtaining incriminating information. These were identifying contradictions in the suspect's account, offering moral justifications/psychological excuses for committing the offence, using praise or flattery and appealing to the suspect's conscience. Interestingly, Leo also found that younger suspects appeared to be more vulnerable to appeals of conscience and justification than older suspects. In contrast, older suspects seemed to be more vulnerable to appeals based on self-interest and the strength of evidence suggesting their guilt.

Leo's results indicate that police investigators in America do indeed use coercive interview techniques and that they are similar in nature to those recommended by Inbau et al. (2001). This is despite the fact that Leo was in the interview room, in the majority of cases, when the interrogation was actually being conducted.

In contrast to Britain, recording of suspect interviews in America is not the norm despite the potential for it to increase the fact finding accuracy of judges and juries (Kassin, Leo, Crocker & Holland, 2003). Inbau et al. (2001) are against the video recording of interviews with suspects and the Federal Bureau of Investigations does not permit it either. This is particularly concerning given Leo's findings that police investigators typically employed coercive and persuasive interviewing techniques.

INVESTIGATOR BIAS

It is clear that coercive and manipulative police interviews still occur in America. However, what is more surprising is that coercive police interviews still appear to occur at times in Britain despite the introduction of PACE and the national PEACE training for officers. It is therefore important to determine the factors that might affect police interviewing styles. One factor that has received attention in the research literature is that of investigator bias, a tendency to view suspects as guilty.

One of the most prominent findings from the research, which is somewhat dated but has yet to be contradicted, is that officers regularly assume suspects to be guilty, even prior to interviewing them, and that the main aim of the interview is to obtain a confession. For example, Moston, Stephenson and Williamson (1992) report that of the 1,067 British police interviews they reviewed, officers were sure of the suspect's guilt at the outset of the interview in 73 % of cases. In addition, the main aim of the interview was to obtain a confession in about 80 % of cases. The main factor associated with this assumption of guilt was the officers' perceived strength of evidence against the suspect. They found that when there was weak evidence the police interviewer was certain of the suspect's guilt in 31 % of cases. When there was moderate evidence interviewers were sure the suspect was guilty nearly 74 % of the time and with strong evidence the interviewers saw 99 % of suspects as guilty. Criminal history was also found to have an influence on officer's certainty of the suspect's guilt with interviewers being sure of the suspect's guilt in 69 % of cases when suspects had no previous convictions and 76 % of cases when suspects had previous convictions (Moston et al., 1992). The results indicate that even when there is weak evidence against a suspect there is often a presumption of guilt prior to the interview commencing.

In America, the use of the Behaviour Analysis Interview to determine whether suspects are likely to be innocent or guilty is common, thus only those suspects perceived to be guilty tend to be formally interrogated. However as Inbau et al. (2001) note, suspects are often perceived to be guilty and are formally interrogated even when the evidence against them is weak. Indeed according to Inbau et al. (2001) holding a presumption of guilt 'has the advantage of provoking a reaction of resentment from the innocent person, whereas a guilty person has a tendency not to demonstrate any resentment and to show certain non-verbal reactions'. As illustrated earlier the Reid Technique recommended for interrogation is designed to elicit a confession from the suspect.

There are a variety of reasons why police officers may aim to obtain confessions from suspects. For example, suspects who confess are much more likely to plead guilty (Phillips & Brown, 1998), obtaining a confession means that time does not have to be spent searching for evidence, many convictions would not succeed without confession evidence (Baldwin & McConville, 1980) and confession evidence is often seen as a prosecutor's most potent weapon (Kassin, 1997). Despite attempts to shift the focus of police interviews away from obtaining a confession, and towards a search for the truth, there is evidence that a confession culture still exists (Cherryman, Bull & Vrij, 2000).

What drives this confession culture and the presumption of guilt? It may be that a presumption of guilt, and thus the desire to obtain a confession, is based on existing evidence such as witness statements or concrete physical evidence. However, when there is weak or no evidence against the suspect, the presumption of guilt may arise from the sometimes erroneous 'information' that is gleaned from a neutral pre-interrogation interview. During such an interview, an investigator makes a decision as to whether or not the suspect's behaviour is deceptive (as advocated in the Behaviour Analysis Interview). Alternatively, investigators may hold preconceived hypotheses or hunches that they wish to test out. Kassin and Gudjonsson (2004) suggest that investigators may rely on crime-related schemas or prototypes of the type of person who might be responsible for a given type of offence and their motive (see Smith, 1991 for an example of how schema and prototypes can distort decision making in legal contexts).

In addition to holding preconceived schemas or hunches, individuals in general are subject to various confirmation biases. Nickerson (1998) describes confirmation bias as 'the seeking or interpreting of evidence in ways that are partial to existing beliefs, expectations, or a hypothesis in hand' (p. 175). This can involve both seeking information that confirms a belief, whilst not seeking, and even avoiding, information that disconfirms the belief. This can in turn create a reality that ultimately supports the original belief. Thus, investigators who begin an interview with the hypothesis that the suspect is likely to be guilty, perhaps based on their crime-related schema, are therefore likely to be susceptible to subsequent selective information searching and biased processing of information.

Snyder and Swann (1978) carried out a series of studies to examine the role of confirmation bias in social interaction. Participants were provided with hypotheses about the personal attributes of others (that the person was an extrovert or an introvert) and were asked to choose questions from a pre-set list to test these hypotheses. In each of the four studies participants used a confirmatory hypothesis-testing strategy, in other words they tended to search for information that would support their initial hypothesis. For example, participants who tested the hypothesis that the other person was an extrovert chose extrovert-oriented questions such as 'What would you do if you wanted to liven things up at a party?' whereas participants who tested the hypothesis that the other person was an introvert chose introvert-oriented questions such as 'What things do you dislike about loud parties'. Additionally, the authors found that it did not matter to participants where their hypotheses originated, how likely it was that the hypothesis would prove accurate, or whether incentives for accuracy were offered, they still relied on confirmatory hypothesis testing.

A further interesting finding from Snyder and Swann (1978) was that when the interviewers asked hypothesis confirming questions, the interviewees tended to answer the questions in ways that appeared to confirm the hypothesis being tested, leading independent observers to judge them as introverted or extroverted according to the hypothesis testers original expectation. Research has indicated that this self-fulfilling prophecy effect operates as a three-stage process. Firstly, a perceiver forms an expectation of the target person, secondly the perceiver behaves in a manner consistent with this expectation and thirdly, the target person adjusts their own behaviour to match the perceiver's expectation. This results in behavioural confirmation of the original expectation (Brehm, Kassin, & Fein, 1999). It should be noted that only when a target person's behaviour has changed in response to the perceiver's actions is this regarded as self-fulfilling prophecy (Nickerson, 1998).

Snyder and Swann's (1978) research indicates that people tend to use confirmatory hypothesis testing strategies to test their hypotheses. In addition, the behaviour of hypothesis testers can influence the target person's behaviour thus resulting in a self-fulfilling prophecy. Although Snyder and Swann's work gives us an interesting insight into confirmation bias, the studies involved a relatively innocuous situation. Kassin, Goldstein and Savitsky (2003) tested this hypothesis in a forensically relevant context using a mock interview procedure. Specifically, they investigated whether presumptions of guilt influenced the conduct of mock interviewers and whether this in turn influenced judgments made by neutral observers about the behaviour of the mock suspects. In this study suspects committed a mock crime (stole $100) or took part in an innocent but related act. Interviewers were led to believe that either most suspects were guilty or most suspects were innocent prior to interviewing the suspects. Neutral observers then listened to the taped interviews, made judgments about whether the suspect was guilty or innocent and rated their impressions of both participants. Kassin et al. (2003) found that interviewers with guilty expectations chose more guilt-presumptive questions to ask suspects than did those with innocent expectations. Post-interview, 42% of the interviewers with guilty expectations judged the suspect as guilty compared to 19% of those with innocent expectations. Interviewers' post-interview ratings indicated that, unknown to them, they tried harder to get a confession when the suspect was innocent and they exerted more pressure on innocent suspects than guilty suspects. Interestingly, innocent suspects saw their interviewers as trying harder to get a confession and as exerting more pressure on them than did guilty suspects.

Kassin et al. (2003) also found that observers rated 76% of interviewers with guilty expectations as guilt-biased compared to 61% of those with innocent expectations. Observers also saw interviewers as more presumptive of guilt when they were paired with actual innocent suspects than with actual guilty suspects. Interviewers with guilty expectations were rated by observers as trying harder to obtain confessions and exerting more pressure on suspects than those with innocent expectations. Observers also rated interviewers as trying harder to obtain a confession and exerting more pressure on the suspect when the suspect was truly innocent rather than guilty. Suspects in the guilty expectation condition were seen as being more defensive, and were more often judged by observers to be guilty, than those in the innocent expectation condition, although the difference was not statistically significant.

Kassin et al.'s (2003) study demonstrates that presumptions of guilt not only affect the type of questions that are used to interrogate a suspect during an interview but also how the suspect's behaviour is subsequently perceived by an uninformed observer. One of the limitations of Kassin et al.'s (2003) study is that interviewers chose their questions from a pre-set list determined by the experimenters. It is therefore not clear whether the same level of bias would exist if interviewers were allowed to generate their own questions. Hill, Memon and McGeorge (2005) therefore examined whether a guilt bias influenced the types of questions interviewers chose to ask a suspect when they were free to generate their own questions, a situation that more closely matches that of real police interviews. They found that interviewers who believed the suspect was likely to be guilty, as opposed to innocent, generated a higher proportion of guilt-presumptive questions to ask the suspect and that these questions were more guilt-presumptive in content. In addition, interviewers who rated the suspect as guilty, as opposed to interviewers who rated the suspect as innocent, were more confident in their ratings of guilt/innocence. This study demonstrates that confirmation bias plays a role in suspect interviews even when interviewers are free to generate their own questions. Although both Kassin et al.'s (2003) study and Hill et al.'s (2005) study shed some light onto the effect that holding a presumption of guilt may have on the subsequent interview, both studies were conducted with a college population. There is therefore a need for further research into the effect that holding a presumption of guilt has on police investigators in order to find out if the above findings are ecologically valid.

Ask and Granhag (2005) proposed that investigators' motivation to arrive at definite conclusions regarding a case (i.e. need for closure) is an important contributing factor to investigative failures. Their research was designed to examine whether the investigating officer's preliminary hypotheses regarding a criminal case, in combination with a need for closure, accentuates confirmation bias. All of the police officers taking part in an advanced training course for criminal investigators received the same material regarding a homicide case. However, the investigator's initial hypotheses about the background of the case were manipulated. Half of the investigators were provided with a potential motive for the prime suspect ('suspect motive' condition); whilst the remaining participants were made aware that there was another potential suspect ('alternative culprit' condition). All investigators also completed the Need for Closure Scale (Webster & Kruglanski, 1994). Ask and Granhag (2005) found that investigators high in need for closure were less likely to acknowledge that evidence was inconsistent with the prime suspect's guilt when they had received a potential motive for the prime suspect ('suspect motive' condition), but were more likely to acknowledge inconsistencies when they were made aware of potential inconsistencies ('alternative culprit' condition). This interaction fell short of statistical significance and therefore should be replicated. However, the data are supportive of the hypothesis that investigators' tendency to seek confirmation of a crime hypothesis increases with the level of need for closure. However, there are two complications to the results. Firstly, the investigators' level of need for closure did not appear to influence the urgency with which the task was completed and therefore may not have exerted much influence on the task. Secondly, the initial manipulation did not affect investigators' perceptions of the suspect's guilt as intended. All investigators, regardless of condition, had a tendency to presume that the prime suspect was guilty even when the possibility of an alternative culprit was made explicit to them. This complication therefore precludes a firm interpretation of the results.

As a result of the investigators' tendency to see the prime suspect as guilty, regardless of condition, a second study was therefore conducted with university students. Ask and Granhag (2005) found that in contrast to the police sample, students were significantly affected by the initial hypothesis manipulation in their ascription of guilt and interpretation of evidence. Those participants in the 'alternative culprit' condition were less likely to view the prime suspect as guilty and were less likely to rate the evidence as implying guilt of the prime suspect than were those participants in the 'suspect motive' condition. Although these results confirm that participants interpret information in line with an initially induced hypothesis, the participants' need for closure did not influence the extent to which the initial hypothesis biased the interpretation of subsequent information. As was the case in the first study, need for closure did not appear to influence the speed with which the participants completed the task, perhaps explaining the lack of effects in these two studies. Research to further examine the impact that need for closure has on cognitive processes in investigative interviews should be carried out.

Despite the difficulty in drawing firm conclusions from Ask and Granhag's study regarding the need for closure, the findings indicated that police investigators tended to presume that the suspect was guilty regardless of possible alternative hypotheses. This is consistent with previous findings (e.g. Leo, 1996; Moston, Stephenson & Williamson, 1992) and highlights the dangers of confirmation bias within an investigative interview where potentially exonerating evidence may be ignored.

Research into the impact that investigator bias can have on suspect interviews is still in its infancy. However, from the research that has been conducted so far it appears that investigator bias can have a negative impact on the search for the truth. Holding a presumption of guilt affects the interviewers questioning style, the response of the interviewee and the perceptions of independent observers with regards to the suspect's guilt. It also appears to hinder the ability of investigators to be open-minded and to consider alternative hypotheses. These findings are extremely valuable in providing an insight into the effect of investigator bias on suspect interviews and have potential implications for developing the focus of investigator training. However, more ecologically valid research is required before the findings can be generalised to real police interviews with suspects.

CONCLUSION

It is likely that a significant number of innocent suspects are formally interviewed. In America investigators rely on the Behaviour Analysis Interview to detect deception, even though officers are only slightly better than chance at detecting deception (Vrij, 2000). *Miranda v Arizona* (1966) established procedural safeguards to ensure that suspects were advised of their right to remain silent and their right to have an attorney present during police interviews. However, recent research shows that a large number of individuals waive their Miranda rights and that innocent suspects are significantly more likely to waive their rights than guilty suspects (Kassin & Norwick, 2004). In addition, it has been shown that adults have problems understanding their Miranda rights especially those adults with mental retardation (O'Connell, Garmoe & Goldstein, 2005). Even those who do understand their rights can self-incriminate themselves if they are suggestible (Gudjonsson, 2003).

Added to this are the pressures placed upon suspects to confess, often as a result of an investigators' presumption that the suspect is guilty, and on occasions leading to false confessions. Once perceived as guilty, innocent suspects are at increased risk of conviction (Kassin, 2005). It would be hoped that the trial process would uncover the suspect's innocence. However, confessions have more impact on jurors than any other form of evidence even when the confession is believed to be coerced (Kassin, 2005). In addition, Kassin, Meissner and Norwick (2005) found that individuals do not exhibit high levels of accuracy in detecting false confessions.

British police forces have taken considerable steps in recent years to try and minimise the occurrence of coercive and manipulative suspect interviews, which have in the past resulted in false confessions. Certainly positive effects of these steps can be seen in studies examining the quality of suspect interviews in Britain and further development of investigative training and supervision packages are underway. Small steps to safeguard suspect rights are also being taken in America, with more states introducing recording of suspect interviews, whether this is compulsory by law or on a voluntary basis. Further research into the impact of investigator bias on suspect interviews in ecologically valid settings will be beneficial to our understanding of confirmation bias and will help to inform future training needs.

REFERENCES

Ask, K. & Granhag, P.A. (2005) Motivational sources of confirmation bias in criminal investigations: The need for cognitive closure. *Journal of Investigative Psychology and Offender Profiling*, **2**, 43–63.

Baldwin, J. (1992) *Video taping police interviews with suspects: A national evaluation. Police Research Series Paper 1*. London: Home Office Police Department.

Baldwin, J. & McConville, M. (1980) *Confessions in Crown Court trials. Royal Commission on Criminal Procedure–Research Study 5*. London: HMSO.

Bedau, H.A. & Radelet, M.L. (1987) Miscarriages of justice in potentially capital cases. *Stanford Law Review*, **40**, 21–179.

Brandon, R. & Davies, C. (1973) *Wrongful imprisonment*. London: George Allen & Unwin.

Brehm, S.S., Kassin, S.M. & Fein, S. (1999) *Social psychology* (4th edn). Boston: Houghton Mifflin Company.

Bull, R. & Cherryman, J. (1995) *Helping to identify skills gaps in specialist investigative interviewing: Enhancement of professional skills*. London: Home Office Police Research Group.

Cherryman, J., Bull, R. & Vrij, A. (2000) *How police officers view confessions: Is there still a confession culture?* European Conference in Psychology and Law, Cyprus.

Clarke, C. & Milne, R. (2001) *National evaluation of the PEACE investigative interviewing course*. Police Research Award Scheme (PRAS/149).

Drizin, S.A. & Leo, R.A. (2004) The problem of false confessions in the post-DNA world. *North Carolina Law Review*, **82**, 891–1003.

Evans, G. & Webb, M. (1993) High profile–but not that high profile: interviewing of young persons. In E. Shepherd (Ed.), *Aspects of police interviewing: Issues in criminological and legal psychology*, **18** (pp. 37–45). Leicester: The British Psychological Society.

Fisher, R.P., Brennan, K.H. & McCauley, M.R. (2002) The cognitive interview method to enhance eyewitness recall. In M. Eisen, G. Goodman & J. Quas (Eds), *Memory and suggestibility in the forensic interview* (pp. 265–86). Mahwah, N.J: Erlbaum.

Granhag, P.A. & Stromwall, L.A. (2004) *The detection of deception in forensic contexts*. Cambridge: Cambridge University Press.

Gudjonsson, G.H. (2003) *The psychology of interrogations and confessions: A handbook*. Chichester: John Wiley & Sons, Ltd.

Hill, C., Memon, A. & McGeorge, P. (2005) *Interviewing suspects: The effect of investigator bias on questioning style*. Paper presented at the Society for Applied Research in Memory and Cognition, Wellington, New Zealand.

Home Office (1985) *Police and Criminal Evidence Act 1984*. London: HMSO.

Home Office (1999) *Youth Justice and Criminal Evidence Act 1999*. London: HMSO.

Home Office (2001) *Achieving best evidence in criminal proceedings: Guidance for vulnerable or intimidated witnesses, including children*. London: Home Office.

Inbau, F.E., Reid, J.E., Buckley, J.P. & Jayne, B.C. (2001) *Criminal interrogation and confessions* (4th edn). Gaithersberg, MD: Aspen.

Irving, B. (1980) *Police interrogation: A case study of current practice. Research studies No. 2*. London: HMSO.

Irving, B.L. & McKenzie, I.K. (1989) *Police interrogation: The effects of the Police and Criminal Evidence Act 1984*. London: The Police Foundation.

Kassin, S.M. (1997) The psychology of confession evidence. *American Psychologist*, **52**, 221–33.

Kassin, S.M. (2005) On the psychology of confessions: Does innocence put innocents at risk? *American Psychologist*, **60**, 215–28.

Kassin, S.M., Goldstein, C.C. & Savitsky, K. (2003) Behavioural confirmation in the interrogation room: On the dangers of presuming guilt. *Law and Human Behaviour*, **27**, 187–203.

Kassin, S.M. & Gudjonsson, G.H. (2004) The psychology of confessions: A review of the literature and issues. *Psychological Science in the Public Interest*, **5**, 33–67.

Kassin, S.M., Leo, R.A., Crocker, C. & Holland, L. (2003) *Videotaping interrogations: Does it enhance the jury's ability to distinguish true and false confessions?* Paper presented at the Psychology & Law International Interdisciplinary Conference, Edinburgh, Scotland.

Kassin, S.M. & McNall, K. (1991) Police interrogations and confessions: Communicating promises and threats by pragmatic implication. *Law and Human Behaviour*, **15**, 233–51.

Kassin, S.M., Meissner, C.A. & Norwick, R.J. (2005) 'I'd know a false confession if I saw one': A comparative study of college students and police investigators. *Law and Human Behaviour*, **29**, 211–27.

Kassin, S.M. & Norwick, R.J. (2004) Why people waive their Miranda rights: The power of innocence. *Law and Human Behaviour*, **28**, 211–21.

Leo, R.A. (1996) Inside the interrogation room. *Journal of Criminal Law and Criminology*, **86**, 266–303.

Leo, R.A. (2004) The third degree and the origins of psychological interrogation in the United States. In G.D. Lassiter, (Ed.) *Interrogations, confessions and entrapment* (pp. 37–84). New York, NY: Kluwer Academic.

Leo, R.A. & Ofshe, R.J. (1998) The consequences of false confessions: deprivations of liberty and miscarriages of justice in the age of psychological interrogation. *Journal of Criminal Law and Criminology*, **88**, 429–96.

McGurk, B., Carr, J. & McGurk, D. (1993) *Investigative interviewing courses for police officers: An evaluation. Police Research Series: Paper No. 4.* London: Home Office.

Memon, A., Vrij, A. & Bull, R. (2003) *Psychology and law: Truthfulness, accuracy and credibility.* Chichester: John Wiley & Sons, Ltd.

Milne, R. & Bull, R. (1999) *Investigative interviewing: Psychology and practice.* Chichester: John Wiley & Sons, Ltd.

Miranda v Arizona, 384 U.S. 336 (1966).

Moston, S., Stephenson, G.M. & Williamson, T.M. (1992) The effects of case characteristics on suspect behaviour during police questioning. *British Journal of Criminology*, **32**, 23–40.

Munsterberg, H. (1908) *On the witness stand.* Garden City, NY: Doubleday.

Narchet, F.M., Coffman, K.A., Russano, M.B. & Meissner, C.A. (2005) *A qualitative analysis of modern police interrogation manuals.* Paper presented at the American Psychology and Law Conference, San Diego.

Nickerson, R.S. (1998) Confirmation bias: A ubiquitous phenomenon in many guises. *Review of General Psychology*, **2**, 175–220.

O'Connell, M.J., Garmoe, W. & Goldstein, N.E.S. (2005) Miranda comprehension in adults with mental retardation and the effects of feedback style on suggestibility. *Law and Human Behaviour*, **29**, 359–69.

Pearse, J. & Gudjonsson, G.H. (1996) Police interviewing techniques at two south London Police Stations. *Psychology, Crime and Law*, **3**, 63–74.

Phillips, C. & Brown, D. (1998) *Entry into the criminal justice system: A survey of police arrests and their outcomes.* London: Home Office.

Russano, M.B., Meissner, C.A., Narchet, F.M. & Kassin, S.M. (2005) Investigating true and false confessions within a novel experimental paradigm. *Psychological Science*, **16**, 481–6.

Scottish Executive (2003) *Guidance on interviewing child witnesses in Scotland.* Edinburgh: Scottish Executive.

Smith, V.L. (1991) Prototypes in the courtroom: Lay representations of legal concepts. *Journal of Personality and Social Psychology*, **61**, 857–72.

Snyder, M. & Swann, W.B. (1978) Hypothesis-testing processes in social interaction. *Journal of Personality and Social Psychology*, **36**, 1202–12.

Softley, P. (1980) *Police interrogation: An observational study in four police stations. Home Office Research Study No. 61.* London: HMSO.

Vrij, A. (2000) *Detecting lies and deceit: The psychology of lying and the implications for professional practice.* Chichester: John Wiley & Sons, Ltd.

Vrij, A., Mann, S. & Fisher, R. (2006) An empirical test of the Behaviour Analysis Interview. *Law and Human Behaviour*, **30**, 329–45.

Webster, D.M. & Kruglanski, A.M. (1994) Individual differences in need for cognitive closure. *Journal of Personality and Social Psychology*, **67**, 1049–1062.

CHAPTER 11

Interrogations and Confessions

GISLI H. GUDJONSSON

INTRODUCTION

The term 'interrogation' is generally used in the literature and in police practice to refer to the questioning of criminal suspects, typically involving a confrontation, whereas the term 'interviewing' is more commonly used in cases of witnesses and victims. Williamson (1993) has proposed the term 'investigative interviewing' to cover both the interviewing of witnesses and suspects. However, in this chapter the term 'interrogation' will be used, as the focus is specifically on the interrogation of suspects for the purpose of potential police prosecution. Here confessions are often crucial in securing a conviction. It is therefore not surprising that interrogators have traditionally focused on obtaining confessions rather than merely gathering information. In this chapter the author will discuss the nature of confessions in the area of criminal justice, review the relevant theories and empirical evidence and show how interrogation can go wrong in terms of producing false confessions.

INTERROGATION

There are a large number of interrogation manuals available for questioning suspects and breaking down resistance (Gudjonsson, 2003a).

Offenders' Memories of Violent Crimes. Edited by Sven Å. Christianson.
© 2007 John Wiley & Sons, Ltd.

Most of these interrogation manuals originate in the USA (Leo, 1992). The basic assumptions made in most police training manuals are that many criminal cases can only be solved by obtaining a confession and unless offenders are caught in the commission of a crime they will be reluctant to confess unless they are interrogated by using persuasive techniques, which are typically comprised of trickery, deceit and psychological manipulation. The main process involved is breaking down denials and resistance, whilst increasing the suspect's desire to confess (e.g. Inbau, Reid, Buckley & Jayne, 2001). The single best-known interrogation technique, which is still used extensively in the USA, is the 'Reid Technique' (Inbau et al., 2001). The Reid Technique employs both interviewing and interrogation. The former is non-accusatory and functions to establish rapport and provides investigative and behavioural information that can be used during subsequent nine-step interrogation to break down resistance of suspects judged to be guilty (Buckley, 2006). Gudjonsson (2003a), Kassin and Gudjonsson (2004) and Kassin (2006) have provided critical appraisal of the Reid Technique, and other similar techniques, and point to its inherent dangers (e.g. being a guilt-presumptive process, over reliance on behavioural signs as indicators of deception, the use of trickery, deceit and theme development, which does on occasion result in false confessions). Most authors of police interrogation manuals ignore the possibility that their recommended techniques could, in certain instances, make a suspect confess to a crime that he or she had not committed, and even argue that they 'don't interrogate innocent people' (Kassin and Gudjonsson, 2004: p. 36).

An innovative approach to police interviewing was implemented in England in 1992, which was developed through the collaboration between police officers, psychologists and lawyers (Williamson, 1994). The mnemonic 'PEACE' was used to describe the five distinct parts of the new interview approach ('Preparation and Planning', 'Engage and Explain', 'Account', 'Closure', and 'Evaluate'). This interviewing approach is largely based on the work of Fisher and Geiselman (1992) into 'The Cognitive Interview', which involves a memory facilitating process based on psychological principles. It is most commonly used with victims and witnesses, but it can also be used with cooperative suspects. The original PEACE interview course lasted one week and it seemed to improve interviewers' skills in meeting legal requirements (i.e. preventing interviews that were coercive and in breach of the Police and Criminal Evidence Act), but there was no distinct improvement in interviewing skills, in obtaining a detailed and probing account from witnesses and suspects (Clarke and Milne, 2001; Griffiths and Milne, 2006). There is now available an advanced three-week training course, which builds on the foundation taught on the basic one-week course. The focus is more on interviewing suspects in serious cases, such as murder and rape. The preliminary outcome of the advanced training is promising in terms of improved overall interviewing skills, but these skills deteriorate to a certain extent over time in complex areas, refresher courses may need to be attended (Griffiths and Milne, 2006). It is also important to recognise that complex interviewing courses are unlikely to be effective in the workplace unless officers regularly practice their newly learned interviewing skills and are provided with feedback and supervision.

THE INTERROGATION OF TERRORIST SUSPECTS

Since the terrorist attacks on the United States on 11 September 2001, interrogation for the purpose of intelligence gathering has had a Government priority (Mackey and Miller, 2004; Rose, 2004). Concerns have been raised about the treatment of prisoners by the military and security service in Afghanistan and Guantanamo Bay in Cuba (Rose, 2004). One experienced American military interrogator has commented: 'But one of the most crucial weapons in the war on terrorism may be the abilities of a relative handful of soldiers and spies trained in the dark art of getting enemy prisoners to talk' (Mackey and Miller, 2004: p. xxii). The same authors claim that 'Fear is often an interrogator's best ally' (p. 8) and 'By the time of our departure from the baking, arid plains of Bagram, we could boast that virtually no prisoner went unbroken' (p. xxv).

The technique described in detail by Mackey and Miller (2004) of current practice by the military is highly coercive in nature and questions must be asked about the real value of these techniques for obtaining reliable information for intelligence gathering (Rose, 2006). Gelles, McFadden, Borum and Vossekuil (2006) and Pearse (2006) have produced informative accounts of the approaches and potential problems involved in terrorist interviews.

CONFESSIONS AND DENIALS – BASE RATES

Kassin and Gudjonsson (2004) argue that confessions are traditionally important in three different contexts: religion, psychotherapy and criminal justice. In this chapter the focus is on confessions within the criminal justice system. Here, in its broadest sense a confession is construed as 'any statements which tend to incriminate a suspect or a defendant in a crime' (Drizin and Leo, 2004: p. 892), which on occasions include denials. Classifying a self-incriminating denial (e.g. denying having been to the scene of crime when the suspect's fingerprints are found there) as an admission is problematic and should be avoided (Gudjonsson, 2003a).

The statement can be either oral or in a written form. A better definition is to use 'Black's Law Dictionary' to distinguish between a 'confession' and 'admission'. It defines a confession as 'a statement admitting or acknowledging all facts necessary for conviction of a crime' and an 'admission' as 'an acknowledgement of a fact or facts tending to prove guilt which falls short of an acknowledgement of all essential elements of the crime.' (cited in Drizin and Leo, 2004: p. 892).

Self-incriminating admissions, not amounting to the suspect accepting responsibility for the crime and giving a detailed narrative account of his or her actions, is not a proper confession. For example, a suspect may admit to having been in the vicinity of the crime or even claim to witness it. Such admissions may be incriminating, but they must be distinguished from confessions. Even the comment, 'I did it' without a detailed explanation, should be treated as an admission and not as a confession.

According to Gudjonsson (2003a) and Kassin and Gudjonsson (2004), most interrogation-elicited statements fall into four groups: *true confessions, false confessions, true denials* and *false denials* (some are difficult to categorise as they may be partially true or partially false). Statements that consist only of 'no comment' replies to questions could not be classified into any of the groups since such a suspect gives no account on which to base such a classification. This four-group classification is particularly useful when researching the psychological factors associated with each group.

The problem with any research into confessions and denials is that there is no way of telling what the base rate for guilt and innocence is among those interrogated. The higher the base rate of guilt among those interrogated the lesser the risk of a false confession occurring. Large scale studies among young college students in Iceland (aged 15–25) have shown a base rate of guilt of between 64% and 67% in three separate studies (Gudjonsson, Sigurdsson, Asgeirsdottir & Sigfusdottir, 2006; Gudjonsson, Sigurdsson, Bragason, Einarsson & Valdimarsdottir, 2004; Gudjonsson, Sigurdsson & Einarsson, 2004). These findings, although limited by their self-report status, suggest that, at least in Iceland, about one-third of youngsters interrogated by the police may be innocent of the crime for which they are questioned. Unfortunately, in real-life criminal cases the base rate of guilt or innocence is rarely known and it is likely to fluctuate according to the nature of the case being investigated (Gudjonsson, 2003a). For example in serious cases such as murder, or in terrorist cases, many innocent people may be arrested and interviewed as potential suspects and this increases the risk of false confession.

MODELS OF CONFESSIONS

There are a number of psychological models available to explain why suspects confess to crimes they have committed. Gudjonsson (2003a, 2006) has discussed these in detail. Only a brief summary of each model will be presented in this chapter. Theoretical models of confessions are important because they assist in understanding why suspects confess to crimes they have committed and generate hypotheses that can be tested empirically. However, each model should be viewed in the context of the following. Firstly, confessing to a crime during custodial interrogation often has serious consequences for the individual concerned. Suspects' self-esteem and integrity are often adversely affected, their freedom and liberty are at risk, and there may be other penalties (e.g. a financial penalty, a community service). In some cases the death penalty is imposed (Ofshe and Leo, 1997a). In view of this it is perhaps surprising that a substantial proportion of all suspects confess during custodial interrogation (i.e. in England the confession rate has remained about 60 % for more than 25 years). Why should this be the case? A number of theoretical models are available to explain why suspects confess to crimes that they have committed.

Gudjonsson (2003a) reviews six models of confessions: 'The Reid Model' (Jayne, 1986); 'A Decision-Making Model' (Hilgendorf and Irving, 1981); 'Psychoanalytic Models' (e.g. Reik, 1959); 'An Interactional Model' (Moston, Stephenson & Williamson, 1992); 'A Cognitive-Behavioural Model' (Gudjonsson, 1989); and 'The Ofshe-Leo Model' (Ofshe and Leo, 1997a). There is some overlap between the different models, although each makes different assumptions about why suspects confess to the police during questioning (e.g. the undoing of deception; outcome of a decision-making process; feelings of remorse; interactions between background; the characteristics of the suspect; nature of the case and contextual factors; the nature of the relationship between the suspect; the environment and significant others within that environment; and interrogative pressure and coercion).

Taken together, the general theme of the models is that suspects confess to crimes when they perceive that the evidence against them is strong, when they need to relieve feelings of guilt, have overcome feelings of shame, when they have difficulties coping with the custodial pressure (i.e. interrogation and confinement) and when they focus primarily on the immediate consequences of their actions rather than the long-term ones. In the context of the models, interrogation is best construed as an interactive process between the suspect, the police and significant others who are present during the interrogation (e.g. lawyers).

INTERROGATION AS AN INTERACTIVE PROCESS

Gudjonsson (2003b) developed a model to describe the interrogation process that would help the expert witness and researcher in evaluating cases of disputed confessions. The Interaction Model shows the kind of factors that need to be considered when evaluating cases of disputed confessions. The three main factors are labelled 'Police factors', 'Vulnerabilities' and 'Support'.

Police Factors

These are factors associated with the custody itself (e.g. the nature and duration of the confinement, sleep deprivation in custody), the interrogation (i.e. the techniques or tactics used by the interrogator, the intensity of the interrogation, duration and number of interviews), and the personality, attitudes and behaviour of the interrogator (e.g. for a review see Gudjonsson, 2002).

Case characteristics (i.e. the seriousness and notoriety of the crime) and the responses of the suspect to the detention and interrogation interact closely with the custodial and interrogative factors. For example, the behaviour of the police is influenced by the nature of the crime they are investigating and how the suspect reacts initially to the detention and interrogation. If a suspect gives an apparently frank confession to the police at the beginning of an interview then there is generally no need for confrontational interaction and challenges. However, if the police do not believe the version of events given by the suspect then there may be confrontation, robust challenges and psychological manipulation aimed at overcoming the resistance and denials (Inbau, et al., 2001; Pearse & Gudjonsson, 1999).

In relation to interviewers' attitudes and demeanor, Holmberg and Christianson (2002) found that interviews rated as 'dominant' were associated with denials, whereas interviews marked by 'humanity' were associated with admissions. This suggests that the style of interviewing influences the outcome of interview. Holmberg and Christianson (2002) hypothesised that when guilty suspects feel they are treated sensitively and with respect they are more likely to confess, particularly when interviewed in relation to sensitive crimes, such as sexual offences and murder. Information gathering interviews, although seen as more cognitively demanding, cause less distress and discomfort than accusatory types of interviews (Vrij, Mann & Fisher, 2006).

It would be expected that for various reasons some offences more frequently attract confessions than others. For example, it would be expected that the highest rate is found for offences where the strength of the evidence against the suspect is likely to be high (e.g. being stopped and found driving while intoxicated, being found in the possession of drugs, being caught shoplifting or committing a burglary). There is some empirical evidence for this (Sigurdsson & Gudjonsson, 1994). In addition, as the offence becomes more serious the stakes in terms of perceived and real punishment rise and this is likely to inhibit some suspects from confessing, particularly when they have access to legal advice (Phillips and Brown, 1998). Conversely, it is exactly in the most serious cases where the duration and dynamics of the interview become more demanding and the risk of coercive interviewing style increases (Pearse & Gudjonsson, 1999).

St-Yves (2006) has recently reviewed the contradictory evidence relating to the confession rate of sex offenders and argues that there are two factors that reduce the likelihood of sex offenders confessing to their crimes. These are feelings of shame and humiliation and the negative attitude of some interviewers towards their crimes. Gudjonsson (2006) argues that some sex offenders, and particularly child molesters, have a strong need to talk about their crimes due to feelings of guilt and this gives the police an advantage. However, they also find it difficult to be open and honest when interrogated due to feelings of shame, which act to inhibit them from confessing. They are therefore torn between feelings of guilt, which encourages them to confess, and feelings of shame, which inhibit them from confessing. Their feelings of shame need to be overcome during the interrogation, which means that sex offenders need to be interviewed sensitively, humanely and skillfully. Any challenges need to be presented in a 'softly' or 'gently' fashion and with apparent understanding of the perpetrator's perspective and emotional needs.

The more serious the offence the more likely the police are to use persuasive techniques to break down resistance (e.g. Evans, 1993; Irving & McKenzie, 1989; Leo, 1996; Pearse & Gudjonsson, 1999). Leo (1996) found that some interrogation tactics were more effective in eliciting a confession than others. The four most significant tactics, each one being successful in over 90 % of cases where utilised, were as follows:

1. Appealing to the suspect's conscience.
2. Identifying and pointing out contradictions in the suspect's denial and story.
3. Offering moral justification or psychological excuse for the crime.
4. Using praise and flattery.

Leo also found a significant relationship between the length of the interrogation and the number of tactics used, on the one hand, and the number of confessions obtained, on the other. Thus, the more time and effort the detective puts into the interrogation process, the greater the likelihood that a confession will be elicited.

Whether or not suspects confess or deny the offence is significantly related to the strength of the evidence against them. Moston, Stephenson and Williamson (1992) found that where the evidence against suspects was rated as 'weak', 76.6 % denied the offence, in contrast to 66.7 % who made self-incriminating admissions where the evidence was rated as 'strong'. This finding is consistent with research among convicted criminals (Gudjonsson & Sigurdsson, 1999), which consistently shows that there are three main reasons why suspects confess to crimes they have committed. Firstly, suspects belief in the strength of the evidence against them. Secondly, the internal need to confess, particularly in violent and sex crimes. Thirdly, custodial (e.g. fear and distress about being detained in custody) and interrogative pressures (e.g. not being able to cope with the interview, wanting the interview to be terminated). In general, suspects confess to a combination of these three factors, but the single most important reason is the suspect's perception of the evidence against him or her (Gudjonsson, 2003a).

Vulnerabilities

These are the specific vulnerabilities of the detainee, which are associated with his or her physical and mental health, as well as more specific psychological vulnerabilities, such suggestibility, compliance, acquiescence, anxiety and antisocial personality traits (Gudjonsson, 2003a). Children and juveniles (Drizin & Colgan, 2004; Redlich, Silverman, Chen & Steiner, 2004) and persons with mental retardation (Fulero & Everington, 2004) are susceptible to giving unreliable accounts of events if not carefully interviewed.

When the English police interview mentally disordered persons and juveniles there are special legal provisions available to ensure that their statements to the police are reliable and obtained properly and fairly. The single most important provision is the presence of an 'appropriate adult' during police questioning (i.e. a person who is independent of the police and is not his or her lawyer). In England and Wales, the current legal provisions are detailed in the Codes of Practice (Home Office, 2003), which accompany the supplement the Police and Criminal Evidence Act 1984 (PACE: Home Office, 1985). Even when the police adhere to all the legal provisions, a judge may on occasion consider it unsafe and unfair to allow the statement to go before the jury (Gudjonsson, 2003a). Here the issue may be whether or not the defendant was 'fit' when interviewed by the police (i.e. whether the suspect was sufficiently physically or mentally well to cope with the questioning and give reliable answers). In cases concerning 'fitness to plead' and 'fitness to stand trial' clear operational criteria are available to guide mental health professionals and the Court. In contrast, until recently there were no established criteria for determining 'fitness for interview' that could be applied by forensic medical examiners (FMEs, also known as police surgeons), psychiatrists and psychologists when assessing suspects at police stations (Gudjonsson, 2005). 'Fitness for interview' is not a term that appears within PACE, and it was first introduced formally into legal in the current Codes of Practice (Code C, Annex G), which became effective on 1 April 2003.

When psychological vulnerabilities are severe or disabling, or when combined with certain other factors, such as lengthy and demanding interrogation, the suspect may be found to be unfit for interview (Gudjonsson, 2005). When this occurs the interview needs to be postponed until the person is fit for interview or suspended altogether.

There is evidence that the duration of detention, nature of the interrogation techniques used, and dynamics in the police interview, are related to the severity of the crime being investigated and it is here that custodial and interrogative factors tap more into psychological vulnerabilities (Gudjonsson, 2003a). Pearse and Gudjonsson (1999) used a special coding frame, 'The Police Interviewing Analysis Framework' (PIAF), to analyse the social interaction between the interviewer and suspect from the tape recordings of real-life interrogation and to identify the techniques that were associated with moving suspects from a position of denial to a confession. Each five-minute segment of interrogation was careful analysed and the results were subjected to a factor analysis. The three most salient factors that were associated with breaking down of resistance were all 'overbearing' in character and were labelled as 'Intimidation' (e.g. maximising the seriousness of the offence and the anxiety of the suspect when denying the offence), 'Robust Challenge' (i.e. repeatedly challenging lies and inconsistencies), and 'Manipulation' (i.e. minimising seriousness of the offence, inducements, theme development). These techniques, which are similar to those recommended by Inbau et al. (2001), were effective in breaking down resistance and securing a confession. However, this was achieved at a considerable risk of the confession being rendered inadmissible by a court due to coercion and the defendant consequently being acquitted. In contrast, there were two further more 'sensitive' styles employed, albeit to a lesser degree, referred to as 'Appeal' and 'Soft Challenge', which proved particularly effective with sex offenders and did not undermine the admissibility of the confession as they were not construed as being coercive.

In a real-life observational study of run-of-the-mill cases at two English police stations, over 170 suspects were psychologically assessed by clinical psychologists prior to their being interviewed by the police (Gudjonsson, Clare, Rutter & Pearse, 1993). All tapes of interviews with the suspects were subsequently analysed to find out what factors were associated with denial and confessions (Pearse, Gudjonsson, Clare & Rutter, 1998). The great majority of the inter- views were very short (i.e. 80 % lasted less than 30 minutes and 95 % were completed within one hour), the confession rate was 58 %, there was little interrogative pressure in the tactics used, and very few suspects moved from a denial to a confession (see Gudjonsson, 2003a). Logistic regression analysis was performed on the data. The dependent (outcome) variable was confession versus denial. The independent vari- ables included the suspect's age, ethnicity, mental state, intelligence, suggestibility, illicit drug taking, criminal history, police interview tactics and presence or absence of a legal advisor. The strength of the evidence against the suspect was not measured in this study.

Two factors were highly predictive of a denial (i.e. the presence of a legal advisor and a previous history of imprisonment), whereas only one variable predicted a confession (i.e. whether the suspect had told the researcher that he or she had taken illicit drugs within 24 hours of arrest). The main implications of the findings are that in the run-of-the-mill English cases where there is little interrogative pressure or persuasion taking place, the great majority of suspects who confess do so right at the beginning of the interview, psychological vulnerabilities, apart from illicit drug taking, which probably makes suspects eager to be released from custody as quickly as possible and therefore more willing to confess, are of little relevance, and having a legal representative and previous experience of imprisonment are strongly associated with a denial. However, in the more serious cases, psychological vulnerabilities and police pressure become much more important (Gudjonsson, 2003a).

Support

The impact of the presence or absence of a lawyer or an appropriate adult during the interrogation needs to be evaluated as a part of the overall custodial environment. The impact of the presence of a solicitor on suspects' behaviour during interrogation is well established (Gudjonsson, 2003a). There is evidence from our current work at police stations that the presence of an appropriate adult in an interview, even if they do not interact much directly in the interview process, influences positively the behaviour of the police and solicitors (Medford, Gudjonsson & Pearse, 2003). Medford et al. (2003) found that the presence of an appropriate adult increased the likelihood that a solicitor would also be present in an interview, there was overall less interrogative pressure in the interview and the solicitor took a more active role in the interview.

HOW INTERROGATIONS CAN GO WRONG

Police interrogation can go 'wrong' in the sense that it results in 'undesirable consequences' for the criminal justice system or the suspect. Gudjonsson (2003a) argues that there are a number of ways in which this can happen. Firstly, a confession, even if true, can be ruled as inadmissible during a suppression (*voire dire*) hearing due to the coercive or oppressive nature of the interrogation. Secondly, interrogation, even if properly conducted, can lead to false confessions. The greater the pressure during the interrogation and confinement the greater the risk of a false confession. Thirdly, coerced confessions can result in resentment and resulting in the suspect retracting it and failing to cooperate with the police in the future. Fourthly, coercion can result in the suspect developing a post-traumatic stress disorder. Fifthly, interrogation techniques that are considered unfair may undermine public confidence in the police. Sixthly, poor interviewing may result in suspects failing to give a confession when they would otherwise do so (e.g. suspects who would have confessed in their own time refuse to confess when they feel they are being rushed or unfairly treated by the police). In other instances, suspects who have already confessed may retract their confession when they feel they are pressured too much to provide further information. This phenomenon is known as 'the boomerang effect' (Gudjonsson, 2003a).

FALSE CONFESSIONS

The evidence that some people are vulnerable to giving a false confession during questioning or confrontation comes from three main sources. Firstly, anecdotal cases histories (e.g., Drizin & Colgan, 2004; Gudjonsson, 2003a). Secondly, self-report studies among prisoners and college student samples (see Gudjonsson, 2003a for a review). Thirdly, laboratory paradigms (Kassin & Kiechel, 1996), which usefully complement the other two kinds of studies in understanding the psychology of false confessions.

Definition

There are different ways of defining a false confession. The most stringent criterion is that the person confesses to a crime of which he or she is completely innocent (Gudjonsson, 2003a). Ofshe and Leo (1997a) define a false confession more broadly:

> . . . as detailed admission to a criminal act that the confessor either did not commit or is, in fact, ignorant of having committed (p. 240).

The Ofshe and Leo definition implies that a false confession can, theoretically at least, be induced from both innocent and guilty suspects. For example, it is possible that a guilty suspect who has no recollection of having committed the alleged crime is considered to be a 'false confessor' when he/she is manipulated into confessing to the details of something of which he/she has no memory. This definition can be useful in practice when assessing cases of disputed confession where the expert witness does not want to make assumptions about guilt or innocence (see Gudjonsson, 2003a, Chapter 23).

Self-incriminating admissions, which do not amount to the suspect accepting responsibility for the crime and giving a detailed account of his or her actions, can result in a wrongful conviction. For example, a suspect may falsely admit to having been in the vicinity of the crime. Such false admissions may be incriminating, but they must be distinguished from false confessions. Ofshe and Leo (1997a) have emphasised the importance of carefully checking the *post-admission narrative* account given by the suspect after he or she has uttered the words 'I did it'. If the detailed description of the confession fits the crime then it gives credibility to the confession, assuming of course that the special knowledge is not due to *contamination* (i.e. the suspect having learned about the case from sources other than direct involvement in the crime). In contrast, if there is a poor fit between the special knowledge and the crime then it may cast doubt on the reliability of the confession. The police and the court often place a great deal of weight on the presence of special knowledge, but the police sometimes communicate such knowledge to the suspect without acknowledging it (Gudjonsson, 2003a).

Frequency

The frequency with which false confessions occur during interrogation in different countries is not known. However, it is documented from anecdotal case histories and miscarriages of justice research that false confessions do sometimes occur for a variety of reasons (Gudjonsson, 2003a). Such confessions are often subsequently retracted, but once a confession has been given to the police the likelihood of a conviction when the case goes to court is greatly increased, even if the confession is disputed at the trial.

A number of high-profile cases of false confessions have been reported (Gudjonsson, 2003a; Kassin & Gudjonsson, 2004). In their review of a large number of proven cases of false confessions in the USA, Drizin and Leo (2004) argue that these are likely to represent 'only the tip of a much larger iceberg' (p. 919). Kassin and Gudjonsson (2004) comment: 'As no one knows the frequency of false confessions or has devised an adequate method of calculating precise incident rates, there is perennial debate over the numbers' (p. 48).

There have been five large-scale studies in Iceland into false confession rates. Gudjonsson and Sigurdsson (1994) and Sigurdsson and Gudjonsson (1996) asked Icelandic prison inmates if they had ever confessed falsely to the police. In both studies, 12 % claimed to have made a false confession to the police some time in their lives. In two community studies among Icelandic college ($N = 1080$) and university ($N = 666$) students, 25 % in each study reported that they had been interrogated by the police. Of those 3.7 % and 1.2 %, respectively, claimed to have made a false confession (Gudjonsson, Sigurdsson, Bragson et al., 2004; Gudjonsson, Sigurdsson & Einarsson, 2004). In the most recent study (Gudjonsson, Sigurdsson, Asgeirsdottir & Sigfusdottir, 2006), involving 10,472 students in further education (aged 16–24), 1898 (18.5 %) claimed to have interrogated by the police at a police station. Of those 641 (7 %) claimed to have made a false confession to the police. The rate of reported false confession was 3 % for those interrogated only once, but was 12 % among those interrogated by the police more than once.

The main difference between the Gudjonsson et al. (2006), study and the two previous community studies (Gudjonsson, Sigurdsson, Bragson et al., 2004; Gudjonsson, Sigurdsson & Einarsson, 2004) is that in the former study it was specifically requested that participants only reported interrogations that took place at police stations. In Iceland suspects, like those in the USA (e.g. Redlich et al., 2004) are sometimes interviewed outside police stations (e.g. in police cars or at the scene of crime), but this procedure is less formal in Iceland (i.e. suspects are not normally read their rights or under arrest) and it was therefore not included in the study. In the previous community studies no distinction was made between interrogation that took place at a police station and those outside. This made the previous methodology less rigorous and probably explains the higher rate of reported interrogation in the two community studies (i.e. 25 % as opposed to 18.5 % in the present study).

In addition to the five studies cited above, in a recent small-scale study conducted immediately after police interrogation at Icelandic police stations, 9 (19 %) out of 47 suspects claimed to have made a false confession to the police at some time in their lives (Sigurdsson, Gudjonsson, Einarsson & Gudmundsson, in press). Taken together, these findings suggest that people who are frequently interrogated by the police are at a particularly high risk of making false confessions. Even those only interrogated once, a small percentage of them claim to have made a false confession to the police.

Richardson (1991), as a part of his M.Sc. Dissertation, asked 60 juveniles living in a residential home in England if they had ever made a false confession to the police. Fourteen (23 %) claimed to have made a false confession to the police. The main reason they gave for having made a false confession was to protect a friend or peer.

Models of False Confessions

Why do people confess to crimes they have not committed, which is clearly against their self-interest? Gudjonsson (2003b) argues that this is typically due to a combination of factors that are associated with the circumstances and nature of the custodial confinement and interrogation, and the suspect's psychological vulnerabilities. Most typically, however, it seems to be the inability of suspects to cope with the custodial and interrogative environment.

There are a number of theories or models of false confession, which were developed on the basis of observations of anecdotal cases reported in the literature, or on a series of individual cases studies (Gudjonsson, 2003a). Munsterberg (1908) was the first to provide a conceptual framework for understanding false confessions (Kassin & Gudjonsson, 2004). He viewed false confessions as a normal reaction to unusual circumstances, such as emotional shock of being arrested, detained and interrogated. Kassin and Wrightsman (1985) and Wrightsman and Kassin (1993) developed a more sophisticated model, which suggested three psychologically distinct types of false confession, referred to as 'voluntary', 'coerced-compliant', and 'coerced-internalised' types. More recently, Ofshe and Leo (1997a, 1997b) have proposed a modified five-level model, which distinguishes between coerced and non-coerced compliant and persuaded confessions. Their model applies to both true and false confessions. Gudjonsson (2003a) proposed a refined version of the Kassin and Wrightsman original model and recommended two changes. Firstly, the term *coerced* should be substituted by the term *pressured* in order to overcome problems related to legal definitions and applications of the term coercion. Secondly, he proposed a bivariate classification system that distinguishes between the three types of false confessions (i.e. voluntary, compliant, and internalised) and categorises the source of pressure (i.e. internal, custodial, non-custodial).

Risk Factors

The risk or vulnerability associated with false confessions can be separated into 'personal' and 'situational' factors (Kassin & Gudjonsson, 2004). Personal risk factors are those associated with the individual characteristics of the suspect. These include such factors as low intelligence, personality, (e.g. suggestibility and compliance), youth, and psychopathology. Recent research also shows that false confessions can form a part of a criminal life style, the delinquency of friends, poor self-esteem and depression (Gudjonsson et al., 2006).

Situational risk factors include physical custody and isolation, the nature of the interrogation techniques used, the process of confrontation and the social support system available during the custodial confinement and interrogation. Sleep deprivation also increases psychological vulnerability to giving in to suggestions and interrogative pressure (Blagrove, 1996). There have been a number of experimental studies, following the innovative study of Kassin and Kiechel (1996), which have demonstrated that the presentation of false evidence can lead some vulnerable people to make a false admission of guilt to crashing a computer, to internalise responsibility for the act, and confabulate details (Forrest, Wadkins & Miller, 2002; Forrest, Wadkins & Larson, 2006; Horselenberg, Merckelbach & Josephs, 2003; Horselenberg, Merckelbach, Smeets, Franssens, Peters & Zeles, 2006; Redlich & Goodman, 2003). These laboratory paradigms, although having limited similarities to real-life interrogations, demonstrate that false confessions can be readily elicited from many apparently normal individuals using subtle tactics. The relationship with personality traits such as suggestibility and compliance has been mixed in these studies, perhaps due to the nature of the samples studied (i.e. they are mainly undergraduate university students) and the low level of pressure in the paradigms used. Redlich and Goodman (2003) demonstrated the role of age and suggestibility as vulnerability factors. In one study fantasy proneness was associated with false confessions (Horselenberg et al., 2006), whilst in another locus of control, anxiousness and authoritarian personality traits were related to internalised false confessions (Forrest et al., 2006).

CONCLUSIONS

Interrogations remain an important investigative tool, but they can go wrong on occasions, including resulting in false confessions. The evidence suggests that suspects confess for three main reasons – perceptions of the strength of the evidence against them, internal pressure, and custodial and interrogative pressure (including techniques using deceit, trickery and psychological manipulation). Usually, suspects confess for a combination of reasons, but perceptions of the strength of evidence is the single most important reason. This has important implication for investigators. Where the evidence against the suspect is weak or flawed, interrogative and custodial pressure increase the risk of false confessions. Investigators should be aware that false confessions do occur on occasions, for a variety of reasons, including suspects wanting to protect somebody else, not being able to cope with the interrogative and custodial pressures, and psychological vulnerabilities (Gudjonsson, 2003a).

REFERENCES

Blagrove, M. (1996) Effects of length of sleep deprivation on interrogative suggestibility. *Journal of Experimental Psychology: Applied*, **2**, 48–59.
Buckley, J.P. (2006). The Reid Technique of interviewing and interrogation. In T. Williamson (Ed.), *Investigative interviewing* (pp. 190–206). Devon: Willan Publishing.
Clarke, C. & Milne, R. (2001) *National evaluation of the PEACE investigative interviewing course. Police Research Award Scheme. Report No. PRAS/149.* Institute of Criminal Justice Studies, University of Portsmouth.

Drizin, S.A. & Colgan, B.A. (2004) Tales from the juvenile confessions front. In G.D. Lassiter (Ed.), *Interrogations, confessions, and entrapment* (pp. 127–62). New York: Kluwer Academic.

Drizin, S.A., & Leo, R.A. (2004) The problem of false confessions in the post-DNA world. *North Carolina Law Review*, **82**, 891–1007.

Evans, F.J. (1993) *The conduct of police interviews with juveniles*. Royal Commission on Criminal Justice Research Report No. 8. London: HMSO.

Fisher, R.P. & Geiselman, R.E. (1992) *Memory enhancing techniques for investigative interviewing: The cognitive interview*. Springfield, IL: Thomas.

Forrest, K.D., Wadkins, T.A. & Miller, R.L. (2002) The role of preexisting stress on false confessions: An empirical study. *The Journal of Credibility Assessment and Witness Psychology*, **3**, 23–45.

Forrest, K.D., Wadkins, T.A. & Larson, B.A. (2006) Suspect personality, police interrogations, and false confessions: Maybe it is not just the situation. *Personality and Individual Differences*, **40**, 621–8.

Fulero, S.M. & Everington, C. (2004) Mental retardation, competency to waive *Miranda* rights, and false confessions. In G.D. Lassiter (Ed.), *Interrogations, confessions, and entrapment* (pp. 163–79). New York: Kluwer Academic.

Gelles, M.G., McFadden, R., Borum, R. & Vossekuil, B. (2006) Al-Qaeda-related subjects: A law enforcement perspective. In T. Williamson (Ed.), *Investigative interviewing* (pp. 23–41). Devon: Willan Publishing.

Griffiths, A., & Milne, B. (2006). Will it all end in tiers? Police interviews with suspects in Britain. In T. Williamson (Ed.), *Investigative Interviewing* (pp. 167–89). Devon: Willan Publishing.

Gudjonsson, G.H. (1989) Compliance in an interrogation situation: A new scale. *Personality and Individual Differences*, **10**, 535–40.

Gudjonsson, G.H. (2002) Who makes a good interviewer? Police interviewing and confessions. In M. Bockstaele (Ed.), *Politieverhoor en Personality-Profiling* (pp. 93–102). Brussel: Uitgeverij Politeia nv.

Gudjonsson, G.H. (2003a) *The Psychology of interrogations and confessions. A handbook*. Chichester: John Wiley & Sons, Ltd.

Gudjonsson, G.H. (2003b) Psychology brings justice. The science of forensic psychology. *Criminal Behaviour and Mental Health*, **13**, 159–67.

Gudjonsson, G.H. (2005) Fitness to be interviewed. In J. Payne-James, R.W. Byard, T.S. Corey & C. Henderson (Eds), *Encyclopedia of forensic and legal medicine. Volume 2* (pp. 169–74) London: Elsevier.

Gudjonsson. G.H. (2006) The psychology of interrogations and confessions. In T. Williamson (Ed.), *Investigative interviewing* (pp. 123–46). Devon: Willan Publishing.

Gudjonsson, G.H. (2006) Sex offenders and confessions: How to overcome their resistance during questioning. *Journal of Clinical Forensic Medicine*, **13**, 203–7.

Gudjonsson, G.H., Clare, I., Rutter, S. and Pearse, J. (1993) *Persons at risk during interviews in police custody: The identification of vulnerabilities*. Royal Commission on Criminal Justice. London: H.M.S.O.

Gudjonsson, G.H. & Sigurdsson, J.F. (1994) How frequently do false confessions occur? An empirical study among prison inmates. *Psychology, Crime and Law*, **1**, 21–6.

Gudjonsson, G.H. & Sigurdsson, J.F. (1999) The Gudjonsson Confession Questionnaire-Revised (GCQ-R): Factor structure and its relationship with personality. *Personality and Individual Differences*, **27**, 953–68.

Gudjonsson, G.H., Sigurdsson, J.F., Bragason, O.O., Einarsson, E. & Valdimarsdottir, E.B. (2004) Confessions and denials and the relationship with personality. *Legal and Criminological Psychology*, **9**, 121–33.

Gudjonsson, G.H., Sigurdsson, J.F. & Einarsson, E. (2004) The role of personality in relation to confessions and denials. *Psychology, Crime and Law*, **10**, 125–35.

Gudjonsson, G.H., Sigurdsson, J.F., Asgeirsdottir, B.B. & Sigfusdottir, I.D. (2006). Custodial interrogation, false confession and individual differences. A national study among Icelandic youth. *Personality and Individual Differences*, **44**, 49–59.

Hilgendorf, E.L. & Irving, M. (1981) A decision-making model of confessions. In M. Lloyd-Bostock (Ed.), *Psychology in legal contexts: Applications and limitations* (pp. 67–84). London: MacMillan.

Holmberg, U. & Christianson, S-A. (2002) Murderers' and sexual offenders' experiences of police interviews and their inclination to admit and deny crimes. *Behavioral Sciences and the Law*, **20**, 31–45.

Home Office (1985). *Police and Criminal Evidence Act 1984*. London: HMSO.

Home Office (2003). *Police and Criminal Evidence Act 1984. Codes of Practice A-E Revised Edition*. HMSO: London.

Horselenberg, R., Merckelbach, H. & Josephs, S. (2003) Individual differences and false confessions: A conceptual replication of Kassin and Kiechel (1996). *Psychology, Crime, and Law*, **9**, 1–18.

Horselenberg, R., Merckelbach, H., Smeets, T., Franssens, D., Peters, G.-J.Y. & Zeles, G. (2006) False confessions in the lab: Do plausibility and consequences matter? *Psychology, Crime & Law*, **12**, 61–75.

Inbau, F.E., Reid, J.E., Buckley, J.P. & Jayne, B.C. (2001) *Criminal interrogation and confessions* (4th edn). Gaithersberg, MD: Aspen.

Irving, B. & McKenzie, I.K. (1989) *Police interrogation: The effects of the Police and Criminal Evidence Act*. London: Police Foundation of Great Britain.

Jayne, B.C. (1986) The psychological principles of criminal interrogation. In F. Inbau, J. Reid & J. Buckley (Eds), *Criminal interrogation and confessions* (3rd edn) (pp. 327–47). Baltimore: Williams & Wilkins.

Kassin, S.M. (2006) A critical appraisal of modern police interrogations. In T. Williamson (Ed.), *Investigative interviewing* (pp. 207–28). Devon: Willan Publishing.

Kassin, S.M., & Gudjonsson, G.H. (2004). The psychology of confessions. A review of the literature and issues. *Psychological Science in the Public Interest*, **5**, 33–67.

Kassin, S.M. & Kiechel, K.L. (1996) The social psychology of false confessions: Compliance, internalization, and confabulation. *Psychological Science*, **7**, 125–8.

Kassin, S.M. & Wrightsman, L.S. (1985) Confession evidence. In S.M. Kassin & L.S. Wrightsman (Eds), *The psychology of evidence and trial procedure* (pp. 67–94). Beverly Hills, CA: Sage.

Leo, R.A. (1992) From coercion to deception: the changing nature of police interrogation in America. *Crime, Law and Social Change: An International Journal*, **18**, 35–59.

Leo, R.A. (1996) Inside the interrogation room. *The Journal of Criminal Law and Criminology*, **86**, 266–303.

Mackey, C. & Miller, G. (2004) *The interrogator's war. Inside the secret war against Al Qaeda*. London: John Murray, Publishers.

Medford, S., Gudjonsson, G.H. & Pearse, J. (2003) The efficacy of the appropriate adult safeguard during police interviewing. *Legal and Criminological Psychology*, **8**, 253–66.

Moston, S., Stephenson, G.M. & Williamson, T.M. (1992) The effects of case characteristics on suspect behaviour during questioning. *British Journal of Criminology*, **32**, 23–40.

Munsterberg, H. (1908) *On the witness stand*. Garden City, NY: Doubleday.

Ofshe, R.J. & Leo, R.A. (1997a) The social psychology of police interrogation. The theory and classification of true and false confessions. *Studies in Law, Politics and Society*, **16**, 189–251.

Ofshe, R.J. & Leo, R.A. (1997b) The decision to confess falsely: Rational choice and irrational action. *Denver University Law Review*, **74**, 979–1122.

Pearse, J.J. (2006) The interrogation of terrorist suspects: The banality of torture. In T. Williamson (Ed.), *Investigative interviewing* (pp. 64–83). Devon: Willan Publishing.

Pearse, J. & Gudjonsson, G.H. (1999) Measuring influential police interviewing tactics: A factor analytic approach. *Legal and Criminological Psychology*, **4**, 221–38.

Pearse, J., Gudjonsson, G.H., Clare, I.C.H. & Rutter, S. (1998) Police interviewing and psychological vulnerabilities: Predicting the likelihood of a confession. *Journal of Community and Applied Social Psychology*, **8**, 1–21.

Phillips, C. & Brown, D. (1998) *Entry into the criminal justice system: A survey of police arrests and their outcomes*. London: Home Office.

Redlich, A.D. & Goodman, G.S. (2003) Taking responsibility for an act not committed: The influence of age and suggestibility. *Law and Human Behavior*, **27**, 141–56.

Redlich, A.D., Silverman, M., Chen, J. & Steiner, H. (2004) The police interrogation of children and adolescents. In G.D. Lassiter (Ed.), *Interrogations, confessions, and entrapment* (pp. 107–25). New York: Kluwer Academic.

Reik, T. (1959) *The compulsion to confess: On the psychoanalysis of crime and punishment*. New York: Farrar, Straus & Cudahy.

Richardson, G. (1991) *A study of interrogative suggestibility in an adolescent forensic population*. Unpublished M.Sc. Thesis, University of Newcastle.

Rose, D. (2004) *Guantánamo. America's war on human rights*. London: Faber & Faber.

Rose, D. (2006). American interrogation methods in the war on terror. In T. Williamson (Ed.), *Investigative interviewing* (pp. 42–63). Devon: Willan Publishing.

Sigurdsson, J.F. & Gudjonsson, G.H. (1994) Alcohol and drug intoxication during police interrogation and the reasons why suspects confess to the police. *Addiction*, **89**, 985–97.

Sigurdsson, J.F. & Gudjonsson, G.H. (1996) Psychological characteristics of 'false' confessors: A study among Icelandic prison inmates and juvenile offenders. *Personality and Individual Differences*, **20**, 321–9.

Sigurdsson, J.F., Gudjonsson, G.H., Einarsson, E. & Gudmundsson, G. (in press) Differences in personality and mental state between suspects and witnesses immediately after being interviewed by the police. *Psychology, Crime and Law*.

St-Yves, M. (2006) Confessions by sex offenders. In T. Williamson (Ed.), *Investigative interviewing* (pp. 107–22). Devon: Willan Publishing.

Vrij, A., Mann, S. & Fisher, R.P. (2006). Information-gathering vs accusatory interview style: Individual differences in respondents' experiences. *Personality and Individual Differences*, **41**, 589–99.

Williamson, T.M. (1993) From interrogation to investigative interviewing. Strategic trends in the police questioning. *Journal of Community and Applied Social Psychology*, **3**, 89–99.

Williamson. T.M. (1994) Reflections on current police practice. In D. Morgan and G. Stephenson (Eds), *Suspicion and silence. The rights of silence in criminal investigations* (pp. 107–16). London: Blackstone.

Wrightsman, L.S. & Kassin, S.M. (1993) *Confessions in the courtroom*. Newbury Park, CA: Sage Publications.

CHAPTER 12

Interviewing to Detect Deception

ALDERT VRIJ AND PÄR ANDERS GRANHAG

INTERVIEWING TO DETECT DECEPTION

In principle, lies could be detected in three different ways: (i) by analysing what people say, (ii) by observing their nonverbal behaviour, or (iii) by measuring their physiological responses. Whichever method is used, lie detectors always face the problem that no cue uniquely related to deception, akin to Pinocchio's growing nose, exists. Rather, different liars show different cues to deceit, and the same liar may show different cues under different circumstances (DePaulo, Lindsay, Malone, Muhlenbruck, Charlton & Cooper, 2003).

The absence of the equivalent of Pinocchio's growing nose has an important consequence. We are, for example, able to record the thermal patterns from people's faces with non-intrusive cameras, a technique called thermal imaging. It has been suggested that this technique could be used to catch liars (Pavlidis, Eberhardt & Levine, 2002). The most straightforward application would be to install thermal imaging cameras at strategic places, such as at check-in desks at airports, and to classify passengers as 'liars' or 'truth tellers' on the basis of their thermal patterns. However, this assumes a unique relationship between deception and thermal patterns, whereas such a relationship

Offenders' Memories of Violent Crimes. Edited by Sven Å. Christianson.
© 2007 John Wiley & Sons, Ltd.

does not exist. Thermal imaging, and other methods that assume the existence of Pinocchio's growing nose, are thus inappropriate for lie detection.

We will argue that for cues to become, to some extent, diagnostic cues to deception, the active involvement of lie detectors is required. The lie detector's task is to increase the likelihood that cues will arise that could be reliably interpreted as cues to deceit (Vrij, Fisher, Mann & Leal, 2006). Lie detectors could achieve this by using particular interview techniques. This chapter discusses the different interview techniques currently employed by lie detectors, and their potential to discriminate between truth tellers and liars. Interview styles can only be effective if they are based upon sound theoretical principles about what are the mental processes of liars and truth tellers, and what differentiates between the two. These theoretical insights will be discussed first, and they will be compared with practitioners' beliefs about deception. When liars and truth tellers realise that observers are trying to establish whether or not they are lying, they may employ certain strategies in order to appear convincing. These strategies will be discussed next. Nearly all research about lie detection interview styles concentrates on physiological lie detection, and we will discuss the two most popular physiological lie detection techniques, the Relevant–Irrelevant Test (RIT) and the Control Question Test (CQT).[1] In this section we will also discuss other physiological devices such as the Stress Voice Analyser and thermal imaging. We will argue that the rationale behind the interview styles used in such techniques (i.e. assuming that certain questions will lead to stronger physiological responses in liars than in truth tellers due to liars' heightened fear of getting caught) is theoretically weak. The final part of this section briefly summarises deception research using brain mapping techniques (e.g., functional magnetic resonance images, fMRI).

Interview styles designed to elicit verbal and nonverbal cues to deceit are virtually nonexistent. We are aware of only two such techniques, the Behaviour Interview Analysis (BAI), and an unnamed technique that we label the Baseline Observation Method (BOM). Both techniques will be discussed and we will argue that the interview styles used in these techniques are also based upon invalid theoretical principles.

When we, the two authors of this chapter, noticed the lack of theoretically sound interview techniques in lie detection, we each went about conducting research in order to fill this gap. Our approaches have

---

[1] See Jelicic and Merckelbach, Chapter 9 of this volume, for a discussion of a third polygraph test, the Guilty Knowledge Test.

common ground: we both design techniques that attempt to make lying cognitively more difficult. Granhag and colleagues' research concentrates on cases where there is some evidence available against a suspect, and how this evidence can be strategically used in interviews for lie detection purposes. Vrij and colleagues concentrate on cases where there is no evidence available. Both research projects are still in progress, and the available research findings, together with ideas for future research, will be discussed.

MENTAL PROCESSES OF LIARS AND TRUTH TELLERS

Zuckerman, DePaulo and Rosenthal (1981) argue that if differences occur between liars and truth tellers in their nonverbal, verbal or physiological responses, this is likely to be the result of liars experiencing at least one of the following three factors: (1) emotions, (2) cognitive load, or (3) attempted control. Each of these factors emphasise a different aspect of deception, and lies may well feature all three factors.

Liars may be afraid of getting caught, depending on the personality of the liar and on the circumstances under which the lie takes place (Ekman, 1985, 2001; Vrij, 2000). For example, people who are confident in their lying skills may experience less fear during deception; and liars may experience more fear in high-stakes situations, where the liar feels that getting away with the lie or getting caught makes a real difference to him or her, than in low-stakes situations, where the liar feels it is not so important whether or not he or she will be believed.

In order to get away with their lies, liars need to provide plausible answers while avoiding contradicting themselves, and tell a lie that is consistent with everything the observer knows or may find out, while avoiding making slips of the tongue. Liars also need to remember what they have said, so that they can say the same things again when asked to repeat their story. They also may feel an urge to control their demeanour so that they will appear honest (as emphasised in the attempted control process, below), and may pay close attention to the target person in order to assess whether they are getting away with their lies. This could be cognitively demanding. The extent to which lying is demanding probably depends on the type of lie. Telling an outright lie (i.e., total falsehoods where the information is completely different from the truth) may be more cognitively demanding than concealing information (i.e., omitting relevant details), and telling an elaborate lie may well be more demanding than providing short yes or no answers. Lying may also be more demanding when the lies are

not well prepared or rehearsed. It also depends on the personality of
the liar. Verbally eloquent people find it less cognitively demanding to
lie than people who are less verbally eloquent (Vrij, Akehurst, Bull &
Soukara, 2002, 2004; Vrij, Edward & Bull, 2001).

Liars may well realise that observers will look at their reactions to judge whether they are lying, and may therefore attempt to
control and influence their reactions so that they will appear credible. To be successful, liars should avoid showing suspicious-looking
responses and should try to display honest-looking responses (Hocking
& Leathers, 1980). It effectively means that liars need to act, hereby
running the risk that they overact and show responses that will appear
planned, rehearsed and lacking in spontaneity. Liars' motivation and
efforts to deliberately control themselves will probably increase when
the stakes increase. Liars' ability to come across convincingly depends
on their personality. For example, expressive people often make a credible appearance, because their spontaneity tends to disarm suspicion
(Riggio, 1986); and people who show positive behaviours (looking into
the eye, avoiding fidgeting, etc.) naturally may also be in a beneficial
position (Vrij, Granhag & Mann, in press).

Although Zuckerman et al.'s multifactor model does a fine job in
pinpointing what constraints liars possibly face, it runs the risk of
being interpreted too simplistically. As DePaulo pointed out, the three
factors (emotions, cognitive load and attempted control) may also influence truth tellers' responses (DePaulo, 1992; DePaulo et al., 2003). For
example, liars may be more afraid in high-stakes situations, but so will
truth tellers. Therefore, given the similarities between liars and truth
tellers, if cues to deception occur, they are ordinarily quite subtle.

PRACTITIONERS' VIEWS ABOUT CUES TO DECEPTION: HOW THEY RELATE TO DIAGNOSTIC CUES TO DECEPTION

A substantial number of studies have been carried out examining how
practitioners such as police officers, prison guards, customs officers, prosecutors and judges think that liars respond. Strömwall, Granhag and
Hartwig (2004) and Vrij, Akehurst and Knight (2006) provide reviews
of these studies. These studies have been carried out in countries all
over the world such as Germany, the Netherlands, Sweden, the United
Kingdom and the United States, albeit mostly with Caucasian participants. A striking and consistent finding is that people across different
occupational groups and different countries do not differ in their beliefs
about deception (The Global Deception Team, 2006). Practitioners typically believe that liars will react nervously with 'looking away' and

'making grooming gestures' being the most popular answers (Strömwall et al., 2004). Laypersons, such as college students or members of the general public, share these views (Strömwall et al., 2004).

Despite these strong beliefs, the outcome of a meta-analysis that examined how liars and truth tellers responded in more than one hundred studies (DePaulo et al., 2003), does not support the assumption that liars show more nervous behaviours than truth tellers. However, these studies were typically carried out in low-stakes settings, and perhaps nervous behaviours will differentiate between liars and truth tellers in high-stakes situations. High-stakes situations have rarely been examined in deception research, but Mann, Vrij and Bull's (2002) study is an exception. They examined the behavioural responses of 16 suspects while they lied and told the truth during their police interviews. The suspects were interviewed in connection with serious crimes such as murder, rape and arson, and were facing long custodial sentences if found guilty. Results revealed that compared to when they told the truth, the suspects exhibited more pauses, fewer eye blinks, and fewer arm, hand and finger movements when they lied (Mann et al., 2002; Vrij & Mann, 2003). Indicators of being tense (such as fidgeting and gaze aversion) did not emerge. The results suggest that the suspects' cues to deception were more likely to be the result of increased cognitive demand, or attempted control, than nervousness. A follow-up study supports this suggestion. Mann and Vrij (2006) showed police officers a selection of the truthful and deceptive clips of Mann et al.'s (2002) study. After each fragment the officers were asked to indicate to what extent the suspect (i) appeared tense, (ii) gave the impression that he or she had to think hard, and (iii) gave the impression that he or she was controlling him or herself. Results revealed that the suspects appeared to be thinking harder when they lied than when they told the truth. They also appeared to be trying to control themselves more when they lied than when they told the truth. However, in contrast to popular beliefs, the suspects appeared more tense when they told the truth than when they lied.

A combination of reasons may explain those findings. The suspects may not only have been nervous when they lied, they also may have been nervous when they told the truth, making it less likely that nervous behaviours will increase during deception. Many of the suspects included in Mann et al.'s (2002) study had a criminal background and had regular contact with the police. Therefore, they were probably familiar with the police interview situation and perhaps this makes it less likely that they will become nervous when they lie. Moreover, suspects in police interviews are typically of below average intelligence (Gudjonsson, 2003), although this probably depends on the type of crime under investigation. There is evidence that less intelligent people will have particular difficulty in inventing plausible and convincing stories (Ekman & Frank, 1993). The suspects therefore may have experienced cognitive demand when they lied. People who are engaged in cognitively difficult tasks almost automatically tend to decrease their movements, because nonverbal communication becomes neglected when cognitive demand increases (Ekman & Friesen, 1972). This decrease in nonverbal communication may also have a physiological explanation, because physiological activity (e.g., heart rate, skin conductance responses) decreases when cognitive demand increases (Leal, van Hooff & Vrij, 2005). Also, deceiving is associated with activating executive 'higher' brain centres such as the prefrontal cortex (Spence, Hunter, Farrow, Green, Leung, Hughes & Ganesan, 2004). Increased activation in these areas inhibits ongoing unnecessary motor

Table 12.1 Examples of non-verbal cues to deception found in published police interrogation manuals

Manual	Non-Verbal Cues to Deception
Gordon & Fleisher (2002)	Problem with eye-contact Touching the nose Restless foot and leg movements
Inbau et al. (2001)	Avoiding eye-contact Frequent posture changes Grooming gestures Placing hands over mouth/eyes
Macdonald & Michaud (1992)	Rubbing the eyes Avoiding eye contact Covering/rubbing the ears
Rabon (1992)	Restless behaviour Tapping of feet Fidgeting Excessive swallowing Avoiding direct gaze
Yeschke (1997)	Shuffling the feet Avoiding eye contact Picking lint from clothes High frequency of blinking
Zulawski & Wicklander (1993)	Moving the chair Abrupt and jerky behaviour Problem with fine motor coordination Cold and clammy hands Using hands to cover mouth Failure to maintain eye contact

behaviours (e.g., fidgeting) (Shallice & Burgess, 1994). Finally, it may be that the suspects actively tried to suppress showing signs of nervousness when they lied.

The question arises of where the apparent incorrect view that liars show nervous behaviours comes from. One explanation is that police manuals express this view. We have summarised the views mentioned in various police interrogation manuals in Table 12.1.

The cues mentioned in these police manuals show an overlap, yet they are not based on scientific findings. None of the behaviours listed in Table 12.1 emerged as cues to deceit in Mann et al.'s (2002) analysis of suspect interviews, described previously. Neither are these the cues that emerged from DePaulo et al.'s (2003) meta-analysis as cues associated with deception.

STRATEGIES USED BY LIARS AND TRUTH TELLERS IN ORDER TO APPEAR CONVINCING

Physiological Countermeasures

The moment people realise that someone else is going to judge whether or not they appear convincing, they may well try to influence their reactions in such a way that they actually do make a credible impression. Such attempts are called countermeasures. Although in principle, both liars and truth tellers could attempt to employ countermeasures, liars are most likely to do so, as truth tellers have the tendency to take their own credibility for granted (DePaulo et al., 2003). Most countermeasures studies have been conducted in physiological lie detection research. Honts and Amato (2002) provide an overview of these studies. One thing that examinees who employ countermeasures in a physiological lie detection test could try to accomplish is to show the same level of 'nervousness' (labelled 'arousal' in physiological terms) for the entire period of the examination. This could be achieved by using drugs. However, showing the same levels of arousal throughout the whole test will result in an 'inconclusive' outcome in CQT polygraph testing, rather than in a 'not-guilty' outcome. In CQT testing, examinees should show larger responses when answering the irrelevant, control questions compared to answering the relevant questions (see next section) in order to obtain a not-guilty verdict. Examinees could achieve this by using physical countermeasures such as self-inflicting physical pain (e.g., tongue biting) or via muscle tensing activities such as pressing the toes against the shoe sole while answering the control questions, because pain and muscle tension will increase arousal. Mental countermeasures, performing mental games such as counting exercises when answering the control questions, could also be used effectively. For example, Honts, Raskin and Kircher (1987) reported that 70 % of their guilty participants were classified as innocent following training to press the toes and bite the tongue, whereas the test results of the remaining 30 % trained guilty participants were inconclusive. In other words, none of the guilty participants who used countermeasures were classified as guilty (whereas 80 % of the guilty participants who did not use countermeasures were classified as guilty). Another study (Honts, Raskin & Kircher, 1994) suggests that mental countermeasures are more difficult to employ than physical countermeasures. Applying counter-measures spontaneously, that is without previous training, appears to be more difficult (Honts & Alloway, in press; Honts & Amato, 2002).

Verbal and Nonverbal Countermeasures

We are aware of four verbal countermeasures experiments (Caso, Vrij, Mann & de Leo, 2006; Vrij et al., 2002, 2004; Vrij, Kneller & Mann, 2000). In all those experiments participants where informed about Criteria-Based Content Analysis (CBCA), which is a verbal veracity assessment instrument, sometimes used as evidence in court (Vrij, 2005b). CBCA experts rate the presence of 19 criteria in verbal state-ments, and the assumption is that these criteria are more likely to occur in truthful than in deceptive statements. In all four experiments, after receiving information about the CBCA method, participants (both liars and truth tellers) were instructed to provide a statement and to include several of those CBCA criteria in their statements. This training appeared to be successful. Coached adult participants obtained higher CBCA scores than uncoached adult participants and differences between liars and truth tellers only emerged in uncoached participants (Vrij et al., 2002, 2004; Vrij, Kneller & Mann, 2000).

We are aware of only two studies examining the effects of using nonverbal countermeasures (Caso et al., 2006; Vrij, Semin & Bull, 1996). In both studies, participants were informed that liars are inclined to decrease their movements. Providing this information turned out to be unsuccessful in prompting participants to adjust their behaviour accordingly. Both liars and truth tellers increased their movements to the same extent, and, as a result, the difference in move-ments between liars and truth tellers (liars made fewer movements than truth tellers) remained the same (Vrij et al., 1996). These findings suggest that nonverbal countermeasures are more difficult to employ than verbal countermeasures, and that is perhaps not surprising. People are more practised in controlling their verbal behaviour than in controlling their nonverbal behaviour (because they exchange information predominantly via words), and, generally, this practice makes people better at controlling their verbal behaviour than their nonverbal behaviour. Moreover, the fact that words are more important than nonverbal behaviour in the exchange of information makes people more aware of what they are saying than of how they are behaving (DePaulo & Kirkendol, 1989). Awareness of one's own behaviour is essential in effectively controlling that behaviour (DePaulo & Kirkendol, 1989).

Strategies Used by Liars and Truth Tellers

There is little research on the strategies liars and truth-tellers use on their own initiative, thus without being trained. This is unfortunate. Learning about strategies and their consequences can help us understand when and why liars' and truth-tellers' responses will differ and when they will not. This knowledge could increase our lie-catching ability.

In studies by Hartwig, Granhag and Strömwall (2005b) and Strömwall, Hartwig and Granhag (2005) suspects (undergraduates) were interviewed by experienced police officers about a mock crime, half of the suspects were guilty and half were innocent. After the interviews, each suspect was asked about his or her strategy. More guilty suspects (over 60 % in Hartwig et al.,'s study and over 90 % in Strömwall et al.'s study) than innocent suspects (37 % in Hartwig et al., and 70 % in Strömwall et al.) said that they had employed a strategy during the interview. It thus seems that innocent suspects trust that, if they only tell the truth, their internal state of innocence will show. They therefore feel less need to plan their behaviour and decide on a strategy to use when being interviewed. However, innocent suspects overestimate the extent to which lie catchers can read their internal state (Hartwig et al., 2005b; Kassin & Norwick, 2004), a tendency that is in line with the illusion of transparency bias, people's tendency to overestimate the extent to which their own thoughts, emotions and other states can be seen by others (Gilovich, Savitsky & Medvec, 1998). This tendency has several important implications for the psychology of confessions (Kassin, 2005).

Guilty suspects thus use strategies more frequently than innocent suspects. When innocent and guilty suspects do use strategies, do they use the same or different strategies? We will focus on verbal strategies. Returning to the study by Strömwall and colleagues (2005), it was found that guilty and innocent suspects differed in terms of verbal strategies. The most common verbal strategy reported by guilty suspects (around 40 %) was to 'keep their story simple', and the most common verbal strategy reported by innocent suspects (around 50%) was to 'keep their story real'. The finding that liars try to keep their story simple is supported by previous research (Granhag & Strömwall, 2002). Hartwig and colleagues (2005a; 2006) have presented more fine-grained analyses of the actual interviews, and these show that guilty suspects avoid mentioning information pertaining to evidence in the free recall to a significantly higher extent than do innocent suspects. In short, guilty suspects practice a strategy of avoiding self-incriminating avoidance, whereas innocent suspects have a strong belief that their innocence will shine through if they tell the truth, and worry less about whether the information they tell is self-incriminating or not.

Are the strategies of avoidance (on the part of guilty suspects), and the strong belief that 'my innocence will show' (on the part of innocent suspects) effective? As will be detailed in the next section, if the interviewer uses the evidence in a strategic manner, the answer is 'no' for guilty suspects and 'yes' for innocent suspects (i.e., it will be possible to distinguish guilty from innocent suspects), but if the interrogator uses the evidence in a non-strategic manner, the answer is 'yes' for guilty suspects and 'no' for innocent suspects (i.e., it will be very difficult to distinguish guilty from innocent suspects).

INTERVIEWING TO DETECT DECEPTION: PHYSICAL LIE DETECTION TECHNIQUES

Physical activity in liars and truth tellers is usually measured with a polygraph. The most commonly recorded responses are sweating of the fingers, blood pressure and respiration (Bull, 1988), which are all measures of arousal. Hence, the polygraph is an arousal detection rather than a lie detection machine.

Relevant–Irrelevant Test

In the Relevant–Irrelevant Test (RIT), two types of questions are asked, crime-relevant questions (e.g., 'Did you kill Chris Smith?') and crime-irrelevant questions (e.g., 'Is today Tuesday?'). Control questions are necessary to ask because people's individual physical responses differ in intensity, just as how people differ in their tone of voice, speech rate, the number of movements they make, and so on. The rationale behind the RIT is that lying examinees will show stronger physiological responses to relevant crime-related questions than to irrelevant questions. They will do this because they are lying when answering the crime-related questions, and this deception will increase arousal due to fear of not being believed. Truthful examinees tell the truth when answering both the crime-related and crime-irrelevant questions, hence, their physiological responses will be the same when answering both questions. However, this theoretical premise has practical drawbacks. A strong physiological response could also occur when truthful examinees answer the crime-related questions, because they too may fear that they will not be believed. What perhaps increases this problem is that polygraph tests are only carried out if no conclusive evidence is available in the case. (In the case of conclusive evidence, a polygraph test is redundant.) This means for innocent persons that they have yet not been able to prove their innocence during the investigation prior to the polygraph test. For them, the outcome of the polygraph test really matters. A guilty verdict would mean that they are still not exonerated from the accusations or suspicions that have surrounded them, and this could have serious negative consequences; such as continuing to be investigated and interviewed about the crime by the police, fear that the truth about their innocence may never be believed, and perhaps negative reactions from family members, colleagues, neighbours, etc. Under such circumstances, heightened arousal may well occur when answering relevant questions. RIT is therefore an inappropriate technique for polygraph testing, and there is agreement amongst polygraph researchers that such a test should not be used (Honts, 1991; Lykken, 1998; Raskin, 1986; Saxe, 1994).

The Control Question Test

The Control Question Test (CQT, also labelled the Comparison Question Test) compares responses to relevant questions with responses to control questions. *Relevant questions* (e.g., 'Did you kill Chris Smith?') are specific questions about the crime. *Control questions* deal with acts that are indirectly related to the crime under investigation, and do not refer to the crime in question. They are meant to embarrass the suspects (both guilty and innocent) and evoke arousal. This is facilitated by giving the suspect no choice but to lie when answering the control questions. Examiners formulate control questions for which, in their view, denials are deceptive. The exact formulation of these questions will depend on the examinee's circumstances, but a control question in an examination regarding a murder might be: 'Have you ever tried to hurt someone to get revenge?' (Iacono & Patrick, 1997), where the examiner believes that the examinee has indeed hurt someone in such a situation at some point in his or her life. Under normal circumstances, some examinees might admit to this (control) wrong-doing. However, during a polygraph examination they will not do so because the examiner will give the examinee the impression that to admit to this would cause the examiner to conclude that the examinee is the type of person who would commit the crime in question, and would therefore consider he or she to be guilty. Thus, the examinee has no choice other than to deny this (earlier) wrongdoing and thus be untruthful in answering the control questions. In case the examinee does admit this earlier wrongdoing, the question will be reformulated. This means that the questions (both control and relevant) will be discussed with the examinee prior to the examination. The examination starts when the examinee makes clear that he or she is happy to answer 'no' to all control and relevant questions.

The CQT is based on the assumption that in *innocent suspects* control questions will generate more arousal than the relevant questions, because they will be more concerned about their answers to the control questions, and because they are lying to the control questions. However, the same control questions are expected to elicit less arousal in *guilty suspects* than the relevant questions. Guilty suspects give deceptive responses to both types of question, but relevant questions represent the most immediate and serious threat to the examinee, which are expected to lead to a stronger physiological response than the control questions.

Several problems have been identified with the CQT polygraph test (Ben-Shakhar, 2002; Vrij, 2000). Firstly, similar to the RIT technique, the chance that innocent suspects will also show heightened arousal to relevant questions cannot be ruled out. Secondly, the test is not standardised, because the control questions that could be asked depend on the type of crime under investigation. When investigating a theft different control questions need to be asked than when investigating a murder. Also, control questions such as 'Have you ever tried to hurt someone to get revenge?' can only be asked to examinees who are known to have hurt someone in the past. The lack of standardisation means that much depends on the skills of the individual polygraph examiner formulating the questions. Thirdly, as discussed earlier, CQT is vulnerable to the use of countermeasures.

The debate about CQT is heated, with both opponents (Lykken, 1998) and supporters (Honts, 2005) expressing strong views. Real-life studies examining the accuracy of CQT testing do reveal a trend where CQT is less accurate at correctly classifying innocent examinees than at correctly classifying guilty examinees (Granhag & Vrij, 2005). In fact, the results for innocent examinees are disappointing with between 59% and 78% of innocent suspects being correctly classified.

Voice Stress Analysers and Thermal Imaging

Sometimes Voice Stress Analysis (VSA) and thermal imaging are presented as alternatives to polygraph techniques. VSA uses microphones attached to computers to detect and display arousal-related voice indices such as intensity, frequency, pitch, harmonics or micro tremors; thermal imaging uses infrared cameras to detect changes in temperature patterns (and thus blood flow) around the eye. SVA and thermal imaging may be better indicators of arousal than the traditional polygraph test measurements (National Research Council, 2003) but this will probably also depend on where the measurements are recorded. For example, better voice pitch recordings will be obtained when the examinee is in a soundproof room than when in a noisy environment.

VSA and thermal imaging can be used overtly (with the examinee's knowledge), but, because voice stress analysers and thermal imaging measure arousal non-intrusively (via microphones and thermal cameras respectively), they can also be used covertly, without the examinee's knowledge.

To introduce VSA and thermal imaging as alternative techniques to the polygraph is misleading because the only difference is in how arousal is measured (the traditional tests measure sweating of fingers, blood pressure and respiration). The similarity with traditional polygraph testing implies that all the limitations with traditional testing, discussed above, also apply to VSA and thermal imaging. The ability to measure arousal non-intrusively has obvious benefits. Arousal data can be measured more quickly (the examinee does not have to be connected to a machine) and without the examinees being aware that they are being assessed. However, covert testing introduces severe limitations. CQT type of questioning, the only type of questioning that is supported by polygraph supporters, cannot be carried out without the examinee's awareness, because the questions need to be discussed with the examinees prior to the examination, and background information about the examinee is necessary (see previously). This implies that, if VSA or thermal imaging tests were to be carried out without having background information about the examinee (which is likely to be the case when used at check-in desks at airports, or by insurance companies when they discuss clients' claims over the telephone), CQT tests cannot be carried out. RIT type of questioning could be used, but this test is disputed even by polygraph supporters. Alternatively, just single questions could be asked (i.e., 'Are you carrying illegal goods in your luggage'?) but this is even less reliable than an RIT test, because no control questions are asked and, as a result, there is no attempt to control for individual differences. Unsurprisingly, the National Research Council (2003) concluded that both voice stress analysis and thermal imaging do not provide acceptable scientific evidence for use in the detection of deception. See http://www.polygraph.org/voicestress.htm for useful information about SVA.

Functional Magnetic Resonance Images (fMRI)

Improvements in neuroscience techniques make it now possible to examine human brain functioning. Brain activity is associated with changes in blood flow and changes in oxygen consumption in the brain and researchers can measure such changes with an MRI scanner. Those scanners, primarily used in hospitals, for example, to detect brain tumours or injuries, are expensive. Conducting fMRI analyses are expensive also and can be time-consuming (sometimes as long as two or three hours per examinee) (National Research Council, 2003). Several lie detection studies have been carried out with such a scanner but they appear somewhat artificial. In a typical study, participants were shown a playing card (5 of clubs) but were asked to deny having seen such a card when they were asked about it whilst in the scanner (Langleben, Loughead, Bilker, Ruparel, Childress, Busch & Gur, 2005). An accuracy rate of 78% was obtained in this study, but such accuracy rates are also found if such 'playing card' lie detection tests are carried out with traditional polygraph equipment measuring sweating, blood pressure and respiration (Ben-Shakhar & Elaad, 2003; MacLaren 2001). Thus in terms of lie detection capacity, fMRI lie detection does not appear to bring us any further than traditional physiological lie detection measures. However, fMRI research has the advantage that it tells us more about what is going on in liars than traditional measures. For example, Spence et al.'s (2004) review of fMRI research showed that lying is associated with activities in 'higher' brain centres such as the prefrontal cortex (see also Davatzikos, Ruparel, Fan, Shen, Acharyya, Loughead, Gur & Langleben, in press; Langleben et al., 2005), which support the concept that (at least in those studies) lying was cognitively more demanding than truth-telling. We believe that this facility, underpinning the theoretical notion about what is going on in liars, is the main advantage of fMRI research (see also Poldrack & Wagner, 2004).

We have no doubt that hopes are raised that fMRI analyses could be used as an accurate lie detection tool, perhaps because people are typically impressed by using such sophisticated equipment. Unsurprisingly, Wolpe, Foster and Langleben (2005) reported that in the United States, defence-related agencies have dedicated significant funds to fMRI lie detection research. However, the fMRI lie detection studies that have been conducted so far have limitations. They are artificial, and the brain regions activated are not only activated during deception (Langleben et al., 2005; Poldrack & Wagner, 2004; Wolpe et al., 2005). In other words, it does not detect lies, but the brain processes that are associated with lying. Such brain processes may also occur when people are telling the truth. Thus, careful interpretation of the results obtained with such tests will therefore always be crucial. As Wolpe et al. (2005) noted, this fact can easily be overlooked in applied settings.

VERBAL AND NONVERBAL LIE DETECTION TECHNIQUES

Behaviour Analysis Interview

The only published interview protocol that we are aware of that is designed to evoke verbal and behavioural responses to deceit is Inbau, Reid, Buckley and Jayne's (2001) Behaviour Analysis Interview (BAI) technique. The BAI technique consists of 15 standardised questions, and the assumption is that innocent interviewees will respond differently to the specialised questions than will deceptive interviewees. Regarding the nonverbal responses, Inbau et al. (2001) assume that liars feel less comfortable than truth tellers in the police interview situation, and, as a result, liars are more likely to show nervous behaviours such as crossing their legs, shifting in their chair, looking away from the interviewer, and performing grooming behaviours when answering some of the 15 questions. Regarding the verbal answers, deceptive suspects are thought to be less helpful in the interview and to not show an appropriate level of concern about being a suspect, whereas truth tellers are more likely to offer helpful information, and show an expectancy to be exonerated (see also Horvath, Jayne & Buckley, 1994). Thus, compared to their innocent counterparts, guilty suspects are thought to be more evasive when they are asked about the purpose of the interview (question 1); less emphatic in their denial of having committed the crime (question 2); more likely to deny any knowledge of whom the culprit might be (question 3); less likely to name another suspect (question 4, because naming someone who the suspect knows is innocent would be an unnecessary lie); less likely to name someone they believe is innocent (question 5, because guilty suspects prefer to surround themselves with other possible suspects); and so on.

The theoretical assumption of BAI is flawed. The premise that liars feel less comfortable than truth tellers in a police interview is not universally accepted by the scientific community. Neither does deception research support the view that liars show more nervous behaviours than truth tellers (DePaulo et al., 2003), even in high-stakes situations (Mann et al., 2002). BAI's assumption that liars would be less helpful than truth tellers is also problematic, as this goes directly against the theoretical premise that liars take their credibility less for granted than truth tellers and are therefore more keen than truth tellers to make a convincing impression (DePaulo et al., 2003). It sounds reasonable that being perceived as unhelpful will look suspicious, therefore, someone may predict that liars will try to avoid appearing unhelpful.

Several experimental studies have provided evidence that the BAI premises are not valid. Kassin and Fong (1999) trained participants to look for the nonverbal cues to deception outlined by Inbau et al., and compared these participants' performance on a subsequent lie detection test with a group of participants who were untrained. The trained participants performed significantly worse than those who received no training. In Mann, Vrij and Bull's (2004) lie detection study, police officers judged the veracity of statements made by lying and truthful suspects during real-life (videotaped) interviews. They found a significant, but negative, correlation between officers reportedly attending to the Inbau et al. nonverbal cues and their accuracy in the lie detection task. In Vrij's (2005a) experiment, an interviewer challenged the veracity of liars' and truth tellers' accounts after they narrated what had happened. When they were then asked to repeat what had happened, more truth tellers than liars refused to do so. In other words, contradicting Inbau et al.'s (2001) assumptions, liars were more helpful than truth tellers. Finally, in Vrij, Mann and Fisher's (2006a) experiment, participants lied or told the truth about an event during a BAI interview. The interviews were coded according to Inbau et al.'s guidelines. The results showed that, compared to liars, truth tellers were less helpful and exhibited more nervous behaviours than liars.

Baseline Observation Method

The Baseline Observation Method, proposed by, amongst others, Inbau et al. (2001) is based upon the premise that there are large individual differences in people's speech and behaviour. Therefore, it may facilitate lie detection if someone's natural truthful speech style and behaviour is known to the observer, so that the behaviour and speech style under investigation can be compared. Inbau et al. (2001) suggest observing the natural verbal and nonverbal behaviour exhibited by suspects during the small talk part of the interview, and to compare this with the responses during the actual investigation. This technique is often employed in police interviews (Moston & Engelberg, 1993). Unfortunately, it is an incorrect use of BOM. Not only do different people behave differently in the same situation (*inter*-individual differences), the same person behaves differently in different situations as well (*intra*-individual differences) (DePaulo, 1992; DePaulo & Friedman, 1998). Small talk and the investigative core of the police interview are fundamentally different. The formal interview matters to suspects, as severe negative consequences may follow if they are not believed. In other words, this is a high-stake situation. The small talk component has no such consequences and is therefore a low-stake situation. People tend to behave differently during low-stake and high-stake situations (Ekman, 1985/2001; Vrij, 1995). When the BOM technique is employed, parts of the interview should be used that are *truly comparable* in terms of stakes. They should also be comparable topic wise, because sometimes the behaviours people show are topic related (Davis & Hadiks, 1985). See Vrij (2006b) for a discussion of the BOM method.

VERBAL AND NONVERBAL LIE DETECTION TECHNIQUES WHERE THERE IS NO EVIDENCE AGAINST THE SUSPECT

Information-Gathering Technique and Reverse Order Interviewing Technique

Our (both authors) interview techniques are based on the theoretical premise (Zuckerman et al., 2001) and empirical findings (DePaulo et al., 2003; Mann et al., 2002) that liars may experience more cognitive load in police interviews than truth tellers. Police interviewers could exploit this by employing interview techniques that further increase the lying suspect's cognitive demand.

First, rather than accusing a suspect (e.g., 'You are lying') interviewers could employ an information-gathering approach (e.g., 'Tell me in as much detail as possible what you did last night'). An accusatory approach has two problems. Firstly, it is likely to result in short replies from the suspect (e.g., 'I am not lying', 'I didn't do it', etc.). Short replies are cognitively easier to formulate than extensive answers (Vrij, Mann & Fisher, 2006b), and are less likely to reveal verbal differences than extensive answers (Vrij, 2005b; Vrij, Mann, Kristin & Fisher, in press). Secondly, truth tellers and liars may well show similar behavioural responses after being accused, because the behaviour caused by the accusation may overshadow possible differences in behaviour caused by lying (Bond & Fahey, 1987; Ekman, 1985/2001; Vrij, 2006).

Information-gathering interview techniques are thus preferable. Cognitive demand could be increased in such techniques by asking specific follow-up questions about the information provided by the suspect in response to the open-ended question (e.g., 'You mentioned that you went to the gym last night, could you please describe who else was there?'). Answering such questions could be more difficult for liars than for truth tellers. The liar's strategy could have been to prepare a fabricated alibi. Asking more questions forces the suspect to provide more details about the alibi, and this could involve including details not previously prepared. In that case the suspects need to elaborate spontaneously, which is cognitively demanding. Obviously, the suspect could always decide to just stick to his or her prepared alibi and not provide any further information (e.g., 'Sorry, I don't know who else was at the gym'). This is unlikely, because not being able to elaborate on a previous statement looks suspicious, and liars attempt to avoid making such an impression. Rather than looking suspicious they may decide to make up more details.

A sophisticated alibi would be to describe an event that the suspect has actually experienced before, albeit not at the time he/she claims. Thus, the gym example mentioned above would be particularly useful if the suspect has indeed been to that gym on previous occasions. The interviewer should be aware of this. Questions such as 'What pieces of equipment did you use at the gym?' are then easy to answer for the suspect. Instead, the interviewer should ask time-specific questions (e.g., 'Could you please describe who else you saw there?') as this is the only aspect of the event the suspect lies about or is unlikely to categorically be able to answer.

Secondly, it is often found in deception research that truth tellers tend to tell their stories in a more *un*structured way than liars (Vrij, 2000, 2005b). That is, liars tend to tell their stories in a more fixed chronological order (this happened first, and then this, and then that, and so on) than truth tellers. It has been suggested that it is difficult for liars to fabricate a story in a non-chronological order (Köhnken, 1999; Steller, 1989; Zaparniuk, Yuille & Taylor, 1995). Lie detectors could exploit this difficulty by asking interviewees to tell their stories in a non-chronological order, for example, in reverse order. Presumably, this novel output order should be relatively easy for truth tellers to generate, since they are not under as much cognitive load, whereas it may be difficult for liars who are burdened by a more severe cognitive load.

Whether these interview styles actually work and will benefit lie detectors is currently unknown. We believe that the efficiency of such interview styles should be empirically tested before they are put into practice. Research is also needed to examine what exactly causes the cognitive load for liars. Is it formulating the lie that causes cognitive load? Or the efforts to control behaviour? Or is it the suspect's observation of the police interviewer in order to find out whether he or she gets away with the lie that causes the cognitive demand? Or is it perhaps a combination of those aspects? Unravelling the determinants of cognitive load could be used to design interview techniques that are specifically tailored to increasing cognitive load concerning those aspects that the suspect finds most demanding.

VERBAL LIE DETECTION TECHNIQUES WHERE THERE IS EVIDENCE AGAINST THE SUSPECT

In cases where there is some evidence against the suspect, this could be used strategically in interviews using an information-gathering style. Kronkvist and Granhag (2005) reviewed 15 police interrogation manuals regarding recommendations on how to best use case-specific facts and evidence, known to interviewers, during a police interview. Very few of the manuals made recommendations, but those that did mentioned that the existing evidence should be disclosed at the outset of the interview in order to make the suspect confess (Inbau et al., 2001; Yeschke, 1997). There are some archival studies that have analysed when the evidence is disclosed during a police interview. In an American study, Leo (1996) showed that disclosure of evidence (accompanied by a suggestion of guilt) was the typical way to start the interview, and occurred in more than 80% of the cases analysed. In a British study, Moston and Engelberg (1993) showed that only a minority of the interviewers disclosed the evidence at the beginning of the interrogation. Archival studies on evidence disclosure thus show mixed, and perhaps culturally specific, results. There may be several reasons behind disclosing the evidence at the outset of the interview. Perhaps, the interviewer perceives the existing evidence as very strong, and believes that the suspect will break down when confronted with such overwhelming evidence. Alternatively, it may be due to frustration or impatience on the part of the interviewer, or poor planning by the interviewer.

In their experiment, Hartwig, Granhag, Strömwall and Vrij (2005) used 58 suspects (undergraduates), half of whom had committed a mock crime (stealing a wallet from a briefcase in a shop) and later denied this, and half of whom had committed no such crime but who had touched the briefcase while visiting the same shop. For half of the guilty suspects and half of the innocent suspects, the interview began by the interviewer confronting the interviewee with the case-specific evidence (two independent witness testimonies, and the fact that their fingerprints had been found on the briefcase), followed by the interviewer's invitation to describe their activities. The remaining two groups (half of guilty and half of the innocent suspects) had the exact same case-specific evidence presented to them after, rather than before, they had told the interviewer about their activities. All interviews were videotaped, and shown to observers (other undergraduates), who were asked to assess veracity.

The results show that observers who were shown videotapes in which the case-specific evidence was disclosed early in the interview achieved significantly lower deception detection accuracy (42.9%), than did those observers who were shown videotapes in which the very same case-specific evidence was disclosed later in the interview (61.75%). Comparing the suspects' statements against the existing case-specific evidence, it was found, for the late-evidence condition, that guilty suspects' statements were significantly more inconsistent with the evidence than were innocent suspects' statements, whereas the same comparison was non-significant in the early evidence condition. Thus, the strategy used in the late-evidence condition (that is, withholding the evidence) created problems for the guilty suspects (their statements became inconsistent with the case-specific evidence). A correlational analysis showed that the observers indeed picked up on these inconsistencies: (a) the more inconsistencies in a statement, the more likely the observers were to assess the suspect as guilty, and importantly, (b) the more inconsistencies in a statement, the more likelihood that observers were correct in their judgements.

In a follow-up study, Hartwig and colleagues (2006) further refined and tested the strategic use of evidence technique (the SUE-technique). The study was conducted with the help of police trainees, who either were or were not trained in strategically using the evidence when interrogating guilty or innocent mock suspects. During the training, the idea behind the SUE-technique was outlined and illustrated with videotaped examples of strategic and non-strategic use of the evidence. The police trainees were trained in both identifying potentially incriminating evidence from case-files and in planning and asking questions concerning the evidence without disclosing it to the suspect. Finally, they were given the opportunity of practising the SUE-technique on each other.

During the experiment, trained and untrained interviewers interviewed innocent and guilty mock suspects. They were not informed who was guilty and who was innocent. The results showed that trained interviewers applied different strategies than did untrained interviewers. When interviewing the mock suspects, trained interviewers (but not untrained) confronted the guilty suspects with the evidence at the end of the interview more often than they did for innocent suspects (due to guilty suspects were more likely to contradict or avoid talking about the evidence than innocent suspects). After being interviewed by trained interviewers, guilty suspects reported having experienced significantly more cognitive demand than did innocent suspects, but after being interviewed by untrained interviewers, guilty and innocent suspects reported to have experienced the same amount of cognitive demand. The differences in the manner of interviewing resulted in that guilty suspects interviewed by trained interviewers were more inconsistent with the evidence compared to guilty suspects interviewed by untrained interviewers. Moreover, the trained interviewers picked up on these inconsistencies: The more inconsistencies in a statement, the more likely the trained interviewers were to have assessed the suspect as guilty, whereas the same correlation was non-significant for untrained interviewers. Finally, trained interviewers obtained a considerably higher deception detection accuracy rate (85.4%), than untrained interviewers (56.1%). In fact, the 85% deception detection accuracy rate is among the highest ever found in deception research.

In essence, the success of the SUE-technique is contingent on liars' and truth-tellers' strategies. The SUE-technique will be successful in pinpointing guilty suspects if they first avoid mentioning the evidence when recalling the event in question (self-incriminating avoidance), and then contradict the existing evidence when asked specific questions (and the research cited above shows that they do). The SUE-technique will be successful in pinpointing innocent suspects if these believe that their innocence will show, and recall the event in question as they remember it (and the research cited above shows that they do). The SUE-technique is still at an early stage, and needs to be refined and tested for a number of contexts and situations. For example, we know little about the extent to which the effectiveness of the SUE-technique is a function of (a) the suspect's certainty about the existing evidence against him or her, (b) the complexity of the crime event, and (c) the delay between the crime event and the interrogation.

CONCLUSION

Since cues akin to Pinocchio's growing nose do not exist, lie detectors will fail in their task if they just look for such cues. Rather, interview techniques need to be employed, for example, to control for individual differences between individuals. We have demonstrated that interview styles designed to evoke arousal in liars will fail, as no questions can be asked that increase arousal in liars but not in truth tellers. Rather, we propose techniques that concentrate on cognitive demand and are created to make the interview situation more difficult for liars than for truth tellers. Often, our proposed techniques oppose the recommendations found in police interrogation manuals. We hope that our techniques will be useful to practitioners.

REFERENCES

Ben-Shakhar, G. (2002) A critical review of the control questions test (CQT). In M. Kleiner (Ed.), *Handbook of polygraph testing* (pp. 103–26). London: Academic Press.

Ben-Shakhar, G. & Elaad, E. (2003) The validity of psychophysiological detection of information with the Guilty Knowledge Test: A meta-analytic review. *The Journal of Applied Psychology*, **88**, 131–51.

Bond, C.F. & Fahey, W.E. (1987) False suspicion and the misperception of deceit. *British Journal of Social Psychology*, **26**, 41–6.

Bull, R. (1988) What is the lie-detection test? In A. Gale (Ed.), *The polygraph test: Lies, truth and science* (pp. 10–19). London: Sage Publications.

Caso, L., Vrij, A., Mann, S. & de Leo, G. (2006) Deceptive responses: The impact of verbal and nonverbal countermeasures. *Legal and Criminological Psychology*, **11**, 99–111.

Davatzikos, C., Ruparel. K., Fan, Y., Shen, D.G., Acharyya, M., Loughead, J.W., Gur, R.C. & Langleben, D.D. (in press). Classifying spatial patterns of brain activity with machine learning methods: Application to lie detection. *Neuroimage*.

Davis, M. & Hadiks, D. (1995) Demeanor and credibility. *Semiotica*, **106**, 5–54.

DePaulo, B.M. (1992) Nonverbal behavior and self-presentation. *Psychological Bulletin*, **111**, 203–43.

DePaulo, B.M. & Friedman, H.S. (1998) Nonverbal communication. In D.T. Gilbert, S.T. Fiske & G. Lindzey (Eds), *The handbook of social psychology* (pp. 3–40). Boston, MA: McGraw-Hill.

DePaulo, B.M. & Kirkendol, S.E. (1989) The motivational impairment effect in the communication of deception. In J.C. Yuille (Ed.), *Credibility assessment* (pp. 51–70). Dordrecht, the Netherlands: Kluwer.

DePaulo, B.M., Lindsay, J.J., Malone, B.E., Muhlenbruck, L., Charlton, K. & Cooper, H. (2003) Cues to deception. *Psychological Bulletin*, **129**, 74–118.

Ekman, P. (1985/2001). *Telling lies*. New York: W.W. Norton.

Ekman, P. & Frank, M.G. (1993) Lies that fail. In M. Lewis & C. Saarni (Eds), *Lying and deception in everyday life* (pp. 184–201). New York, NJ: Guilford Press.

Ekman, P. & Friesen, W.V. (1972) Hand movements. *Journal of Communication*, **22**, 353–74.

Gilovich, T., Savitsky, K. & Medvec, V.H. (1998) The illusion of transparency: Biased assessments of other's ability to read one's emotional states. *Journal of Personality and Social Psychology*, **75**, 332–46.

Gordon, N.J. & Fleisher, W.L. (2002) *Effective interviewing and interrogation techniques*. London: Academic Press.

Granhag, P.A. & Strömwall, L.A. (2002) Repeated interrogations: Verbal and nonverbal cues to deception. *Applied Cognitive Psychology*, **16**, 243–57.

Granhag, P.A. & Vrij, A. (2005) Deception detection. In N. Brewer & K. Williams (Eds), *Psychology and law: An empirical perspective* (pp. 43–92). New York, NJ: The Guilford Press.

Gudjonsson, G.H. (2003) *The psychology of interrogations and confessions: A handbook*. Chichester: John Wiley & Sons, Ltd.

Hartwig, M., Granhag, P.A., Strömwall, L.A. & Vrij, A. (2005) Detecting deception via strategic disclosure of evidence. *Law and Human Behaviour*, **29**, 469–84.

Hartwig, M., Granhag, P.A., Strömwall, L.A. & Kronkvist, O. (2006) Strategic use of evidence during police interrogations: When training to detect deception works. *Law and Human Behaviour*, **30**, 603–19.

Hartwig, M., Granhag, P.A. & Strömwall, L.A. (2005). *Guilty and innocent suspects' strategies during police interrogations*. Manuscript submitted for publication.

Hocking, J.E. & Leathers, D.G. (1980) Nonverbal indicators of deception: A new theoretical perspective. *Communication Monographs*, **47**, 119–31.

Holmberg, U. & Christianson, S.A. (2002) Murderers' and sexual offenders experiences of police interviews and their inclination to admit or deny crimes. *Behavioral Sciences and the Law*, **20**, 31–45.

Honts, C.R. (1991) The emperor's new clothes: The application of the polygraph tests in the American workplace. *Forensic Reports*, **4**, 91–116.

Honts, C.R. (2005) The psychophysiological detection of deception. In P.A. Granhag & L.A. Strömwall (Eds), *Deception detection in forensic contexts* (pp. 103–23). Cambridge, England: Cambridge University Press.

Honts, C.R. & Alloway, A. (in press) Information does not affect the validity of a Comparison Question Test. *Legal and Criminological Psychology*.

Honts, C.R. & Amato, S.L. (2002) Countermeasures. In M. Kleiner (Ed.), *Handbook of polygraph testing* (pp. 251–64). London: Academic Press.

Honts, C.R., Raskin, D.C. & Kircher, J.C. (1987) Effects of physical countermeasures and their electromyographic detection during polygraph tests for deception. *Journal of Psychophysiology*, **1**, 241–7.

Honts, C.R., Raskin, D.C. & Kircher, J.C. (1994) Mental and physical countermeasures reduce the accuracy of polygraph tests. *Journal of Applied Psychology*, **79**, 252–9.

Horvath, F., Jayne, B. & Buckley, J. (1994) Differentiation of truthful and deceptive criminal suspects in behaviour analysis interviews. *Journal of Forensic Sciences*, **39**, 793–807.

Iacono, W.G. & Patrick, C.J. (1997) Polygraphy and integrity testing. In R. Rogers (Ed.), *Clinical assessment of malingering and deception* (pp. 252–81). New York: The Guilford Press.

Inbau, F.E., Reid, J.E., Buckley, J.P. & Jayne, B.C. (2001) *Criminal interrogation and confessions, 4th edn*. Gaithersburg, MD: Aspen Publishers.

Kassin, S.M. (2005) On the psychology of confessions. Does innocence put innocents at risk? *American Psychologist*, **60**, 251–8.

Kassin, S.M. & Fong, C.T. (1999) 'I'm innocent!': Effects of training on judgments of truth and deception in the interrogation room. *Law and Human Behavior*, **23**, 499–516.

Kassin, S.M. & Norwick, R.J. (2004) Why people waive their Miranda rights: The power of innocence. *Law and Human Behavior*, **28**, 211–21.

Köhnken, G. (1999, July). *Statement validity assessment*. Paper presented at the pre-conference program of applied courses 'Assessing credibility' organised by the European Association of Psychology and Law, Dublin, Ireland.

Kronkvist, O. & Granhag, P.A. (2005) *The use of evidence during interrogation- What do we learn by reading police interrogation manuals?* Manuscript under preparation.

Langleben, D.D., Loughead, J.W., Bilker, W.B., Ruparel, K., Childress, A.R., Busch, S.I. & Gur, R.C. (2005) Telling the truth from lie in individual subjects with fast event-related fMRI. *Human Brain Mapping*, **26**, 262–72.

Leal, S.M., van Hooff, J. & Vrij S.A. (2005) *Cognitive demand, arousal and the compensatory blink: Implications for deception research.* Manuscript submitted for publication.

Leo, R.A. (1996) Inside the interrogation room. *Journal of Criminal Law and Criminology*, **86**, 266–303.

Lykken, D.T. (1998) *A tremor in the blood: Uses and abuses of the lie detector.* New York, NJ: Plenum Press.

Macdonald, J.M. & Michaud, D.L. (1992) *Criminal interrogation.* Denver; CO: Apache Press.

MacLaren, V.V. (2001) A quantitative review of the guilty knowledge test. *The Journal of Applied Psychology*, **86**, 674–83.

Mann, S. & Vrij, A. (2006). Police officers' judgements of veracity, tenseness, cognitive load and attempted behavioural control in real life police interviews. *Psychology, Crime, & Law*, **1**, 307–19.

Mann, S., Vrij, A. & Bull, R. (2002) Suspects, lies and videotape: An analysis of authentic high-stakes liars. *Law and Human Behavior*, **26**, 365–76.

Mann, S., Vrij, A. & Bull, R. (2004) Detecting true lies: Police officers' ability to detect deceit. *Journal of Applied Psychology*, **89**, 137–49.

Moston, S. & Engelberg, T. (1993) Police questioning techniques in tape recorded interviews with criminal suspects. *Policing and Society*, **3**, 223–37.

National Research Council (2003) *The polygraph and lie detection.* Committee to Review the Scientific Evidence on the Polygraph (2003). Washington, DC: The National Academic Press.

Pavlidis, J., Eberhardt, N.L. & Levine, J.A. (2002) Seeing through the face of deception. *Nature*, **415**, 35.

Poldrack, R.A. & Wagner, A.D. (2004) What can neuroimaging tell us about the mind? Insight from prefrontal cortex. *Current Directions in Psychological Science*, **13**, 17–181.

Rabon, D. (1992). *Interviewing and interrogation.* Durham; NC: Carolina Academic Press.

Raskin, D.C. (1986) The polygraph in 1986: Scientific, professional, and legal issues surrounding acceptance of polygraph evidence. *Utah Law Review*, **29**, 29–74.

Riggio, R.E. (1986) Assessment of basic social skills. *Journal of Personality and Social Psychology*, **51**, 649–60.

Saxe, L. (1994) Detection of deception: Polygraph and integrity tests. *Current Directions in Psychological Science*, **3**, 69–73.

Shallice, T. & Burgess, P. (1994) Supervisory control of action and thought selection. In L. Weiskrantz, A. Baddeley & D. Alan (Eds), *Attention, selection, awareness and control: A tribute to Donald Broadbent* (pp. 171–87). New York NJ: Clarendon Press.

Spence, S.A., Hunter, M.D., Farrow, T.F.D., Green, R.D., Leung, D.H., Hughes, C.J. & Ganesan, V. (2004) A cognitive neurobiological account of deception: Evidence from functional neuroimaging. *Philosophical Transactions of the Royal Society of London*, **359**, 1755–62.

Steller, M. (1989) Recent developments in statement analysis. In J.C. Yuille (1989). *Credibility assessment* (pp. 135–54). Deventer, the Netherlands: Kluwer.

Strömwall. L.A., Granhag, P.A. & Hartwig, M. (2004) Practitioners' beliefs about deception. In P.A. Granhag & L.A. Strömwall (Eds), *Deception detection in forensic contexts* (pp. 229–50). Cambridge: Cambridge University Press.

Strömwall, L.A., Hartwig, M. & Granhag, P. (2005) To act truthfully: Nonverbal behaviour and strategies during a police interrogation. *Psychology, Crime & Law*, **11**(4), 353–361.

The Global Deception Team (2006) A world of lies. *Journal of Cross-Cultural Psychology*, **3**, 60–74.

Vrij, A. (1995) Behavioral correlates of deception in a simulated police interview. *Journal of Psychology: Interdisciplinary and Applied*, **129**, 15–29.

Vrij, A. (2000) *Detecting lies and deceit: The psychology of lying and its implications for professional practice*. Chichester: John Wiley and Sons, Ltd.

Vrij, A. (2004) Invited Article: Why professionals fail to catch liars and how they can improve. *Legal and Criminological Psychology*, **9**, 159–81.

Vrij, A. (2005a) Cooperation of liars and truth tellers. *Applied Cognitive Psychology*, **19**, 39–50.

Vrij, A. (2005b) Criteria-based content analysis: A qualitative review of the first 37 studies. *Psychology, Public Policy, and Law*, **11**, 3–41.

Vrij, A. (2006a) Challenging interviewees during interviews: The potential effects on lie detection. *Psychology, Crime, & Law*, **12**, 193–206.

Vrij, A. (2006b). Nonverbal communication and deception. In V. Manusov & M.L. Paterson (Eds), *The handbook of nonverbal communication*. Thousand Oaks, CA: Sage Publications.

Vrij, A., Akehurst, L. & Knight, S. (2006). Police officers', social workers', teachers' and general public's beliefs about deception in children, adolescents and adults. *Legal and Criminological Psychology*, **11**, 297–312.

Vrij, A., Akehurst, L., Soukara, S. & Bull, R. (2002) Will the truth come out? The effect of deception, age, status, coaching, and social skills on CBCA scores. *Law and Human Behavior*, **26**, 261–83.

Vrij, A., Akehurst, L., Soukara, S. & Bull, R. (2004) Let me inform you how to tell a convincing story: CBCA and Reality Monitoring scores as a function of age, coaching and deception. *Canadian Journal of Behavioural Science*, **36**, 113–26.

Vrij, A., Edward, K. & Bull, R. (2001) Stereotypical verbal and nonverbal responses while deceiving others. *Personality and Social Psychology Bulletin*, **27**, 899–909.

Vrij, A., Fisher, R., Mann, S. & Leal, S. (2006). Detecting deception by manipulating cognitive load. *Trends in Cognitive Sciences*, **10**, 141–2.

Vrij, A., Granhag, P.A. & Mann, S. (in press). Good liars. *Review of Policy Research*.

Vrij, A., Kneller, W. & Mann, S. (2000) The effect of informing liars about criteria-based content analysis on their ability to deceive CBCA-raters. *Legal and Criminological Psychology*, **5**, 57–70.

Vrij, A. & Mann, S. (2001) Telling and detecting lies in a high-stake situation: The case of a convicted murderer. *Applied Cognitive Psychology*, **15**, 187–203.

Vrij, A. & Mann, S. (2003). Deceptive responses and detecting deceit. In P.W. Halligan, C. Bass & Dakley (Eds), *Malingering and illness deception: Clinical and theoretical perspectives* (pp. 348–362). Oxford: University Press.

Vrij, A., Mann, S. & Fisher, R. (in press). An empirical test of the behaviour analysis interview. *Law and Human Behavior*.

Vrij, A., Mann, S. & Fisher, R. (2006a) An empirical test of the Behaviour Analysis Interview. *Law and Human Behavior*, **30**, 329–345.

Vrij, A., Mann, S. & Fisher, R. (2006b) Information-gathering vs accusatory interview style: Individual differences in respondents' experiences. *Personality and Individual Differences*, **41**, 589–99.

Vrij, A., Mann, S., Kristen, S. & Fisher, R. (in press) Cues to deception and ability to detect lies as a function of police interview styles. *Law and Human Behavior*.

Vrij, A., Semin, G.R., & Bull, R. (1996) Insight in behavior displayed during deception. *Human Communication Research*, **22**, 544–62.

Wolpe, P.R., Foster K.R. & Langleben, D.D. (2005) Emerging neurotechnologies for lie-detection: Promises and perils. *The American Journal of Bioethics*, **5**, 39–49.

Yeschke, C.L. (1997). *The art of investigative interviewing*. Newton, MA: Butterworth-Heinemann

Zaparniuk, J., Yuille, J.C. & Taylor, S. (1995) Assessing the credibility of true and false statements. *International Journal of Law and Psychiatry*, **18**, 343–52.

Zuckerman, M., DePaulo, B.M. & Rosenthal, R. (1981) Verbal and nonverbal communication of deception. In L. Berkowitz (Ed.), *Advances on experimental social psychology*, volume 14 (1–57). New York, NJ: Academic Press.

Zulawski, D.E. & Wicklander, D.E. (1993) *Practical aspects of interview and interrogation*. Boca Raton, FL: CRC Press.

CHAPTER 13

Crime Features and Interrogation Behaviour among Homicide Offenders

PEKKA SANTTILA AND TOM PAKKANEN

Being able to predict with some certainty whether the suspect is going to confess or not at the onset of an interrogation would provide the police with the opportunity of better tailoring the interviewing strategy to be adapted depending on the expected behaviour of the suspect. It is the aim of the present chapter to look at the possibility of making such predictions based on the objective features of the crime that the suspect is accused of. The so called offender profiling framework is based on the assumption that the crime scene behaviour of the offender reflects, in addition to situational influences, the motivational dynamics of the offence as well as the stable personality and cognitive features of the offender. Therefore, to the extent that behaviour during an interrogation also reflects such features, it should be possible to find links between crime features and interrogation behaviour. A preliminary attempt using a sample of Finnish homicide offenders who have committed a difficult-to-solve offence will be used. The sample was restricted to this subgroup of offenders as predicting the interrogation behaviour of suspects is most acute in these cases.

Offenders' Memories of Violent Crimes.   Edited by Sven Å. Christianson.
© 2007 John Wiley & Sons, Ltd.

Confessions are an important part of evidence in solving difficult crimes such as homicide. Of course, confessions are more likely in cases where the evidence against the offender is stronger (Moston et al., 1992) and when they might actually not be needed for a conviction. Nevertheless, Gudjonsson (2003), in reviewing the relevant literature (see also Chapter 11 in this book) suggests that confession evidence is either crucial or important in solving about 20 % of criminal cases, providing the police with evidence that would otherwise not have been available. It is, therefore, in the interests of the police to try to induce the suspect to confess. However, there are many reasons for criminal suspects not to do so (Gudjonsson, 2003). In homicide cases in particular, the legal sanctions are generally severe. Depending on the background of the offenders and the circumstances of the offence, the offence may negatively affect the general reputation of the offenders and their relationships with family and friends. In some cases, the offenders may even be reluctant to admit to themselves that they have committed an especially heinous crime. Finally, the offender may have fears of revenge on the part of the relatives of the victim or accomplices who would be implicated in a confession. In spite of these inhibitory factors, confessions are relatively common. Two large UK studies (Moston et al., 1992; Phillips & Brown, 1998) found the proportion of offenders confessing or otherwise admitting to the crime to be 0.42 and 0.55, respectively. There are suggestions, however, that confessions are less likely the more serious the crime is. Both Neubauer (1974) and Mitchell (1983) found that suspects were more likely to confess to property as opposed to violent offences. The aim of the present study was to see whether the likelihood of confessing would vary as a function of the characteristics of the offender, and the homicide type.

A number of theoretical models for why confessions occur have been proposed. Moston et al. (1992) suggest that the background characteristics of the suspect as well as the characteristics of the offence are relevant for understanding when confessions are likely and when they are unlikely. Also, the age and sex of the suspects as well as their personality are assumed to be relevant.

Gudjonsson's (2003) cognitive-behavioural model of confession suggests that the stress associated with being questioned is important for understanding confession behaviour. Suspects who have committed a serious offence may be distressed by the nature of the conduct itself. The emotional experiences of guilt and shame are particularly relevant. According to the model, the motivational effects of the two emotions differ from each other. The feeling of guilt motivates towards reparative action including confessing. On the contrary, the feeling of shame has the reverse effect decreasing the motivation for revealing what has happened. Different types of homicide may be differentially associated with these two types of feelings and should, therefore, also differ in terms of the likelihood of a confession taking place. It was expected that offenders committing a more instrumental homicide would be less likely to give themselves up or to confess but more likely to deny their involvement. As instrumental offenders may be more likely to have an antisocial background, the offence may not be out of character for them and, consequently, they may be less likely to feel guilt for their behaviour. These offenders use their victims in order to satisfy their needs: the victims themselves are not important and, consequently, feelings of guilt, which might lead to surrendering, are less likely. By contrast, it was expected that offenders committing a more expressive offence would exhibit the opposite pattern. They would be more likely to confess and less likely to deny their involvement in the offence. Expressive features suggest that that the person of the victim is important. Therefore, guilt is a more likely emotion in these cases. The exception was expected to be those offences where the victim had been hidden as this may suggest an antisocial background even if the offence otherwise could be classified as expressive. The results of Santtila et al. (2003) suggest this to be the case. In terms of the feelings of guilt and shame, it may be interesting to see how these are affected by the passage of time since the offence. Feelings of guilt may subside as the offender is able to come up with rationalisations for the offence thereby making a confession less likely. The feeling of shame should, however, not be likewise affected as the consequences of revealing the offence for self-image and self-esteem remain the same, independent of the passage of time.

Sex offences may have a different pattern of confessing compared to other types of offences. For example, Sigurdsson and Gudjonsson (1994) found that sexually motivated offences were associated with lower confession rates than other offences. In a further study, offenders guilty of rape were less likely to confess than other violent offenders, whereas child molesters were the most likely to confess (Gudjonsson & Sigurdsson, 2000). However, Mitchell (1983) found sexual offenders to be more likely to confess than non-sexual offenders. In the present sample, the sexually motivated murders resembled rapes more in terms of the age of victim and the level of aggression than they resembled child molesting suggesting that homicides with sexual features would be associated with lower confession rates compared to other homicides. When considering Gudjonsson's (2003) model of confessing and the role of feelings in it, it should be especially likely that sexually motivated crimes would be associated with feelings of shame, increasing the chances of denial. Self-report studies (Gudjonsson & Bownes, 1992; Gudjonsson & Petursson, 1991; Gudjonsson & Sigurdsson, 1999) of the reasoning offenders have for confessing suggest that after the perception of the strength of evidence the police have against the suspect, internal pressures (feelings of guilt about the offence as well as relief associated with confessing) were the most important determinants of confessions. The results of the studies further suggested that sex offenders had an especially strong need to confess because of internal pressures but were also the most inhibited about confessing because of the perceived severe personal and other consequences. This would suggest that some may confess directly whereas others may maintain their denial for long periods of time.

The relationship between age of the suspect and likelihood of confessing is unclear. Pearse et al. (1998) found that younger suspects were more likely to confess compared to older. However, the relationship between age and the likelihood of confessing disappeared when other case characteristics were controlled for. Younger suspects could be expected to be less equipped psychologically to cope with the demand characteristics of the situation because of their immaturity. In most of the studies looking at age and confessing, the type of crime has not been controlled for limiting their applicability to cases of homicide. It seems that no clear expectation can be formed on the basis of previous studies concerning the relationship between age and the likelihood of confessing in homicide cases that have required extensive investigative activity.

Phillips and Brown (1998) found in a UK study that suspects belonging to ethnic minorities were less likely to confess than non-minority suspects. Also, Pearse et al. (1998) reported that the proportion of non-minority suspects confessing was higher than that of minority suspects even though the difference was not statistically significant. Lack of trust towards the police has been suggested as a possible explanation (Phillips & Brown, 1998). It may also be that discrimination leading to a disadvantaged socio-economic position may result in minority homicide offenders having a more extensive anti-social background, making them more likely to resist confessing for this reason.

An extensive criminal background irrespective of minority status has been found to be related to a decreased likelihood of confessing in some studies (e.g. Softley, 1980) but not in all. Research by Moston et al. (1992) suggests that it is specifically previous prison experience and not convictions as such that is the relevant factor in understanding the effects of criminal background on confessing. It may be that fear of going to prison is the primary causative factor here

(Gudjonsson, 2003). Also, those with previous convictions may be more likely to be aware of their legal rights and through their familiarity with the interrogative situation are more likely to be able to cope with the associated social pressures (Gudjonsson, 2003). Again, there are studies that suggest that the opposite is true (e.g. Baldwin & McConville, 1980). It may be that suspects with previous convictions believe that it is more advantageous to confess and that their denials would be futile in any case.

The moderating effect of the type of offence has not been considered thoroughly. Extrapolating from the confession model of Gudjonsson (2003) it may be that instrumentally motivated homicides are committed by offenders who have extensive criminal backgrounds and are especially antisocial, even belonging to organised criminal groups. This may make them especially likely to resist confessing. This would suggest that an association between criminal background and resistance to confessing would be found in the present study. In contrast, offenders without criminal background were expected to be more likely to have committed an expressive homicide and to confess in order to reveal their feelings of guilt.

These expectations have to some extent been confirmed in a previous study looking at an unselected sample of 502 Finnish homicides (Santtila et al., 2003). Almost half (46 %) of the offenders confessed to the offence in its entirety whereas approximately 6 % denied any involvement. The rest neither admitted to the offence in its entirety nor denied any involvement. The offenders were less likely to give themselves up or to confess in cases involving sexual violence. Also, surrendering was unlikely in relation to a homicide in which something was stolen from the victim. Both these offence types have usually been classified as instrumental as the motivation is not only to harm the victim. Further, the results indicated that in an expressive homicide in which a firearm had been used, total denial was unlikely. However, in expressive homicides that involved the hiding of the body, the behaviour of the offenders was contrary to expectations: they were behaving more similarly to the offenders who had committed an instrumental homicide. An alternative explanation to the pattern of findings is that expressive offenders are more likely to leave incriminating evidence behind them and that this may be the main reason for their confession. It is also possible that the associations identified in an unselected sample would not be born out in difficult-to-solve homicides, which include more instrumental offence types who could overall be expected to be less likely to confess and more likely to maintain denial throughout interrogations.

In terms of personality factors, Gudjonsson and Sigurdsson (1999) have suggested that personality disordered offenders are less cooperative with the police and, therefore, more likely to at least initially resist confessing. In fact, offenders with a personality disorder in homicide cases were found to have tried the hardest to cover up their crime and to avoid detection (Gudjonsson & Petursson, 1982). On the contrary, offenders who saw the crime as inconsistent with their own view of themselves had a higher internal need to confess. When considered in the context of homicide, it can be argued that homicides with instrumental features are especially likely to have been committed by offenders with personality disorders as instrumental features are often associated with planning and explicit criminal motivation, i.e. the homicide is not totally inconsistent with the view the offender holds of himself. Therefore, such features are expected to be associated with denying responsibility. Homicides with expressive features with no ulterior instrumental motives are more likely to be related to interpersonal conflicts (e.g. jealous rage) and were, therefore, not expected to be associated with antisocial personality features in the offender. Consequently, higher levels of confessing would ensue.

The characteristics of the victim may also be informative in predicting the interrogation behaviour of the offender. A previous study (Santtila et al., 2004) showed that it was possible to predict the likelihood of the offender having a criminal record on the basis of victim characteristics related to antisocial lifestyle. For example, the victim having a criminal record made it more likely that the offender also had a criminal record. Such associations are understandable as a substantial proportion of homicides take place in situations where both the offender and the victim have an antisocial lifestyle and know each other. Also, to the extent that antisocial background of the offender is related to antisocial victim characteristics in the present report, it could be expected that such victim characteristics would be related to an increased likelihood of denial and decreased likelihood of confessions. This is because the offender is likely to have a more extensive antisocial history with associated antisocial personality features, which in their turn modulate the interrogation behaviour of the offender. Apart from the antisocial personality features, these offenders also have experience of interrogations making them therefore more likely to be able to resist any pressures that the situation creates.

In addition to exploring associations on a variable-by-variable basis between crime features and interrogation behaviour, we investigated the associations between interrogation behaviour to homicide types as the latter were defined in Pakkanen et al. (2006). These authors showed, using a Mokken scaling analysis of the same data as the present report, that difficult-to-solve homicides could be divided into four main groupings – expressive, antisocial, instrumental in terms of monetary profit and instrumental in terms of sexually abusing the victim – on the basis of features of the offences. In the expressive offences, violence had been utilised to solve a personal conflict between the offender and the victim.

There were two expressive homicide types. The first, *expressive/rage* -type, consisted of variables suggesting high emotional content. In this type of homicide the offender had used an excessive amount of violence needed to kill the victim. There were multiple wounds on different body areas, most commonly caused by a sharp weapon. The second, *expressive/jealousy*-type consisted of variables that tell of a relationship between the offender and the victim. The offender and the victim had either been married or were currently in a relationship and lived together. There were many victims in these cases, quite often a male and a female victim suggesting a triangle situation where the offender had (or had had) a relationship with the female victim and was motivated by jealousy of her relationship with the male victim.

Three homicide types were classified as antisocial. In the first of these, a *antisocial/expressive*-type, the offender had restrained the victim by binding the victim's legs or feet, and had taken actions to prevent being caught (moved the body, moved the victim while the victim was still alive, burned the murder scene). In this type, the victim was commonly homeless and had a criminal record, suggesting these cases were disputes of the 'underworld'. An *antisocial/execution*-type reflected increased instrumentality: the victim was killed with a handgun, most commonly brought to the murder scene, and removed from the scene after the killing by the offender. The level of instrumentality seemed to be even higher *in the antisocial/forensic awareness* -type of homicide. It consisted of variables suggesting a more organised homicide. The offender had gone to lengths to cover his tracks: the body was transported away from the murder scene and buried in an uninhabited area.

There were also three instrumental homicide types related to monetary profit. These all had money in common: the offender had rummaged through the victim's belongings, killed the victim in association with a robbery and stolen the victim's belongings. The *instrumental/opportunistic*-type suggested a crime where the offender had rummaged through the victims belongings after the killing. The damage caused to the victim's face and head suggest a personal connection aspect in the crime, making this type of killing expressive. The *instrumental/robbery*-type included killings that happened in association with a robbery, most commonly in the victim's own home suggesting that the offender had broken in to the victim's home and killed the victim in order to prevent getting caught. The victim was retired and lived alone. The offender had used a blindfold during the robbery, possibly to prevent the victim from identifying him. Lastly, the *instrumental/forensic awareness*-type suggested a more instrumental approach to the killing: the offender had again taken steps to ensure eluding capture. The victim was bound and suffocated and found immersed in water. The offender had stolen belongings from the victim, both identifiable and unidentifiable. These two offence types are very closely related in terms of their motivational dynamics. However, the analyses we conducted suggested keeping them apart.

The two last scales both included sexual elements. The killings occurred in association with a rape and the victim was found naked. In the *instrumental/opportunistic* sex-type the victim was most commonly a female, found partially stripped, raped and strangled. Damage was done to both the genitals and throat of the victim. In the *instrumental/relationship*-type the victim was found naked and had been strangled with an object, as opposed to strangulation with bare hands as was more commonly the case in the first scale of the theme. Again: using a weapon for the strangulation suggests a more instrumental approach in the killing.

The present report aimed at exploring whether crime features would be differentially related to the likelihood of confessing within the sample. The following predictions were made:

General predictions:

(1) Instrumental homicide types and crime features will be associated with a decreased likelihood of confessing.
(2) Expressive homicide types and crime features will be associated with an increased likelihood of confessing.

Specific predictions:

(3) Minority offenders will be less likely to confess.
(4) Criminal background will be associated with an increased likelihood of denial.

(5) Sexual homicide types and crime features will be associated with a decreased likelihood of confessing.
(6) Victim characteristics related to antisocial lifestyle will be associated with a decreased likelihood of confessing.
(7) The likelihood of confessing decreases with the passage of time since the offence.

METHOD

Cases

The sample consisted of 71 separate Finnish homicide investigations obtained from the electronic crime-reporting database of the Finnish National police. Each offender–victim interaction was coded as a separate case. Thus, in an investigation where two offenders had killed two victims, a total of four cases were coded, yielding a total $N = 93$ for the whole sample. There were two series of two homicides each in the material. This method of coding does produce dependencies between certain cases, but the effects on the conclusions should be negligible. Of the total of 85 offenders, 94 % were male with a mean age of 29.33 years $(SD = 10.33$ years), the youngest being 14 years of age, and the oldest 55 years old. The female offenders were on average 31.00 years old $(SD = 13.42)$, ranging from 13 years to 49 years of age. Most of the victims, 48 out of 74 (65 %), were also male. On average, the male victims were 40.67 years old $(SD = 15.82)$, the youngest victim being 8 years old, and the oldest being 78 years old. The female victims (35 %) had a mean age of 37.60 years $(SD = 17.97)$, the age ranging from 1 year of age to 79 years.

All cases of homicides during the years 1991–2001 were included in the preliminary search. The first search yielded a total of 1,017 solved cases; 234 cases of murder and 783 cases of manslaughter. The sample selection process was thereafter conducted in two steps. In the first step, all the cases were skimmed through to exclude 'open and shut' cases, for example where the offender was caught at the crime scene with witnesses and confessed upfront as the police arrived. In many of these cases the offender himself was the one who had reported the killing. This initial exclusion left us with 300 cases. The pre-trial investigation protocols for these cases were ordered from the respective police districts. In the second step, the records for each case were read through more thoroughly to determine whether the case had been hard to solve or not resulting in the sample described above. The procedure is reported in detail in Pakkanen et al. (2006). No interrater reliability checks were possible due to data security as well as practical constraints at this phase.

Variables

The variable list was based on Salfati's (Salfati, 1998) research and on previous research on Finnish homicide (Santtila et al. 2001; Santtila et al., 2003). The variables were coded from the pre-trial investigation protocols. Details of the procedure can again be found in Pakkanen et al. (2006). The variables included in the present study were:

Offender behaviour during the interrogation. This main dependent variable of the present study had three categories: (1) The offender confessed immediately after the onset of the interrogation; (2) The offender denied his or her responsibility first, but confessed later during the interrogation(s); (3) The offender maintained denial of responsibility throughout the interrogation(s).

Offender characteristics. The offender characteristics that were used in the present study were selected on the basis of research referenced in the introduction. These were: (1) The age of the offender; (2) Criminal record variables; (3) Offender being foreigner/refugee/immigrant. Two additional variables that were thought to reflect antisociality were also included: (1) Serial murderer; (2) Income. Obviously, the latter variable has a number of other determinants but it was taken as a proxy of the level of antisociality of the offenders.

Circumstantial features and victim characteristics. A number of circumstantial features of the offence that were thought based on the findings of Santtila et al. (2001; 2003) to reflect the level of planning and resolve of the offender were included: (1) Body was found in countryside/uninhabited area; (2) Point of fatal encounter between the offender and the victim was not known; (3) Body was found at the murder scene; (4) The murder took place during the night. Features (1) and (2) were thought to suggest an offender who had planned the offence more carefully and who would most probably have a highly antisocial background whereas variables (3) and (4) were thought to reflect a less-planned homicide type. In addition, the variables (5) Number of days that passed from the killing to the beginning of interrogation, and (6) Time it took to catch the offender, were thought to be associated positively with a more forensically aware and antisocial offender and were, therefore, also used in the analyses.

The three victim variables that were included were: (1) The age of the victim; (2) Victim's criminal record; (3) Victim being foreigner/refugee/immigrant. It was thought that variables (2) and (3) would be related to offender interrogation behaviour in the same manner as the corresponding characteristics of the offenders themselves.

Homicide types. The homicide types that were derived in Pakkanen et al. (2006) were also used in the present study. The types have been described in the introduction. In addition to using the types, the effect of the individual variables defining the different types on the interrogation behaviour of the offender was also investigated. The complete list can be found in Pakkanen et al. (2006). Associations between the crime scene behaviour of the offenders and their behaviour during subsequent interrogations were assessed in two complementary ways. Firstly, the mean scores of the three interrogation behaviour groups on the 10 scales reflecting different homicide types were compared. The scale scores indicate the number of behaviours the offenders had presented in that particular scale with higher scores indicating a stronger presence of the features of a particular homicide type. Secondly, associations between interrogation behaviour and individual crime scene behaviour were assessed. The behaviours have been grouped under the scales of which they form a part.

The mean case-wise interrater reliability estimated using Cohen's κ values (Brennan & Hays, 1992; Cohen, 1960) from a random sample of five cases coded by two independent coders was 0.72 ($SD = 0.13$; *Minimum* 0.59, *Maximum* 0.89) indicating good interrater reliability. All the individual κs were statistically significant.

Statistical Analysis

χ^2–tests were used to explore the relationships between the dichotomous variables reflecting offender and victim characteristics, circumstantial features, individual crime features and the offender interrogation behaviour variable. The associations between the interrogation behaviour variable and continuous offender and victim characteristics, circumstantial features as well as the scale scores reflecting different homicide types were analysed using One-Way ANOVA. These analyses were repeated using the non-parametric Kruskal-Wallis Test due to the uneven distribution of the different interrogation behaviour categories. Duncan's multiple range post-hoc tests were used to explore the differences between the groups in more detail. Interrelationships between dichotomous variables were computed using the φ-correlation coefficient (r_ϕ), between a dichotomous and a continuous variable using the point-biserial correlation coefficient (r_{pbs}), and between two dichotomous variables using the Pearson product-moment correlation coefficient (r).

RESULTS

Description of the Nature of the Sample

In the following frequencies, the sample of 93 cases (i.e. all offender-victim interactions) are included. In the typical homicide in the present sample, multiple acts of violence had taken place ($n = 79$, 84.9%). A weapon was used in most cases ($n = 75$, 80.6%), it was found by the offender at the murder scene ($n = 51$, 54.8%), and taken from the scene after the killing had taken place ($n = 56$, 60.2%). The homicide typically took place on a weekday ($n = 52$, 55.9%) during the day ($n = 51$, 54.8%). In approximately half of the cases the offender(s) had rummaged through the victim's belongings ($n = 50$, and 53.8%), and stolen identifiable ($n = 46$, 49.5%) and unidentifiable objects ($n = 45$, 48.4%). In more than half of the cases the body was found outside ($n = 49$, 52.7%), but sometimes indoors in an apartment ($n = 37$, 39.8%). The point of fatal encounter, where the offender and the victim had met prior to the killing taking place, was most commonly indoors ($n = 69$, 74.2%) at someone's home ($n = 41$, 44.1%). The killing took place at the point of fatal encounter in approximately half of the cases ($n = 49$, 52.7%).

The sample comprised of a total of 85 individual offenders. The typical offender in the present sample was male, lived in the same city where the offence took place, and was under the influence of alcohol during the time of the offence. In most of the cases he moved on foot. The majority of the offenders were employees, while unemployed offenders made up a bit more than a third of the sample. Just over half of the offenders knew their victims prior to the killing. The most common charges in the offenders' criminal records were charges of violent offences and theft.

Characteristics of the Offenders and their Behaviour during Interrogation

Overall, 47.1% (40 out of 85 offenders) of the offenders confessed straight away, 48.2% (41 out of 85 offenders) denied the offence first but confessed later during the interrogations, and 4.7% (4 out of 85 offenders) denied the offence throughout the interrogations. The low proportion of offenders denying the offence throughout the interrogations may be related to the fact that these were solved homicides where the guilt of the offender had been proven making it most often an unproductive strategy to keep denying the offence.

Offender characteristics that were related to interrogation behaviour are shown in Table 13.1. Serial murderers, offenders of foreign origin and those who had a background of prior criminal record for sexual or drug-related offences were overrepresented among deniers. Some of these offender characteristics were interrelated. Serial murderers were likely to have a background of sexual offences ($r_\phi = 0.39, p < 0.001$) whereas offenders of foreign origin were likely to have a background of drug-related offences ($r_\phi = 0.45, p < 0.001$). The associations of these variables with denying responsibility were, consequently, not independent of each other.

The age of the offenders was also significantly related to their behaviour during the interrogation (Table 13.2). Those who consistently denied any wrong-doing during the whole interrogation were younger than those who first denied but later confessed. Young offenders were also likely to have a background of drug-related offences (correlation between age and drug-related criminal record: $r_{pbs} = -0.22, p < 0.040$) again suggesting that the associations these two variables had with denying guilt were interrelated. Again, of course, the low number of denying offenders presents a problem for the analyses.

Table 13.1 Associations between the characteristics of the offenders and their behaviour during interrogation

		Behaviour during interrogation			
		Confessed	Denied>Confessed	Denied	χ^2
Serial	No	40	40	2	26.98 ***
	Yes	0	1	2	
Offender foreigner/ refugee/ immigrant	No	38	40	2	15.00 ***
	Yes	2	1	2	
CR for sexual offences	No	38	39	0	39.49 ***
	Yes	0	1	1	
CR for drug-related offences	No	36	38	2	11.30 **
	Yes	2	2	2	

Note. CR = criminal record

Table 13.2 Associations between the age and income of the offenders and their behaviour during interrogation

	Confessed [a]		Denied>Confessed [b]		Denied [c]		F	Kruskal-Wallis χ^2
	M	SD	M	SD	M	SD		
Offender age at killing	26.60 [a,b]	9.92	31.32 [a]	9.78	22.25 [b]	2.06	3.33*	6.84*
Income per month (euros)	282.64 [a,b]	309.44	413.03 [a]	343.38	0.00 [b]	0.00	2.67+	5.61+

[a] $n = 39-40$, [b] $n = 38-41$, [c] $n = 3-4$. Means with different superscripts differ significantly (Duncan's multiple range test, $p < 0.05$).

There were also differences in terms of the income of the offenders behaving differently during interrogation (Table 13.2). Offenders who denied the offence were all without income whereas those who first denied and then confessed earned an average of 413 €/month. Those who confessed straight away fell in between the other two groups. Income was positively related to age ($r = 0.37$, $p < 0.001$) again explaining the association at least partly.

Circumstantial Features of the Offences, Victim Characteristics and the Behaviour of the Offenders during Interrogation

A number of circumstantial offence features were related to offender interrogation behaviour (see Table 13.3). Offenders who had disposed of the body of the victim in uninhabited areas or, more generally, in the countryside, were more likely to deny their responsibility throughout the interrogations than other offenders. The same was true of cases where the point of fatal encounter was not known. These two offence features were associated with each other ($r_\phi = 0.48$, $p < 0.001$). Instead, when the victim was found where the murder took place total denial of responsibility was less probable. Total denial of responsibility was also less probable when the offence had taken place during the night. These two features were not significantly related so their associations with interrogation behaviour can be seen as independent. Also, it should be noted that the body was unlikely to be found at the scene of the murder both when the area was uninhabited or countryside ($r_\phi = -0.59$, $p < 0.001$) and when the point of fatal encounter was unknown ($r_\phi = -0.49$, $p < 0.001$).

Table 13.3 Associations between circumstantial crime features and the behaviour of the offenders during interrogation

		Behaviour during interrogation			
		Confessed	Denied>Confessed	Denied	χ^2
Body found: countryside/ uninhabited	No	35	32	0	16.71***
	Yes	5	9	4	
Body found: murder scene	No	6	6	4	18.10***
	Yes	34	35	0	
Night: 24:00 till 5:59 a.m.	No	15	27	3	7.35*
	Yes	25	14	1	
Point of fatal encounter not known	No	39	38	0	40.95***
	Yes	1	3	4	

Further, the amount of time that had passed from the killing until the beginning of the interrogations was related to how the offenders reacted during them. Interrogations that resulted in a confession took place in approximately a month ($M = 29.93$ days, $SD = 98.33$) since the killing whereas interrogations in which the offender continued to deny any responsibility took place after more than four months ($M = 128.67$ days, $SD = 44.56$) had passed. Offenders who changed from denial to confession were interrogated for the first time when more than two months ($M = 74.41$, $SD = 354.11$) had passed since the killing. The differences were statistically significant (Kruskal-Wallis $\chi^2 = 8.17$, $p < .05$).

The time it took to catch the offender after the offence was coded using the following categories: < 2h (2.4%), 2–12h (2.4%), 12–24h (5.9%), 24h–5d (41.2%), 6–10d (11.8%), 11–30d (21.2%), > 30d (15.3%). Most of the offenders in this sample were thus caught after 24 hours had passed since the offence (89.5%). This delay was associated with the interrogation behavior of the offenders as assessed by a Kruskal-Wallis Test ($\chi^{2[2]} = 11.96$, p < 0.003). Those caught after a longer time had passed after the offence were more likely to maintain their denial throughout the interrogations.

Three victim characteristics were associated with continued denial on the part of the offender. The victim having a criminal record or being of foreign origin were predictive of the offender denying responsibility (see Table 13.4). These features were statistically associated

Table 13.4   Associations between victim characteristics and the behaviour of the offenders during interrogation

		Behaviour during interrogation			
		Confessed	Denied>Confessed	Denied	χ^2
Victim had a	No	32	36	1	9.48**
criminal record	Yes	8	5	3	
Victim was foreigner/	No	40	41	2	41.48***
refugee/immigrant	Yes	0	0	2	

($r_\phi = -0.29$, $p < 0.004$) indicating that homicide victims of foreign origin were likely to have a criminal record. Also, the victims of offenders who denied their responsibility were younger ($M = 25.33$ years, $SD = 4.62$) than victims of offenders who confessed immediately ($M = 41.00$ years, $SD = 19.97$) or first denied and then confessed ($M = 42.56$ years, $SD = 15.69$). The differences were statistically significant (Kruskal-Wallis $\chi^2 = 4.14$, $p < 0.05$).

The Behaviour of the Offenders at Crime Scene and their Behaviour during Interrogation

A number of associations were found between scores on the homicide-type scales and the interrogation behaviour of the offenders (see Table 13.5). Offenders who immediately confessed to their offences had committed homicides with more *expressive/rage* features than offenders who consistently denied their responsibility. Those who changed from denial to confession fell in between these two groups. The individual crime scene behaviours that significantly contributed to this result can be seen in Table 13.6 under the heading 'Expressive/rage'. The individual variables are related to the use of a sharp weapon in an excessive manner so as to cause several wounds especially to the torso of the victim.

Instead, offenders who denied their involvement were more likely to commit offences that contained features suggesting forensic awareness (*antisocial/forensic awareness*) and instrumental motivation (*instrumental/forensic awareness, instrumental/opportunistic*). Many of the individual variables included in these scales had significant bivariate associations with interrogation behaviour. Again, these variables are listed in Table 13.6 with the exception of one of the variables forming the *antisocial/forensic awareness* scale, namely the body

Table 13.5 Associations between the offence types and the behaviour of the offenders during interrogation

	Confessed[a]		Denied>Confessed[b]		Denied[c]		F	Kruskal-Wallis χ^2
	M	SD	M	SD	M	SD		
Expressive/rage	3.68[a]	2.29	2.44[a,b]	1.64	1.00[b]	0.00	6.15**	10.64**
Expressive/ jealousy	0.68	1.19	0.78	1.11	0.00	0.00	0.88	2.98
Antisocial/ expressive	4.10	3.83	3.07	2.59	4.25	2.06	1.11	1.63
Antisocial/ execution	1.33	1.10	1.24	1.16	0.50	1.00	0.98	2.35
Antisocial/ forensic awareness	0.68[a]	1.14	0.78[a]	0.99	2.50[b]	0.58	5.50**	9.64**
Instrumental/ opportunistic	2.38	1.94	2.29	1.94	1.00	0.00	0.95	1.95
Instrumental/ robbery	4.18[a]	2.63	3.59[a]	2.18	0.00[b]	0.00	5.74**	10.64**
Instrumental/ forensic awareness	1.90[a]	1.97	1.56[a]	1.27	6.00[b]	3.46	11.71***	6.97*
Instrumental/ opportunistic sex	1.20[a]	1.74	1.61[a]	1.58	3.75[b]	4.35	3.63*	2.87
Instrumental/ relationship	0.15	0.43	0.17	0.50	0.25	0.50	0.09	0.46

[a] $n = 39-40$, [b] $n = 38-41$, [c] $n = 3-4$ Means with different superscripts differ significantly (Duncan's multiple range test, $p < 0.05$).

being found in an uninhabited area or countryside, which is presented in Table 13.3 as it is a circumstantial feature and not a crime scene behaviour as such. As expected, all of them were also at the individual level associated with an increased likelihood of the offender denying all responsibility for the offence.

Robbery related homicides were an exception among the instrumental homicide types. These cases were associated with decreased likelihood of denial and increased likelihood of confession. One of the features belonging to this scale, namely the body being found at the murder scene, was associated with an increased likelihood of confession (see Table 13.3 for this association).

Kicking the victim several times was associated with an increased likelihood of an immediate confession (see Table 13.6) even if the scale to which it belongs was not significantly associated with interrogation behaviour.

Table 13.6 Associations between the behaviour of the offenders at the crime scene and their behaviour during interrogation

		Behaviour during interrogation			
		Confessed	Denied>Confessed	Denied	χ^2
		Expressive/rage			
Sharp weapon used	No	33	41	4	8.58*
excessively	Yes	7	0	0	
Sharp weapon	No	18	26	4	6.03*
excluding kitchen	Yes	22	15	0	
knives and axes used					
in the killing					
Victim sustained	No	20	29	4	6.24*
several wounds to the	Yes	20	12	0	
same body area					
Damage to torso	No	9	19	4	11.85**
	Yes	31	22	0	
		Antisocial/expressive			
Offender had kicked	No	24	36	4	9.79**
the victim several	Yes	16	5	0	
times		Instrumental/forensic awareness			
Body found: immersed	No	35	35	0	19.65***
in water	Yes	5	6	4	
Binding object brought	No	39	40	2	19.20***
by offender	Yes	1	1	2	
Binding object found	No	36	40	2	11.22**
at scene by police	Yes	4	1	2	
Hands bound	No	35	40	2	10.51**
	Yes	5	1	2	
Legs bound	No	39	41	2	26.99***
	Yes	1	0	2	
Suffocation by other	No	32	38	2	6.42*
methods than	Yes	8	3	2	
strangulation		Antisocial/forensic awareness			
Forensic awareness	No	27	24	0	6.97*
	Yes	13	17	4	
		Instrumental/opportunistic sex			
Strangulation with	No	36	28	2	7.35*
hands	Yes	4	13	2	
Killing occurred in	No	39	40	2	19.20***
association with a rape	Yes	1	1	2	
Victim found partially	No	37	33	2	6.16*
unclothed	Yes	3	8	2	

Vaginal penetration	No	37	38	2	8.11*
achieved/attempted	Yes	3	3	2	
Offender had	No	39	40	2	19.20***
ejaculated	Yes	1	1	2	
during the act					
Damage to genitals	No	39	38	2	12.51**
	Yes	1	3	2	

DISCUSSION

Overall, the proportion of deniers was very low (4.7%; 4 out of 85 offenders) and at the same level as in a previous study looking at an unselected sample of Finnish homicides (Santtila et al., 2003). This is somewhat surprising considering that the present sample included homicide cases that had been difficult to solve. Therefore, it was expected that the sample overall consisted of better-planned offences suggesting more antisocial offenders. However, antisocial offenders may, due to their experience be better able to assess the evidence against them and, therefore, to decide when it is a good idea to confess in an attempt to obtain a more lenient sentence (Baldwin & McConville, 1980).

Partly confirming the first general prediction, a number of instrumental or antisocial homicide types and crime features were associated with a decreased likelihood of confessing to homicide in the present sample. The *antisocial/forensically aware* and the *instrumental/forensic awareness* and the *instrumental/opportunistic* homicide types had statistically signficant associations with interrogation behaviour in the predicted direction. These results are in accordance with the idea that instrumentally committed homicides are generally associated with less guilt probably due to the egosyntonic nature of the offence behaviour even though guilt was not directly assessed in the present study. However, the robbery homicide did not exhibit the predicted pattern. It may be that in robbery cases there is more evidence against the suspects, for instance, in the form of surveillance tapes, making it futile for them to deny the offence. Also, the *antisocial/expressive-* and *antisocial/execution*-types were not associated with denial. As these homicide types suggest an antisocial background, it may be that the decision to confess may in some of these cases be a more rational decision based on previous experience with evaluating evidence obtained by the police.

The instrumental homicide types were related to interrogation behaviour in the predicted manner. In addition, a number of individual crime features related to careful planning and a probable antisocial background evidenced similar associations. A hidden body and an unknown point of fatal encounter were both indicative of a denying offender. Theses features are arguably suggestive of planning and care taken in the execution of the offence. Hiding the body may be especially important for the offender when there is a relationship between the offender and the victim that might lead the police to investigate the former. Even though a relationship between the offender and the victim is often associated with the homicide being expressive, the association of hiding the body with an increased likelihood of denying goes to show that a simple instrumental/expressive dichotomy is not satisfactory when analysing homicide from a profiling perspective.

As expected, criminal background of the offender was associated with an increased likelihood of denial. As minority offenders as well as younger offenders were more likely to exhibit some types of criminal background, it was not surprising that these features were also connected with an increased likelihood of denial, contradicting the findings of Pearse et al. (1998) regarding the age of the offender. Their explanation for the negative association between age and likelihood of denying was psychological immaturity. This may well be true with a general sample of different types of offences but does not seem to hold for homicides. In addition, those without income were more likely to deny their responsibility. A possible explanation for this association is that at least some (registered) income can be seen as a proxy variable for a minimum level of social integration and that such integration is less likely to be associated with severe antisociality.

One of the sexual offence types, the *instrumental/opportunistic* sex-homicide was associated with increased denial as predicted. However, the *instrumental/relationship*-homicide did not evidence a similar association. It may be that the base rate of the latter homicide type was too low for an association to become statistically significant. This result is in accordance with the results of Sigurdsson and Gudjonsson (1994) but contradicts those of Mitchell (1983). The unclear pattern of results may partly be due to the conflicting pressures in relation to inhibitions about confessing due to shame associated with an offence of a sexual nature and the guilt of having committed such a crime. The skills of the interviewer may be particularly pertinent in these cases. The interviewers should maintain a nonjudgemental stance towards the offender in order not to increase any feelings of shame. Also, accentuating the depravity of a particular offence is probably going to be counterproductive. The results of the present study suggest that shame may be more important in association with homicides. However, it may also be that homicides of a sexual nature may be indicative of quite advanced antisocial development and this may explain the finding.

The *expressive/rage*-homicides were, as predicted, associated with an increased likelihood of confessing to the offence without delay once the offender had been caught. As these offences are likely to be out of character for the offender, feelings of guilt may be overwhelming and lead to the confession in accordance with the model presented by Gudjonsson (2003). Also, as predicted, individual features reflecting an expressive-homicide type were associated with an increased likelihood of confessing. Finding the body at the murder scene as well as the murder taking place during the night were such features. Not attempting to move and hide the body suggest possible feelings of panic following the offence by the offender, implying little or no planning and less experience with criminal processes and thereby the importance of hiding evidence after an offence. Tentatively, we felt that a night-time killing is more likely to be unplanned and committed in association with an argument under the influence of alcohol whereas day-time killings may be more indicative of an antisocial lifestyle. The results supported this understanding of the dynamics of homicide at least for the present sample.

The passage of time was related to the likelihood of confessing as predicted: the more time had passed, the less likely it was that the offender would confess to the homicide. The possibility of differences in the strength of evidence between the offences where the offenders were caught and interrogated at different times cannot be excluded. However, we suggest here as a tentative explanation the different time courses of the emotions of shame and guilt from the model of Gudjonsson (2003) with guilt abating over time with no necessary change in the experience of shame.

The results have practical implications for conducting homicide investigations: reasonable guesses could be made based on the crime scene actions of an offender regarding the effectiveness of appeals in the media for the offender to surrender himself, and regarding the importance of interview planning due to the increased chance of the offender denying their involvement in the offence. However, these suggestions should be interpreted with caution, as the sample size was quite small and as several other factors (most importantly the strength of evidence against the suspect) that could not be controlled in the present study, which might affect the offender's post-offence behaviour.

REFERENCES

Baldwin, J. & McConville, M. (1980) *Confessions in Crown Court trials. Royal Commission on Criminal Procedure Research Study No. 5.* London: HMSO.

Brennan, P.F. & Hays, B.J. (1992) The Kappa statistics for establishing interrater reliability in the secondary analysis of qualitative clinical data. *Research in Nursing and Health*, **15**, 153–8.

Cohen, J. (1960) A coefficient of agreement for nominal scales. *Educational and Psychological Measurement*, **20**, 37–46.

Gudjonsson, G.H. (2003) *The psychology of interrogations and confessions: A handbook.* Chichester: John Wiley & Sons, Ltd.

Gudjonsson, G.H. & Bownes, I. (1992) The reasons why suspects confess during custodial interrogation: Data for Northern Ireland. *Medicine, Science, and the Law*, **32**, 204–12.

Gudjonsson, G.H. & Petursson, H. (1982) Some criminological and psychiatric aspects of homicide in Iceland. *Medicine, Science, and the Law*, **22**, 91–8.

Gudjonsson, G.H. & Petursson, H. (1991) Custodial interrogation: Why do suspects confess and how does it relate to their crime, attitude and personality? *Personality and Individual Differences*, **12**, 295–306.

Gudjonsson, G.H. & Sigurdsson, J.F. (1999) The Gudjonsson Confession Questionnaire-Revised (GCQ-R): Factor structure and its relationship with personality. *Personality and Individual Differences*, **27**, 953–68.

Gudjonsson, G.H. & Sigurdsson, J.F. (2000) Differences and similarities between violent offenders and sex offenders. *Child Abuse and Neglect*, **24**, 363–72.

Mitchell, B. (1983) Confessions and police interrogation of suspects. *Criminal Law Review, September*, 596–604.

Moston, S., Stephenson, G.M. & Williamson, T.M. (1992) The effects of case characteristics on suspect behaviour during questioning. *British Journal of Criminology*, **32**, 23–40.

Neubauer, D.W. (1974) Confessions in Prairie City: Some causes and effects. *Journal of Criminal Law and Criminology*, **65**, 103–12.

Pakkanen, T., Santtila, P., Mokros, A. & Sandnabba, N.K. (2006) *Profiling hard-to-solve homicides: Identifying dimensions of offending and associating them with statistical variables and offender characteristics.* Manuscript submitted for publication.

Pearse, J., Gudjonsson, G.H., Clare, I.C.H. & Rutter, S. (1998) Police interviewing and psychological vulnerabilities: Predicting the likelihood of a confession. *Journal of Community and Applied Social Psychology*, **8**, 1–21.

Phillips, C. & Brown, D. (1998) *Entry into the criminal justice system: A survey of police arrests and their outcomes.* London: Home Office.

Salfati C.G. (1998) *Homicide: A behavioral analysis of crime scene actions and associated offender characteristics.* Unpublished doctoral thesis. University of Liverpool, UK.

Santtila, P., Canter, D., Elfgren, T. & Häkkinen, H. (2001) The structure of crime scene actions in Finnish homicides. *Homicide Studies*, 363–87.

Santtila, P., Häkkinen, H., Canter, D. & Elfgren, E. (2003) Classifying homicide offenders and predicting their characteristics from crime scene behavior. *Scandinavian Journal of Psychology*, **44**, 107–18.

Santtila, P., Runtti, M. & Mokros, A. (2004) Predicting the presence of a criminal record from indicators of victim antisocial lifestyle in homicides. *Journal of Interpersonal Violence*, **19**, 541–57.

Sigurdsson, J.F. & Gudjonsson, G.H. (1994) Alcohol and drug intoxication during police interrogation and the reasons why suspects confess to the police. *Addiction*, **89**, 985–97.

Softley, P. (1980) *Police interrogation: An observational study in four police stations. Home Office Research Study No. 61*. London: HMSO.

CHAPTER 14

Memory-enhancing Techniques for Interviewing Crime Suspects

RONALD P. FISHER AND VALERIE PEREZ

INTERVIEWING COOPERATIVE SUSPECTS TO ELICIT CRIME-RELEVANT DETAILS

Solving crimes often follows a three-step process. Shortly after the crime, police interview victims and witnesses in an attempt to elicit extensive, relevant information about the crime. When physical evidence is available, e.g., bullet casings or fingerprints, police examine these information source to learn more about the crime. Finally, if all goes well, and a suspect emerges, police may interview the suspect to see if he or she admits or denies guilt.

Psychological research has made extensive progress in the area of interviewing victims and witnesses to elicit case-relevant information (e.g., Eisen, Quas & Goodman, 2002; Fisher & Geiselman, 1992). We also have learned much about interviewing suspects to elicit confessions – or to exonerate innocent suspects (see Kassin & Gudjonsson, 2004). We know precious little, however, about interviewing suspects for the purpose of eliciting crime-relevant information. This is most unfortunate, because suspects are likely to know more about the crime than anyone else. We examine here this potentially rich source of information.

Offenders' Memories of Violent Crimes. Edited by Sven Å. Christianson.
© 2007 John Wiley & Sons, Ltd.

Currently, there is almost no laboratory research on interviewing suspects, largely because of the ethical difficulties of setting up controlled experiments in which volunteer participants are interviewed after being accused of committing a crime. Therefore, we shall rely heavily on the research in related areas of criminal investigation (mainly from interviewing victims and witnesses) and then extrapolate from these studies to the unknown world of interviewing suspects. Much of this chapter, therefore, will be speculative.

We assume that, under some conditions, suspects are willing to volunteer information. This may occur for a variety of reasons. Suspects who are innocent should be motivated to convey to the police as much truthful information as possible about the crime so as to redirect the investigation away from themselves and toward the real perpetrator. Innocent suspects who were someplace other than the crime scene when the crime occurred should be motivated to provide details of their whereabouts in order to exonerate themselves. Even suspects who are guilty of the crime may want to assist in the investigation. This may occur because they feel guilty or ashamed of their role in the crime and wish to do something positive to compensate for their earlier transgression. They may feel overwhelmed by the investigative process and want to free themselves of the oppressive burden of being the suspect of an investigation. Finally, in some instances, suspects are offered a plea agreement by the prosecution, wherein the suspect provides valuable information about the crime in exchange for a lighter sentence. For example, a small-time drug dealer may be offered a reduced sentence in exchange for detailed information about the activities of a major drug lord. In such instances, the suspect's leverage to barter information for a reduced sentence may depend on the quality of the information that he or she provides.

This chapter is directed toward interviewing such cooperative, guilty suspects for the purpose of eliciting complete and accurate descriptions of the known crime or series of crimes. In a few instances, where interviewing techniques have multiple uses (to elicit more information from cooperative suspects and also to detect deception), we will take a minor detour toward the issue of detecting deception. Generally, though, we leave it to our more knowledgeable co-authors of this volume to develop more sophisticated analyses of detecting deception and eliciting confessions.

When suspects are motivated to be truthful and provide accurate, detailed descriptions, interviewers should be able to apply many of the same procedures as when they interview other voluntary respondents, namely, witnesses and victims. We begin our analysis then by examining a known effective procedure for interviewing cooperative respondents, the Cognitive Interview (CI: Fisher & Geiselman, 1992). We then explore how the CI should be altered to meet the specific needs of interviewing suspects.

COGNITIVE INTERVIEW

We take as our starting point the CI, as it has been shown reliably in laboratory and field studies to enhance witness recollection in comparison to techniques used by many police officers in the UK (e.g., George & Clifford, 1992) and the USA (e.g., Fisher, Geiselman & Amador, 1989), and also in comparison to other recommended interview protocols (e.g., Milne & Bull, 2003). Naturally, there is some disagreement about the utility of the CI. Some researchers have failed to find that the CI outperforms the control interview (e.g., Memon, Holley, Milne, Koehnken & Bull, 1994). Others have questioned whether the CI lowers the witness's output threshhold and induces the witness to guess (Memon, Wark, Holley, Bull & Koehnken, 1997). Finally, some police think that it may take too long to conduct the entire CI, and so it may be impractical in some situations (Kebbell, Milne & Wagstaff, 1999). On balance, though, the CI has proven to be highly successful. In Kohnken, Milne, Memon and Bull's (1999) metaanalysis, the CI outperformed the comparison interview in 54 of 55 cases. This is unlikely to be the product of increased guessing, as the overall accuracy rate was slightly *higher* with the CI (85 % accuracy) than with the comparison interview (82 % accuracy). Although the CI may take somewhat longer than other interview protocols, we expect this not to be problematic, and especially when interviewing suspects, because: (a) in high-profile cases, there is ample time to conduct the interview, especially late in the investigation when the interview is conducted with the suspect (not the witness); (b) given the total amount of time that police spend on the entire investigation, the addition of a few minutes to conduct the interview represents only a small fraction of the total time invested; and (c) when there is limited time, a streamlined version of the CI can be conducted that saves time, but at minimal cost to the amount of information elicited (Davis, McMahon & Greenwood, 2005). For a more thorough discussion of these issues, see Fisher, Falkner, Trevisan and McCauley (2000) and Fisher, Brennan and McCauley (2002). In overview, given the unbalanced support the CI has received within the research community, and the number of law enforcement and investigative agencies worldwide that provide training in the CI (see Fisher & Schreiber, 2007), it appears that this is a reasonable starting point to develop a method for interviewing suspects.

The following is a thumbnail sketch of the CI; for a more complete description, see Fisher and Geiselman (1992). We describe the CI here in the language of interviewing suspects, although the CI was developed initially to interview victims and witnesses. Motivated suspects, however, should face many of the same social, cognitive and communication problems as do witnesses and victims. As such, many of the concepts underlying effective interview techniques with witnesses and victims should hold equally well with suspects. After describing the core elements of the CI, we will elaborate on some elements that are unique to interviewing motivated suspects.

Social Dynamics

Suspects who have committed a crime are asked to convey information that may result in a loss of liberties. Even suspects who receive plea bargains, where describing their involvement in the crime may not necessarily lead to a loss of liberties, are still being asked to describe an unpleasant experience. In either event, recalling these experiences must create some anxiety. Two critical features mark this social interaction. Firstly, suspects must be psychologically comfortable with the interviewer as a person to go through the mental effort and emotional distress of describing self-inculpating experiences. Secondly, there are social and knowledge-based inequalities between the suspect and the interviewer: The interviewer (e.g., police officer) generally has higher social or expert status, which normally dictates that the interviewer should control the interview.[1] The suspect, however, has more first-hand knowledge of the crime event, which normally dictates that the suspect should control the interview. Resolving this apparent conflict is critical for a successful interview.

Developing Rapport

Suspects are often asked to provide detailed descriptions of intimate, personal experiences that have potentially serious consequences

---

[1] Although the police will generally have greater social status than the suspect, there may be some instances in which the suspect has greater social status. For instance, in economic crimes, a well-paid banker suspect may have higher social status than the police investigator. Nevertheless, we expect that the police officer's greater expert status *within the context of the investigation* would dictate that the police officer is expected to dominate the interview's social dynamics. Certainly, though, there should be more uncertainty about relative status in this context than in most other non-economic crimes. We assume that the balance of status will also depend on the unique personalities of the interviewer and suspect.

(e.g., conviction, imprisonment). The decision to cooperate may be especially difficult for suspects, because they are requested to give this self-effacing information to police officers, who are complete strangers. Compounding the problem, the police officer's official appearance (badge, uniform, gun) may create a psychological barrier between the officer and the suspect, perhaps increasing the suspect's reluctance to reveal personal, potentially incriminating information. To overcome this natural barrier, police investigators should invest time at the outset of the interview to develop meaningful, personal rapport with the suspect (Collins, Lincoln & Frank, 2002), a feature often absent in police interviews (Fisher, Geiselman & Raymond, 1987).

Whether meaningful, personal rapport is established is often determined in the initial moments of the interview, when first impressions are formed (St-Yves, 2006). For both police investigators and suspects these first impressions are likely to be influenced by pre-existing biases. Suspects – especially guilty ones – may assume that the investigator's intent is simply to elicit incriminating information; consequently, suspects may regard the investigator as a threat. Police investigators, meanwhile, may take for granted a suspect's guilt (St-Yves, 2006). This can occur for a variety of reasons. If a suspect has a criminal record, for example, guilt might be inferred based on one's belief that people are consistent. Once police investigators presume guilt, they are likely to adopt an accusatory or dominant interviewing style, an approach that may increase suspects' reluctance to provide information (Holmberg & Christianson, 2002).

There are several steps that investigators can take to overcome these preconceptions, including keeping an open mind and building rapport (St-Yves, 2006). First, it is crucial that the investigator remains objective, presuming neither guilt nor innocence. This neutral, open-minded approach should contribute to the overall success of the investigation by preventing tunnel vision, the tendency to fixate on a particular suspect or crime schema (St-Yves, 2006). An open-minded approach should also facilitate rapport development. Research suggests that rapport-building behaviours, such as warmly welcoming the suspect and clearly communicating the interview's purpose, are components of a humane interviewing style, which may promote an increased willingness to cooperate (Holmberg & Christianson, 2002). For rapport to contribute to the overall success of the interview, however, it must be maintained. Investigators can achieve this by paying attention (actively listening to the suspect's responses), maintaining a professional demeanor and preserving the suspect's dignity (St-Yves, 2006).

Little research has examined the influence of rapport on the accuracy and completeness of suspects' responses in forensic interviews.

We can, however, extrapolate from some eyewitness research, which suggests that rapport increases the amount of information elicited. Equally important, rapport increases the amount of information without reducing accuracy (Collins et al., 2002). In this study, Collins et al. assigned participants to either neutral or abrupt interviews, or five minutes of rapport building in which interviewers spoke with a gentle tone, addressed subjects by name and assumed a relaxed posture. Participants in the rapport-building condition provided more information during free recall, and also subsequently produced significantly fewer incorrect details during cued recall, than did those in the neutral and abrupt conditions. A similar finding occurred in Henson, Cannell and Lawson (1976), who assigned participants to either neutral or rapport-building interviews. In the rapport-building interview, interviewers expressed respect, interest, understanding, a non-critical attitude and positive feedback. Once again, the rapport-building interviews elicited more information than did neutral interviews.

Recent retrospective studies by Holmberg and Christianson (2002) suggest that suspects, like witnesses, may also provide valuable information when rapport is established. These authors asked convicted offenders to describe the nature of their pre-trial interaction with police investigators. Two interviewing styles were identified based on the offenders' responses: dominant and humane. Offenders interviewed in a humane manner, in which rapport was established and suspects were treated with respect, were more likely than those interviewed in a dominant manner to admit their involvement in the offence. Because this was an observational study, and not an experimental study, it is difficult to determine whether suspects' increased willingness to cooperate was in fact caused by the investigators' use of rapport-building strategies or whether the two measures were merely associated with one another. Certainly, however, these findings are compatible with the argument that rapport development may encourage suspects to be more forthcoming during forensic interviews.

Active Suspect Participation

Guilty suspects have extensive first-hand information about the target event. Therefore the suspect, and not the interviewer, should be doing most of the mental activity during the interview. In practice, however, police interviewers often dominate the social interaction with suspects by asking many accusatory questions that elicit only brief denials and render suspects mentally inactive (Moston & Engelberg, 1993). This may be more characteristic of suspect interviews conducted within the US, and less so in the UK (Vrij, Mann, Kristen & Fisher, in press). Interviewers can induce suspects to take more active roles and to volunteer lengthier statements by adopting an information-gathering style of interview, and specifically by: (a) explicitly requesting suspects to volunteer information; (b) asking open-ended questions; and (c) not interrupting suspects during their narrative responses. Interviewers who adopt this information-gathering style of interviewing may find that the resulting, longer responses also provide more verbal and non-verbal cues for detecting deception (Vrij, Mann & Fisher, 2006. Asking open-ended questions, as opposed to confronting suspects with specific accusations, also permits investigators to detect the different response strategies used by liars and truth-tellers. For instance, Hartwig, Granhag, Strömwell and Vrij (2005) found that not confronting suspects with specific accusations, but rather allowing suspects to provide an undirected free recall, led to strategically different kinds of response by guilty and innocent suspects. Specifically, guilty suspects provided vaguer and less detailed responses than did innocent suspects, presumably to reduce the amount of self-incriminating information they generated, and to provide fewer details that might be disproved. Sensitivity to these different response strategies should result in better discrimination between liars and truth-tellers (Hartwig, Granhag & Strömwell, in press).

Memory/general Cognition

Investigators do not have contact with suspects until after a crime has occurred. Therefore, for cognitive theory to be useful to enhance suspect recollection, it must focus on the retrieval phase of memory – as opposed to most mnemonics, which are implemented at encoding (Bower, 1970; Higbee, 1977). Secondly, both the suspect and the interviewer are engaged in demanding cognitive tasks: The suspect is attempting to recall and describe in detail a complex event; the interviewer is listening for details and subtleties within the suspect's response, formulating questions and noting the suspect's answers. Because these tasks are demanding, suspects' and interviewers' limited cognitive resources must be used efficiently.

Context Reinstatement

According to the encoding specificity principle, memory retrieval is most efficient when the context of the original event is reinstated at the time of recall (Tulving & Thomson, 1973). Therefore, at the beginning of the interview, interviewers should instruct suspects to mentally recreate their affective, physiological, cognitive and emotional states that existed at the time of the original event. For innocent suspects, the original context may be their alibi location, including other people who may have been at the same location. For guilty suspects, the original context is the crime scene. Context reinstatement might also be implemented by conducting the interview at the scene of the alibi or at the scene of the crime.

Limited Mental Resources

People have only limited mental resources to process information (Baddeley, 1986; Kahneman, 1973). Performance therefore suffers when we engage in several difficult tasks at once. Suspects may conduct superficial searches through memory, because they are concurrently listening to the interviewer's questions. Interviewers may fail to process subtle nuances within a suspect's response, because they are concurrently generating hypotheses about the crime and formulating questions.

Information-processing errors that are brought about by reduced mental resources should occur more frequently for deceptive than truthful suspects, as lying generally requires more cognitive resources than does telling the truth (Vrij, Fisher, Mann & Leal, 2006). For instance, liars must keep track of past statements to ensure that their current statements are consistent with what they have already told the investigator; liars may also be monitoring their own non-verbal behaviour to ensure that they are not 'leaking' any clues about their deception; finally, liars may be monitoring the investigator's non-verbal behaviour to determine whether they are 'getting away' with their lie. In like fashion, *interviewers* who believe that the suspect may be lying – and therefore monitor the suspect's behaviour for subtle cues that indicate lying – should also have fewer cognitive resources available than interviewers who believe that the suspect is being truthful. As a consequence of these reduced cognitive resources, interviewers who believe that their suspect is lying will have more difficulty listening to the content of the suspect's responses than interviewers who believe that the suspect is telling the truth. It may therefore be easier for a second investigator one who is observing but not actually conducting the interview (i.e., not having to use cognitive resources to formulate questions or an interview strategy), to monitor the suspect's verbal and non-verbal behaviours for signs of deception and also to understand the content of the suspect's responses (e.g., Granhag & Strömwall, 2001).

When interviewing cooperative suspects who are motivated to be truthful, interviewers can minimise overloading suspects' mental resources by refraining from asking questions while suspects are searching through memory, and generally by asking fewer but more open-ended questions. Asking fewer questions should also increase the interviewer's efficiency by not deflecting his or her mental resources from the task of listening to the suspect's description. Interviewers can also promote more efficient use of suspects' limited mental resources by encouraging them to close their eyes when recalling (Bekerian & Dennett, 1997) and by minimising physical distractions, such as phone calls during the interview.

Suspect-compatible Questioning

Each suspect's mental representation of an event is unique. During the commission of a crime, some suspects may focus on the victim, whereas others may focus on the surroundings. If a crime is committed by several perpetrators acting in a group, each perpetrator may have a different role. If so, each suspect would have a different representation of the crime, probably emphasising his or her unique role within the group (see Neisser, 1981). For instance, one suspect may have been responsible for instructing the victims, while another suspect might have taken the money, and yet another suspect was the lookout. To enhance a suspect's recall of the critical event, interviewers should tailor their questions to the mental representation of each particular suspect and not ask all suspects the same set of questions.

The accessibility of event details also varies systematically throughout the course of the interview. A suspect's memory for the actions taken by an accomplice, for instance, should be more accessible when the suspect is thinking about the accomplice than when the suspect is thinking about leaving the crime scene in a getaway car. In general, event details will be most accessible when they are perceptually related to the suspect's current mental image (Pecher, Zeelenberg & Barsalou, 2003). Interviewers therefore should be sensitive to the suspect's currently active mental image, so as to time their questions most efficiently. This may require interviewers to defer asking questions about investigatively relevant details until later in the interview, when the suspect's mental image is compatible with the questions.

Multiple Retrieval

Suspects will rarely exhaust their knowledge of the critical event in one interview, even if they indicate that they cannot remember

any more. Conducting a second or third interview should therefore generate new recollections, a common finding in laboratory
research (reminiscence: Gilbert & Fisher, 2006; Scrivner& Safer,
1988). Furthermore, these new recollections are likely to be accurate,
especially if they are produced in response to open-ended questions
(Fisher & Patterson, 2004). Sometimes, investigators doubt the accuracy of these newly found recollections, based on the assumption that
memory should become weaker with the passage of time. However,
unless there is a strong belief that the suspect is lying, or the newly
found recollection directly contradicts an earlier statement, one should
assume that these new recollections are accurate.

Varied Retrieval

Different retrieval cues may access different properties of a complex
event (Anderson & Pichert, 1978). Therefore, suspects should be
encouraged to think about events in many different ways, for instance,
thinking about the event in different temporal orders (forward or
backward) or from different spatial or personal perspectives (from the
suspect's perspective or from the victim's perspective; Gilbert & Fisher,
2006). Similarly, events may be represented conceptually, especially
for the person who planned the crime strategically, and also in terms
of their sensory properties (Paivio, 1971). Suspects should therefore be
encouraged to describe the event in terms of its meaningful or conceptual properties and also in terms of its various sensory properties. In
general, the more different ways suspects think about an event, the
more details they should recall.

One of the fortuitous spinoffs of the CI recommendation to ask
witnesses to describe events in both chronological and backward
order (Geiselman, Fisher, MacKinnon & Holland, 1985) is that this
varied-order technique has sometimes led to suspects unintentionally
revealing their involvement in a crime. Several American and Swedish
police (Christianson, personal communication, 24 January 2006) have
noted that guilty suspects who initially denied their involvement in a
crime (when asked to describe the crime in chronological order) later
implicated themselves (as being central actors in the crime) when
asked to describe the crime in reverse order. We surmise that these
suspects had practised narrating a fictitious rendition of the crime
prior to their first police interview, so that when the police interviewer asked them initially to describe the crime, the suspects reported
their rehearsed rendition of the story (in which they did not play a
central role). When they were later asked to narrate the story in backward order, which they had not practised prior to the interview, they

accidentally reported a truthful but unrehearsed version of the story, revealing their involvement in the crime. Thus, the varied-order technique, which we initially proposed to enhance cooperative witnesses' recollection, also appears to assist in detecting deception.

Metacognitive Monitoring

People can monitor the accuracy of their knowledge well, and can maintain high accuracy if they are not actively encouraged to guess (Koriat & Goldsmith, 1996). To promote high accuracy in recall, interviewers should instruct suspects explicitly not to guess, but rather to indicate that they 'don't know'. Furthermore, interviewers should refrain from applying social pressure on suspects to volunteer extensive information simply to create the appearance of being helpful or to comply with their obligation in a plea bargain. Such pressure is likely to generate incorrect testimony, which may send the investigation in the wrong direction. We suspect that this may have occurred during the early days of the American incursion into Iraq, when Iraqi informants generated faulty reports of weapons of mass destruction. From an investigator's perspective, it is usually preferable for suspects to make errors of omission (failing to report details) than to make errors of commission (reporting incorrect details). Keeping errors of commission at an acceptably low level, however, requires that suspects use their metacognitive skills properly and edit out of their reports those facts that they are not certain of.

Minimising Constructive Recall

At times, memory is a constructive process, whereby the rememberer incorporates information from other (non-target) sources to construct the target episode (Bartlett, 1932; Bransford Franks, 1971; Loftus & Palmer, 1974; see also Roediger & McDermott, 1995, that all remembering is constructive). For instance, suspects may incorporate knowledge gathered from other suspects or the media to help construct their memories of a crime. More important, suspects may also acquire and use information from the interviewer based on his or her verbal or non-verbal behaviour (Ceci & Bruck, 1993). Interviewers should therefore be careful about not leaking information to suspects either through facial gestures or other non-verbal behaviours or by making suggestive comments.

As we will note later, suspects may have committed other crimes in the past, in which case they may incorporate information from other crimes into their narration of the current crime. Similarly, if they have had extensive exposure to crime, either from their personal involvement or from communicating with other criminals, suspects may have developed a schema about the 'standard' method to commit a crime (Bartlett, 1932). Investigators should attempt to discourage suspects from such schema-driven constructive recall, and instead, encourage them to describe their knowledge of the specific crime in question. Reinstating the context of the specific crime should promote such episodic retrieval, rather than the more generic schema-driven reconstruction. Investigators might also ask suspects, especially after they provide a 'standard' *modus operandi*, whether they simply 'know' that these details occurred or whether they 'remember' that the details occurred specifically in the crime under investigation (Gardiner, 1988).

Communication

For police interviews to be effective, investigators must communicate their investigative needs to the suspect. Suspects must also communicate their unique knowledge of the target event to the investigator. Ineffective communication will lead suspects to withhold valuable information or to provide irrelevant, imprecise or incorrect answers.

Promoting Extensive, Detailed Responses

Police interviews require suspects to describe people, objects and events in more detail than civilians normally do in casual conversation. Inducing such an extraordinary level of description requires that police convey this goal explicitly, which they rarely do. To compound the problem, suspects may withhold information because they do not know what is relevant for a police investigation. To minimise suspects' withholding information, interviewers should instruct suspects to report everything they think about, whether it is trivial, out of chronological order, or even if it contradicts earlier statements.

If contradictions do arise within a suspect's testimony, interviewers should defer resolving these contradictions until late in the interview. Investigators often attack these contradictions immediately in their zeal to expose the suspect's lie, as inconsistency is frequently taken as an indicator of lying (Granhag, Strömwall & Jonsson, 2003). Doing so, however, may either severely damage any rapport that has been developed between the suspect and interviewer, or it may discourage suspects from volunteering information freely in the future. Both of these possible effects militate against the investigator's goals. It is preferable to allow suspects to tell their entire story first, and then to resolve contradictions after having collected as much information as possible.

Code-compatible Output

Interviewers and respondents often exchange ideas using only the verbal medium and fail to use other media that might convey information more effectively. Some people, however, have poor verbal skills and are more expressive non-verbally. Children, the elderly, and new immigrants are primary examples of people who have only limited ability to express themselves verbally. Requiring them to use only the verbal medium impairs their ability to describe events. Likewise, some actions or objects are difficult to describe verbally, as there are no simple, common words or expressions that convey the ideas adequately – even for people with good verbal skills (Leibowitz, Guzy, Peterson & Blake, 1993). Again, limiting the interview exclusively to the verbal medium, and not making use of non-verbal media, reduces the quality of information gathered.

Ideally the response format should be compatible with the suspect's mental representation of the event, thereby minimising the need to transform his or her mental representation into an overt response (cf. ideo-motor theory, Greenwald, 1970). For example, if an event is inherently spatial (e.g., location of objects within a room), then suspects should respond spatially, e.g., by drawing a sketch of the room, or by placing model objects within a (model) room. If the event is an action, suspects might better respond motorically, by attempting to duplicate the original action. In general, the more directly suspects can convey their knowledge, the more accurate and precise will be their response.

COGNITIONS UNIQUE TO GUILTY SUSPECTS

Guilty suspects, those who have actually participated in the crime, should differ in important ways from victims or witnesses, and so the interview should reflect their unique cognitive representations of the crime. Next, we describe several characteristics that are unique to guilty suspects and suggest how the interview might be altered accordingly.

Premeditated Crimes

For many victims and witnesses, crimes are unexpected events that happen without warning, and so do not permit any forethought. Indeed, sometimes witnesses are not even aware that a crime has been committed until long after the crime has occurred. By comparison, perpetrators who commit premeditated crimes have an opportunity to develop a strategic plan long before committing the crime. For instance, they may think about the timing of the various components of the crime to be certain that they can complete the crime before the police arrive. They may consider whether to take implements (e.g., weapons, vehicles, carrying cases, maps, documents, masks, etc.) to ensure the crime's success. In general, the more skill that is required to enact a crime successfully, and the more skillful is the criminal, the more he or she will have thought about the details of the crime prior to the act itself. As a result of this premeditation, perpetrators should think about the crime at a deeper, more semantic level than will victims and witnesses, for whom the event is probably experienced at the sensory and emotional levels (Craik & Lockhart, 1972). Questions and retrieval cues that relate to the meaningful, planful nature of the event should therefore be more successful for interviews with suspects than for interviews with victims and witnesses (Fisher & Craik, 1977; Tulving & Thomson, 1973).

For guilty suspects who premeditated a crime, the context of the crime includes not only the crime itself, but also the planning phase. Therefore, when interviewers 'reinstate the context' of the crime, they should initially reinstate the context of the pre-crime plan. In doing so, interviewers should ask suspects to reconstruct the pre-crime plan and to think about the decisions they made leading to the plan. For instance, they might ask suspects to think about whether they considered alternative plans and if so, why they favoured the final plans over the alternatives. If several accomplices constructed the plan, suspects might consider the suggestions of the various planners.

As a result of pre-planning, perpetrators may have an expectation or schema of how the crime should unfold (Bartlett, 1932). If so, they should be acutely aware during the crime of anything that goes awry or not according to plan (Alba & Hasher, 1983). To take advantage of this heightened awareness, interviewers should ask suspects to think about: (a) the planned version of the crime; and (b) any events that violated their expectations and perhaps necessitated a change in plans; or (c) how they altered their plans during the crime.

Post-crime Meditations

Professional criminals, whose livelihood depends on being able to commit similar crimes in the future, may review the crime events afterward. These post-crime thoughts are likely to focus on unexpected events that may have sabotaged the crime. Perpetrators may consider what they should do differently next time to reduce their chances of being caught. This is comparable to sophisticated organisations retrospectively analysing ill-fated decisions, in order to avoid making such strategic errors in the future. These post-crime meditations should facilitate later memory of the crime in much the same way that rehearsing innocuous events is known to enhance memory (e.g., Raaijmakers & Shiffrin, 1980). Victims and witnesses may also engage in post-crime rehearsal, but more so as a set of sensory experiences than as a strategically orchestrated sequence of activities. The deeper, more semantic nature of the perpetrator's post-crime meditations should serve to preserve the crime actions better for criminals than for victims or witnesses (McDaniel, Kowitz & Dunay, 1989). Interviewers can make use of these post-crime thoughts by encouraging suspects to think not only about the crime itself but also about their relevant thoughts following the crime.

SCOPE OF CRIMINAL'S PERCEPTUAL EXPERIENCE

We expect that perpetrators will concentrate on different aspects of the crime than victims and witnesses. For instance, perpetrators may focus on the victims' behaviours, whereas victims and witnesses may focus their attention on weapons (Steblay, 1992) and on the perpetrators' behaviours. Perpetrators may also be particularly sensitive to the passage of time and to the physical layout of the crime scene, because these factors may dictate whether the crime is successful or whether the perpetrators are apprehended. In a similar fashion, if a crime is committed by a group of people, the perpetrator in charge may have different perceptions than the subordinate perpetrators. Following the principle of suspect-compatible questioning, which we described earlier, interviewers should direct their questions toward those aspects of the crime that are particularly salient for the individual suspect being interviewed.

MULTIPLE PERPETRATORS

Crimes committed by multiple perpetrators have a different dynamic than those committed by one individual, because the perpetrators act interdependently with one another, as a group (e.g., Perpetrator X tied up the victim while Perpetrator Y pointed the gun at them, and Perpetrator Z took their money). Criminals should therefore be relatively aware of how their actions coordinated with one another, and especially if they planned the crime in advance. This should be even more so for the group leader, the person who orchestrated the group's activities. Interviewers can make use of this property by: (a) asking each suspect how his or her role in the crime integrated with the roles of the accomplices; and (b) asking the suspects to describe the crime from their own perspective, but also from the perspectives of the other members of the team (see the earlier section on varied retrieval).

As with interviews with multiple victims and witnesses, interviews with multiple suspects should be conducted with each suspect separately to avoid contaminating one another's memory (Technical Working Group: Eyewitness Evidence, 1999). Conducting the interviews separately with each suspect also avoids social loafing, whereby each suspect does not put forth maximal effort in the memory task, but relies on the other suspects to do the mental work necessary for an effective interview (Karau & Williams, 1993). Finally, conducting the interviews separately allows the investigator to corroborate the responses across suspects, which should provide some insights about the veracity of their statements.

One of the difficulties of interviewing perpetrators who acted in groups is that they probably spoke to one another shortly after committing the crime, potentially tainting one another's recollection (e.g., Gabbert, Memon, Allan & Wright, 2004). Unfortunately, if the suspect's memory has been altered by exposure to an accomplice's recollection of the crime, it is unlikely that even highly successful retrieval techniques will gain access to the pre-altered knowledge (see Fisher et al., 2002).

FREQUENCY OF OCCURRENCE AND SOURCE MONITORING

Victims and witnesses are unlikely to experience more than one or two crimes in their lives (unless they work at a convenience store or live in a high-crime area), whereas criminals may participate in several crimes across their criminal 'careers'. As a result, criminals are expected to make more source-monitoring errors, confusing the details of one crime with another (Johnson, Hashtroudi & Lindsay, 1993). Criminals should also forget the details of the crime more rapidly than victims and witnesses, for whom the crime is a unique experience. As a result of their many related experiences, criminals may rely more on a schema-driven constructive memory, whereas victims and witnesses may rely more on an episodically based retrieval process (Alba & Hasher, 1983; Fisher & Chandler, 1984; Fisher & Cuervo, 1983). Assisting the suspect to recall the details of a particular crime, and minimising the influence of schema-based reconstruction, should benefit from reminding the suspect of some unique details associated with a particular crime.

We note an apparent conflict between two claims: (a) criminals who commit premeditated crimes should remember these acts relatively well, because they have processed the events at a deep, semantic level (Craik & Lockhart, 1972); and (b) criminals who have committed many related crimes should be subject to source-monitoring errors (Johnson, et al., 1993). We believe that both of these principles operate at any one time, although each principle works to counteract the other. Thus, criminals who have planned a crime thoroughly should remember the crime better than criminals who commit opportunistic crimes that entail no preplanning. On the other hand, criminals who have committed a greater number of crimes, and especially if the crimes are similar to one another (e.g., serial car theft), should experience more source-monitoring errors, or even complete omissions, than criminals who have committed fewer crimes. Whether the level-of-processing principle (predicting good memory) or the source-monitoring principle (predicting poor memory) dominates depends on the specific parameters of each case: How much preplanning did the criminal engage in? How many similar crimes did the person commit? In the next section, we offer a novel approach to assisting suspects to recall a series of related crimes.

MOTIVATING RELUCTANT SUSPECTS

It is obvious that most guilty suspects have disincentives to volunteer information. A critical ingredient in suspect interviews then is to give them sufficient motivation to participate. One such motivator is to enter into a plea bargain so that suspects may gain something by volunteering information. In cases of serial crimes (e.g., serial car theft), for instance, the prosecution may offer a plea bargain to the suspect such that, if the suspect confesses to a limited number of crimes and assists the prosecution to solve the other cases, the prosecution will drop the charges for all but a few cases. If the suspect accepts the offer, he or she must still remember and describe in detail all of the bargained-for crimes. Not surprisingly, recalling many events from a common set of elements (e.g. 30 car thefts) can easily tax the suspect's memory (Watkins & Watkins, 1976). In the next segment, we describe an interviewing strategy and validation study to assist recalling individual events from a large, common pool.

Phillips and Fisher (August, 1998) simulated the task of assisting suspects to recall a large pool of serial crimes by asking college seniors to recall all of the classes they had taken in their college career – typically about 30. The experiment was conducted in two phases: In Phase I we gathered normative data from one set of students to create effective retrieval cues for recalling college courses, and in Phase II we tested these retrieval cues to see if they enhanced the recall of another group of college students. Our strategy was to create retrieval cues that are strong associates of the to-be-remembered (TBR) courses, but specific enough so that they are not associated with too many courses (cue overload: Watkins & Watkins, 1976).

In Phase I, we asked a group of students to think of courses they had taken in college and to list the most outstanding characteristic of each course. Typical characteristics included: receiving a very high (or low) grade, unusual time of day (very early or very late), established a good friendship with a fellow student, thought the teacher was very interesting (or very boring), was surprised at the content of the course. Almost all of the named characteristics reflected that the course was in some way unique, at either the high end or the low end of some salient dimension (grade, time of day, friendship, interesting/boring, etc.). A few of the named characteristics were idiosyncratic (e.g. spilled coffee during lecture), however, most of the characteristics converged on only a few dimensions. We then identified the five most commonly indicated characteristics and used them in the second phase of the experiment, as retrieval cues for other students to recall their college courses.

In Phase II, the validation phase, we gave another group of students (retrieval assistance group) 20 minutes to list all of the college courses they had taken. After this initial free recall, we provided the students with the specific cues we had gathered in Phase I and gave them 15 minutes to think of any additional courses. In the control group, the students did the same initial 20-minute free recall, listing all of their courses. This was followed by a second, 15-minute free recall period to recall any additional courses, but where we provided no additional cues. The results showed two interesting data patterns. Firstly, both groups recalled some courses in the second recall period that they did not recall in the initial free recall (reminiscence), which supports the 'multiple retrieval' suggestion we noted earlier. Secondly, and more importantly, in the second recall period, the retrieval-assistance group remembered almost 15% more new courses than did the control group. Furthermore, the accuracy of these recollections was extremely high (fewer than 10% were fabricated), as determined by comparing students' recollections with their official university records. Our results, then, support the notion that one can assist people to recall a large set of similar items by providing retrieval cues based on another group's recollections of similar experiences.

Criminal investigators might use a parallel, two-phase strategy to assist suspected serial criminals to recall a long list of related crimes. Following the logic of the Phillips and Fisher study (August, 1998), investigators would first create a set of potential retrieval cues, and then provide these retrieval cues to the current suspect. To create the potential retrieval cues, investigators would find imprisoned criminals who had committed crimes similar to the current case. The investigators would then ask these criminals to think about specific crimes that they had committed in the past and to indicate some outstanding characteristic of each crime. (Presumably, these criminals would be given immunity for the recalled crimes.) Typical answers might be: It was the first armed robbery I committed, I was almost caught by police, I did not have the proper tools. The investigators would then construct a list of the most frequently noted characteristics. The resulting characteristics (dimensions that criminals use to assess crimes) could then be given to the current suspect to assist his or her memory for the as-yet-unrecalled crimes.

Two potential concerns pointed out by Holmberg (personal communication, 24 January 2006) might require some creativity to implement this strategy. First, given the demands of investigating a serious crime (e.g., rape), the crime investigators may not have ample time to interview the imprisoned criminals to collect the requisite normative data. We suspect that these interviews could be conducted by the investigators' assistants or other members of the law enforcement system who are not overwhelmed by the demands of the current investigation. Furthermore, we expect that, in time, a thorough catalogue of normative data would have developed for each possible crime, so that the investigator could access these norms directly from an existing archive. The second problem, which is potentially more dangerous, is that providing these retrieval cues to the suspects may be construed as asking leading questions, and inducing false memories. We can think of two approaches to this question. Firstly, this is an empirical question, and so it would be valuable to conduct an innocuous, simulated laboratory study to determine whether or not the cues promote false memories. Secondly, if the retrieval cues do induce false memories, perhaps we can modify the retrieval cues so they are more neutral, thereby reducing their suggestiveness. For instance, instead of asking suspects whether they required a weapon to commit any crimes, we might ask suspects to think about whether the *presence or absence* of a weapon was important in committing any crime. We leave it to our readers to devise alternative ways to adapt this procedure. In practice, the police should request legal counsel to determine the legality of the recommended procedure.

Future Directions

Progress in the area of interviewing suspects will depend on developing adequate research paradigms to study this sensitive area. We expect progress to come from the convergence of two forms of study: experimental laboratory research and analysis of real-world interviews with suspects.

Of the two research paradigms, the more difficult will be to create an ecologically valid, experimental procedure that captures the motivational disincentives and high arousal faced by guilty suspects, and yet is ethically acceptable for research with volunteer participants. We believe that a good starting point for such a paradigm is the procedure used by Russano, Meissner, Narchet and Kassin (2005) to examine the effects of police interrogation procedures on possible coerced confessions. In Russano et al., student participants were placed in a situation in which they were enticed to cheat by breaking the explicitly stated rules of the experiment not to share information with another participant (a confederate who requested assistance during the experimental session). In Russano et al., most students did 'cheat' and assisted the confederate. These student participants were then confronted by the experimenter with evidence to support the conclusion that they violated the stated rule. The students were then asked to 'confess' to having broken the rule. Some student participants did not violate the experimental rule (did not share information with the confederate), but they were, nevertheless, suspected of doing so by the experimenter. Although the goal of the current chapter is not to elicit confessions, but rather to elicit descriptions about the targeted event, the Russano et al. paradigm may be useful for our purposes in that it establishes, in a controlled environment, the necessary conditions of arousal and disincentives for volunteering information.

One might also examine the lie-detection literature (see Granhag & Vrij 2005), for a recent review) to see if an acceptable paradigm can be adapted for our purposes. We suspect that in most of those studies, the disincentive to be truthful (not earning a small monetary bonus) does not adequately duplicate the necessary conditions faced by real-world suspects. Perhaps there are other experimental paradigms that we are unaware of that duplicate these conditions effectively.

A second source of insight to developing more effective suspect interviews is to analyse real-world criminal investigations. Because these are official police investigations, they are not bound by the same ethical and practical constraints as conducting experimental research with volunteer participants. As such, they capture completely the high arousal faced by suspects and the full-fledged disincentives they have for volunteering information. Much of this research examines suspects' retrospective recollections of their feelings at the time of the interview, and excellent progress has been made by Holmberg and Christianson (2002) using this paradigm.

Although high in ecological validity, this research is limited because (a) it depends on suspects' later retrospective reports and (b) it is observational. The concerns about using retrospective reports are that (a) suspects may not be aware of some of their thoughts and reactions to the interviewers' questioning style (Nisbett & Wilson, 1977) and (b) if much time has elapsed between the initial interview and debriefing the suspect, some of the suspect's original reactions may have been forgotten or over time, may have been altered by post-interview experiences (Loftus, 1979), or may be subjected to other biases in decision-making, e.g., the need for consistency (Ross, 1989). The obvious concern with observational research is that it is difficult to determine cause and effect. For instance, we do not know whether the observed correlation between interviewer style (dominant or humane) and suspect's behaviour (confess or not; feelings of self worth; cooperation) indicates that dominant interview styles promote undesirable suspect behaviour (e.g., not cooperative) or whether the direction of causality is the reverse: Suspects' undesirable behaviour causes interviewers to adopt a more dominant style.

An alternative research approach to analysing real-world suspect interviews is to conduct micro-analyses of the records of these interviews, either audio tapes, video-tapes or written transcriptions. In such analyses, the researcher notes the suspect's answers to specific questions. The results of this type of micro-analysis allows researchers to examine questions such as: Whether suspects provide more extensive responses when interviewers develop better rapport? Are suspects' responses more informative when interviewers encourage them to supplement their verbal responses with non-verbal actions? Do suspects volunteer more information when interviewers explain the expected social dynamics (suspects should volunteer information without waiting for the interviewer to ask a question) than when no explanation is provided? This type of textual analysis of transcribed interviews has been used successfully to analyse interviews of cooperative witnesses (e.g. Fisher, et al. 1987; Fisher, et al., 2000; George & Clifford, 1992). We believe that a similar type of detailed analysis might also be fruitful for suspect interviews. Naturally, this research methodology also suffers from the observational nature of the task and the difficulty of establishing causality. For instance, we may find that open-ended questions are associated with more informative answers than are closed questions; however, we cannot say for certain whether the questions promote different answers, or whether suspects who provide more informative answers encourage interviewers to ask more open-ended questions.

It is clear that both of these research paradigms are limited. Experimental, laboratory research cannot easily capture the arousal level and motivational disincentives for suspects in real-world conditions. The alternative approaches, retrospective surveys of suspects and textual analysis of recorded suspect interviews, suffer from distortions associated with memory or with the failure to identify the direction of causality. As with many other scientific issues, our knowledge will progress best by examining the convergence of findings across research paradigms.

EXTENDING THE RESEARCH BEYOND CRIMINAL INVESTIGATIONS

We have couched our description of the research exclusively in terms of criminal investigation. However, the basic problem of gathering information from suspects exists in many domains. For example, in the area of accident investigation, pilots, who may be responsible for fatal airplane crashes, are often interviewed to elicit information about the accident. Not surprisingly, pilots may be reluctant to volunteer information if it leads to their being identified as the primary cause of the accident. Similarly, military leaders or business decision-makers, whose errors of judgement may be responsible for the loss of lives or millions of dollars, may be interviewed to determine how or why their critical decision was made. They, too, have strong disincentives to volunteer extensive and accurate information. Because the underlying psychological processes are similar across all of these domains, we believe that the ideas we have developed in this chapter should generalise to many different human actions and decisions. We hope that we have generated some valuable ideas to develop progress in these critical investigations.

REFERENCES

Alba, J.W. & Hasher, L. (1983) Is memory schematic? *Psychological Bulletin*, **93**, 203–31.
Anderson, R.C. & Pichert, J.W. (1978) Recall of previously unrecallable information following a shift in perspective. *Journal of Verbal Learning & Verbal Behavior*, **17**, 1–12.
Baddeley, A.D. (1986) *Working memory*. Oxford: Oxford University Press.

Bartlett, F.C. (1932) *Remembering: A study in experimental and social psychology*. Cambridge: Cambridge University Press.

Bekerian, D.A. & Dennett, J.L. (1997) Imagery effects in spoken and *written recall*. In D. Payne & F. Conrad (Eds), *Intersections in basic and applied memory research* (pp. 279–89). Mahwah, NJ: Erlbaum.

Bower, G.H. (1970) Analysis of a mnemonic device. *American Scientist*, **58**, 496–510.

Bransford, J.D. & Franks, J.J. (1971) The abstraction of linguistic ideas. *Cognitive Psychology*, **2**, 331–50.

Ceci, S.J. & Bruck, M. (1993) Suggestibility of the child witness: A historical review and synthesis. *Psychological Bulletin*, **113**, 403–39.

Collins, R., Lincoln, R. & Frank, M.G. (2002) The effect of rapport in forensic interviewing. *Psychiatry, Psychology and Law*, **9**, 69–78.

Craik, F.I. & Lockhart, R.S. (1972) Levels of processing: A framework for memory research. *Journal of Verbal Learning & Verbal Behavior*, **11**, 671–84.

Davis, M.R., McMahon, M. & Greenwood, K.M. (2005) The efficacy of mnemonic components of the *Cognitive Interview*: Towards a shortened variant for time-critical investigations. *Applied Cognitive Psychology*, **19**, 75–93.

Eisen, M.L., Quas, J.A. & Goodman, G.S. (2002) Memory and suggestibility in the forensic interview. Mahwah, NJ: Lawrence Erlbaum Associates, Publishers.

Fisher, R.P., Brennan, K.H. & McCauley, M.R. (2002) The cognitive interview method to enhance eyewitness recall. In M. Eisen, G. Goodman & J. Quas (Eds), *Memory and suggestibility in the forensic interview* (pp. 265–286). Mahwah, NJ: Erlbaum.

Fisher, R.P. & Chandler, C.C. (1984) Dissociations between temporally-cued and theme-cued recall. *Bulletin of the Psychonomic Society*, **22**, 395–7.

Fisher, R.P. & Craik, F.I. (1977) Interaction between encoding and retrieval operations in cued recall. *Journal of Experimental Psychology: Human Learning & Memory*, **3**, 701–11.

Fisher, R.P. & Cuervo, A. (1983) Memory for physical features of discourse as a function of their relevance. *Journal of Experimental Psychology, Learning, Memory, and Cognition*, **9**, 130–8.

Fisher, R.P., Falkner, K.L., Trevisan, M. & McCauley, M.R. (2000) Adapting the cognitive interview to enhance long-term (35 years) recall of physical activities. *Journal of Applied Psychology*, **85**, 180–9.

Fisher, R.P. & Geiselman, R.E. (1992) *Memory enhancing techniques for investigative interviewing: The cognitive interview*. Springfield, IL, England: Charles C. Thomas, Publisher.

Fisher, R.P., Geiselman, R.E. & Amador, M. (1989) Field test of the cognitive interview: Enhancing the recollection of actual victims and witnesses of crime. *Journal of Applied Psychology*, **74**, 722–7.

Fisher, R.P., Geiselman, R.E. & Raymond, D.S. (1987) Critical analysis of police interviewing techniques. *Journal of Police, Science and Administration*, **15**, 177–185.

Fisher, R.P. & Patterson, T.D. (November, 2004) *The relationship between consistency and accuracy of eyewitness memory*. Paper presented at Psychonomic Society, Minneapolis, MN.

Fisher, R.P., & Schreiber, N. (2007) Interviewing protocols to improve eyewitness memory. In M. Toglia, R. Lindsay, R.D. Ross & J. Reed (Eds), *The handbook of eyewitness psychology: Volume One. Memory for events* (pp. 53–80). Mahwah, NJ: Erlbaum Associates.

Gabbert, F., Memon, A., Allan, K. & Wright, D.B. (2004) Say it to my face: Examining the effects of socially encountered misinformation. *Legal and Criminological Psychology*, **9**, 215–27.

Gardiner, J.M. (1988) Functional aspects of recollective experience. *Memory & Cognition*, **16**, 309–13.

Geiselman, R.E., Fisher, R.P., MacKinnon, D.P. & Holland, H.L. (1985) Eyewitness memoryenhancement in the police interview: Cognitive retrieval mnemonics versus hypnosis. *Journal of Applied Psychology*, **70**, 401–12.

George, R. & Clifford, B.R. (1992) Making the most of witnesses. *Policing*, **8**, 185–98.

Gilbert, J.A.E. & Fisher, R.P.(2006). The effects of varied retrieval cues on reminiscence in eyewitness memory. *Applied Cognitive Psychology*, **20**, 723–39.

Granhag, P.A. & Strömwall, L.A. (2001) Deception detection based on repeated interrogations. *Legal and Criminological Psychology*, **6**, 85–101.

Granhag, P.A. Strömwall, L.A. & Jonsson, A. (2003) Partners in crime: How liars in collusion betray themselves. *Journal of Applied Social Psychology*, **33**, 848–68.

Granhag, P.A. & Vrij, A. (2005). Detecting deception. In N. Brewer & K.D. Williams (Eds), *Psychology and law: An empirical perspective* (pp. 43–92). London: The Guilford Press.

Greenwald, A.G. (1970) Sensory feedback mechanisms in performance control: With special reference to the ideo-motor mechanism. *Psychological Review*, **77**, 73–99.

Hartwig, M., Granhag, P.A. & Strömwall, L.A. (in press) Guilty and innocent suspects' strategies during police interrogations. *Psychology, Crime & Law*.

Hartwig, M., Granhag, P.A., Strömwall, L.A. & Vrij, A. (2005) Detecting deception via strategic disclosure of evidence. *Law and Human Behaviour*, **29**, 469–84.

Henson, R., Cannell, C.F. & Lawson, S. (1976) Effects of interviewer style on quality of reporting in a survey interview. *The Journal of Psychology: Interdisciplinary and Applied*, **93**, 221–7.

Higbee, K.L. (1977) *Your memory: How it works and how to improve it.* Oxford: Prentice-Hall.

Holmberg, U. & Christianson, S.Å. (2002) Murderers' and sexual offenders' experiences of police interviews and their inclination to admit or deny crimes. *Behavioral Sciences & the Law*, **20**, 31–45.

Johnson, M.K., Hashtroudi, S. & Lindsay, D.S. (1993) Source monitoring. *Psychological Bulletin*, **114**, 3–28.

Kahneman, D. (1973) *Attention and effort.* Englewood Cliffs, NJ: Prentice-Hall.

Karau, S.J. & Williams, K.D. (1993) Social loafing: A meta-analytic review and theoretical integration. *Journal of Personality and Social Psychology*, **65**, 681–706.

Kassin, S.M. & Gudjonsson, G.H. (2004) The psychology of confessions: A review of the literature and issues. *Psychological Science in the Public Interest*, **5**, 33–67.

Kebbell, M.R., Milne, R. & Wagstaff, G.F. (1999) The cognitive interview: A survey of its effectiveness. *Psychology, Crime and Law*, **5**, 101–15.

Kohnken, G., Milne, R., Memon, A. & Bull, R. (1999) The cognitive interview: A meta-analysis. *Psychology, Crime and Law*, **5**, 3–27.

Koriat, A. & Goldsmith, M. (1996) Monitoring and control processes in the strategic regulation of memory accuracy. *Psychological Review*, **103**, 490–517.

Leibowitz, H.W., Guzy, L.T., Peterson, E. & Blake, P.T. (1993) Quantitative perceptual estimates: Verbal versus nonverbal retrieval techniques. *Perception*, **22**, 1051–60.

Loftus, E.F. (1979) The malleability of human memory. *American Scientist*, **67**, 312–20.

Loftus, E.F. & Palmer, J.C. (1974) Reconstruction of automobile destruction: An example of the interaction between language and memory. *Journal of Verbal Learning & Verbal Behavior*, **13**, 585–9.

McDaniel, M.A., Kowitz, M.D. & Dunay, P.K. (1989) Altering memory through recall: The effects of cue-guided retrieval processing. *Memory & Cognition*, **17**, 423–34.

Memon, A., Holley, A., Milne, R., Koehnken, G. & Bull, R. (1994) Towards understanding the effects of interviewer training in evaluating the cognitive interview. *Applied Cognitive Psychology*, **8**, 641–59.

Memon, A., Wark, L., Holley, A., Bull, R. & Koehnken, G. (1997) Eyewitness performance in cognitive and structured interviews. *Memory*, **5**, 639–56.

Milne, R. & Bull, R. (2003) Interviewing children with mild learning disability with the cognitive interview. *Issues in Criminological & Legal Psychology*, **26**, 44–51.

Moston, S. & Engelberg, T. (1993) Police questioning techniques in tape recorded interviews with criminal suspects. *Policing and Society*, **3**, 223–37.

Neisser, U. (1981) John Dean's memory: A case study. *Cognition*, **9**, 1–22.

Nisbett, R.E. & Wilson, T.D. (1977) Telling more than we can know: Verbal reports on mental processes. *Psychological Review*, **84**, 231–59.

Paivio, A. (1971) *Imagery and verbal processes*. New York: Holt, Reinhart, & Winston.

Pecher, D., Zeelenberg, R. & Barsalou, L.W. (2003) Verifying different-modality properties for concepts produces switching costs. *Psychological Science*, **14**, 119–24.

Phillips, M.R. & Fisher, R.P. (August, 1998) *Enhancing cooperative suspects' memories of crimes: A cued recall approach*. Poster presented at the 106th annual convention of the American Psychological Association, San Francisco, CA.

Raaijmakers, J.G.W. & Shiffrin, R.M. (1980) SAM: A theory of probabilistic search of associative memory. In G. Bower (Ed.), *The psychology of learning and motivation: Advances in research and theory*, Volume 14. New York: Academic Press.

Roediger, H.L. & McDermott, K.B. (1995) Creating false memories: Remembering words not presented in lists. *Journal of Experimental Psychology: Learning, Memory, and Cognition*, **21**, 803–14.

Ross, M. (1989) Relation of implicit theories to the construction of personal histories. *Psychological Review*, **96**, 341–57.

Russano, M.B., Meissner, C.A., Narchet, F.M., & Kassin, S.M. (2005) Investigating true and false confessions within a novel experimental paradigm. *Psychological Science*, **16**, 481–6.

Scrivner, E. & Safer, M.A. (1988) Eyewitnesses show hypermnesia for details about a violent event. *Journal of Applied Psychology*, **73**, 371–7.

Steblay, N.M. (1992) A meta-analytic review of the weapon focus effect. *Law and Human Behavior*, **16**, 413–24.

St-Yves, M. (2006) The psychology of rapport: Five basic rules. In T. Williamson (Ed.), *Investigative interviewing: Rights, research, regulation*. Devon (UK): Willian Publishing,

Technical Working Group: Eyewitness Evidence (1999) *Eyewitness evidence: A guide for law enforcement*. U.S. Department of Justice, Office of Justice Programs, National Institute of Justice. NCJ 178240.

Tulving, E. & Thomson, D.M. (1973) Encoding specificity and retrieval processes in episodic memory. *Psychological Review*, **80**, 359–80.

Vrij, A., Fisher, R., Mann, S. & Leal, S. (2006) Detecting deception by manipulating cognitive load. *Trends in Cognitive Sciences*, **10**, 141–2.

Vrij, A., Mann, S. & Fisher, R.P. (2006) Information-gathering vs accusatory interview style: Individual differences in respondents' experiences. *Personality & Individual Differences*, **41**, 589–99.

Vrij, A., Mann, S., Kristen, S. & Fisher, R.P. (in press) Cues to deception and ability to detect lies as a function of police interview styles. *Law & Human Behavior*.

Watkins, M.J. & Watkins, O.C. (1976) Cue-overload theory and the method of interpolated attributes. *Bulletin of the Psychonomic Society*. **3**, 289–91.

Wells, G.L., Lindsay, R.C.L., Turtle, J.W., Malpass, R.S., Fisher, R.P. & Fulero, S.M. (2000) From the lab to the police station: A successful application of eyewitness research. *American Psychologist*, **55**, 581–98.

CHAPTER 15

Interviewing Offenders: A Therapeutic Jurisprudential Approach

ULF HOLMBERG, SVEN Å. CHRISTIANSON AND DAVID WEXLER

INTRODUCTION

Discussing a strong emotional event, such as having committed murder, is very different than having a typical conversation. After all, committing a violent act, like murder, is one of the most severe forms of antisocial behaviour. There are many obstacles an individual must overcome when reporting about such an event. Firstly, the individual must want to begin the search for memory details that he or she has vigorously avoided. It is common for offenders, as well as among victims of repeated sexual and physical abuse, to develop mechanisms to avoid thinking about such an event. Over time, the individual's active avoidance strategies, such as stop-thinking activity, suppression and others, may make his or her links and associations to the specific details of the event less robust (e.g., Wegner, Quillian & Houston, 1996).

Offenders' Memories of Violent Crimes. Edited by Sven Å. Christianson.
© 2007 John Wiley & Sons, Ltd.

Secondly, the individual must confront the memories of the crime. This is not just a matter of confronting one's own feelings and the victim's reactions, but also of confronting the past (e.g., strong negative childhood memories of being rejected, abused, alone and deeply secluded). Most homicide offenders do not share their personal negative experiences and have developed skills from childhood that enable them to avoid thinking about such events (e.g., distortion, displacement, stop-thinking activity). This results in fewer cues to other types of autobiographical memories and experiences; and thus, the offender does not easily retrieve detailed memories of the crime.

Thirdly, the offender needs a recipient to listen to his or her traumatic memories. This person must be skilled in listening to reports of gruesome and shocking experiences. Finding such a listener may be hard because details of murder are not easy for any listener to hear; and the listener may disclose, either verbally or non-verbally, that it is difficult for him or her to learn of such details.

Police officers often seek a confession that, from their perspective, is an ideal starting point for a perpetrator to tell his story about the crime. Most offenders, however, are not focused on the crime and most of them do not want to confess. Instead, they want to be understood and to understand how the situation happened. This is especially true for reactive (impulsive) homicide offenders (see Chapters 1 and 3 this volume), who are often traumatised by the crime (Pollock, 1999). Against this background, it is counterproductive when police officers preoccupy themselves with confessions rather than truth seeking because by doing so they end up treating the suspect with disrespect and lack of empathy. Condemnation by the police officer will often turn the suspect's attention away from the crime and promote avoidance. The suspect focuses on the interrogators and their insults and provocations. It is not surprising that some offenders claim amnesia. Such claims could be construed as a strategy for psychological survival, as a way to handle both the past, which has led to the act of crime, and the immediate present, being a murderer and being interviewed by a confronting police officer.

This chapter discusses the outcome of offenders' reports about crimes as a function of investigators' different styles of interviewing and the impact on the offenders' psychological well-being based on the complexity of remembering and sharing violent offences. By way of introduction, the case of 'Bert' makes the problem more explicit.

THE CASE OF 'BERT'

At lunchtime one day in the nineties in Sweden, Bert phoned his social worker and told her that he had found his best friend dead. The social worker called the police; and later that day the police arrested Bert as a suspect in his friend's death. That evening a police officer interviewed Bert and began his questioning with, 'Bert, tell me what you have been through today'. Bert began describing what he had done early in the morning, but after 15 seconds the police officer interrupted Bert with questions. For the next 20 minutes, the police officer asked Bert a number of questions searching for the reasons he may have killed his friend. Invoking a confession-seeking approach, the police officer repeatedly asked the same kinds of questions, becoming louder and louder with each one. By trying to solve the problem (to reach Bert's confession) in a first level of abstraction, the officer did more of the same within the system of communication; and the efforts to solve the problem became circular. Watzlawick, Weakland and Fisch (1974) described such efforts, that is, repeatedly asking the same kinds of questions, as a means to solve the problem of a first order change. This police interview resulted in a conflict. As the police officer continuously asked the same questions, it forced Bert to conclude that the officer was just trying to 'grill' him; and so Bert became silent.

The next day, Bert was present at the court proceeding where it was argued that his friend had been strangled to death. Therefore, the police transferred the case to an experienced homicide investigator who interviewed Bert in a calm and more empathic manner. During this second police interview, Bert was silent and showed depressive symptoms regarding the fact that his friend was dead. The homicide investigator invited Bert to talk about his feelings and validated Bert's right to mourn the death of his friend. During this process, Bert stated several times that he did not know how his friend had died. According to the problem-solving theory of Watzlawick et al. (1974) and searching a change of the second order (a non-circular problem-solving approach), the homicide investigator initiated a communication about communicating. Instead of using the confession-seeking method utilised by the first police officer, the investigator initiated a conversation with Bert about how painful memories can make it difficult to talk about certain events. During the next interview, Bert stated that he had painful memories of a gurgling sound and that if this gurgling sound had not been present, his friend would likely be alive. Because the investigator was empathic, Bert was able to explain remorsefully how he had panicked as he was strangling his friend.

DOMINANT AND HUMANITARIAN INTERVIEWING

While many studies of US and UK police interview methodologies have taken place, unfortunately only a few studies have explored the Swedish methodology of conducting police interviews. The National Police Board or the Ministry of Justice has not undertaken any initiatives to formally evaluate or develop new methods for police interviews.[1] Of course, the law regulates the time and manner in which police interviews may be conducted, as well as the obligations a police interviewer has towards an interviewee. But, no one in Sweden has conducted research, evaluations and development as Hill and Memon describe from the American and British perspectives (see Chapter 10 in this volume).

Regarding training, although the Swedish Police Academy has offered a three week-long course in advanced police interview techniques for about the past 10 years, not many police officers (less than 100 per year) have taken this course. Since 1998, both the advanced courses and the basic interview training programme at the police academies use a textbook authored by Christianson, Engelberg and Holmberg (1998). The authors utilise Investigative Interviewing including the PEACE-model (see Chapter 10) and the Cognitive Interview (see Chapter 14) theories in their textbook. Hypothetically, Swedish police interviews are mostly in line with the standard method, based mainly on the questioning as described by Clifford and George (1996). It is also likely that some officers have adopted a humanitarian approach grounded in investigative interviewing as described by Christianson et al. (1998). However, we do not know which techniques the Swedish police use because no one conducts continuous evaluations of their practices.

The different styles of interviewing Bert, not only exemplify a first and a second order change in these police interviews, but are also examples of dominant and humanitarian interviewing approaches. In a written interview with 83 convicted murderers and sexual offenders, Holmberg and Christianson (2002) found that these men perceived their police interviews as either *dominant* or *humanitarian* experiences. In the dominant experience, these offenders perceived their interviewers as impatient, rushing, aggressive, brusque, nonchalant,

---

[1] Recently, the National Police Board distributed (Spring 2006) a manual about interviewing sexual offenders. The manual is lacking in its theory and scientific ground, for example, the manual establishes that sexual offenders use nine masks (e.g., Mr Good guy, Mr Angry, etc.) to *manipulate* and *blockade* police interviewers. Police officers are recommended to learn these masks and use them *instinctively* when interviewing suspects. Moreover, in the efforts to reach suspects confessions, police officers are recommended to minimise verbal expressions with a negative meaning and maximise expressions that can be seen as positive.

unfriendly, deprecating (in the article described as dissociating) and condemning. In the humanitarian experience, the offenders characterised their interviewers as cooperative, accommodating, positive, empathic, helpful and engaging. Additionally, the offenders who experienced the humanitarian approach perceived themselves as being respected by the interviewers, which resulted in them considering themselves as friendly, obliging, acknowledging, cooperative, non-aggressive and confident during the process. In contrast, those offenders who experienced the dominant interview style perceived themselves as being anxious and found they were frightened, stressed, sleepless, paralysed and unconfident during the process.

Furthermore, Holmberg and Christianson found a significant positive relation between the humanitarian interviewing style and the offenders' admissions of crime, while there was a weak non-significant relation between a dominant approach and the offenders' denials of crime. That study also revealed that there was a significant positive relation between the offenders' experiences of being respected and admitting to a crime, whereas there was no significant relation found between the offenders' experiences of feeling anxious and admitting guilt.

The way in which the police officer conducted the first interview with Bert is in line with the dominant approach. Because this approach can make interviewees anxious (Holmberg & Christianson, 2002), the police can be seen as anti-therapeutic agents. In Holmberg and Christianson's study, it was found that the interviewees who felt that the interviewers had rushed them for answers, with no time for reflection, and seemed to lack obliging manners resulted in the interviewees perceiving that there was an external pressure to admit (Gudjonsson, 2004; Gudjonsson & Petursson, 1991; Gudjonsson & Sigurdsson, 1999). Such findings are in line with Moston and Engelberg's (1993) study showing that confrontational interviews extort negative outcomes. Likewise, it shows that the police officer neglected the psychological and social aspects of the interviewing procedure (Finkelman & Grisso, 1996). However, when the investigator conducted the next interview, he utilised a humanitarian approach that is associated with offenders' feelings of respect and can result in admissions (Holmberg & Christianson, 2002). The humanitarian approach corresponds with the ethical interview (Shepherd, 1991) and can be seen as linking with several concepts of therapeutic jurisprudence.

THERAPEUTIC JURISPRUDENCE

Therapeutic jurisprudence (TJ) is a growing movement within the philosophy of law and within the legal and judicial practice areas. Its roots can be seen as anchored to the American legal realism developed in the first half of the 20th century. As early as 1908, Roscoe Pound, a Harvard jurist, had criticised the existing jurisprudence, which he called mechanical jurisprudence (MJ) that conceptualised the law as an autonomous discipline (Finkelman & Grisso, 1996). Pound proclaimed that MJ 'lived' its own sovereign life and that the consequences of a crime were only seen in legal terms. Sociological jurisprudence (Dow, 2000; Finkelman & Grisso, 1996) then developed as a reaction against MJ. Sharing much with sociological jurisprudence, TJ focuses on human problems and conflicts and urges police officers, prosecutors and other legal actors to understand that conflicts produce social and psychological effects on the individuals involved. TJ sees the law and its procedures as therapeutic agents because the law and its execution often generate therapeutic or anti-therapeutic consequences (Petrucci, Winick & Wexler, 2003). In the late 1980s, Professor David Wexler and Professor Bruce Winick founded TJ based on the mental health law. By this perspective, the law and the execution of legal procedures became to be seen in the context of behavioural sciences (Petrucci et al., 2003).

The purpose of TJ is to execute legal procedures such that they promote the social and psychological well-being of the individual involved in a juridical action (Wexler, 1996b). The idea is that legal actors can use theories and empirical knowledge from the behavioural sciences that can influence the practice of the law. In such a way, the jurisprudence may be seen as a therapeutic tool to promote psychological well-being in the legal practice.

An example of how TJ can be practiced in law enforcement is in the investigations of sexual assaults where the suspects often deny the crimes, especially in cases of child sexual abuse. As long as the suspect denies the crime and argues that nothing has happened, he or she does not explain the conflict that arose between the suspect, the crime victim and society. Suspects' disinclination to admit sexual assaults does not only relate to their own perspective of the committed crime that is seen as especially heinous, but also to the fact that police investigators often expect denials from these suspects (see e.g., Kassin, Goldstein & Savitsky, 2003; Kassin & Gudjonsson, 2004; Meissner & Kassin, 2002).

Police officers may also mistakenly interview these suspects in an anti-therapeutic counterproductive way. For example, a man convicted for sexually assaulting his daughter described how the police officer interviewed him: 'he (the police officer) didn't ask a question, in fact, once he asked me, 'why do you think she (the reviewer) acts like this,' he *declared*, he said to me like this, '*what you have done here*', he said, '*that's serious*' (Holmberg, 2004, p. 10). Such a confrontational approach is anti-therapeutic and may awaken the suspects' avoidance. Instead of expecting suspects' denials, one may argue that such behaviour should be seen as a self-enhancing cognitive distortion, expressed in terms of denials and minimisations of the allegations (Baumeister, Catanese & Wallace, 2002; Simon, 1995). This cognitive distortion can be analysed like the crime committed, for example, an investigator should invite the suspect to talk about his or her needs and emotions related to the incident (Benneworth, 2003). In this way, the analysis may reveal what hinders the suspects to discuss the incident.

Such analysis may be conducted through *meta-communication*, that is to communicate about the communication, where hindrances may be identified and solved. In this way, a police interviewer, as well as a suspect, may be aware of one's own and of the other's cognitions and meta-cognitive experiences, based in misperceptions, misinterpretations and neglected needs (Salonen, Vauras & Efklides 2005). The meta-communicative analysis may reveal the suspect's needs to talk about the crime event. For example, a convicted rapist described his encounter with a police officer who recognised his needs and emotions. In his own words, he expressed the situation as, 'then I got some questions and I started to narrate, she (the police officer) had a little of, a little of broad-mindedness. *She showed respect*, I felt that it was something more than just a job, like, now interrogation – bang boom and nothing more, but *she might possibly talk about it*' (Holmberg, 1996). Thus, by talking about the suspects' hindrances and needs, the investigator may promote to a second order change of the problem (Watzlawick et al., 1974), where after the suspect may express his view of what happened. If the investigator does not make such an effort, it may contribute to more cemented denials and problem avoidance from the suspect.

TJ scholarship often deals with law reform itself. But a very important branch of TJ work takes the law as given and seeks ways in which the law's application or implementation can be improved to further its therapeutic power. Until now, TJ's emphasis on applying the law therapeutically has dealt with judges and lawyers. Here, however, we extend it to law enforcement.

Thus, criminal behaviour and subsequent police interviews relate not only to legal issues, but also to social and psychological aspects as described by TJ (Finkelman & Grisso, 1996; Wexler, 1996a). TJ and the humanitarian approach both promote the physiological and psychological well-being of the individual involved in the juridical action (Wexler, 1996b) because they both have an interest in treating offenders as human beings by recognising their behaviour and needs. Additionally, these styles provide a problem-oriented approach comparable to ethical interviewing (Shepherd, 1991) and cognitive interviewing (Fisher & Geiselman, 1992, see also Fisher & Perez, Chapter 14 in this volume). Regarding ethical interviewing (EI), Shepherd argued that the EI approach lends itself to professional investigations. It also facilitates an investigative quality associated with a greater degree of success in crime prevention, detection and conviction of guilty criminals. This approach rests on ethical principles, signifying that the individuals show respect and treat each other as equal human beings with the same rights to dignity, self-determination and free choice. It also emphasises empathy, which means treating each other from the perspective of mutual understanding. The humanitarian approach, revealed by Holmberg and Christianson (2002), is in line with ethical interviews.

When an investigator interviews a suspect in the humanitarian style (Holmberg, 2004; Holmberg & Christianson, 2002) it promotes rapport and therefore, allows the interviewee to provide information as was found by research conducted by Collins, Lincoln and Frank (2002) and Butler et al. (2003). Additionally, Benneworth (2003) demonstrated, in line with the humanitarian approach, that a police officer who uses open-ended questions about relationships and assists the offender in recreating an emotional history facilitates admission. Such an approach enhances the individual's prospects for rehabilitation and psychological well-being, which is in line with TJ (Petrucci et al., 2003; Wexler, 1996a, 1996b, 1996c, 2000; Winick, 2000).

It follows that the dominant style is considered anti-therapeutic because it may hinder an interviewee's ability to recreate the context of an event (see, e.g., Baddeley, 1998; Christianson, 1992; Fisher, 1995; Fisher & Geiselman, 1992). Soukara, Bull and Vrij (2002) examined 40 experienced detectives' perspectives on interviewing uncooperative suspects and found that 80 % of the officers rated the *social skills* of the interviewer as being very important requirements for conducting successful interviews. An anti-therapeutic dominant approach may indicate the interviewers lack social skills, whereas a therapeutic jurisprudential and humanitarian approach may confirm that the interviewers have strong social skills. The therapeutic humanitarian approach may actually enable the interviewee to recreate and recollect the event. In turn, this may provide for the interviewee's psychological well-being and therefore, enable the interviewee to work through very stressful experiences. Although hypothesised, it is likely that Bert's opportunity to perceive psychological well-being would have been higher when he was interviewed by the second humanitarian interviewer compared to the first dominant interviewer. This is because the humanitarian approach may provide the offender with the mental space to work through the event that resulted in the crime, and in turn provide for his psychological well-being, which is an important component of TJ.

WELL-BEING AND SENSE OF COHERENCE

Ann Elisabeth Auhagen (2000) asked herself if her life makes sense and if she can discover any sense in her life. These questions relate to the concept of the meaning of life. Auhagen argues that the meaning of life is a multidimensional construct of an individual's perception of his or her life, which is positively correlated with well-being and can be empirically measured. Zika and Chamberlain (1992) investigated the meaning of life with several measures including both positive and negative well-being dimensions; and Debats, Drost and Hansen (1995) combined a qualitative and a quantitative method in their study of the construct. Results from both studies show that the meaning of life is mainly positively associated with psychological well-being, and Debats et al. suggest a salutogenic approach in studies of mental health. Auhagen (2000) argues that Antonovsky's construct *sense of coherence* (SOC), based on a salutogenic perspective, offers an appropriate way to define and, with its instrument, to measure the meaning of life and psychological well-being.

In line with Auhagen, Gana (2001) argues that SOC measures an individual's mental health, well-being and coping capacity. Gana studied 193 adults regarding their adversity (anxiety, worry and stress), psychological well-being and SOC. By correlation analysis and structural analysis, Gana showed that adversity and stressful experiences had no direct effect on psychological well-being, but did so indirectly by a mediator, the SOC. Gana concludes that the effects of stressful events on psychological well-being are buffered in the SOC, which Antonovsky (1984, 1987) conceptualised as a global orientation. By this, an individual may perceive and express his or her pervasive, continuing and dynamic feelings of confidence in whether life is predictable and whether all will work out as the individual can reasonably expect.

The SOC comprises the three components, *comprehensibility, manageability and meaningfulness* (Antonovsky, 1984). The first cognitive component, comprehensibility, refers to the extent to which individuals perceive information, about themselves and the social environment, as structured, predicable and comprehensible. The second instrumental component, manageability, refers to whether an individual perceives his or her personal and social resources as sufficient to cope with demands posed by internal and external stimuli. The third motivational component, meaningfulness, is the emotional counterpart to comprehensibility that refers to what extent individuals feel that their lives make sense emotionally and to the degree they perceive stressful experiences as worthy to invest time, energy and effort. According to a person's world view, the SOC is relatively stable over time. But traumatic events often change how an individual perceives his or her life and consequently, also change that person's SOC, which becomes more prominent after severe multiple traumas (Schnyder, Büchi, Sensky & Klaghofer, 2000; Snekkevik, Anke, Stranghelle & Fugl-Meyer, 2003). Senkkevik et al. also found that low SOC was associated with psychological distress, anxiety and depression. On the other hand, high SOC relates to lower scores on perceived stress and negative affectivity and to higher scores on positive affectivity and life satisfaction (Pallant & Lae, 2002).

Additionally, Pallant and Lae showed in their study that the short 13-item form of the SOC (see Antonovsky, 1987) has high reliability, construct validity and incremental validity and is useful for well-being measures. In our view, the measure of sense of coherence seems to be an appropriate instrument to measure the psychological well-being in TJ.

SENSE OF COHERENCE IN MURDERERS AND SEXUAL OFFENDERS

In Holmberg and Christianson's (2002) study about murderers' and sexual offenders' experiences from police interviews, the murderers and sexual offenders also completed a SOC form to measure their psychological well-being. The original 29-items SOC form was modified leaving 12 items on the questionnaire (nos. 4, 5, 6, 8, 9, 12, 13, 14, 16, 17, 26 and 29), comprising 4 items each for measuring comprehensibility, manageability and meaningfulness. The 43 murderers and 40 sexual offenders in Holmberg and Christianson's study also completed this modified 12-item SOC form that had an acceptable internal consistency, $\alpha = 0.78$. The score of these 12-item SOC form ranged from a minimum of 20 to a maximum of 80. For the total sample of 83 offenders, the mean of sense of coherence was 51.1 (*SD* 12.95) and there was no significant difference between murderer and sexual offenders. Those 29 participants (35%) who reported that they had been physically punished/assaulted as a child showed a significant lower SOC ($m = 46.0$, $SD = 7.97$) compared with those who had not ($m = 53.6$, $SD = 14.01$), $t(80) = 3.11$, p<0.01. Those 29 men (35%) who reported traumatic childhood experiences of being psychological assaulted/outraged also reported a lower SOC ($m = 46.4$, $SD = 12.76$) than those without such experiences ($m = 54.0$, $SD = 11.99$), $t(77) = 2.63$, $p < 0.01$. Moreover, 9 offenders (11%) revealed that they had been sexually abused as a child; and these men showed the lowest SOC ($m = 38.4$, $SD = 12.83$) among all participants that differed significantly from those who had not been sexually abused ($m = 52.9$, $SD = 11,71$), $t(77) = 3.45$, $p < 0.01$. Of these 83 offenders, 27% reported that they had been abused through a combination of assaults (physical, psychological and/or sexual) as children.

Relying upon therapeutic jurisprudence and psychological well-being, the question is raised whether murderers and sexual offenders differ in SOC depending on how they perceived their police interviews. Holmberg and Christianson (2002) revealed, through principal component analyses (PCA), that murderers and sexual offenders perceived their interviews as either being characterised by humanity or dominance, which then resulted in the interviewees either feeling respected or anxious during the process. A regression analysis shows that the humanitarian approach relates to reactions of being respected ($R^2 = 0.54$, $\beta = 0.78$, $p > 0.01$). Having the PCA factor respected dichotomised on the quartiles, an independent variable was created representing four groups of participants that had felt respect in a low, somewhat, moderate and high degree. Participants that had been maltreated and abused in their childhood were excluded; so early experiences of maltreatment would not affect the SOC related to police interviews.

Regarding SOC, a one-way analysis of variance revealed a significant difference between groups. Those men who had felt themselves highly respected showed a significant higher sense of coherence ($m = 66.7$, $SD = 7.19$) compared with those that had felt themselves less respected ($m = 51.1$, $SD = 7.82$; $m = 54.1$, $SD = 11.61$; $m = 56.1$, $SD = 7.49$), $F(3, 33) = 5.60$, $p < 0.01$. Holmberg and Christianson (2002) also found a significant relation between the murderers' and sexual offenders' perceptions of a humanitarian police interview as well as feelings of being respected and admissions of crime. Those admitting offenders showed a significant higher SOC ($m = 60.3$, $SD = 11.59$) than denying offenders did ($m = 51.7$, $SD = 12.04$), $t(37) = 2.26$, $p < 0.05$. Besides the higher SOC, admissions may also be seen as an advantage as it was for an offender convicted of sexually abusing his twin daughters. He described the advantage of admission in a therapeutic way, 'your children come back to you, emotionally. You can never be brought together with a child you have exposed to something like this, if you do not admit and accept your responsibilities. Moreover, if you care ever so little about your children, you have only to admit. There is nothing else. You can't move back to your family where you have called your daughter a liar' (Holmberg, 1996).

In sum, murderers and sexual offenders that had been maltreated and abused in childhood showed a lower psychological well-being in terms of SOC than those murderers and sexual offenders without such experiences. It was also shown that, with control for childhood maltreatment, offenders who experience a humanitarian police interview may have feelings of being respected that were associated with a higher psychological well-being. Obviously, this study has not revealed any direction of causality, but an association between perception of respect and SOC. It may be possible that a police interviewer's humanitarian approach towards an interviewee causes the interviewee's feelings of being respected that, in turn, generates a high SOC. Moreover, the original source of the humanitarian experiences may be with the interviewee him or herself because if he or she behaves in a humanitarian and respected way, the police interviewer might respond in the same way, resulting in a high SOC. On the other hand, the interviewees' perceptions of dominance and anxiety in the police interview may evoke strong negative feelings or memories from a history of being rejected, abused, alone and deeply secluded, therefore causing a low SOC whether the original source was the police interviewer or the interviewee.

An example of how a dominant police interviewer evokes strong negative feelings is the case of Robert, a suspect for the sexual homicides of a young girl and a young woman of which Robert denied being the perpetrator despite the fact that the police found DNA on the victims' bodies. During the years when he was growing up, Robert was badly beaten and psychologically maltreated by his mother and father. To avoid the severe maltreatment, he sometimes ran out in the woods and stayed there for several days. During the police interview, the police officer asked Robert what his mother might think about him as a suspect of two sexual homicides. Robert responded by saying, 'it is not interesting what that hag thinks'. The officer insisted upon talking about Robert's mother, but Robert retired into himself and refused to talk about his mother.[2] The negative feelings or anxiety that the officer evoked caused avoidance based on Robert's history of being rejected, maltreated, alone and deeply secluded. Such avoidance in the

---

[2] The interviewer also asked the suspect to speculate about the victims' parents thoughts and feelings about him or the thoughts his grown-up son might have about him being a suspect of these gruesome crimes.

police interview is counterproductive and obviously anti-therapeutic. Instead, the officer should have approached Robert in a humanitarian way that related to interviewees' feelings of being respected. An interviewee's feelings of respect relate to admissions; and admitting perpetrators show an association to a higher psychological well-being.

It may be argued that the interviewee's perceived experiences of humanity and respect can be an expression of a police officer's confession seeking interviewing strategy. This may be true in some cases, but in Holmberg and Christianson's study the offenders who felt highly respected also reported a higher SOC than those who felt less respected one or more years after their police interviews. It is likely that an offender who was treated by a simulated humanitarian approach realised this after conviction and a year or more in prison, and consequently, reported in this study a perception of low SOC based on bitterness. Moreover, investigations of murders and serious sexual crimes most often comprise several police interviews requiring the police interviewer and the suspect to spend several hours together. A pilot study where Holmberg (1996) interviewed 20 convicted rapists indicated that offenders can detect simulated humanitarian-like approaches and accordingly react with a bitterness based on perceptions of trickery and deceit.

SUMMARY

Humanity and respect in police interviews that promote admissions should not only be seen from investigative and legal perspective because it is likely that therapeutic jurisprudential derived admissions also promote experiences where a murderer or a sexual offender may work through the crime committed. Hereby, such admissions may enhance the memory as well as facilitate the psychological well-being of the suspect.

There is a need for further research regarding psychological well-being in therapeutic jurisprudence because Holmberg and Christianson's study (2002) only showed a relationship between perceptions of the police interview and psychological well-being. It is important to define this concept and find methods to measure psychological well-being in the legal context because it will offer a greater opportunity to develop legal methods and procedures.

The use of the modified SOC instrument in this study may have somewhat weakened the results compared to when the original 29-items SOC form is used. However, this study indicates that psychological well-being in legal context can be measured and further research suggests using different standardised instruments to identify more deeply the psychological well-being in therapeutic jurisprudence.

This research may be regarded as a new dimension of TJ scholarship. It deals not with law reform *per se*, but rather with that branch of TJ scholarship concerned with applying the law therapeutically through the roles and behaviours of legal actors. Here, we have expanded these roles and behaviours to now include those of police officers conducting interviews of suspects. Prior TJ work has been concerned with employing an 'ethic of care', developing 'respectful relationships' and affording offenders procedural justice in the form of 'voice' and 'validation' (Winick & Wexler, 2003). Those concepts have typically been discussed in connection with courts and lawyers. In this chapter, we explored these concepts in the context of police investigative methods.

The humanitarian/dominant investigative distinction can be nicely situated within the conceptual framework of TJ and the research presented here is in keeping with TJ's call for empirical work to aid the understanding of the law in action (as opposed to knowing only the law 'on the books'). Furthermore, our use of the 'sense of coherence' concept is very much in keeping with TJ's call for researchers to explicate and justify their measures of psychological well-being.

Thus, we hope our chapter has shed light on how the TJ perspective can contribute to the work of law enforcement (and vice versa). Indeed, going beyond the present chapter, if we look to the context of the entire volume, we can also see the potential relevance of TJ in accessing and eliciting offender memories of crime.

ACKNOWLEDGEMENTS

For valuable comments and suggestions regarding the work with the text to this chapter we express our gratitude to Kathleen Dostalik, University of Arizona.

REFERENCES

Antonovsky, A. (1984) The sense of coherence as a determinant of health. In J.D. Matarazzo, S.M. Weiss, J.A. Herd, N.E. Miller & S.M. Weiss (Eds), *Behavioral health; A handbook of health enhancement and disease prevention*. Chichester: John Wiley & Sons, Ltd.

Antonovsky, A. (1987) *Unrevealing the mystery of health*. San Francisco: Jossey-Bass.

Auhagen, A.E. (2000) On the psychology of meaning of life. *Swiss Journal of Psychology*, **59**(1), 34–48.

Baddeley, A. (1998) *Human memory; Theory and practice.* Boston, MA: Allyn and Bacon.

Baumeister, R.F., Catanese, K.R. & Wallace, H.M. (2002) Conquest by force: A narcissistic reactance theory of rape and sexual coercion. *Review of General Psychology*, **6**(1), 92–135.

Benneworth, K. (2003 July) Who 'tells the story' in the police-paedophile investigative interview and the encouragement of suspect denial. Paper presented at the Psychology & Law International, Interdisciplinary Conference, Edinburgh, UK.

Butler, E.A., Egloff, B., Wilhelm, F.H., Smith, N.C., Ericson, E.A. & Gross, J.J. (2003) The social consequences of expressive suppression. *Emotion*, **3**(1), 48–67.

Christianson, S.Å. (Ed.) (1992) *The handbook of emotion and memory: Research and theory.* Hillsdale, NJ.: Lawrence Erlbaum Associates Publishers.

Christianson, S.Å., Engelberg, E. & Holmberg, U. (1998) *Avancerad förhörs- och intervjumetodik.* Stockholm: Natur och Kultur.

Clifford, B.R. & George, R. (1996) A field evaluation of training in three methods of witness/victim investigative interviewing. *Psychology, Crime & Law*, **2**, 231–48.

Collins, R., Lincoln, R. & Frank, M.G. (2002) The effect of rapport in forensic interviewing. *Psychiatry, Psychology and Law*, **9**(1), 69–78.

Debats, D.-L., Drost, J. & Hansen, P. (1995) Experiences of meaning of life: A combined qualitative and quantitative approach. *British Journal of Psychology*, **86**(3), 359–75.

Dow, D.R. (2000) The relevance of legal scholarship: Reflections on judge Kozinski's musings. *Houston Law Review*, **37**, 329–40.

Finkelman, D. & Grisso, T. (1996) Therapeutic jurisprudence: From idea to application. In D.B. Wexler & B.J. Winick (Eds), *Law in a therapeutic key.* Durhamn, NC: Carolina Academic Press.

Fisher, R.P. & Geiselman, R.E. (1992) *Memory-enhancing techniques for investigative interview; The cognitive interview.* Springfield: Charles C. Thomas Publishing.

Fisher, R.P. (1995) Interviewing victims and witnesses of crime. *Psychology, Public Policy and Law*, **1**(4), 732–64.

Gana, K. (2001) Is sense of coherence a mediator between adversity and psychological well-being in adults? *Stress and Health*, **17**, 77–83.

Gudjonsson, Gisli H. (2004) The psychology of confessions: A review of the literature and issues. *Psychological Science in the Public Interest*, **5**(2), 33–67.

Gudjonsson, G.H. & Petursson, H. (1991) Custodial interrogation: Why suspects confess and how does it relate to their crime, attitude and personality. *Personality and Individual Differences*, **12**, 294–306.

Gudjonsson, G.H. & Sigurdsson, J.F. (1999) The Gudjonsson Questionnaire – Revised (GCQ-R): Factor structure and its relationship with personality. *Personality and Individual Differences*, **27**, 953–68.

Holmberg, U. (1996) Sexualbrottsförövarens upplevelser av polisförhör. Report No.7:1996, Kristianstad University.

Holmberg, U. (2004) Police interviews with victims and suspects of violent and sexual crimes; Interviewees' experiences and interview outcomes. Stockholm University: Dissertation

Holmberg, U. & Christianson, S.Å. (2002) Murderers' and sexual offenders' experiences of police interviews and their inclination to admit or deny crimes. *Behavioral Sciences and the Law*, **20**, 31–45.

Kassin, S., Goldstein, C.C. & Savitsky, K. (2003) Behavioral confirmation in the interrogation room: On the dangers of presuming guilt. *Law and Human Behavior*, **27**(2), 187–203.

Kassin, S.M. & Gudjonsson, G.H. (2004) The psychology of confessions: A review of the literature and issues. *Psychological Science in the Public Iinterest*, **5**, 33–67.

Meissner, C.A. & Kassin, S.M. (2002) 'He's guilty!': Investigator bias in judgments of truth and deception. *Law and Human Behavior*, **26**(5), 469–80.

Moston, S. & Engelberg, T. (1993) Police questioning techniques in tape recorded interviews with criminal suspects. *Policing and Society*, **3**, 223–68.

Pallant, J.F. & Lae, L. (2002) Sense of coherence, well-being, coping and personality factors: Further evaluation of the sense of coherence scale. *Personality and Individual Differences*, **33**, 39–48.

Petrucci, C.J., Winick, B.J. & Wexler, D.B. (2003) Therapeutic jurisprudence: An invitation to social scientists. In D. Carson & R. Bull (Eds), *Handbook of psychology in legal contexts* (pp. 579–601). Chichester: John Wiley & Sons, Ltd.

Pollock, Ph.H. (1999) When the killer suffers: Post-traumatic stress reactions following homicide. *Legal and Criminological Psychology*, **4**, 185–202.

Salonen, P., Vauras, M. & Efklides, A. (2005) Social interaction–What can it tell us about metacognition and coregulation in learning? *European Psychologist*, **10**(3), 199–208.

Shepherd, E. (1991) Ethical interviewing. *Policing*, **7**, 42–60.

Schnyder, U., Büchi, S., Sensky, T. & Klaghofer, R. (2000) Anotonovsky's sense of coherence: Trait or state? *Psychotherapy and Psychosomatis*, **69**, 296–302.

Simon, L.M.J. (1995) A therapeutic jurisprudence approach to the legal processing of domestic violence cases. *Psychology, Public Policy, and Law*, **1**(1), 43–79.

Snekkevik, H., Anke, A., Stanghelle, J.K. & Fugl-Meyer, A.R. (2003) Is sense of coherence stable after multiple trauma? *Clinical Rehabilitation*, **17**, 443–54.

Soukara, S., Bull, R. & Vrij, A. (2002) Police detectives' aims regarding their interviews with suspects: Any change at the turn of the millennium? *International Journal of Police Science & Management*, **4**(2), 100–14.

Watzlawick, P., Weakland, J., & Fisch, R. (1974) *Change; Principles of problem formation and problem resolution*. New York: Norton.

Wegner, D.M., Quillian, F. & Houston, C.E. (1996) Memories out of order: Thought suppression and the disturbance of sequence memory. *Journal of Personality and Social Psychology*, **71**, 680–91.

Wexler, D.B (1996a) Therapeutic jurisprudence and the criminal courts. In D.B. Wexler & B.J. Winick (Eds), *Law in a therapeutic key*. NC: Carolina Academic Press.

Wexler, D.B (1996b) Reflections on the scope of therapeutic jurisprudence. In D.B. Wexler & B.J. Winick (Eds), *Law in a therapeutic key*. Durham, NC: Carolina Academic Press.

Wexler, D.B (1996c) Therapeutic jurisprudence and changing conceptions of legal scholarship. In D.B. Wexler & B.J. Winick (Eds), *Law in a therapeutic key*. Durham, NC: Carolina Academic Press.

Wexler, D.B. (2000) Practicing therapeutic jurisprudence: Psychological soft spots and strategies. In D.P. Stolle, D.B. Wexler & B.J. Winick (Eds), *Practicing therapeutic jurisprudence; Law as a helping profession* (pp. 45–67) Durham, NC: Carolina Academic Press.

Winick, B.J. (2000) Therapeutic jurisprudence and the role of counsel in litigation. In D.P. Stolle, D.B. Wexler & B.J. Winick (Eds), *Practicing therapeutic jurisprudence; Law as a helping profession* (pp. 309–24.) Durham, NC: Carolina Academic Press.

Winick, B.J. & Wexler, D.B. (2003) *Judging in a therapeutic key: Therapeutic jurisprudence and the courts.* Durham, NC: Carolina Academic Press.

Zika, S. & Chamberlain, K. (1992) On the relation between meaning in life and psychological well-being. *British Journal of Psychology*, **83**(1), 133–45.

Index